THERAPY *With* DIFFICULT CLIENTS

THERAPY *With* DIFFICULT CLIENTS

Using the Precursors Model to Awaken Change

FRED J. HANNA

American Psychological Association
Washington, DC

First Printing, July 2001
Second Printing, January 2003
Third Printing, October 2005
Fourth Printing, February 2008

Published by
American Psychological Association
750 First Street, NE
Washington, DC 20002
www.apa.org

To order
APA Order Department
P.O. Box 92984
Washington, DC 20090-2984
Tel: (800) 374-2721,
Direct: (202) 336-5510
Fax: (202) 336-5502,
TDD/TTY: (202) 336-6123
On-line: www.apa.org/books/
E-mail: order@apa.org

In the U.K., Europe, Africa, and the Middle East, copies may be ordered from
American Psychological Association
3 Henrietta Street
Covent Garden, London
WC2E 8LU England

Typeset in Goudy by World Composition Services, Inc., Sterling, VA

Printer: Port City Press, Inc., Baltimore, MD
Cover Designer: RCW Communications, Falls Church, VA
Technical/Production Editor: Jennifer L. Macomber

Library of Congress Cataloging-in-Publication Data
Hanna, Fred J.
Therapy with difficult clients : using the precursors model to awaken change / Fred J. Hanna.
p. cm.
Includes bibliographical references and index.
ISBN 1-55798-793-9 (alk. paper)
1. Impasse (Psychotherapy) 2. Attitude change. I. Title.
RC489.I45 H36 2001
616.89'14—dc21 2001022415

British Library Cataloguing-in-Publication Data
A CIP record is available from the British Library.

Printed in the United States of America

CONTENTS

PREFACE

The subject of therapeutic change and resistance to change has been a primary interest of mine for more than three decades. I consider it one of the most intriguing and extraordinary of the vast range of phenomena that constitute human life. I have studied therapeutic change as a therapist, a researcher, and as a consultant. I have also investigated it informally through dozens of interviews of people who have achieved change outside of therapy as well as others who attempted to change but never quite accomplished it.

It is relatively easy to apply the many effective therapeutic techniques with clients who are willing and involved in the change process. However, one of the most challenging aspects of therapy is working with clients who have little interest in change, or who think that change is a waste of time, or who somehow have come to believe that change is a threat to their personal freedom or the core of their being. This area is one of the most important for the further development of psychotherapy. After surveying the field, I believe that there is a need for more techniques and approaches to help such clients and the therapists who work with them.

The many theories of psychotherapy, from behavioral to psychodynamic and from existential to family systems, are remarkably instructive and descriptive of the subtleties and complexities of human thought, feeling, behavior, and relationships. There is no substitute for the study of the great insights these theories catalog and represent. Add to those the more recent integrative and eclectic approaches to psychotherapy, and one has a rich and wide spectrum of perspectives on human problems and predicaments. Nevertheless, the classic theories and the innovative integrative approaches do not delve deep enough, nor do they go far enough in capturing the essential structures and dynamics of change. We remain in great need of the knowledge of what makes people change. Doing therapy with difficult clients serves as a constant reminder.

My investigations of therapeutic change and difficult clients have revealed a host of subtle processes that affect change. These processes seem to take place at a level beyond the cognitive and affective. They tend to be easily overlooked, even though a focus on them can be of great help in facilitating change. Such subtle processes go largely unacknowledged in routine psychotherapy not so much because they are hidden but because they are pervasive. Their pervasiveness also makes them difficult to identify and articulate. For example, what are the subtle processes that move a callous and cruel man from nearly exclusive self-centeredness toward opening to the feelings and views of others? What are the dynamics that make an involuntary, defiant, court-ordered client wake up to become aware of a problem and involved in therapy? What brings a helplessly depressed person to the point of realizing that depression is something that can be influenced and relieved? Similarly, when a client is sitting on the fence between taking responsibility and blaming others, what nudges the person toward responsibility? These are difficult questions and certainly require further research, but we now know that such changes result not from a single process but a combination of many.

A major purpose of this book is to identify seven of these processes and move them from the vague to the defined. I have called the processes *precursors* because they seem to herald the arrival of change. When the precursors dawn, change seems also to be on the horizon. I hope to outline the intricate and variable manner in which the precursors act interdependently to produce change. To help therapists in their use of this model, I propose a clinical assessment tool that reveals which of the precursors is missing in the client who is not achieving change. Finally, I provide techniques for implementing each precursor in accordance with the assessment. This is the essence of the precursors approach to therapeutic change. The precursors are offered as an aid to clients for whom therapy is a painful and fruitless struggle.

I want to make it clear that these precursors are neither my invention nor my discovery. They were recognized long before the dawn of psychotherapy. I have only shown how they interact and described an array of techniques that stimulate the precursors in clients who may not otherwise achieve positive change. I share these techniques and approaches in the hope that they will help difficult clients achieve change sooner rather than later.

ACKNOWLEDGMENTS

I have been inspired by many people in this field. Some I have met, and others I have not. I am grateful to them for providing insights that have helped me find my path in this fascinating and gratifying work. The pioneering insights of Jerome Frank are now legendary, and I am deeply grateful to him for the extraordinarily helpful conversations we have had. I thank George Howard for his wisdom, his innovative research, and his progressive ideas concerning psychotherapy. When I was a graduate student, he took me under his wing and patiently answered dozens of questions. He helped shed light on a path that would have taken me many years to find on my own.

I also thank Hal Arkowitz, who encouraged me to write the original article on which this book is based. He did more than merely validate my ideas about the precursors; he helped me deepen them. Michael Mahoney's comments on my work have been of great value. His deep and global view of psychotherapy and its potential has been a rich source of insight to me for many years. I express my heartfelt thanks to him for his invaluable suggestions concerning the original draft of this book. I have also found the work of Arnold Lazarus to be a source of instruction and learning. I have ever admired his insights and his bold thinking and commentary on psychotherapy, as well as his therapeutic wisdom. In this same vein, I have been inspired by the thoughts and perspectives of such people as Larry Beutler, Robert Elliott, Carlo DiClemente, Marvin Goldfried, John Norcross, James Prochaska, Daniel Robinson, and Hans Strupp.

My collaboration with Kaisa Puhakka has been nothing less than extraordinary. Her mentoring has been invaluable, and I am deeply thankful to her for teaching me the subtleties of object relations therapy. Most of all, she has always been willing to take part in a vital interchange of ideas that was part of our perennial quest to understand the human predicament. Her help with the manuscript has also been of great value.

I owe a debt of gratitude to Al Ottens, who has always been there for insightful comments, support, and reassurance. I also thank Martin Ritchie, Chris Aanstoos, and Lorean Roberts for their professional and personal support.

My wife, Constance Hanna, a wonderfully effective and empathic therapist, has kept me practical and concrete. Her wisdom, editing, and advice on the manuscript have been wonderful. I also thank two professional philosophers from whom I benefited enormously. Ramakrishna Puligandla taught me the subtleties and liberating potential of dialectical philosophy from the viewpoints of both Kant and Nagarjuna. James Daley, now-deceased friend and mentor, taught me the insider's perspective on phenomenology as a philosophical discipline and its implications for psychology. Studying with him brought Husserl and Heidegger alive, especially in terms of dialectics and ontology. My study with both of these men afforded great insight into the nature and goals of psychotherapy.

In terms of the manuscript itself, I thank APA Books editors Margaret Schlegel for her original interest in the book and Linda McCarter for her enthusiasm and insightful suggestions, which were of great help in improving the book's style, substance, and organization.

My colleagues at Johns Hopkins University also deserve acknowledgment for supporting me during the time of writing this book. My thanks, in no particular order, go to Mary Guindon, Larry Larsen, Michael Rosenberg, Shelley Ingram, Deborah Carran, Larry David, Alan Green, and Gloria Lane. My mother, Julia Hanna, provided great support and encouragement, and she has my deepest gratitude.

THERAPY *With* DIFFICULT CLIENTS

INTRODUCTION

Arnold A. Lazarus (1990) once wrote that psychotherapy is "still in the dark ages" (p. 356). In terms of what we actually know about the nature of positive change and how to help people achieve it as quickly and smoothly as possible, this assessment remains more or less accurate. For psychotherapy to rise to a new level, it is necessary to consider a range of potential paths that lead to a more complete view of how people change. This book is intended as a step toward an enhanced understanding of what brings about beneficial change in human beings. Although it will not bring the field out of the "dark ages" of which Lazarus spoke, its promise lies in the fact that it concentrates on change itself, and not on theories of change, techniques, or stages of change. This book is about the catalysts that bring therapeutic change into being.

Therapeutic change is the raison d'être of psychotherapy. It is arguably the most important defining characteristic of psychotherapy. Bereft of the concept of change, psychotherapy loses its meaning. Change is not only psychotherapy's essence and purpose, it is also its primary criterion for gauging success. Historically, too much attention has been devoted to theories and techniques, rather than what actually brings about therapeutic change. If psychotherapeutic change is such a crucial aspect of therapy and counseling, it is extremely important to understand its nature. Curiously, it is relatively easy to define at a superficial level, so much so that on the surface it may appear rather simple. In fact, it is a remarkably complex and intricate phenomenon.

A working definition of *psychotherapeutic change* is a beneficial, positive alteration in thoughts, behaviors, feelings, or interpersonal interaction that leads to improved or more effective coping or functioning and greater satisfaction with one's outer and inner life. In general, it is anything that constitutes an improvement to a person's life in terms of feeling, thinking, behaving, or relating. Change can be as simple as getting along with one's supervisor, learning to manage one's time, or feeling better after talking about a problem. It can be as profound as conquering major depression, recovering from an addiction, overcoming the devastating effects of abuse, or finding meaning in a seemingly empty existence.

There is a more global, developmental aspect as well. Therapeutic change is at the basis of a wide number of human actions and intentions far beyond the scope of therapy. It has to do with finding satisfaction or fulfillment in life. People seek love so as to achieve therapeutic change. They attend college, travel the world, and pursue careers for that purpose. It is so fundamental to desire change that one could make the case that it is behind a vast range of human pursuits.

The acquisition of desired possessions is related to therapeutic change. People use alcohol or drugs, in many cases, in the illusory hope of therapeutic change. Drugs produce changes in feeling, perceiving, thinking, behaving, and relating. If drugs had no such effect, people would not show the slightest interest in using or abusing them. People seek therapy for the same reasons. Ultimately, perhaps, therapeutic change is a process of making life more enjoyable or meaningful.

The irony is that with more than 100 years of research and practice and nearly 500 theories of and approaches to psychotherapy (see Hanna, 1994; Omer & London, 1988), we know relatively little about the intricate details of the change process itself. Much of this knowledge remains to be discovered. In the past 15 years, researchers have spent much time and effort demonstrating that psychotherapy helps bring about change, but little research has examined the mechanisms that actually produce change. Most of the work has focused on how change happens within the relationship, through techniques, by various standard approaches, or through the new integrative theories or systems of therapy. Another avenue in recent years has been the development of approaches to particular populations such as people with disabilities, elderly people, or people of color.

A recognized problem in conducting such research is that most outcome studies do not model or represent psychotherapy as it is described in the literature (Persons, 1991). In other words, what practicing therapists do is not always what gets studied. Thus, outcome research does not always present a clear picture of how change comes about in routine therapy sessions. Gendlin (1986) pointed out that an alternative to looking at outcomes is to examine the *microprocess* moments of therapy, that is, those specific and significant frames of therapy in which change manifests. These moments can become lost in outcome studies, which look at general results. Of course, both outcome and microprocess are important, but this book is more concerned with microprocesses that stimulate change.

FUNDAMENTAL QUESTIONS

A more thorough understanding of the intricacies of therapeutic change may be the most important step toward improving the effectiveness of therapy. Procedures can then be developed that derive from that new and vital knowledge. When it comes to using techniques, therapists still rely, for the most part, on those that have been cataloged in the various theories such as behavioral, Gestalt, Adlerian, or cognitive. Are there undiscovered change principles that can lead to the development of more effective techniques and more efficient use of the techniques we have?

There are some fundamental questions about change that need to be addressed in this regard. Why is it that some clients change relatively quickly in therapy, whereas others make little, if any, progress? Why is change painfully difficult for some clients and comparatively easy for others? Why do some clients welcome change, but others resist and struggle against it every inch of the way? Why do some clients achieve core personality changes, whereas others make relatively minor, linear adjustments? Why do some clients recognize that therapeutic change is important but others see it as threatening? And how can the most beneficial change be produced in the shortest amount of time, especially in this age of managed care?

At this point in the development of psychotherapy, we have answers to these questions, but they are incomplete. I hope to persuade the reader that if we thoroughly understood the answers to these questions, therapists might be able to help clients produce change more quickly and efficiently. The latter point is one of universal concern to psychotherapy and research. I once heard researcher Michael Mahoney say that therapy is the most difficult profession there is. Like chess, it is relatively easy to learn its principles and maneuvers, but it is incredibly difficult to master.

PRECURSORS OF CHANGE

This book offers one approach to these fundamental questions by suggesting a set of seven variables, called "precursors," that seem conducive to psychotherapeutic change. A *precursor* is generally defined as something that goes before and in some way announces the coming or arrival of something else. I refer to these seven variables as precursors because their presence indicates the imminent manifestation of change and then renders change itself possible through the better known processes. The seven precursors are not focused around the therapist, theories, or techniques. Each has to do with client-specific factors, that is, what the client brings to the session. The precursors of change are largely concerned with pivotal processes within the person on which change depends. Each has empirical validation. The seven precursors, which are defined briefly in chapter 2 and in detail in chapter 3, are as follows:

1. a sense of necessity,
2. a willingness or readiness to experience anxiety or difficulty,

3. awareness,
4. confronting the problem,
5. effort or will toward change,
6. hope for change, and
7. social support for change.

The precursors, taken together, form a comprehensive picture of how people change and why they do not. These ingredients, working in various combinations, seem to regulate the speed, intensity, and magnitude of therapeutic change (Hanna & Ritchie, 1995).

REGULATORS OF CHANGE

The seven precursors can be considered regulators of the change process (see Hanna & Ritchie, 1995). In other words, the more they are present in a person, the more quickly change will occur, and in some cases, the deeper that change will be in the psyche of the person. The precursors assessment form presented in chapter 4 is an application of the precursors model that helps clinicians determine which precursors need to be developed or implemented to bring about change.

Each precursor can be formulated in different ways and with different terms and jargon, but I have tried to keep them as theory free as possible. In fact, they are assumed by all the theories and techniques of counseling and therapy. The precursors are pervasive; one can pick up virtually any book on therapy that contains successful case examples, and the precursors will be very much in evidence in each of those cases. And in unsuccessful cases, the precursors will be absent. There may be more precursors than those discussed in this book, but these seven seem to be key ingredients of change.

I have often been asked how the precursors model of change relates to the transtheoretical stage model of Prochaska, Norcross, and DiClemente (1994; see also Prochaska & DiClemente, 1982; Prochaska, DiClemente, & Norcross, 1992). There is no question that this team of researchers has made an excellent contribution to our understanding of the various stages of change. These stages progress from the precontemplation and contemplation stages to the preparation, action, and maintenance stages. This is an important, descriptive, and helpful model.

By contrast, the precursors model is concerned with outlining what brings change about at all. The precursors of change are the factors that must be present for any advancement along the stages to occur. The precursors move the person to progress along the stages, and if the person regresses, it is because the precursors have waned.

In the transtheoretical stage model, Brogan, Prochaska, and Prochaska (1999) stated that the initial precontemplation stage is the most difficult, and people in this stage are most likely to lack progress in therapy. This book focuses primarily on clients in this stage and sheds light on how and why they do not progress. Of course, the precursors model is no final answer by any means. There remains much to learn about the nature and function of psychotherapeutic change (see Goldfried, Castonguay, & Safran, 1992; Stiles, Shapiro, & Elliott, 1986), including the discovery of additional, and perhaps more potent, precursors. Nevertheless, the precursors model in combination with the stage model form a reasonably clear picture of the change process in accord with our current level of knowledge. The two models fit together well.

Although I refer to this set of pivotal change factors as "precursors," it should be understood that they are functions or actual conditions perceived to be present, or not, within a person. They are not personality traits or client characteristics, such as ego strength or hardiness. Confronting the problem, one of the most powerful of the precursors, is something that a person does, or not, in real time. It is not something that is a part of a person's personality makeup. Anyone, with any kind of personality, disordered or not, can do this to some degree, assuming that there is nothing physiological that would prevent it.

Taken as a group, the precursors can be viewed as a set of interdependent, necessary conditions for therapeutic change. Without these being present in a client, change is not likely to occur regardless of how great the therapist, how potent the theory, how close the relationship, or how capable the person.

DIFFICULT OR RESISTANT CLIENTS

The test of any model of change is whether it will apply to difficult clients. The precursors model of change is presented precisely for the purpose of working with people who find change to be difficult or intolerable or a source of pain, inconvenience, or failure. Traditionally, such clients have been referred to as "resistant," an idea now well accepted by a wide range of therapists (Mahoney, 1991). Unfortunately, this term carries the needless connotation that a lack of change is somehow due to the client's recalcitrance, active or passive aggressiveness, or defiance. When therapeutic change does not occur, it may not be because the client is resistant; the person may simply have remained uninformed about its benefits, may feel undeserving of its results, or may be vigorously engaged in self-protection. Like communication or social skills, some people may never have learned how to change or to accept help. I have encountered some clients who never learned the fundamental lesson that therapeutic change is something valuable and helpful.

The precursors perspective reframes the idea of resistance as a condition where there are too few precursors present and operative in a person. From this perspective, a resistant client is more aptly recast as a difficult client. A *difficult client* is a person for whom change is not forthcoming in therapy. From the precursors perspective, a difficult client is a person who displays what might be called "change deficits" and can be helped with education about the precursors and a variety of techniques specifically designed to increase the presence of the precursors. One of the major points of this book is that a client is likely to be considered difficult to the degree that he or she lacks the seven precursors. When the precursors become established, that person will no longer be likely to be perceived as difficult or resistant.

PRECURSORS ASSESSMENT

The precursors assessment, fully described in chapter 4, is a therapy tool that can help therapists determine which of the seven precursors are missing in a difficult client and which need to be established or increased. The assessment is rated by the therapist, with the help of the client when appropriate. The assessment enables the therapist to see how the precursors combine and interact and provides a relatively clear picture of what is needed for a particular client to achieve change. Therapist and client then can work toward implementing and increasing the missing precursors using the treatment suggestions provided in the clinical sections of this book.

UNIQUE ASPECTS OF THE PRECURSORS MODEL

Several aspects of the precursors model are rather unique. One is that the model concentrates solely and completely on a set of change principles without focusing on stages, theories, or personality traits. Powerful calls for this kind of approach were made in the 1980s and still have not been fully realized. Stiles et al. (1986) called for new approaches to identify a common pool of change mechanisms. In a workshop held by the National Institute of Mental Health (NIMH) in 1986 (see Wolfe & Goldfried, 1988), 14 psychotherapy researchers suggested that research be conducted "on the actual change processes that take place in psychotherapy" (p. 449). They also called for research designed to delineate and elucidate common and unique factors among and across the various theories. Yet another of their recommendations was that research be conducted to develop a taxonomy of effective change processes. The precursors approach is indeed a taxonomy of effective change processes that exist among and across virtually all the schools of psychotherapy, and the model holds true for change independent of therapy as well, as Gendlin (1986) advised.

Beutler (2000), 14 years later, noted that researchers have continued to call for orienting therapy around change principles and reiterated the importance of doing so. The precursors model is, perhaps, the first model based purely on change principles. However, rather than addressing the "common factors" of therapy, another popular topic in current psychotherapy, this book addresses the common factors of change itself.

Therapists Have Precursors, Too

Another unique aspect of this model is that therapists and helpers can also be rated according to their own precursors of change. Because the precursors can vary from problem to problem, and from day to day, a therapist can be very much oriented toward change with one client and less so with another. I have often seen this in my consulting practice in various community agencies. An entire chapter of this book is dedicated to rating therapists according to their precursors, which can enhance an understanding of how therapists contribute, or not, to the change process in that client (see chapter 5). The precursors assessment form can thus help determine how helpful a particular therapist is with a particular client at a particular time. This application may be of service in the supervision of therapists and counselors in training.

In addition, this book reintroduces the needlessly vague but important concept of countertransference as "therapist interference" with the change process, and we will see how therapists can use their own feelings and reactions to client behaviors and statements in a therapeutic manner. Another consequence of understanding the precursors of change is that the knowledge gained sheds indirect light on the characteristics of the most effective, or "master" therapists. A complete model of therapeutic change would be able to define the kind of therapist who is most adept at facilitating it. As we shall see, the precursors model makes the characteristics of effective therapists stand out in bold relief and helps us to better understand exactly what it is that they do. Some of this discussion is based on research by developmental psychologists on the subject of wisdom, and it has profound implications for the training and development of therapists and counselors (see chapter 7).

A Metacognitive View of Change

The precursors model is also unique in that it is the first change model, to my knowledge, that fully considers metacognitive aspects of change. Much fuss has been made over cognition or thinking in psychotherapy in the last 30 years, and rightfully so. Students are taught from their first courses that change in behavior and feeling stems from changing thoughts and beliefs about events. With a few exceptions, however, metacognition has seldom been considered as related to producing change. Rather than addressing thinking and thought processes, metacognition has to do with thinking about thinking, psychological acts, or what were once called "acts of consciousness" (Husserl, 1913/1982), those inner decisions about where to direct awareness, the act of regulating one's behaviors and thoughts, thinking about thinking, and the awareness of awareness (Hanna, Giordano, Dupuy, & Puhakka, 1995). Cognition alone cannot account for metacognitive functions of the human psyche (Slife, 1987), and some disorders, such as depression, may be related to metacognitive processes (Slife & Weaver, 1992).

Several of the precursors take these vital human functions into account as part of producing change. Interestingly, when change is viewed from a metacognitive perspective, it takes on a new aspect: Change looks more and more like a skill. Behavior therapists have long emphasized the importance of skill building. In the metacognitive context, change itself is a skill, and mastery of the precursors is tantamount to mastery of therapeutic change itself (Hanna, 1996).

Techniques Oriented Around Change Principles

Another unique aspect of this book is the array of techniques it describes for implementing the precursors. It is unusual for techniques to be cataloged in terms of change principles. In this book, a chapter is devoted to techniques designed to establish the presence of each of the seven precursors. Many of the techniques have not been previously described, whereas others are more familiar techniques adapted specifically for bringing about the presence of precursors in difficult clients.

Precursors in Group and Family Therapies

The precursors model is not limited to work with individuals. It is also applicable in group therapy and in family therapy. The precursors can be assessed and identified not only with each individual member of the group or family, but also with the group or family as a whole. A group will display a configuration of precursors of its own. Whitaker held that a family has its own character as an entity in its own right (quoted in Simon, 1985). Therapy groups can be seen in the same way. Thus, the precursors model and assessment can help a therapist working with difficult groups and families as well.

PERSON AS THE PRIMARY FOCUS

People change without a therapist, without an identified theory, and without a close relationship (Hanna & Ritchie, 1995; Norcross & Prochaska, 1986a, 1986b). Thus, a model of therapeutic change should be able to account for and describe change outside of psychotherapy and counseling. Too often, thinking about therapeutic change is limited to the context of psychotherapy and counseling, and this is a mistake. Our research has found that if people possess, develop, or implement the precursors, change will occur with or without a therapist. Thus, if change can occur without an empathic therapist, and without a professional theory or approach, then change is largely in the domain of the person.

From a precursors perspective, for change to manifest, it does not matter if the person is in therapy or not. The precursors precede, regulate, and influence the better-known change processes cataloged in psychotherapy. Most of these change processes are from the classical theories; examples are insight, catharsis, changes in beliefs or thoughts, reinforcement, exposure, desensitization, problem-solving, the act of acceptance, working through transference, and the corrective emotional experience. Without the precursors, these latter change processes are not likely to take place.

Human Being as Active Agent

The precursors model of change makes great use of the concept of *active agency*, the view that human beings function as agents, actively influencing both their own minds and their environments (see Harré, 1984; G. S. Howard, 1986; Robinson, 1985). The behaviorist view of human beings leaned more toward a mechanistic or deterministic conception of human beings as merely effects of and responses to environmental forces. The latter perspective did not allow for the idea that human beings actually determined or shaped events in their lives, only that their environments and events determined and shaped them. This perspective, albeit useful in its way, is limited (G. S. Howard, 1986; Mahoney, 1989). In the past two decades, it has steadily diminished in popularity.

In parallel with the decline of this view, the active agency conception has been gaining increasing attention and confirmation during the past 15 years. The idea was central to the older approaches of Rogers and Adler and is now becoming widely accepted. People are indeed influenced by the world, just as much as they are agents influencing that same world in return. Researcher George Howard once told me that his many studies have shown that when it comes to predicting human behavior, the best method we have is to ask the person what he or she is going to do.

In truth, the idea of active agency in psychology has been around for over a century. It was at the basis of the psychology of William James, for example, and is assumed in almost all the major schools of psychotherapy today. In fact, many historians of psychology believe that contemporary psychology in general is now returning to the approaches and conceptions found in James's (1890/1981) classic *Principles of Psychology* (Hergenhahn, 1996).

Metacognition also rests comfortably within the active agency conception, especially with regard to the realm of awareness, making decisions, consciously changing thoughts, exerting effort, forming and reforming mental images, and deliberately acting on the body and its impulses to enact new behaviors. Nowhere are such processes better described than in James's classic book.

The precursors model shows how research confirms active agency and how therapeutic change depends to a large degree on it. Bohart and Tallman (1999) observed that "clients in varying degrees can solve their own problems, come up with their own ideas, and actively contribute to the therapy process by investing their own creative understanding in whatever the therapist is doing" (p. xiv). The precursors model shows how to stimulate this process in clients who are not at all disposed toward change.

The precursors approach views resistance as a choice, as a lifestyle, or as an active seeking and maintaining of self-protection (Mahoney, 1991). Resistance can also be quite creative. Sometimes people seek therapeutic change through misguided means and inaccurate knowledge, and in the process appear to be resisting change at all costs. The truth may be that they are trying to improve but are using the wrong knowledge base and methods, as in the case of abusing drugs or joining a cult. That so much of human change turns out for the worse is often for this reason.

Thus, change is not always therapeutic. For so many difficult clients, almost every experience of change they have ever undergone is negative and acutely associated with pain, suffering, loss, or oppression. Abuse causes change, as do violence and neglect. Even though psychotherapy holds no intention to produce these negative experiences, in a difficult client's mind, psychotherapy's tacit promise of change might be tantamount to the threat of pain by association. Therefore, in this private logic, all change, even positive change, seems guaranteed to be a painful, unbearable experience and should be avoided or deflected at any and every opportunity in order to protect oneself from it. Such a mindset is largely devoid of the precursors of change. Part of the process of establishing the precursors involves overriding and moving beyond such negative associations. Many of the techniques offered in the clinical sections are designed to do exactly that.

DEGREE OF CHANGE: FIRST ORDER AND SECOND ORDER

Depth of change can vary. Although first-order and second-order change are defined a bit differently by different authors, the essential meaning is consistent (Watzlawick, Weakland, & Fisch, 1974). *First-order change* is linear, surface, uncomplicated, straightforward change that takes the form of an adaptation or adjustment. For example, a woman learns new communication skills with which to better get along with her daughter, or a man learns to be assertive with his supervisor.

Second-order change, on the other hand, is profound. It can be defined as a sweeping, deep structure or core change in an individual (Lyddon, 1990). This kind of change affects a person's core self or mode of being or his or her essential worldview. Second-order change radiates into and transfers across the wide array of a person's personality traits, compartmentalizations, activities, and interests. Our research findings agreed with Lyddon's in that second-order change often initially involves intense turmoil or stress that is directly related to internal conflicts of considerable magnitude. These initial conditions are enough to threaten the person's equilibrium and psychological stability prior to the change itself. In other words, second-order change arises, often but not always, out of a crisis. It is also associated with advancement across stages of development (Gilligan, 1982; Hanna et al., 1995). Our research found that the precursors are intimately involved with the occurrence of both first-order and second-order change (Hanna & Ritchie, 1995).

More than two decades ago, Marks (1978), in an often-cited summary of the effectiveness of behavior therapy, noted that the potential of classical therapies to produce major change is relatively weak. He wrote that an important goal for the field should be to develop new therapies that lead to a greater magnitude and intensity of change. When psychotherapy and counseling evolve to the point where almost any client who is free of organic brain damage can derive benefit relatively quickly, deeply, and with relative ease, the discipline will have taken a quantum leap. The suggestion offered by Marks was to explore and develop new approaches that can lead to such results. The model outlined in this book, applied to difficult clients, is not a quantum leap in itself, but is based on the research of second-order change experiences. It is offered to point the way to one possible and perhaps promising avenue of approach toward that goal.

MAJOR POINTS OF THE BOOK

There are several central points in this book that I ask the reader to consider. I list them here as a preparation for the chapters that follow.

1. The presence of the precursors makes therapeutic change possible. Without the precursors, change is unlikely in a client.
2. The absence of even one precursor can inhibit the progress of therapy. When the missing precursor is implemented, therapy can progress more smoothly.
3. Client resistance, no matter how one defines the term, indicates a lack of precursors of change.
4. The precursors regulate the rate, intensity, and magnitude of therapeutic change. The more they are present, the more change is likely to occur.
5. Therapy with difficult clients often involves the use of a different set of skills than therapy with clients who are motivated or involved in the therapy process.
6. With many difficult clients, it is helpful to first establish precursors that are missing or deficient before proceeding to routine therapy approaches.
7. Difficult clients need particularly effective relationship skills on the part of the therapist and a level and degree of empathy that often surpass what is necessary for more willing and involved clients.
8. A therapist's lack of precursors can negatively affect the progress of therapy. Therapists can inadvertently inhibit the level of precursors of clients in a number of ways.
9. A remarkable number of techniques can be used to increase the presence of each of the seven precursors.
10. Therapeutic change is a skill. Clients can learn to do it as a matter of course, and then practice it on their own.

ORGANIZATION OF THE BOOK

This book is divided into five sections. Part I introduces the model. Chapter 1 discusses and reframes the idea of client resistance. Chapter 2 sets up the precursors model. In chapter 3, the details of each of the seven precursors are provided. Each precursor is defined and described according to how it brings about change. The clinical markers of each precursor are also provided to help therapists detect their presence and absence in clients. This latter feature is important for using the assessment.

Part II describes the use of the precursors assessment form. Chapter 4 is devoted to the use of the form with difficult clients and provides several examples. Chapter 5 describes the use of the form to determine the level of precursors of a therapist working with a particular difficult client. In this chapter, examples are given of how the therapist's absence of precursors can have a direct bearing on the climate, tone, and success of therapy.

Part III is the first of two clinical applications sections. Chapter 6 lists important guidelines and tips for forming the therapeutic relationship with difficult clients. Chapter 7 reframes the idea of countertransference as "therapist interference" and shows how to use therapist reactions to clients in a positive manner, as well as how to manage one's own personal issues that inevitably get evoked by difficult clients. Chapter 8 discusses multicultural and gender issues from the too-often neglected viewpoint of oppression. The hidden "benefits" of oppression are discussed with the goal of liberating clients of oppressed groups beyond mere adaptation or adjustment.

Part IV of the book is the second of the clinical applications sections. In many respects, this is the heart of the book. Each chapter provides techniques and practices for the establishment and enhancement of a particular precursor. A list of techniques is given for each precursor.

Finally, Part V of the book discusses some of the problems currently facing psychotherapy and how these can be understood in terms of the precursors model. Advantages of the precursors model are also discussed.

I

UNDERSTANDING DIFFICULT CLIENTS, THERAPEUTIC CHANGE, AND RESISTANCE

1

WHAT MAKES A CLIENT DIFFICULT?

The first duty of a therapeutic model of change is to elucidate both the process of how people change and the process of how they remain the same. Its second duty is to show how change can be achieved where there are many factors working against it. In other words, for a model of change to be worth its therapeutic salt, it should illuminate how to work with clients who are considered to be difficult.

The precursors model attempts to meet each of these challenges, but there is a curious twist: When a client is undergoing change and responding well to the therapy process and procedures, there is little or no need for the precursors approach. Whatever approach the therapist is using is probably just fine. In fact, this may be the case with more than a third of all clients, who respond to just about any professional approach (A. A. Lazarus, 1990). We know from research that all of the major approaches seem to work about equally well, with the exception of a few specifically effective applications for particular disorders, such as exposure for phobias or lithium for bipolar disorder.

The irony is that if not for difficult clients, therapy could become quite automatized, and virtually any client would benefit from just about any competently applied theory. Indeed, some computer therapy programs have been successful with clients, and clients have even reported experiencing "therapist understanding" in a computer program (Selmi, Klein, Greist, Sorrell, & Erdman, 1990). Similarly, bibliotherapy also seems to be quite effective and helpful in a way that does not require live therapists (Christensen & Jacobson, 1994). But these approaches would not be likely to work with difficult clients. Computer therapy programs do not have the finesse or skill required in work with a defiant or passive–aggressive client. It is simply too soon to start automatizing therapy for all clients (Silverman, 1996).

What I intend to show in this chapter is that the reason for success in the cases in which change is occurring is that the precursors are already amply present and well in operation. Both computers and people can do therapy with these clients. However, with difficult, undermining, manipulative, unwilling, or involuntary clients, the precursors are hardly present, if at all. Computer programs and bibliotherapy will not do the job. The therapeutic mandate proposed in this book is to implement the seven precursors of change so that more conventional approaches can begin to take root.

One of the most serious problems facing the field of psychotherapy is that approximately 40% of clients terminate therapy prematurely, that is, before the time agreed on by client and therapist (Garfield, 1994). Several authors believe that lowering this rate is crucial to improving psychotherapy (e.g., Prochaska et al., 1994). If we understood therapeutic change well enough to be able to easily handle impasses, we would have fewer premature exits. Understanding and successfully dealing with resistance is crucial to this goal.

REFRAMING CLIENT RESISTANCE AND DIFFICULTY

The term *resistance* is now generally understood by a wide range of therapists (Mahoney, 1991). But what is it really? Bugental and Bugental (1984) associated resistance with the fear of change. They credited Freud for originally pointing out "what every therapist discovers: The patient who comes seeking desperately for help soon bends every effort to defeat help being given" (p. 54). Historically, Freud viewed resistance as an inner dynamic that leads people to repress and avoid any painful or uncomfortable material in the unconscious. In this context, virtually everyone displays some kind of resistance.

As time went on, however, the term was commonly applied to clients who did not make satisfactory progress in psychotherapy. Currently, it is commonly applied to clients who are defiant, unruly, stubborn, undermining, ambivalent, apathetic, or deceptive in their attempts to avoid change. A good working definition of *resistance* is "the patient's efforts to obstruct the aims and process of treatment" (Walrond-Skinner, 1986, p. 298). In the past few years, resistance as a term has become less popular, and resistant clients have been more humanely and accurately referred to as "difficult," both to themselves and therapists. In the context of this book, a *difficult client* is one for whom change is not forthcoming in spite of the therapist's and client's efforts to achieve it.

Change is difficult enough for people in general. Attempting to keep things the same is generally easier than making things different. Many people find the prospect of change to be upsetting, threatening, overwhelming, painful, ill advised, impossible, or just plain silly. Whatever the reason, if a person does not find the prospect of change appealing, change is not likely to be forthcoming. Assuming that people are to some degree free agents, imposing change on a person, regardless of professional credentials, looks like punishment or even fascism to a client who is not convinced that it will help. Such clients fight hard to preserve whatever precious freedom and self-determination they have left. They dig in their heels and engage in a power struggle with the therapist, seeking to avoid any kind of surrender to a person they do not trust.

Resistance as Self-Protection

In his classic book *Human Change Processes* (1991), Mahoney pointed out that people who actively fight beneficial change do so because their beliefs and general outlook are so delicately in balance that change appears as a threat so great that it could cause collapse, and with it the loss of functioning and mental equilibrium. Interpreted in a slightly different way, to the client for whom change is not appealing, the prospect of change, therapeutic or otherwise, represents the onset of a crisis. *Crisis* has been defined as an event or events that cause cognitive, emotional, and environmental turmoil so great that the person goes into a kind of shock called "disequilibrium" (Janosik, 1986). Examples of such events are the death of a child, abuse, suicidal ideation, or tragedies caused by natural disasters. Crisis work consists not of enhancing the person's coping skills and range of functioning, but in restoring that person to his or her precrisis level of coping and functioning.

Some clients experience a different kind of disequilibrium as a result of the perceived threat of change. They have feelings of instability and uncertainty, wild emotional swings, and loss of control. Clients of this bent understandably get angry, oppositional, and spiteful toward a therapist or anyone who pushes them to change. I have found that some of these clients are suffering from a previously unidentified trauma and are still trying to hold things together to get along in the world. From this perspective, it is wise to reframe difficulty and resistance as a form of self-protection rather than subtly or not so subtly implying that such clients are being stubborn or misguided.

Clients "Trained" to Be Difficult by Their Therapists

When a client is not changing, it is often for an excellent reason, and it could be that a therapist is indirectly bringing about the problem. The following case descriptions present a few examples of clients whose therapists played a role in their difficulty. Two of these case examples will be re-examined in greater detail in chapter 5, where the therapists are rated on the precursors assessment form.

Beth was a woman in her late 30s who was losing her home because of financial losses and losing her children to a former husband, who was falsely accusing her of abusing them. She was frantic. Her previous therapist had insisted that she explore issues of childhood, which were causing her current problems. The implicit promise was that if she resolved her childhood issues, her current problems would also resolve. Beth was an angry, suspicious, and bitter client, who was still desperate for help.

Her new therapist found it perfectly reasonable that Beth was unwilling to explore her childhood and her emotions. What she needed from therapy was a problem-solving approach. Beth had been "resistant" to anything else and was very difficult to work with. But with the new therapist, she worked hard to resolve the real-time problems in which she was immersed. Beth's resistance was caused by the first therapist's misguided insistence on the "proper" treatment.

A different example of therapist-initiated "resistance" is the case of Kurt, a 31-year-old male therapist, and his client Janey, a female university senior in her mid-20s. Janey was highly cooperative in answering questions in her early sessions with Kurt, and early on she seemed to value her therapy sessions. She freely and openly discussed her issues and problems. Her major complaint was that the men in her life verbally mistreated and did not respect her. She claimed to be worried about this issue and wondered if she would ever find someone who really loved her. She was articulate, feminine, and attractive, easily identified her beliefs and feelings, and reported several seemingly important insights. On the other hand, there was a certain naïveté about her and a tendency to smile even while in pain and to laugh with a shrill, almost tinny tone.

After 20 therapy sessions, change was not apparent. She still allowed her current male partner to verbally abuse her, and she complained of the same problems from session to session. Finally, she stopped showing up for sessions and did not return telephone calls.

In attempting to understand all this in supervision, Kurt discovered, reluctantly and with no small amount of embarrassment, that he harbored a hidden belief, formed in high school, that "girls with fake laughter" and who "smiled for no reason" were "stupid" and not likely to ever achieve any kind of significance in their lives other than "finding a husband." He realized that this bias slipped out in various ways in his interactions with Janey, and although he never did or said anything overtly disrespectful, he never led her to be correspondingly difficult. That is, she was compliant and agreeable on the surface but never really moved toward change. He also realized that if he had provided Janey with the skills to cope with and confront her current male partner, she might have benefited more from those 20 sessions.

A quite different example involves Jerry, a pleasant 30-year-old man who reported feeling "lost" and "wayward" about the lack of direction in his life. Although quite intelligent, he had no career plans, and nothing seemed to inspire him to want to do anything with his life. Nancy, his therapist, had nine years of experience working in a university counseling center. In supervision, she reported, after 16 sessions, that he was so "totally passive" and so "resistant" to help that she could not get him "to do anything" at all about his problem.

When asked to report her real feelings about the client, she was embarrassed to report that she found him "irritating" and "maddening" to work with, and she disliked the way he talked so slowly and deliberately, as though he were "picking each word, one by one." To her credit, she felt quite badly about her feelings toward him, but also said that she was not able to help and suggested referring Jerry to another therapist.

The supervisor recommended that she write down all the people in her life of whom Jerry reminded her. The next week, she reported with a sense of relief and astonishment that Jerry reminded her of her sexually abusive brother, from whom she had cut herself off 20 years earlier. After this supervision, she no longer considered Jerry to be resistant or difficult, and he began to make progress. In fact, she began to like him. At one point, Jerry told her that she seemed "nicer." This therapist learned a valuable lesson.

Such examples show how clients can be difficult because of the therapist's faulty perceptions or an inappropriate or ill-advised approach. The therapists were not immediately aware of their own contributions to their clients' perceived resistance. It is extremely important to emphasize this aspect of difficulty and resistance in therapy.

Clients Difficult All on Their Own

In many cases the client is difficult in spite of the best efforts of the most competent therapists, and three are described in the following case examples. Diagnoses from the *Diagnostic and Statistical Manual of Mental Disorders* are deliberately omitted so that a distinct picture of the person can emerge without labels or clinical categories. We will re-examine these cases in chapter 5.

Tommy

Tommy, age 29, was tall, blond, handsome, charming, quite humorous, and thoroughly self-centered. He was married to Julie, whom he described as a loving and devoted wife and caring mother of their three children. His wife and he had been "fighting," and she insisted that he go to therapy.

Tommy hated himself for cheating on her at every opportunity, but he would not, or could not, stop. He would sometimes criticize her for being stupid and foolish, but when challenged, he would say, "My wife is a saint." He said it was "only natural" for men to cheat on their wives. He reported that one of his friends had advised him to seek therapy because he was so unhappy and because he was "throwing away a good woman." A salesperson who regularly made house calls as part of his work, Tommy was so good at concealing his activities that Julie had no inkling of his promiscuity. Tommy, meanwhile, showed neither preference nor prejudice regarding the women he seduced. Whether they were thin, obese, white, or of color, he loved to charm and exploit women.

Tommy boasted of his lovemaking ability and frankly said that such talents were wasted on a wife. Then, in almost the same breath, and in an explosion of guilt, he ruthlessly criticized and condemned himself for being a liar and a phony. He believed, as a Christian, that he was headed "straight to hell" for his many affairs. His fear of hell seemed to trouble him more than his infidelity, much more so, it appeared, than any potential harm done to his family or marriage. Tommy had been to three therapists trying to rid himself of his anxiety. He had apparently competed with and fought his therapists at every turn. In a tone of voice that combined both bravado and shame, he claimed that none of his therapists were of any help at all.

His current therapist deduced that his apparent interest in therapy amounted to the improbable goal of reducing his anxiety without changing his behaviors. Beyond what he stated, his chief goal for therapy seemed to be reassurance that he would indeed make it to heaven, that his behaviors were really OK, and that he was a good person. He had also confided in his minister but found no support for his promiscuity.

Joy

Joy identified herself as a "former showgirl" from the Lake Tahoe region in Nevada. She was in her late 30s, slim, with dark hair and bright blue eyes. She was heavily into the occult and new age pursuits, believing that she was highly clairvoyant and psychically gifted. She had been involved with several new age cults. She was actively and avowedly celibate and freely admitted to a contempt for men, although she dressed seductively. She also claimed that she was destined to find her "soul mate" sometime in the next year. She had been to many psychics and astrologers but had decided to seek therapy as a way of opening the psychological blocks that stood in the way of her realizing her "destiny" as an occult "adept."

In therapy, her insistence on staying "positive" was so strong that she avoided any disclosure that was associated with negative emotion or inferred weakness, as such things ran counter to the list of new age affirmations that she repeated to herself each day. She seemed interested only in discovering how she could undo the lingering negative "vibrations" of the destructive people of her past. These included her family, ex-husband, and many of what she called "false friends." She assumed that psychotherapy could teach her how to completely cut herself off from all negative emotions and influences, especially her parents. Joy was also highly demanding and wanted instant results. Quite rigid in her thinking, she often lectured her therapist on new age principles, which she said were superior to those of psychotherapy. Not surprisingly, Joy reached a rather dramatic impasse in her therapy after eight sessions, showing considerable impatience and correctly claiming to have derived no benefit.

Ricky

Ricky was 18 years old and a member of a street gang. He was tall, handsome, and muscular and had been placed in an outpatient adolescent drug and alcohol treatment program when he was 17. He was addicted to crack cocaine and was on probation for its possession and sale. He was a father to at least three children born of adolescent girls. He reported quite factually that all women loved him, and he blatantly and proudly admitted, after some coaxing, that he liked to impregnate young girls. It was also clear that he had supplied many young people with drugs and had committed other crimes, although, according to his probation officer, he had not been brought up on these charges.

He had an outwardly pleasant demeanor and smiled in a cocky, self-assured manner. But there was a coldness about him as well—a deeply disturbing lack of warmth or engagement that sometimes evoked visceral reactions of intimidation in the therapists in the program. Ricky never exhibited any overt violence. However, with any kind of confrontation of his behaviors or attitudes came a subtle nonverbal threat of intimidation. He had a way of cocking his head and curling his lip in a silent, smiling snarl whenever questioned about his lifestyle or his attitudes. These defiant behaviors seemed to open a window into a deep, smoldering hostility. Ricky was highly intelligent and manipulative. He displayed an extraordinary sense of entitlement that was, of course, part of his criminal mindset. In therapy, it soon became clear that he was immersed in a deep hatred of the world and people in general. Therapy to him was a form of control and punishment to be outwitted and thwarted at all costs. He often told his therapist, "I ain't gonna let you f--- with my head."

Difficult Indeed

The above examples describe people who were extraordinarily difficult to engage in therapy. Standard therapeutic approaches were of no help, and each client was adept at strangling the therapeutic change process. Even those who recognized that change was necessary did not want the kind of change that psychotherapy offered.

AT THE ROOTS OF DIFFICULTY AND RESISTANCE: ONTOLOGICAL CORE BELIEFS AND IMPLICIT LEARNING

Difficulty or resistance to change has to do with a person's fundamental belief system and specific beliefs, which are formed so early in a person's life that the seeds of its formulation are sown before he or she learns to speak. Such preverbal beliefs about the nature of the world and life itself can be extremely powerful in forming a person's attitude toward life and living. These specific beliefs are called *ontological core schema* (Ottens & Hanna, 1998) because they are beliefs about the nature of reality itself and about some of the fundamental aspects of being alive. They take the form of preverbal judgments formed about such fundamental subjects as awareness, love, people, self, problems, and the world in general. Karr-Morse and Wiley (1997) cited evidence that beliefs and attitudes toward violence, for example, can be formed before age two, long before verbal expression takes place. Examples of some of these fundamental preverbal beliefs that directly affect the psychotherapy process are "interactions with people cause pain," "awareness of a problem only makes it worse," and "people don't care about anybody."

Implicit learning (Dowd & Courchaine, 1996), which is related to the earlier idea of implicit theory formation (Wegner & Vallacher, 1977), is similar to ontological core schemas or beliefs. *Implicit learning* is a process, engaged in by virtually all human beings, wherein complex concepts and beliefs are formed that are not encoded or structured in the mind in a verbal format. These beliefs are also formed at an age so early that they "are not easily accessible via language" (Dowd & Courchaine, 1996, p. 164) and are thus highly difficult to address in therapy that relies solely on talking. Because much of therapy is a verbal process, this may explain why change is so often difficult to achieve through language-bound techniques or methods.

Through implicit learning, people form a set of assumptions that serves as a platform on which a person's entire meaning system can rest. These assumptions are often highly emotionally charged and if challenged will evoke vehement reactions ranging from protest and defiance to betrayal and hurt. As Dowd and Courchaine put it, "The involvement of older, more primitive knowing systems may occur whenever strong affect is present" (p. 173). If those primary, fundamental assumptions do not change, then neither will the person. There is an old saw that one should never discuss religion or politics in casual conversation; these topics, like many discussed in therapy, evoke deep emotional responses, or what Burns (1980) called "hot thoughts." In my experience, implicit knowledge can be changed, but only with care and extreme courtesy, and usually permission from the client must be deliberately and openly sought beforehand.

For example, I once had a client, Catherine, who held a doctoral degree in psychology and who was a psychotherapist in her own private practice. She was extremely self-aware and articulate. Somehow, she came to be convinced that no one would ever be there for her when she really needed them, not even her best friends. When I asked, she said that even when her friends had been supportive and there for her, she always considered it surprising and unlikely. She had felt deep emotional anxiety over this issue and had consistently framed and described it as a problem in trusting others. Being familiar with her highly admirable qualities and knowing her to be a trusting person, I eventually became highly suspicious of this view. When I asked her if trust might not be the real problem, she became quite upset with me and insisted that trust had been a problem all her life and that she was insistent on working through it.

I then asked her if she noticed how upset she became when I asked the question. She nodded. I asked her if she would be willing to explore that but said that if at any point she thought it was a waste of time to pursue this, to let me know and we would move on. She agreed. I then asked her to hold on tightly to that feeling of upset and protest toward my question and to follow it into her mind. Being highly aware, she was easily capable of such a directive. I then asked her to allow any memory images to emerge that might be related to this feeling. In a moment she began to cry. She was soon relating memory images in which she was in her crib crying, and waiting for her mother to come to her. But her mother never came, and she remembered being horribly alone and deeply despondent, abandoned, and unloved. It was during this time, she said, that she formed a belief that no one is reliable and that people cannot be counted on to be there in times of need. She estimated that she was about a year to 18 months old.

Of course, it is not important whether the memory is accurate, or if it actually occurred, or if that was her actual age at the time. Adler (1956) noted many decades ago that early memories need not be real for a person to obtain therapeutic benefit from examining them. It is the ontological belief about people that was at the heart of the problem, regardless of the story content.

After this session, Catherine called her mother and told her about this early memory. Her mother, as Catherine related the story to me, was quite surprised, and told her how bad she had felt listening to her baby cry for long periods. She said that she did not attend to her because the conventional wisdom at the time was to avoid spoiling the child by deliberately letting her cry, which allegedly would make the child more self-reliant. Seeing and dismissing the ontological core belief was of great value to Catherine, but when she heard her mother more or less verify her memory, it was of great significance indeed.

CLIENT VARIABLES AS CRUCIAL INFLUENCES ON THERAPY SUCCESS

The case examples illustrate the wide range of manifestations of difficulty and resistance. But there is a highly important angle to consider: the qualities and characteristics that the client brings to therapy. These are commonly referred to as *client variables*.

As nearly as can be determined from research evidence, client variables are the most powerful influences on successful outcomes in therapy (Bergin & Lambert, 1978; Frank, 1974; Lambert, 1992; O'Malley, Suh, & Strupp, 1983). There is considerable evidence that these are also the most important factors on which to focus a model of change. Client variables include personal qualities, environmental influences, and what the client actually does in therapy and in life. About 55% of possible influences on the outcome of therapy seem to depend on the personal qualities and characteristics of the client (see Hanna, 1996; Lambert, 1992). People can and do change on their own without the help of a therapist of any persuasion (Norcross & Prochaska, 1986a, 1986b), and the skills and influence that a therapist brings to the session are not nearly so important as the client's contribution. After all, it is the client who ultimately does the work and who makes the changes. But the eternal question is, What kind of client is likely to change? If we knew the answer to this question, we could to some extent predict who will respond to therapy and who will not.

The Search for Personality Traits

Some researchers have believed that personality traits or qualities have more of an influence on therapy results than any other conditions. Some of these traits are viewed as leading to positive therapy results and others as obstructing the progress of therapy. Recently, some researchers (e.g., Beutler & Clarkin, 1990; Garfield, 1994) cataloged a variety of desirable client traits such as hardiness, coping ability, locus of control, ego strength, positive attitude, interpersonal reactance, and other personality patterns. Beutler and Clarkin (1990) noted how little had been written about negative qualities—the "qualities of patients which serve a . . . limit-setting function on motivation and compliance across treatment modes, settings, and formats." They went on to say, "It is commonly assumed that certain patient qualities bode poorly for mental health treatment, while others are seen to be necessary characteristics for benefiting from our services" (p. 67). If this is indeed the case, it would seem a good idea to isolate what qualities predict or bode well for successful results, as well as those that do not. Unfortunately, this quest does not seem to have been particularly fruitful, as much of the research in this area has been inconclusive (Garfield, 1994).

Rather than give up, however, it may be wise to redirect the search toward qualities that are not bound to personality traits or types, and the precursors are such qualities. These qualities should be capable of being displayed by anyone capable of change, and that means almost anyone at all. The qualities should also be relatively free of theoretical allegiance in terms of jargon or labels. For example, "ego strength" is a psychodynamic concept not easily translated into more widely understood terms, although it does seem to bear a resemblance across paradigms to the concept of coping ability. Much preferred would be a theory-free, common language formulation of this phenomenon.

In addition, such qualities should be readily recognizable in their own right. Unlike personality traits, a person might have these characteristics today and be without them tomorrow. These could then be pointed to as distinctly identifiable, direct influences on change. Our research indicates that the precursors fulfill these criteria (Hanna & Ritchie, 1995).

Client Involvement and Motivation

According to current research, two client qualities seem to be major indicators of successful outcomes. Many studies have demonstrated the importance of the involvement of the client in working in therapy (Garfield, 1994). O'Malley et al. (1983) found that "patient involvement showed the most consistent relationship with outcome" (p. 585). They defined *involvement* as active participation and cooperation, without hostility, negativity, or distrust of the therapist. The results of this study were borne out by later studies by Gomes-Schwartz (1978); Kolb, Beutler, Davis, Crago, and Shanfield (1985); and Reandeau and Wampold (1991). In their review of the literature, Orlinsky, Grawe, and Parks (1994) found that cooperation by the client related positively to outcome in 71% of findings cited in their review. Bergin and Garfield (1994) concluded that it is the client, more than the therapist, who implements the change process, and that without the active involvement of the client, nothing the therapist does will have any effect. They added that success is not a question of whether therapy works, but whether the client works in therapy to make change happen.

What these studies teach us is that if a client is not involved in the therapy process, he or she is not likely to achieve any significant degree of therapeutic change. When this involvement is active and engaged, according to Bohart and Tallman (1999), the client's own self-healing process takes over.

Another client variable is usually referred to as "motivation," which has also been found to be present in instances of successful outcome (Luborsky, Crits-Christoph, Mintz, & Auerbach, 1988). Maslow (1970) recognized the importance of motivation, and Blum (1988) saw it as related to a move toward freedom. Cullare (1996) noted that motivation is the opposite of resistance. It is not at all surprising that Orlinsky and associates (1994) found that when clients identified and reported the presence of their own motivation, it was related to a positive result in 80% of the findings they investigated.

Unfortunately, motivation is one of those concepts that is deceptively simple on the surface but is actually quite difficult to define. Rosenbaum and Horowitz (1983) observed that motivation is "sufficiently fuzzy so that almost any variable can be thought of as relevant" (p. 351). They noted that motivation is not a simple commodity and that it is difficult to identify how it actually manifests in therapy. The same is true, unfortunately, for involvement. It is necessary to further unpack both of these important concepts so that they can be used and implemented by therapists. This task is a major function of the precursors model.

Motivation, Involvement, and the Use of Techniques

Study the vast number of theories, procedures, and techniques used in psychotherapy, and one finds that most assume some degree of motivation and involvement on the part of the client. In the above cases of Tommy, Joy, and Ricky, involvement was lacking in all three, and motivation was either absent, in the case of Ricky, or alloyed and misdirected in spite of a stated interest in change by Tommy and Joy. Techniques typically used with clients, such as role playing, the empty chair, identifying and disputing irrational beliefs or dysfunctional cognitions, behavioral contracting, desensitization, and so on usually will not work with a client who is unmotivated and uninvolved. Without involvement and motivation, few techniques are likely to be effective, in spite of the therapist's level of skill. That is why positive outcomes seem to be related to these variables.

As an example, I have encountered many clients who steadfastly refused to engage in role plays. They thought such an exercise was "useless" or "stupid" and simply would not do it. The empty chair, not surprisingly, was viewed with even more disdain. I have many times heard the statement, "I ain't talking to no empty chair!" The same has been true for many difficult clients' attitudes toward other techniques as well. Never mind that research has shown role plays, for example, to be a powerful change-producing technique. If the client is not involved or motivated, little is going to happen.

In view of all of these issues, the field is clearly in need of broader and deeper understanding of why people change and why they do not. In the chapters that follow, a model will be presented as one way to undercut motivation, involvement, and the hundreds of theories of therapy, linking each to the primary functions and conditions that are the precursors of change.

2

TOWARD A MODEL OF CHANGE FOR DIFFICULT CLIENTS

To make use of research findings that show the importance of client variables, especially motivation and involvement, these variables need to be further examined so as to be readily applicable in therapy. Their vagueness makes it difficult to derive applications from current conceptualizations. However, as motivation, involvement, and related variables become unpacked, what emerges is a set of functions and conditions that a client might engage or hold that are specifically conducive to therapeutic change. These are, of course, the precursors. The precursors can give definition, detail, and applicability to research findings on motivation and involvement and other client variables.

In this chapter, I review the seven precursors and their definitions. I explore the advantages of shifting the focus of therapy from a theoretical perspective toward change itself, with the precursors model being an example of such a shift. I briefly review the current state of psychotherapy theory and techniques. I then describe the precursors model and its potential to expedite therapy with difficult clients and examine the idea of therapeutic change as a skill that can be learned and refined. The chapter continues with a discussion of metacognition in the context of therapeutic change and of the need to use a different set of skills when working with difficult clients.

THE SEVEN PRECURSORS TO CHANGE

The precursors model envisions the following seven elements as necessary for therapeutic change to occur:

1. A *sense of necessity* is a felt sense of urgency or need on the part of the client that change take place. In the person's assessment, current conditions are not at all satisfactory and must give way to a different set of circumstances.

2. A *willingness or readiness to experience anxiety or difficulty* is the client's recognition that he or she is willing to feel the discomfort that comes with change. *Defensiveness*, the diametric opposite to this precursor, is usually defined as an attempt to avoid anxiety. When this precursor is present, anxiety or difficulty is not resisted but directly experienced, in the knowledge that doing so is necessary for change to occur.
3. *Awareness* is knowing that a problem exists and having a good sense of what that problem or issue is, as well as of the thoughts, feelings, and behaviors connected with it. Awareness is the opposite of denial or obliviousness. Without it, a person has no idea where to direct his or her resources toward change. With awareness, a client can pinpoint areas of dysfunction or need and identify relevant thoughts, feelings, and behaviors.
4. *Confronting the problem* is the culmination of awareness but is not the same. Confronting is the steady and deliberate attending to and observing of anything that is intimidating, painful, or confusing, in spite of the inclination to avoid, shun, or act out. It is operative when a client is looking at a problem squarely and directly and continues to observe, explore, or investigate it until he or she grasps its essence.
5. *Effort or will toward change* indicates action actually taken toward solving the problem. It is the expending of energy as well as the movement made. It also involves the will in the sense of making a commitment, coming to a decision, and initiating action. Effort manifests in two domains: the mind, in changing one's thoughts and attitudes, or the world, in coping with real-life situations.
6. *Hope for change* is the client's realistic expectation that change can, and will probably, occur. It is not wishing, longing, desiring, or yearning. The hopeful client sees the possibility of change and the path to accomplish it. This recognition has the power to motivate even an apathetic client, especially if that client also has a sense of necessity.
7. *Social support for change* consists of being engaged in confiding, supportive relationships that are dedicated to the well-being and improvement of the client. Social support paves the path toward therapeutic change when those relationships function to enhance and inspire the presence of each of the other precursors.

AT THE BASIS OF THEORY

The precursors approach is not a theory per se, but a model. It is a compilation of a set of change characteristics and their implications. The precursors are prior to and underlie all the major theories of psychotherapy, making them applicable across theories, and in that sense this model is part of the psychotherapy integration movement. For many years researchers and clinicians sought to improve psychotherapy along the lines of theory. The search for a new, global theoretical perspective took up the attention of many researchers and clinicians. In the process, the field accumulated nearly 500 theories and approaches, of which 50 or so could be considered to be major.

It is now clear that the once lofty ideal of the global theory of psychotherapy has lost its luster. The past 20 years have seen a shift toward integrating theories and approaches. The shift probably began with the classic study by Smith and Glass, in 1977, which found no evidence that any one of the major theories is more effective than any of the others.

Little evidence has accumulated to dissuade researchers from the idea that all of the major schools of psychotherapy, from psychoanalysis and Adlerian to cognitive and behavioral, are roughly equivalent in effectiveness (see Stiles et al., 1986; Wampold et al., 1997). Since the Smith and Glass study, it has been generally acknowledged that the field entered a "post-theoretical" era (Omer & London, 1988). We now have a host of approaches that are characterized by categories and terms such as *eclectic*, *integrative*, *transtheoretical*, and containing the *common factors* of therapy. All have made valuable contributions.

For example, A. A. Lazarus's (1976, 1989b, 1996) development of technical eclecticism streamlined psychotherapy, allowing for concentration on effective techniques with a minimum of theory. Wachtel's (1977) theoretical integration of behavioral and psychoanalytic therapies showed how two seemingly incompatible theories can work together in relative harmony. The common factors approach, pioneered by Frank, is an attempt to find what each of the major theories has in common, seeking the middle path between advocating techniques and combining theories (see Frank, 1961; Frank & Frank, 1991; Grencavage & Norcross, 1990). Among many important observations, Frank pointed out that a rationale or myth (theory) is necessary to explain the healing process for a client. Finally, the stages of change, outlined by Prochaska, Norcross, and DiClemente in their various articles and books, indicated how change takes place at various stages of therapy (e.g., Prochaska et al., 1994).

However, Norcross (1990) pointed out a decade ago that this focus of attention on combining and integrating theories and treatments has given rise, indirectly and inadvertently, to a host of new and additional theories of the integrative and eclectic variety. The sheer number (well over 50) of such solutions has added even greater complexity to the theoretical picture and, in some ways, has rendered the original problem worse than before. Nevertheless, the original theories, as well as the integrative approaches, continue to provide a vast treasure of insights concerning psychotherapy and human behavior.

Realigning Psychotherapy Theories Around Change

It is now generally recognized that dogmatically insisting on the "Truth" of any of psychotherapy theory is a mistake born of philosophical naïveté (see Hanna, 1994; G. S. Howard, 1986; R. B. Miller, 1983). Many theories take positions that were abandoned by the discipline of philosophy long ago. *Cognitive therapy theory*, for example, traditionally subscribes to the primacy of cognition, the idea that cognition is more important than behavior or affect in approaching various psychological problems. This view has its roots in the centuries-old philosophy of rationalism, the idea that the world is based on rational principles and amenable to rational speculations and explanations, held by philosophers such as Descartes and Spinoza. However, there is little or no reason to believe that cognition really is primary, and recent developments in cognitive therapy indicate a trend toward including affective experiencing (see Mahoney & Lyddon, 1988; Ottens & Hanna, 1998). Research by Zajonc (1980) and A. A. Lazarus (1989b), for example, has shown that cognition and affect are interdependent and that affect and even sensations can precede cognition in many cases.

The opposite of rationalism is *empiricism*, or the idea that we must rely on the senses to understand the world. Ultimately, empiricism led to a philosophy known as *logical positivism*, in which its original intent was to abandon any metaphysical or other statement or theory that could not be verified by scientific inquiry. Karl Popper (1963), the noted philosopher of science, once told Nobel Laureate Peter Medawar that logical positivism takes the naive position that "the world is all surface" (Medawar, 1984, p. 101) and that mind or mental states need not be considered. Philosophy abandoned logical positivism decades ago due to its reductionistic, overly simplistic outlook on the world.

The idea of mentalism in behaviorism is a prime example of this simplistic conception. For years, the use of the term *mind* was not allowed in psychology and was looked down on as shortsighted and unenlightened. Research, however, has made it ever more clear that our perceptions and sense experiences are directly affected by our thoughts and beliefs. Nevertheless, much of experimental psychology is still bound up with and by positivist assumptions (G. S. Howard, 1986; Mahoney, 1989).

Current theories of psychotherapy neither capture nor contain truth any better than those older philosophies. They contain too many elements of metaphysics. Both religion and psychotherapy theory are inextricable from metaphysics, one of the most perpetually perplexing domains of human knowledge (Hanna, 1994; R. B. Miller, 1983; O'Donohue, 1989; Tjeltveit, 1989). *Metaphysics* is, simply stated, the seeking or study of knowledge that is beyond the capacity of science to verify. Most theories of psychotherapy contain metaphysical elements that cannot be verified by science, such as the id, the self-actualizing tendency, or the collective unconscious. The self is also a metaphysical construct that Adler (1956), as well as the philosopher Hume (1739/1978), poignantly called into question. Kant (1787/1929) showed in his classic *Critique of Pure Reason* that reason alone cannot provide the solutions to metaphysical problems. William James (1907) also repeatedly showed in his various treatises that reason was not capable of solving metaphysical problems. James, whom Alfred North Whitehead (1925, 1938) hailed as one of the four most important philosophers in all of history, developed pragmatism as a dialectical means of coping with and transcending theoretical and conceptual conundrums.

Pragmatism, in a psychotherapy context, is a dialectical mode of thinking that fluidly moves between and among theories, without any attachment beyond the immediate therapeutic situation. In the Jamesian tradition, what is true is so in terms of its pragmatic value. For example, the highly praised idea of human free will is a metaphysical position that has pragmatic value in therapy. The problem is that our fascination with theories obscures the need for the focus on what actually produces change. It is in James's pragmatism and his radical empiricism that the precursors approach finds its inspiration.

I have described in much greater detail elsewhere (Hanna, 1994) how the major theories of psychotherapy are deeply entrenched in metaphysics and how an approach based on James's philosophy of radical empiricism might liberate it. From a Jamesian perspective, if therapeutic change is indeed at or near the essence of psychotherapy, perhaps there is good reason to focus the development of therapy models and speculation around therapeutic change itself, what produces it and what enhances it. This is the heart of the precursors approach, and it is no surprise that researchers have been advocating this for more than a decade. However, the question remains for psychotherapy integrationists: What do we do with all these theories?

Theories Are for Clients

From a precursors perspective, the classical theories of psychotherapy are better reserved for use by clients than by therapists. Clients, for example, have much to gain by understanding that thinking influences feeling and behavior. Of course, cognitive therapy theory is not absolute truth, but many clients have used its ideas to effectively overcome their difficulties. As Frank observed, the healing process seems to require some kind of rationale or myth to serve as an explanation of a psychological problem, and the theory of each therapeutic approach provides a different rationale or myth. Thus, depressed clients can benefit, for example, from the 19th-century James–Lange theory of behavior, which states that if one acts confidently or happily, eventually one begins to think and feel that way as well. Similarly, clients can respond positively to existential and Gestalt explanations, just as they do with those of Adlerian and family systems.

Theoretical explanations have healing value in themselves—as reframes—and should be readily available for clients who might be able to benefit from them when their situation warrants. Of course, students and practicing therapists should also study them, but not to the degree that they would actually believe in the ultimate truth of any one of them. Dialectical philosophers such as James, Heidegger, and Husserl have shown that theories possess no truth value in and of themselves. Theories are for clients, and the realization that the so-called truths of psychotherapy can be framed, reframed, "jargonized," and "rejargonized" from a variety of perspectives can liberate therapists from entrenchment in any one theory. That liberation allows for a fluid, dialectical movement between and among therapy approaches, with the needs of the client dictating the therapeutic approach chosen. This is a primary assumption of the psychotherapy integration perspective. Unfortunately, however, many therapists continue to cling to a single approach, in spite of the difficulties this brings (Beutler, 2000).

Carl Whitaker (1976), the renowned family therapist, believed that theories were ultimately destructive to therapy. He put it this way: "My theory is that all theories are bad except for the beginner's game playing, until he gets the courage to give up theories and just live" (p. 154). Whitaker believed that adherence to a theory is a way of avoiding the anxiety of simply not knowing what the truth about human beings really is. Strean (1993) was even more direct:

> It is helpful for practitioners to study carefully their affinity to a particular theoretical perspective or therapeutic model as well as their abhorrence of other perspectives and models. When our clients idealize and/or

> denounce certain individuals, or certain "isms" with a great deal of affect, we try to help them resolve their infantile attachments and overdetermined hatred. (p. 14)

Precursors View of Psychotherapy Theory

The precursors model is neither antitheoretical nor anti-intellectual. The precursors model allows and encourages a therapist to incorporate any or all theories and techniques as appropriate. Each of the theories makes use of the precursors, although seldom making an effort to recognize or identify them. Search the more than 400 theories of psychotherapy, and one finds that the precursors of change are always presupposed. Read the hundreds of successful case studies cited by therapists in books and articles, and the precursors are there and operative in those clients, regardless of the theory espoused. Theories are best suited to use with clients for their therapeutic benefit. It has long been held that scientific psychotherapy needs to be more aware of the implications of philosophy (see, for example, R. B. Miller, 1983).

AT THE BASIS OF TECHNIQUES

Techniques abound in psychotherapy. Role playing, the empty chair, identifying and disputing dysfunctional cognitions, behavioral contracting, guided imagery, systematic desensitization, flooding, and self-monitoring are just a few. Just as the various theories assume the existence of the precursors, psychotherapy techniques are implemented with the assumption that the precursors are present in the clients who engage in techniques. However, this assumption is almost never stated as such. In the broad psychotherapy literature, the precursors are only seldom mentioned in the context of being necessary for techniques to work. Implementing techniques with a client who has none of the precursors would not be much different than doing therapy with a client who is sound asleep. Just as theories might be oriented around change, it may also be advantageous to orient techniques around change itself in the form of functions such as the precursors. As in the case of theories, the precursors are at the basis of techniques; constantly assumed but seldom acknowledged.

Empirically Validated Treatments

A relatively recent approach, admirably related to an attempt to solve or bypass the theoretical dilemma, has been for researchers to isolate those techniques in psychotherapy that have research support, eventually eliminating those that do not. At first glance, this sounds entirely reasonable. A list of techniques that can be relied on by therapists as scientifically sound would be most useful. For example, we have long known that exposure or systematic desensitization techniques seem to be best for specific phobias.

However worthy this project seems, it has been criticized (see, for example, Beutler, 2000; Drozd & Goldfried, 1996; Silverman, 1996; Strupp, 1997) as being premature and shortsighted. Silverman, editor of a major psychotherapy journal, noted that there was a hidden bias of ideology behind this movement that is destructive to the actual purpose of determining the effective treatments. The bias, he noted, is toward behavioral and cognitive approaches, with an implicit condemnation of all other practitioners and schools of therapy. He went on to say that this seemingly worthwhile effort is actually entrenched in a dogmatic, rigid belief that the behavioral and cognitive approaches are superior and that because of this all other approaches should be abandoned.

In other words, this "research" solution is flawed by the recurrent problem of theoretical favoritism. In addition, Garfield (1998) noted that the focus on empirically supported treatments, as it is being currently done, runs the risk of ignoring crucial client and therapist characteristics and their effects on outcomes. In support of this, Anderson and Strupp (1996) found that the most effective therapists occasionally violated manual guidelines for the sake of therapeutic change. Thus, while admirable in its intent, the effort to catalog scientifically sound techniques may be a bit too simplistic in its current conception and needs to account more for the complexities and ambiguities of psychotherapy (Davison, 1998).

The Precursors Perspective

Beutler (2000) reported a work group's conclusions on empirically validated treatments that were in direct agreement with the approach in this book. One of the conclusions was to "focus more on understanding the basic principles and strategies of change than on theoretically linked techniques" (p. 1002). From a precursors perspective, techniques, empirically validated or not, are dependent on the precursors of change for their effectiveness. If a client has no sense of necessity, is not ready for or willing to experience any difficulty in therapy, thinks that there is no problem at all, and will not look at it or do anything about the problem or issue, virtually none of those empirically validated treatments will work. The therapist's task then shifts toward getting the client to the point where the technique in question can take hold and be engaged. If the precursors are present and the relationship is sound, the technique will probably be effective.

The reason the major schools of therapy are more or less equivalent is rather simple: All have a more or less equal grasp on change itself. The same is generally true for techniques. Whether theory or technique, each requires, draws from, and makes use of the precursors. The absence of precursors means the absence of change. Any therapy, any procedure, or any approach that evokes, inspires, or brings to emergence the primary prerequisites of change will tend to be a valid therapy. And the therapist who encourages the presence of precursors will be an effective therapist regardless of his or her training and theoretical background. Furthermore, because up to 85% of what occurs in psychotherapy is common to all approaches (Strupp, 1996), what researchers are actually studying when comparing so-called different therapies amounts to the difference between chicken noodle and chicken rice soups.

The precursors underlie and run through the background of therapy theories, but they are seldom focused on as goals in themselves. I am not saying that the precursors should be the focus of all approaches; that would be quite inaccurate. The emphasis of a focus on precursors becomes relevant when working with difficult clients, who lack the precursors necessary to make standard therapy approaches successful. In the overall effort to improve the effectiveness of therapy in general, the precursors may play a role.

PRECURSORS AS COMMON FACTORS OF CHANGE

Twenty years ago, Goldfried (1980) wrote that "there exist certain 'timeless truths,' consisting of common observations of how people change. These observations date back to early philosophers and are reflected in great works of literature" (p. 996). Goldfried went on to refer to these as "robust phenomena, as they have managed to survive the distortions imposed by the therapists' varying theoretical biases" (p. 996). Although similar to Goldfried's observations, the precursors named in this book are not so much common factors of therapy as common factors of therapeutic change itself. This list of precursors may be more important than a catalog of common factors of therapy.

Another way of looking at the precursors is that in many cases they are necessary conditions for change (Hanna & Ritchie, 1995). There are many well-known change processes that receive much attention in psychotherapy and are commonly linked to the improvement of clients. Examples are insight, catharsis, cognitive restructuring, emotional arousal, reinforcement, exposure, problem-solving, the act of acceptance, working through transference, and the corrective emotional experience. Although important, without the primary mindset and functions such as a sense of necessity, awareness, or the exertion of effort, few if any of these processes will ever be brought into play.

Some evidence for the operation of the seven precursors was provided by a study (Hanna & Ritchie, 1995) that compiled 32 variables cited in the psychotherapy literature as having the capacity for producing change. Participants were screened for having undergone a major, significant moment of therapeutic change, and then were asked to rate those 32 variables on what we called a perceived potency scale. Rather than have participants rate the variables on a typical Likert scale ranging from very little to very much, we wanted to get a rating that addressed their perceived sense of cause.

We devised a new scale based on, and allowing for, perceived causal relationships between variables and events. The ratings on the five-point scale were *not present* = 0; *present but not a factor in change* = 1; *somewhat of a factor* = 2; *a definite factor* = 3; *a necessary condition for change* = 4; and *a sufficient condition for change* = 5. We concluded that several of the 32 variables may regulate both the rate and magnitude of therapeutic change; these are now identified as the precursors of change. The precursors are the variables that the participants perceived as being necessary conditions or prerequisites for their experiences of major change. They easily identified the perceived causal potency of these variables relative to their own experiences of change. A quick definition of a precursor was given in the introduction, but it is time now to attend to this in more detail.

Defining Precursor of Change

A *precursor* is defined as a prerequisite or precondition that precedes and indicates the approach of a phenomenon yet to take place. A precursor of psychotherapeutic change is a prerequisite or precondition that precedes and indicates the occurrence of change processes in a person, whether in or out of therapy. These precursors seem to be present in clients who are involved and interested in engaging in and continuing the therapy process. Conversely, when these variables or common factors of change are not present, clients are likely perceived as resistant, difficult, unmotivated, or indifferent. Thus, these precursors are pivotal elements of the therapeutic change process (Hanna, 1996, pp. 232–233).

The precursors model is simply a framework to house these change functions. The model itself is rather like a display case; the primary objects of attention are the precursors themselves and their interactions.

Interaction and Interdependence

The precursors model has the advantage of not being linear. One criticism of the common factors approach to therapy is that it tends to be limited to a linear view of how therapy and therapeutic change take place (Arkowitz, 1992b). In other words, it does not take into account the many complex processes that occur within therapy and within the people who seek to benefit by it. The precursors, as common factors of change, are not to be seen as independent and isolated from each other, but as interdependent variables that overlap in both meaning and function. They can combine and recombine in an extraordinary number of ways, and they also vary in degree of presence from case to case or problem to problem.

For example, a client who has reached a therapeutic impasse has an adequate presence of two precursors, awareness and a sense of necessity, but is largely lacking all the others. Clients with this characteristic are common but can be quite confusing. When other change ingredients such as confronting and being willing to experience anxiety are added to the mix, there may be just enough to initiate the change process. Conversely, the precursors of awareness and a sense of necessity, when lacking, can often be bolstered by social support and hope.

In another example, a client will not approach or talk about a particular problem. Adding a sense of necessity can drive confronting the problem to greater depths and can inspire the willingness to experience anxiety or difficulty as well.

Precursors interact in clients in dozens of ways. In addition, different precursors can vary in intensity and magnitude in different areas of a person's life. For example, in my own case, I tend to be reasonably high in precursor ratings when it comes to working on personal issues but quite low with regard to exercise and health. Another example is a person who is high in awareness but low in a sense of necessity when it comes to the need to quit drinking. On the other hand, when it comes to saving his or her marriage, that same person might have a high sense of necessity but very little awareness of the problems of the marriage. Each person can have a different configuration of precursors for each of his or her particular problems, another reason why therapeutic change in general is so difficult to map.

In addition, precursors are not static, but can wax and wane throughout various stages of therapy. They can be powerfully present one day and nowhere to be found the next. They can even vary in strength from minute to minute in the same session. This variability is another reason for the need to study microprocesses in research. In the case of clients "trained to be difficult" by their therapists, the precursors can almost literally be observed to diminish in the presence of a therapist the client does not trust or with whom the client is angry. Many teenagers, for example, are quite difficult to engage in therapy, and I have watched them act out or protest when they are told that they must work with a counselor with whom they feel no rapport. Precursors literally vanish on the spot. Even with therapists whom they do trust, clients can bring a different level of precursor presence

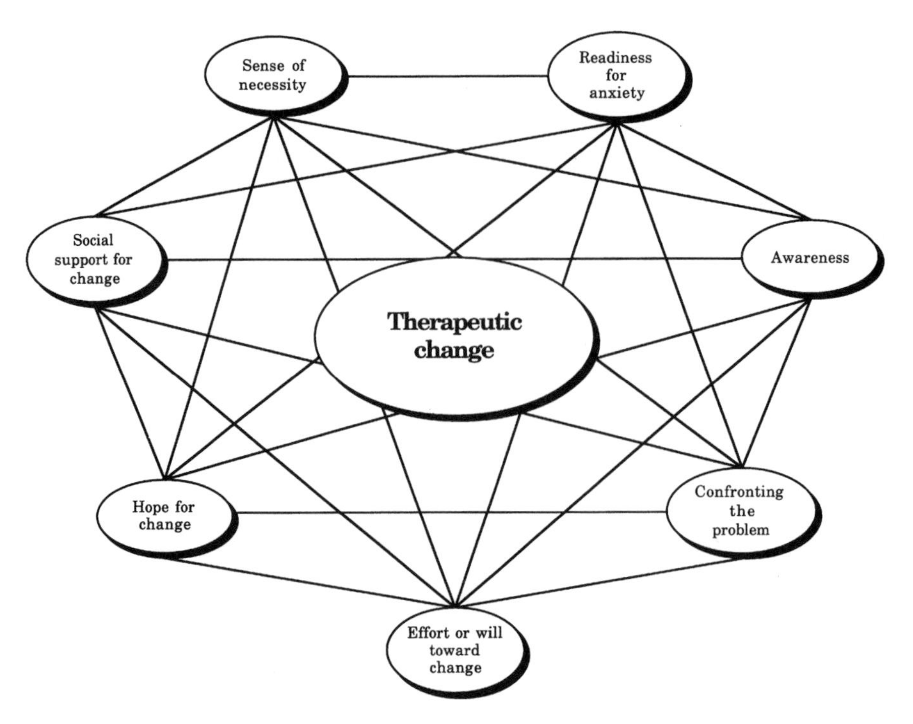

Figure 1. The precursors and their interconnection, interaction, and interdependence on each other and therapeutic change.

each day to therapy. I have observed this phenomenon many times when consulting in community agencies.

CHANGE AS A SKILL

The active agent conception of the human being views therapeutic change as being something intentional and purposeful on the part of the client. Change is not necessarily something that occurs in a person according to a mathematical equation. It does not proceed in the same fashion as a physics experiment or the motion of billiard balls. Of course, mathematical equations and physics formulas do indeed describe much of the activity of the world, but they do not yet adequately describe human beings. Specifically, they do not take into account that active agents—human beings—are the ones who write the equations and the formulas, do the experiments, and set the billiard balls in motion. We understand only half of the process of change if we do not attend to the powers that set change into motion, intentionally, purposefully, and with choices.

I have found that people can learn how to change like they learn how to communicate or to have gratifying relationships. Therapeutic change can be taught as a skill and developed and honed as a skill. Like any other, some people have this skill and some people do not, and those who do not can learn to develop it. Some people may have it but do not seem to be aware of it. Others have told me they know it is there but have no idea how to engage it. I have worked with people who are more than willing to talk about problems, even diagram them, and describe their feelings, but never seem to make a move toward change. They mostly remain dissatisfied and unhappy, but when asked they often say that they do not know how to change.

A different set of people have learned the skill of change through life lessons that were hard earned. They accomplish change in spite of low self-esteem and in the presence of high adversity. Other people, unaware and unknowing, await change as something to magically arrive, rather like the coming of Santa Claus, and are disappointed when they find out that it is actually ordinary people like themselves who deliver the goods. These are all symptoms of a lack of precursors.

A primary message of the precursors model of change is that education is often necessary with difficult clients so that they can know how change works. Education about the change process provides a map and a rationale and is often effective (see Bohart & Tallman, 1999; Garfield, 1994). One of the fundamental mistakes made in psychotherapy and counseling is to assume that clients understand change processes. If they did, change might be accomplished much quicker and easier on a routine basis. At first glance it may seem a little silly to educate a difficult client about change when in fact some may not care in the slightest. No doubt this is true in some instances. However, therapists using an active agent approach treat human beings as if they have choices and options. Change is one such choice, and if change looks to the client like it is in his or her best interest, that change will have a better chance of manifesting.

METACOGNITIVE ASPECTS OF CHANGE

Many precursors of change are not cognitive, nor affective, nor behavioral. They are metacognitive (Hanna & Ritchie, 1995), and this is an important aspect of the attempt to move into and beyond motivation and involvement and beyond theory and techniques. *Metacognition* can be defined as the psychological acts of recognizing, deciding, monitoring, and attending to self-regulation, self-instruction, and the processing of experience, memory, and attention (Flavell, 1979). It is knowing about knowing or thinking about thinking or, in the case of memory, remembering that one once remembered.

Most important for the investigation of change, it can also be defined as "the skill or ability to 'be aware of being aware' " (Pesut, 1990, p. 109).

Metacognition involves the processing of self-talk and self-communications, as well as the vital areas of self-awareness and the deautomatization of habits and reactions (Meichenbaum & Asarnow, 1979). Many metacognitive functions involve subtle acts of willing, not in the sense of free will, but in the sense of intending the exertion of mental effort. The precursors most associated with metacognitive functions are willingness or readiness to experience anxiety or difficulty, awareness, confronting the problem, and effort or will toward change.

The field of education has demonstrated that learning makes use of metacognitive functions. It may also be that the same is true for therapeutic change. In one of the few studies of metacognition related to therapeutic change, Slife and Weaver (1992) found that deficits in metacognitive skills may play a role in the occurrence of depression. What this means from a precursors perspective is that it is not only what a person believes (cognition) that can lead to depression, but also the metacognitive control of attention and awareness. Slife and Weaver also found that metacognitive skills were not related to or the same as cognitive skills. Thus, a person can be more intelligent and insightful but less capable of change than someone far less intellectually gifted but more metacognitively skilled. This is perhaps why heavily intellectualizing clients so often find it difficult to change.

Our research provided evidence that metacognitive factors play a significant role in therapeutic change (Hanna et al., 1995). For example, the readiness or willingness to experience anxiety or difficulty is directly related to client involvement. Our research indicates that one wills oneself to experience the anxiety that comes with change and continuously monitors levels of anxiety and awareness of the limits of one's affective tolerance to avoid being overwhelmed. These are all metacognitive functions. The awareness precursor is among the most obvious of the metacognitive aspects of change. Sometimes a client makes a decision to allow his or her perceptions to penetrate and enter the field of consciousness; this is essentially the decision to become aware of a problem, and it is highly metacognitive.

For example, a client may be surrounded by indications that his or her negative statements and behaviors are harming loved ones. That data do not "register," however, until the person allows that data into his or her awareness through selectively attending to that part of his or her life. That profound and fascinating process of allowing that data to register can sometimes be crucial to the manifestation of cognitive dissonance and the decision to stop destructive acts.

Metacognition is also involved with the classic defense mechanisms. Virtually all therapists have seen instances where denial (refusing awareness), repression (pushing something out of awareness), and other defenses are literally suspended for certain periods of time, resulting in the active engagement of the client in the therapy process for those brief moments. A metacognitive process is occurring in such instances. The core beliefs connected with protecting the person's psychological system are suspended or held in abeyance through a subtle decision process. A purpose of the precursors approach is to be able to engage and extend that suspension or abeyance process, so that change can be activated through the implementation of needed precursors.

The question may arise as to the difference between ontological core beliefs and metacognition. It has been my observation that the metacognitive function is prior to those core beliefs and forms the core beliefs, ontological or otherwise. In the same vein, it is also the metacognitive function that ceases, changes, and replaces core beliefs. It is important to note, however, that once those beliefs are in place, they can be extremely binding if no metacognitive functions are engaged to alter them. This is obvious in the case of clients who are rigid and inflexible. Metacognition ultimately seems intrinsic to the concept of the active agent.

There is another highly relevant and important lesson that metacognition can provide to therapists. In many cases, a person is highly capable of directly influencing and changing his or her feelings and moods. One need not have to depend on the mediating effects of changing thoughts or behaviors to change feelings and emotions. Change of feelings can come about not only through the usual, well-documented cognitive and behavioral processes; it can also come about through direct and deliberate alteration of feelings. One study found that among people who suffer from dysphoria—a combination of depression and anxiety—action-oriented people were able to exert direct influence over their emotions (Rholes, Michas, & Shroff, 1989). More passive people were not so able to influence their emotions. This finding is supported by Kuhl's (1984a, 1984b) studies of metacognition. The precursors model takes into account the possibility of direct change.

The term *metacognition* has its problems, and the phenomenon might be better described by terms such as *wisdom* (see Sternberg, 1990; Hanna & Ottens, 1995) or *dialectical thinking* (Slife, 1987). No matter what we call it, this is an area of great potential for further research.

A DIFFERENT SET OF SKILLS

When motivation and involvement are absent in the client, the therapist's task is to get the client to participate or cooperate in therapy. There are times when getting a client to become even slightly interested in therapy is a major accomplishment and can lower resistance. Getting a client interested in therapy requires a different set of skills than applying the steps of a particular technique or manual. A therapist has to shift to a different modality of approach with a client who is unwilling to follow an established regimen or routine. In such cases, therapeutic skills such as persuasion and influence are necessary to get the client on track. Unfortunately, these skills are not consistently taught in universities.

In work with difficult clients, extraordinary relationship skills are required. Empathy must be sufficiently advanced that the client feels understood by the therapist, even when the therapist does not even slightly agree with the client. The therapist may even experience nausea or visceral discomfort while empathizing with clients who display unsavory or extremely destructive attitudes. Nevertheless, without the ability to reach and make that vital connection with a difficult client, little or no change is likely.

It is a mistake to place one's trust solely in techniques when working with difficult clients. Mahoney (1991) referred to the needless overemphasis on techniques as "technolatry" (p. 252). Without the relationship, techniques are likely to fall flat and not take hold. Put in a more elegant way, "techniques per se are inert unless they form an integral part of the therapist as a person" (Strupp, 1978, p. 314).

CONCLUSION

There are a host of styles of being difficult. Many clients desperately want to change but find the process too painful and fight it at each juncture. Others are not forthrightly resistant or difficult at all; they would change, but they just don't see the point. For yet others, change seems a pleasant prospect but involves too many sacrifices to appear desirable. Another style is to see change as a hindrance to an established way of being. These people often see the therapist as an enemy intruder, there to confuse and confound.

For people with criminal histories, therapeutic change is the same as an admission of weakness and guilt and is to be avoided at all costs. It is also a threat to their "freedom" to do whatever they want, whenever they want, to any victim they choose. Another style of difficult client simply does not believe that change is possible—for anyone—and therefore devotes nothing to it, other than lip service, to a judge, employer, or spouse, as the case may be.

Many of these clients are tremendously difficult to engage. A few are almost inaccessible. The skills needed to work with such clients and engage them in therapy are seldom taught in graduate programs and are almost always learned on the job. Thus, the ability of psychotherapy to reach such clients more quickly and effectively represents one of the growth paths of the entire discipline. It is a primary goal of the precursors approach.

3

THE PRECURSORS MODEL: SKILLS AND FUNCTIONS OF CHANGE

The seven precursors are not arranged in this book or in the assessment in their order of potency or in the order in which they occur. They are arranged in the order presented simply because they are easiest to describe in that sequence. The precursors are present in clients in different configurations for different moments of change, and even for the same person, different precursors have varying influence from one instance of change to the next.

In this chapter, each of the seven precursors is examined, together with

- their philosophical origins in terms of the robust phenomena to which Goldfried (1980) referred,
- the ways each precursor produces change,
- how to recognize the presence and absence of each in a client,
- stories of significant change accomplished by people who participated in our research (see Hanna et al., 1995) and verified as accurate by each participant, and
- clinical markers and the descriptions necessary for rating each precursor on the precursors assessment form.

At the time of this writing, I am not certain which of the precursors is the most potent, although according to the participants interviewed, confronting the problem seems the most influential. This is by no means conclusive, however, as some precursors, such as social support and hope, seem to have a more subtle and pervasive impact on psychotherapeutic change than is immediately apparent.

PRECURSOR 1: A SENSE OF NECESSITY

If necessity is the mother of invention, it may also be the mother of therapeutic change. Most people do not desire therapeutic change for recreational purposes. Even though it can be a wonderful experience, people do not seek therapy in the same way they seek out diversions like shopping or sporting events. Therapeutic change often requires a degree of sacrifice and disruption of routine. It also has a degree of uncertainty and mystery. Generally, before contemplating or entering therapy, a person will to some degree consider it necessary. This sense of necessity is one of the primary ingredients of motivation. Without it, a person is not likely to seriously pursue change beyond trifling with it or giving it mere lip service.

Definition and Description

A sense of necessity is not merely an intellectual matter of priorities or values. It has a definite affective component. It can be defined as a felt sense of urgency regarding the need for change. It is a recognition of the importance of replacing the current set of circumstances with different ones. There is a palpable feeling that the current conditions in one's inner life (e.g., sadness or anxiety) or outer life (e.g., intimidation or threat) are in some way unacceptable if left unattended. The sense of necessity comes from assessing a situation, whether of emotion, mind, or environment, and declaring that it must be altered or ceased. A sense of necessity can influence needs as various as a child's having to get acceptable grades in school to a man's realizing that he has to be nice to his wife to avoid divorce. Other examples are the desire to rid oneself of depression or the recognition that one's drinking has to stop.

The emergence of a sense of necessity is a remarkable occurrence in a human being. Some of the people I have interviewed on this topic (see Hanna et al., 1995) remembered the exact moment of emergence with great detail, including where it arose and how they responded to it, as much as 22 years after the incident. A sense of necessity is more than mere motivation: It is a driving force for change and is a major factor in many of the great reforms or transformations in history, personal or political.

In 15 of the 20 significant therapeutic change experiences we examined (Hanna & Ritchie, 1995), participants reported that a sense of necessity was present in all 20 of those experiences and influential in 19. In terms of its perceived causal potency, it was rated as a necessary condition in 15, or 75%, of those incidents. In other words, according to our participants, 15 of those 20 moments of significant change would not have taken place at all without this vital condition. Thus, 95% of those moments of change had this precursor as an active ingredient.

Other authors have also mentioned the importance of this quality or condition in bringing about change (McMullin, 1986; Power, 1981; Whitaker, 1989). The ancient philosopher Epictetus (c. 130/1944) mentioned that the recognition of necessity was in itself a guide for human action and that it was the key to human freedom. With regard to therapeutic change, a sense of necessity may be what leads a person to seek freedom from limiting circumstances of many varieties. But a certain amount of inspiration is necessary. For example, no one in their right mind would put their hands in a fire if asked. However, if an infant were seen to be wandering into flames, most people would consider it necessary to risk the flames to save the child. Because therapy often involves dealing with painful memories, confusing thoughts, and intimidating situations, people will not generally contemplate such unpleasant things without a sense of necessity. People tend to avoid pain unless there is some perceived necessity to face it. A sense of necessity can lead people to take the actions intended to bring about change.

For example, a battered wife who feels trapped may often debate whether it is necessary to leave her husband or change conditions in her life. She feels a sense of necessity, but it is not particularly strong. However, when she begins to see the damage caused to her children by witnessing their mother being beaten, her sense of necessity for change strengthens sufficiently to lead her to decide that change is necessary in the form of consulting a friend or seeking a shelter. The battered mother might not value her own well-being enough to consider change necessary, but she considers her children to be of the utmost importance, so that saving them makes any risk tolerable, the threat of suffering notwithstanding. For change to occur, it is not so important what brings about the sense of necessity, only that it occur.

How a Sense of Necessity Leads to Change

When someone recognizes that change is necessary and that things must not continue as they are, a thoroughly remarkable event—a reorganization of the person's perceptions and values—takes place. This new alignment orients priorities and actions toward the immediate implementation of change. The way to change may not be clear and the means of change may be obscure, but the person is certain of one thing: that change must take place sooner rather than later.

A Significant Moment of Change Involving a Sense of Necessity

I once interviewed, as part of our research (Hanna et al., 1995), a 41-year-old recovering alcoholic who had not touched alcohol or drugs in 10 years. He informed me that a sense of necessity was crucial on the day he decided to seek recovery, which he said was the most important day of his life. He had abused drugs and drunk to excess daily for 15 years. Then he woke up one Sunday morning with a broken tooth and stitches in his face. He was badly hung over and "broke again." He had no recall of the previous evening, and his two sons told him he had been drinking. While chasing neighborhood kids who were calling him "a drunk," he tripped while climbing a fence and fell face first onto the concrete.

When he heard what his sons were telling him he felt a deep sense of shame and did not want to believe it. He even took a drink to try to get rid of the shameful feelings, but on this day the drink did not have its desired effect. This time was different. For the first time in his life, he said, "I thought about killing myself and not hurting these people [his family] any more."

The realization that he was hurting his family instilled him with a sense of necessity that basically informed him that his drinking and drugging behavior could not and must not continue. He reoriented his life toward avoiding alcohol and drugs, put himself into treatment, and became involved in Alcoholics Anonymous. To his credit, he was still sober at the time of the interview.

When a sense of necessity arises in such a moment, something profound and deeply meaningful takes place. Within the person, the cognizance dawns that something is desperately wrong and needs to be set to right. This is accompanied by a feeling of urgency, and perhaps a sense of desperateness as well, that leads to a certainty that change must occur.

Part of this sense of "wrongness" can be viewed as a response to cognitive dissonance (Festinger, 1957). This is an idea that has been around for decades and remains quite popular. *Cognitive dissonance* arises when two mutually exclusive or incompatible beliefs or perceptions are present in a person, producing a feeling of discomfort or anxiety. The discomfort motivates the person to desire a reduction in the level of discomfort. This sometimes leads to action and sometimes not. It has been closely tied to the process of therapeutic change (Axsom, 1989).

When a client displays little or no sense of necessity, cognitive dissonance is the therapist's friend. There are ways to bring about cognitive dissonance in a person and with it a carefully nurtured sense of necessity (to be discussed in chapter 9). When cognitive dissonance does occur, the goal is to inspire the person to act to reduce the level of discomfort, rather than merely to desire its reduction. An amazing, and puzzling, phenomenon is how some people deal with cognitive dissonance by seeking to resolve it, whereas others simply ignore it. One possible explanation is that if the cognitive dissonance is not sufficient to disturb the person's core beliefs about how life, relationships, beliefs, and actions should be, it may cause little sense of necessity for change.

A sense of necessity emerges when a person assesses a situation and concludes that the circumstances, feelings, thoughts, or conditions should not or must not be allowed to proceed on their current course. When a client reaches such a point, a primary motivational force becomes present and operational as a precursor of change. However, according to our research, this precursor alone does not seem to have sufficient power to produce change.

As a necessary condition for change, this precursor needs the other precursors to actually accomplish change. I have known many examples where a person can have a full-blown sense of necessity and a tremendous sense of urgency but never accomplishes therapeutic change, because the other precursors are missing. Nevertheless, our investigations have shown that therapeutic change is not likely to occur without the presence of this precursor.

Clinical Markers: How to Recognize a Sense of Necessity

Sometimes the easiest way to gauge the presence or absence of a sense of necessity is simply to ask the client. Some difficult clients are quite willing to answer this question honestly and forthrightly, but others obviously may not. If the direct question does not produce satisfactory results or if the client is manipulative or dishonest, therapists can look for certain behavioral markers in clients' nonverbal and verbal communications.

Nonverbal cues can be quite apparent from the very beginning of therapy, even during an initial telephone conversation. A client who feels a sense of necessity may have a tone of urgency in his or her voice or demeanor regardless of the problem described. This urgency might take the form of an intense determination or a plea for help.

A client with a sense of necessity is alert and attentive during the session and actively listens to what the therapist says. He or she may seek clarification of a question or statement by the therapist. Such a client may make eye contact, although people of some cultures avoid eye contact, as do many motivated children and adolescents. Posture, I have found, can sometimes be indicative but also is not reliable, as some clients may have a high sense of necessity but may be suffering from depression or fatigue. In addition, a client with a high sense of necessity will be inclined to be on time for sessions, but a gender issue should be taken into account: Many women find child care needs to be a great hindrance to attending therapy.

The clearest indicator of a client's sense of necessity is the importance they ascribe, either directly or indirectly, to change. Of course, this assumes that the client is being honest and is not scheming or being manipulative, as in the case of clients attempting to graduate (i.e., escape) from substance abuse treatment programs. Aside from dishonesty, clients are often quite happy to inform a curious therapist about their level of necessity for change, even when being difficult in other ways.

If a person believes that change is important or that action needs to be taken when things go awry, this is an indicator that the person will be likely to assess a specific situation as in need of correction or change.

Whether the client's locus of control is internal or external does not affect this precursor; it matters not whether the person considers the problem as being caused by the environment or by his or her own doing. Thus, a client with a high sense of necessity may blame another for his or her problems, although this belief may indicate a lack of other precursors, such as awareness and the readiness for anxiety or difficulty.

When a sense of necessity is present, certain emotions and feelings can be used as clinical indicators. The most obvious is a fear that if change does not occur, some tragedy will ensue. This fear is in itself a motivating influence to produce change. In some people the fear manifests as a frantic preoccupation with the need for change to take place. In other cases, the person broods or even mopes. Apprehension, foreboding, or agitation may also manifest with the sense of necessity for change. Anxiety, of course, is typical, especially when accompanied by cognitive dissonance.

How to Detect the Absence of a Sense of Necessity

A lack of interest in change is the most obvious indicator of a low sense of necessity. When a sense of necessity is absent, there is little or no recognition of a need to change. Change appears to be entirely unnecessary or a waste of effort and time. The client may express a lack of concern, indicating directly or indirectly that the prospect of change is neither important nor pressing. When a sense of necessity is missing, a person can be listless, inattentive, and lackadaisical. He or she will often put off or see no point in carrying out homework assignments and may be late for or miss sessions altogether. The client's living conditions or problems may seem intolerable to the therapist, but the client will seem resigned and apathetic.

The person with no sense of necessity may imply or say, "It's no big deal," or "There's no need to get excited," or "It's not a problem." The person may make a statement that indicates a core belief that inhibits this precursor: "Nothing really matters anyway" is an example (see a more complete list of core beliefs in chapter 9). Such a client will also find little need to form a working therapeutic bond with the therapist, a quality associated with positive outcomes (Orlinsky et al., 1994).

Beyond Necessity

A sense of necessity will bring a person to seek therapy and indeed to seek help of almost any type, from fixing a muffler to getting one's computer repaired. However, simply having or recognizing the need is by no means a guarantee that change will occur. It is only an admission or recognition that change is needed. In many cases, it is just a beginning. There are six other precursors that work interdependently, and in conjunction with, a sense of necessity.

PRECURSOR 2: WILLINGNESS OR READINESS TO EXPERIENCE ANXIETY OR DIFFICULTY

Many difficult clients want change to occur but, paradoxically, without having to change anything. They may have become fixed in a way of living or coping that has become quite automatized and unconscious. They have worked hard to get things the way they are in their lives and are not about to allow some therapist to wreak havoc with their carefully ordered, tightly knit system of thinking and behaving. This can be true of criminals or executives.

Readiness for change consists metaphorically of rolling up one's sleeves, gritting one's teeth, and preparing to get one's hands dirty. Contrary to popular belief, talking about a problem does not always constitute "the talking cure"; talking is not always enough to produce change. Many clients talk about problems indefinitely, session after session, but nothing seems to change. This is not so much the fault of the client as a faulty approach.

Willingness or readiness to experience anxiety or difficulty is probably the most difficult of the seven precursors to understand, even though it has been recognized for a long time. Fortunately, that difficulty is not a hindrance. Research participants in our studies claimed to have understood this precursor quickly and intuitively. It is often the missing ingredient in the most puzzling of difficult clients, and consideration of this factor aids therapists not only in understanding their lack of progress but in providing approaches and techniques that can help.

Definition and Description

Willingness or readiness to experience anxiety or difficulty can be defined as openness to allowing the change process to occur, accompanied by a preparedness to feel the anxieties, emotions, and difficulties that routinely manifest as a result. This precursor involves a metacognitive willing and intending to tolerate and even welcome emotional pain, confusion, or intimidation and involves a surrendering to the change process itself. It is the diametric opposite of *defensiveness*, which is usually defined as effort to avoid anxiety due to some kind of threat.

When this precursor is present, the client directly acknowledges anxiety rather than evading or shunning it. Further, the client acknowledges the difficulty that comes with change and is willing to tolerate it so that change can take place. This precursor sounds a lot like the ancient notion of courage, with the added aspects of persistence and perseverance.

Openness, as opposed to defensiveness, was positively related to successful outcomes in approximately 75% of findings in the literature review by Orlinsky and associates (1994). If the person is not ready to meet the difficulties inherent in the change process, he or she will balk at any movement in that direction. In his classic book on change, Mahoney (1991) referred to readiness as "openness to experience" (p. 342) and pointed to it as a pivotal quality that enables change to take place. Mahrer (1985, 1986, 1989) built a viable and direct therapy approach around this principle, which seems to be at the heart of his experiential therapy. Orlinsky et al. (1994) found that affective experiencing was positively related to outcome in three sets of findings. Of course, Frank (1961) originally pointed out that a common factor of any successful therapy involves the client becoming emotionally aroused in some way. This precursor is also related to the "corrective emotional experience" that many psychodynamic therapists emphasize as central to change (Alexander & French, 1974). When this precursor is present, the talking cure catharsis is more likely to take place. It is important to bear in mind that this precursor is not limited to the outright experiencing of emotions and feelings, the prior willingness to do so opens the door to those experiential aspects. The willingness is metacognitive.

Participants in our studies reported that willingness or readiness to experience anxiety or difficulty was highly influential in bringing about the instances of change under examination. None of our participants had any difficulty understanding its definition and use. In 15 of the 20 incidents or stories, change would not have occurred without the readiness or willingness to experience anxiety or difficulty (Hanna & Ritchie, 1995), where it was rated by participants as a necessary condition. In four of the remaining five, it was rated as influential in bringing about change, and it was reported as present even in the one exception. Thus, of 20 examples of significant therapeutic change, this precursor was an active influence in 95% of them and present in all.

Anxiety Often Accompanies Change

The process of introducing change into a rigid mindset often requires that some confusion and disorder result. The same is true for a mindset that is chaotic and disjointed. Both types of client are likely to resist change, even though they may be in desperate need. Therapeutic change appears to such clients as confusion and disorder, when it is actually a process of establishing a higher degree of order and function and is a natural part of the process of improvement.

For example, when one does spring cleaning, disorder manifests in the displacement of furniture and household items while sweeping and dusting. If the disorder is resisted, the improvement cannot take place or is significantly hindered. Cleaning sometimes initially requires making a mess. Similarly, to an out-of-shape, unconditioned body, the early part of a physical exercise program looks more like pain and stress rather than muscle toning and cardiovascular health.

Likewise, when one's habitual thoughts and behaviors are required to be altered, some mental confusion and disorder are inevitable and often produce anxiety. A mindset that is filled with dysfunctional beliefs and painful memories is in delicate balance. When one is not secure in the first place, the mere thought of altering one's beliefs or dredging up memories can produce a sense of unease or difficulty that reverberates throughout the entire mental framework. If one fights this process, change does not occur. Thus, in the real world, if a therapist, judge, spouse, probation officer, or teacher requires or recommends a change in thinking or behavior, some people perceive such a recommendation as an insult or attack. This anxiety can arise as a factor in clinical practice. If a client can be educated to recognize and be willing to experience such anxiety and disorder, he or she will likely be more amenable to a change process.

Philosophical Roots

This precursor has some interesting philosophical grounding. Martin Heidegger (1927/1962) was probably the first to describe it and note its importance for change. One of the most important philosophers of the 20th century, Heidegger wrote the classic, deeply insightful book *Being and Time*. Much of this book was highly psychological in nature, and Heidegger defined and noted the importance of achieving authenticity as a human being and outlined how to achieve it. Heidegger (1927/1962) used the term *resoluteness* to describe a being "ready for anxiety" (p. 343) and an emerging from a sense of "lostness" (p. 345) toward authenticity. He said that to be resolute, one has to follow one's own growth path, which often requires going against the grain of empty habits as well as social pressures and demands. He used the term *fallen* to indicate a person who has given in to societal and personal inclinations toward avoidance and disingenuousness. Resoluteness involves recognizing those inclinations and pressures, refusing to be carried away by them, and choosing instead to move steadfastly toward authentic being. *Resoluteness* would actually be quite acceptable as the name for this precursor if it were slightly more descriptive.

Owning the Problem

It has often been noted in the psychotherapy literature that a client will begin to make progress when he or she "owns" the problem and stops complaining about it or blaming others for it. A person *owns the problem* when he or she acknowledges and accepts that it is real and must be addressed. There is also an awareness component; the person recognizes that the problem is within the domain of his or her own region of responsibility. *Responsibility* can be defined as the willingness to take charge, control, or command of any memory, thought, image, problem, behavior, relationship, or feeling. When a person takes responsibility for a problem or issue, he or she is much more likely to see the issue through to its solution.

Acceptance of a problem or issue is a major aspect of 12-step programs, with the AA (Alcoholics Anonymous) literature strongly citing acceptance as a powerful influence on abstinence and recovery from alcoholism and drug addiction (Alcoholics Anonymous, 1976). From this perspective, acceptance is often looked on as a spiritual endeavor, although it does not need to be regarded from that perspective (Hanna, 1992). The act of acceptance can also be a necessary condition for some kinds of therapeutic change, as it was in 25% of the 20 major change experiences in our study (Hanna & Ritchie, 1995).

When a client has a sense of necessity but is not willing to experience anxiety or difficulty, the client will typically want the therapist to do most of the work. It is like knowing that the house is in dire need of cleaning but not being willing to go to all the trouble to clean it. Such a client will "dump" rather than describe their issues and problems. Dumping is characterized by exaggeration of the problem's severity, a desire to be rescued from the problem, and very little willingness to own the problem or issue. Such clients are avoidant of important or key issues and prefer to keep things at a superficial level. They may claim that therapy is not helping and blame the therapist for the lack of change. Deep down, these clients are experiencing pain and discomfort and want therapy to provide the magic wand to make it all go away. They may even mistakenly believe that therapy is designed and intended to enable them to avoid pain and discomfort.

How Readiness for Anxiety Leads to Change

Willingness or readiness to experience anxiety or difficulty involves a surrendering to the process of change itself: The person lets go of established routines and habitual behaviors or thought patterns and is open to the possibility of forever altering these routines, habits, and patterns. But the key contribution to change itself is that act of heaving oneself into the realm of the unknown. With therapeutic change, especially second-order change, awareness of the unknown causes no small amount of anxiety. Thus, the willingness to admit oneself into the disarray that comes with the disruption of established and settled mindsets and behaviors is an essential act in the change process.

For change to occur, a client must be willing to "give up or modify clinging to the past" (Strupp, 1988, p. 78) and welcome the new or unfamiliar.

Negative feelings and anxieties must be acknowledged as they arise. Over time, the client learns to assimilate and integrate problem experiences under new headings or schema, so what was once disordered becomes understandable, no longer rejected but acknowledged and accepted (Elliott et al., 1990).

The psychodynamic term *working through* has now become a household expression. Although many things can be worked through, it is this precursor that facilitates the process. The presence of this precursor readies the person to reduce hesitance, break though self-imposed limits, and take command of the uncomfortable emotions that result. This precursor does not cause these acts, which will become clear when we examine the precursor of effort or will. However, just as the will can lead one to take such "risky" actions as going white-water rafting or riding a giant roller-coaster, the willingness to experience anxiety or difficulty also involves the engaging of risk.

When this precursor is abundant, it can produce a sense of adventure that makes the change endeavor not only possible but pleasurable. Even though a person is examining the effects of, for example, physical abuse, experiences of failure, or destructive behaviors, this precursor provides the sense of exploration and discovery that often marks the chief difference between cooperative and difficult clients. The latter have to be coaxed and persuaded. The former often have to be held back and paced.

For example, a suicidal, highly rigid client was referred to me by a hospital after discharge from its psychiatric unit. When he first came, he said simply, "I know I need to change, just tell me what to do and I'll do it." Because of his rigidity, the process became very difficult for him at times, because what he thought was going to change was not at all what really needed his attention. His sense of necessity was high, but his willingness to experience anxiety was quite low. I often had to remind him of his initial statement to me when he began to hold to his old ways. In effect, I asked him to surrender to the process. This often brought him back to the task at hand, and progress would resume. I used this client's sense of necessity to establish the willingness or readiness for anxiety or difficulty. More on the clinical implementation of this precursor will be given in chapter 10.

The discussion so far of willingness or readiness to experience anxiety or difficulty has described the change process from the perspective of inner experience. Worldly or environmental perspectives must also be tolerated. For example, a passive, submissive client had a considerable degree of anxiety when he contemplated confronting a friend who was ridiculing him. The anxiety was so paralyzing that it completely inhibited the person from acting to stop the ridicule. Yet if he did not manage his anxiety and cope with this problem, the situation might have continued indefinitely. The willingness to experience anxiety often opens the door for the confronting precursor.

Another example is that of a woman I worked with who was compulsively shopping, running up credit card bills to the point of bankruptcy.

Because compulsive shopping usually is accompanied by the secondary gain of fun and anxiety reduction, the mere thought of imposing some discipline on spending was an action that flooded her with mixed feelings. Those feelings included anxiety and shame about spending too much and an unwillingness to lose the fun and satisfaction of spending money. She began to feel emptiness and despair at the thought of no more shopping. For change to manifest, she needed to tolerate those feelings of anxiety, shame, and emptiness and to manage them so that self-regulation and self-management could take effect.

A Significant Moment of Change Involving Readiness for Anxiety

The change potential of the willingness or readiness to experience anxiety or difficulty is well illustrated in the following significant moment of change (Hanna et al., 1995). Beverly, a 32-year-old woman, and one of her two children were being severely emotionally, and sometimes physically, abused by her husband. In great fear for years, she finally decided that she must leave him and did so unannounced during the day while he was at work. She moved herself and her children to a town 600 miles away without his knowledge.

He traced her and followed her to that city, and he repeatedly threatened by telephone to shoot and kill her with one of his many firearms. He called her regularly to inform her of her daily activities and tell her that she was in the crosshairs of his rifle. He also followed her to her job and falsely reported to her employer by telephone that he was an FBI agent and that she was about to be arrested for selling drugs, and requested their cooperation. He had flowers sent to her place of employment charged to her own credit card. He also stole her car (which she never got back) and terrorized her in a number of other ways, including vandalizing the cars of two friends who were visiting her at the time. Finally, she contacted the FBI, who recorded some of his death threats, and he fled and had not been in contact with her for more than 10 years.

According to Beverly, this man had her immobilized until she realized that it was death that was at the source of her fears. She realized that she had to be willing to face death itself to escape this man. As she put it, "I was pushed to the brink in facing my fears." Having described herself as having been a person who worried a lot, she reported that she had since become "very low key" and had learned to "live in the present." Through such processes as enduring the situation, not reacting in the way her husband expected, working with the police and the FBI, and informing her employer of the situation, she acquired a sense of "inner control" as she withstood the threats and phone calls. She said, "I am not the same person. I learned about survival . . . It [the experience] absolutely altered the way I am today.

Because of that horribleness, I am a better person." She reported that this was probably the most valuable experience of her life in terms of lessons learned and coming to terms with death.

Clinical Markers: How to Recognize Readiness for Anxiety

Although willingness or readiness to experience anxiety or difficulty is probably the most difficult of the precursors to gauge or clinically assess, there are some signs that can be looked for to discern its presence. Like a sense of necessity, this precursor can also be detected simply by asking clients to assess its presence in themselves. Once the client has described the nature of the desired change, the therapist can ask a simple question such as, "Are you willing to go through the difficulty necessary to make this change?" If the client is not being manipulative or attempting to deceive the therapist, chances are the therapist will get an answer that can help with the assessment. Many clients are quite able and willing to inform a therapist about their willingness to experience turbulent affect or painful memories.

One of the most obvious behavioral manifestations of this precursor is an eagerness to "dive in" to the problem or issue. The client will display a markedly high level of tolerance of pain or discomfort, as if he or she knows that one "has to get through this" and that this is what has to be done. Such clients are active and cooperative during sessions and communicate to the therapist that they are willing to undergo or suffer through the tough issues without backing off. In many respects, these clients will appear courageous, and their resoluteness and steadfastness often evoke the admiration and respect of their therapists.

Intrinsic to the mindset of this precursor is the belief that problems are solved by holding one's ground and not avoiding or running. Clients with this precursor believe that positive change is worth the sacrifice and difficulty that comes with it. Conversely, the belief that anxiety or discomfort are always to be avoided directly negates the operation of this precursor. Another cognitive aspect of this precursor is the belief that opening oneself to the unknown can have positive results. A client who is willing to experience anxiety or difficulty is more likely to explore the unknown, whether by probing the recesses of mind or by testing new behaviors in new environments.

A person high in this precursor generally believes that taking a risk is a valuable and important part of living life and achieving one's goals. Such a person believes the old saying "nothing ventured, nothing gained" and lives by it from a psychological perspective. In terms of anxiety, a person with an ample amount of this precursor believes that it is not intimidating or intolerable, but something that is a source of new lessons to be learned and new self-knowledge to be gained. At its most optimum levels, a person views anxiety not as a threat but as a challenge that holds the promise of a reward of insight and enhanced understanding.

One of the most important affective markers is a mastery of fear. The client may be intimidated by the prospect of change and may even express outright fear of it, but the fear is not so intimidating that it inhibits the act of enduring the discomfort. Another way that this precursor might manifest in the midst of difficult moments in therapy is as perseverance. The client will persist in the task at hand regardless of the anxiety aroused by the prospect of becoming aware of painful issues or problems.

Ideally, a person with a willingness or readiness to experience anxiety or difficulty is also able to express emotion in a way that results in catharsis. The person is aware of various feeling states and is close to the inner source of emotions and feelings. This precursor also allows a person to explore emotions directly as an activity in itself, and not only as a means to isolating thoughts and behaviors. Some people may be more willing to explore certain emotions at the expense of others. For example, some men may be more willing to discuss anger, whereas some women would be more likely to shy away from this emotion (J. B. Miller, 1986). The opposite may be true of sadness. Thus, gender may influence some aspects of this precursor.

How to Detect the Absence of Readiness for Anxiety

When the willingness or readiness to experience anxiety or difficulty is absent, the client may believe that therapy is too difficult or that the therapist, however reasonable, is just too demanding. Such a client may be inclined to miss or to be late for sessions, not so much because a sense of necessity is lacking as because he or she wishes to avoid the inherent difficulties connected with change. Thus, avoidance is a major feature of the lack of this precursor.

The absence of a willingness or readiness to experience anxiety or difficulty can drain the change potential from what Schofield (1964) called "therapeutic conversation." Just because a client is willing to talk about a problem does not mean that he or she is willing to experience the anxiety or difficulty associated with it. Some clients seem to have a kind of defense mechanism that shields them from or filters out the hurt and the pain connected with an issue so that they can talk about it with some composure. Specifically, when the talk is not "curing," the person often seems remote, even though he or she may be intellectually active and engaged and even analyzing the problem. The remoteness comes from a hesitance to experience the emotions or feelings associated with and aroused by the issue at hand. This emotional distancing from the problem is often accompanied by a distancing from the therapist as well. A solid therapeutic relationship is crucial to closing this distance.

In the case of substance abuse treatment programs, some clients learn the proper treatment language and use it to tell therapists and counselors exactly what they want to hear. Such clients' ostensibly honest and heartfelt testimony is mere lip service designed to manipulate the staff into granting early, undeserved graduation. In such cases, a pivotal missing ingredient is assessment of the willingness to experience anxiety or difficulty.

Other difficult clients are willing to acknowledge that a so-called problem is there but insist that there is "no need to get into it." They will insist that the problem can be solved without much effort. A classic example is the alcoholic who says, "I can quit drinking any time I want." Such clients are not willing to admit how difficult abstinence is or to experience the anxieties and discomfort involved. Of course, it may also be true that the person simply does not know how difficult it may be, in which case the next precursor, awareness, comes into play.

When a willingness or readiness to experience anxiety or difficulty is missing, a client may become elusive and evasive with the therapist and may resist probing questions of troubled areas. The client may often divert the therapist's questions toward "safer" topics on which to focus or elaborate. Often the client is not aware of such diversions, but at other times the client is quite aware, and questioning him or her about such diversions is perfectly acceptable and often productive.

At other times, the client becomes annoyed or irritable and engages in rationalizations in the honest belief that the therapist is causing him or her needless pain and anxiety. This indicates a mindset or belief system that anything worth pursuing should not be uncomfortable or painful. Classical traits of the difficult, resistant client will be observed in such cases. More core beliefs to be disputed are provided in chapter 10.

PRECURSOR 3: AWARENESS

Many philosophers have noted that awareness is the most fundamental aspect of life. If we do not have awareness, we don't have much of a life. Awareness is the means through which we discover life itself. The qualities and characteristics of awareness have been extolled in wonder and in awe since the time of the ancients. Although behaviorists attempted to dismiss it, the fact is that without awareness, none of their research or writing would ever have taken place (Wann, 1964). Even to dismiss awareness as insignificant requires awareness in order to do the dismissal.

As a precursor of change, awareness of a problem or issue is a vital and essential element of the psychotherapy process. Without it, self-determined change would probably never directly take place. It is the diametric opposite of that frustrating and baffling defense mechanism that therapists refer to as *denial.* When awareness is fully present, only denial is denied.

Definition and Description

Awareness is so fundamental that any definition of it is ultimately circular, but it is necessary to at least attempt to define it. *Awareness* is the cognizance, recognition, or knowledge of any mental or physical object, relation, or event. It can also be defined as the subjective aspect of neurological activity, although we would, of course, have no idea of what neurological activity is without our being aware enough to study it. For our purposes, *awareness* is interchangeable with the term *consciousness.*

As a precursor of change, awareness is a bit easier to define. Awareness has to do with a client's recognition of or clarity of perception about a problem. It is the function that brings a mental, emotional, or environmental issue in from the edge of consciousness and into focused detail. In general, awareness is the identification or pinpointing of issues or relationships that are in need of addressing as part of the therapeutic process and its tasks.

Although this is a somewhat narrow definition, there are two subfactors that expand and further define its purview. The first is the awareness that there is a problem at all. Many clients simply are unaware and unsuspecting that a problem exists, even when the problem is quite severe, such as a personality disorder. Few people who lack awareness of a problem or issue seek therapy on their own, and most such clients have been referred by a spouse, judge, employer, or friend. For such people, the first order of business is usually to determine some issue or problem that needs attention.

The second subfactor of awareness involves the nature of the problem. The person may be aware that something is wrong but has no idea what. In such cases, a person may even have a high sense of necessity and readiness for anxiety. However, without awareness to pinpoint the region or area on which to focus, the client will show a certain amount of vagueness and lack of clarity about what to address. Such a person may come to therapy to try to determine if there is indeed anything to address at all. This kind of client secretly wants the therapist to say, "You are fine. There is really nothing wrong, and you can go home."

In general, the awareness precursor also includes the ability to identify problem behaviors, emotions, and beliefs or cognitions, as well as interpersonal and family issues in need of remedy. Once a person can accurately size up a problem or issue, he or she can assess with reasonable accuracy its relationship to certain behaviors and cognitions. Awareness of a problem also involves recognizing its origins and contributing factors and properly attributing responsibility for problems or issues without blaming. There is obviously some overlap here with the willingness precursor.

Awareness is the first stage of cognitive dissonance, which often initiates the change process. In other words, awareness must be operative before there can be any recognition of contradiction or incongruency.

It is not surprising that awareness has been identified as a common factor closely tied to the change process across the wide range of therapies (Goldfried, 1995; also see Drozd & Goldfried, 1996; Hanna & Puhakka, 1991; Kottler, 1991). In our study, participants reported that of their 20 clear instances of change, awareness was influential in all 20. It was perceived to be a necessary condition in 14 of the moments of significant change and was discerned to be a sufficient condition in an additional two. This finding suggests that awareness not only is helpful in people going through the process of change, but also has a direct influence on making it happen. In another study, Burnett (1999) asked participants what they learned from counseling and therapy. Participants pointed to awareness, in the form of identification of problems, as a skill that facilitated change.

Consciousness Raising

Increasing awareness is often referred to in therapy and counseling literature as *consciousness raising,* which has been cited as a common factor across therapy approaches (Kottler, 1991; Prochaska et al., 1992). Freud attributed awareness to the functioning of the ego. Of course, the concept of the ego and awareness was around long before Freud, and he himself studied it under Franz Brentano (Hergenhahn, 1996), who was also the teacher of the founder of phenomenology, Edmund Husserl. The philosophical discipline of phenomenology made consciousness the central focus of study.

Consciousness raising is present in virtually every form of psychotherapy and counseling other than pure operant conditioning. It has to do with attaining increased clarity of perception of thought processes, mental images, feelings, emotions, interpersonal interactions, and environmental conditions. Awareness also involves recognizing the effects of one's own actions on any of these aspects of life. It is a critically important aspect of existential and humanistic therapies, which claim a long tradition of emphasizing this phenomenon. Awareness as consciousness raising is an indispensable part of behavior therapy as well, which makes use of such techniques as self-monitoring and self-observation for the purpose of bringing a person to discern more fully and precisely the nature of behaviors or reactions, ranging from problem drinking and cigarette smoking to irrational fears or phobias. Behavioral techniques that make use of exposure would hardly be workable if not for awareness. It is here that much of therapeutic change originates.

Awareness as Consistent

Many philosophers have described the advantages of this precursor. It is one of the robust phenomena to which Goldfried (1980) referred and easily qualifies for the category that he called "timeless truths" (p. 996). Awareness was praised and celebrated in the *Upanishads* (Nikhilananda, 1963), one of the oldest religio–philosophical works known. It was also praised by other ancient Asian philosopher–psychologists such as Buddha, Shankara, and Patanjali (see Gupta, 1998; Hanna, 1993, 1995), who saw conscious awareness as a passive witness of all phenomena of mind and the world. Western philosophers also wrote of awareness in the form of consciousness; it is a theme in the writings of Plotinus, Kant, Husserl, and Sartre.

One of the most remarkable things phenomenologists have discovered about awareness is its amazing consistency. When present, awareness itself seems not to change in its essential character, regardless of what is being contemplated (Merleau-Ponty, 1962), even during drug experiences. In other words, the content of awareness changes and can be altered by various mental states and drug influence. But as a function, awareness itself stays consistent. This is a subtle but important point.

As we know, awareness can contemplate a tremendous range of phenomena, both physical and psychological. Psychological phenomena include mental images, thoughts, desires, intentions, and even hallucinations and delusions. They include the emotions as well, from sadness and grief to enthusiasm, joy, and happiness. Awareness of physical phenomena makes use of the senses to contemplate the sights, sounds, smells, tastes, and touch of, for example, music, mountains, oceans, city traffic, living beings, and inanimate objects. Physical sensations such as headaches, dizziness, nausea, motion, gooseflesh, and sexuality are other examples. Thus, awareness is tremendously consistent and yet versatile, capable of attending to and beholding a fantastic array of phenomena, without itself being altered in its essential character.

The founder of phenomenology as a discipline, Edmund Husserl (1913/1982, 1936/1970), was probably the first to recognize this characteristic of consistency. *Phenomenology* can be defined as the study of conscious experience and of consciousness itself. As a philosophy, it was a major influence on existential thinkers and, ultimately, humanistic and existential psychologists. In the field of experimental psychology, Powers (1973) made a startlingly similar discovery about the consistency of awareness and expressed it quite well:

> Awareness seems to have the same character whether one is being aware of his finger or of his faults, his present automobile or the one he wishes Detroit would build, the automobile's hubcap or its environ-

mental impact. Perception changes like a kaleidoscope, while that sense of being aware remains quite unchanged. (p. 200)

When a client begins to realize that his or her awareness can contemplate almost anything without having to become ensnared or entrapped by it or within it, a sense of freedom and empowerment emerges that can be quite powerful. Therapists can use awareness in calling almost any phenomenon into play for a client to consider or contemplate. This primary psychotherapeutic principle is at the heart of and binds theoretically opposite therapies such as existential and behavioral. Psychotherapy itself could hardly function without it.

Empathy as a Form of Awareness

From the perspective of psychotherapy, empathy is intimately related to and intertwined with awareness. *Empathy*, or the inferential knowledge or perception of how or what another person is perceiving, thinking, or feeling, is a form of awareness. In the precursors model, empathy falls under the awareness category. People who have a reasonable amount of it are more likely to engage others in harmonious social interactions than those who lack the awareness necessary to recognize the cues and indicators of the thoughts, feelings, and responses of others. This has important implications for people with antisocial, narcissistic, borderline, and histrionic personality disorders, where lack of empathy can be a major concern.

How Awareness of the Problem Leads to Therapeutic Change

Lack of awareness is essentially psychological blindness and deafness. Awareness renders change possible. It plucks a problem out of the realm of the obscure and drops it into the clear light. Awareness illuminates, elucidates, and enables recognition of detail. It gives substance to shadow and form to oblivion. People lacking in the awareness precursor have for the most part shut off the process of knowing and growth. When there is no awareness of the existence of a problem, therapeutic change occurs only by accident or through a process that does not require consciousness, such as pharmacotherapy or pure operant conditioning.

When awareness is present, the problem or difficulty can be identified, expediting change. The more details a client can recognize in a problem or issue, the easier it is for him or her to manage and direct the problem or issue and to maneuver around potential pitfalls and snares. For example, when a battered wife becomes more aware of how her husband reacts to certain situations, she learns to maneuver around those sensitive topics. As her awareness becomes more acute, she also learns the mechanisms that her husband uses to entrap her and how her life has become limited by his actions. Eventually, as her awareness increases in therapy, she learns how she can maneuver herself out of her marriage.

Awareness can thus be liberating. In such instances, the increase of awareness is the metacognitive equivalent of learning how to negotiate one's way through a cognitive and interpersonal minefield. Each successive increase in awareness reveals the position and placement of other mines, which can then be avoided on the way to freedom.

In some people, change can come about simply by becoming aware of something they were not aware of before. If I become aware that my temper scares and alienates my children, that may be enough to enable me to start managing my temper outbursts. For these people, awareness is enough. But for most clients who find change difficult, awareness is helpful but not sufficient. Nevertheless, awareness often calls into play the resources within a person that promote the natural inclination to solve a problem. It is fundamental to and begins the process of integrating differing aspects of a person's thoughts or behaviors. When awareness is operative, images, emotions, feelings, sensations, thoughts, behaviors, relationships, and environmental conditions take on a clarity that enhances problem solving simply by providing more information. To oversimplify for the sake of illustration, lack of awareness is no more than lack of information.

Although it is true that behaviorists can manipulate change in a person through conditioned responses to stimuli, that change is entirely dependent on a largely unchanging environment to maintain those new behaviors. I have seen people change in inpatient drug and alcohol treatment programs, only to revert when subjected to the old environmental reinforcers because no cognitive integration took place. With awareness, change can become stable because new cognitive structures are integrated with older knowledge and experience.

Metacognitive Aspects of Awareness and Change

Awareness is one of the most important of the metacognitive aspects of therapeutic change. It has to do with the detecting, seeing, and observing, in one's inner eye, of cognitions, beliefs, and thoughts. Perhaps the most important metacognitive aspect of awareness has to do with what needs to be observed and where to direct attention. Whether a client is avoiding or dealing with an issue pivots on the phenomenon of awareness. In this regard, the awareness precursor is tremendously powerful.

In many ways, awareness is integral to all the other precursors. To the degree that a client can learn to detect such things as emotional difficulties, unresolved issues, problem behaviors, harmful relationships, dysfunctional thoughts, anxieties, and negative environmental influences and stressors, the mere potential for change gains entrance into the realm of the imminently real. That detection process is metacognitive. Chapter 11 describes in detail how the ability to develop such abilities can be improved through therapy, which can help to increase the momentum of change, even if seldom sufficient for change to occur in and of itself.

There is another metacognitive feature of awareness: the ability to step back from a problem, emotion, obsession, or compulsion. Many clients are so enmeshed and immersed in a situation, behavior, thought, feeling, or sensation that they can contemplate or think of little else. One of the most valuable aspects of awareness involves the action of taking a step back and viewing a problem, emotion, or obsessive or compulsive pattern dispassionately (Goldfried, 1995; Rychlak, 1982). This essential action of stepping back is a primary ingredient of therapeutic change and creativity.

A. T. Beck (1976) referred to this stepping back as "distancing," not in the negative sense of avoiding but in the sense of getting an overview. This has also been described as taking a "broad" or sometimes "overarching view." By removing oneself from confusions and mental entanglements, one can, as is often said, "get some perspective." For cognitive therapists, it is the act of stepping back in one's mind and viewing thoughts or beliefs connected with an event or emotion.

Without the precursor of awareness, the presenting problem will appear vague, overly generalized, or indistinct, and the progress of therapy will likely be more slow, tedious, and difficult. More important, therapy techniques are likely to be ineffective to the degree that clarity of the problem is not attained. Without a focal point for techniques, the entire exercise may appear pointless to many difficult clients. Thus, it is often wise, in the initial stages, to devote some time to defining and clarifying the presenting complaint, problem, or symptom.

A Significant Moment of Change Involving Awareness

The following example of a woman's significant moment of change illustrates the mechanism of coming to awareness and the accompanying action of stepping back from the problem. As she put it, her awareness came "in a flash."

After nine years of marriage, she noticed that she "was becoming increasingly depressed." As time went by, she said, "It became obvious that I was in a state of depression." This depression was accompanied by a series of illnesses in the form of "infections" that were "perplexing to several doctors." Although these illnesses were more "annoying" than "life threatening," one infection did become rather serious. The combination of medicine she was taking as well as her depression had made her "lethargic." Her husband was "noncommunicative," and she had been consistently "rebuffed" whenever she tried to talk to him. His habitual manner of dealing with her attempts to communicate was to "say nothing." He also consistently refused her requests to attend marital therapy.

Her change began just after her most serious bout with an infection. "I was standing in my kitchen next to my kitchen stove—I remember staring at one of the burners," she reported. Then the "realization hit me that because my life was in such a disarray that I was dying . . . not so much physically dying; mentally and emotionally I was dying." She went on: "I realized I had to take any step necessary to change my situation. I felt fairly certain that divorce was the answer." Soon after that realization she initiated divorce proceedings, and "all my physical problems dissipated . . . the medication started to work." She reported that she "healed and felt great within one to two months." She had not had a similar illness since.

In summarizing her change, she related, "I was denying myself an opportunity for true happiness. I couldn't say that I didn't matter anymore—that life—being happy—was very important to me." She also reported that she realized, "I'm the only one who can create my happiness." She arranged her life so as to maintain some control over it from that moment on. She recognized that the change was sparked by the initial awareness of her circumstances, which in turn stimulated the presence of other precursors. All of this culminated in a determined and intense inspiration and action toward change.

Clinical Markers: How to Recognize Awareness

When a person possesses a high degree of awareness of the problem or difficulty, it is relatively easy to detect. Such clients have little problem identifying or detailing a problem or issue. Once again, they do not always change, so change should not be looked for as a clinical marker.

When awareness is amply present, the client is able to identify thoughts and feelings with ease. Such a client is alert and catches on to where a therapist may be going with a particular technique or series of questions. There will be a sense of certainty about the person, a poise that manifests as an air of assurance and even confidence. The person may show that assurance even when depressed, discouraged, or stressed. The person will generally respond quickly to queries regarding behaviors, feelings, or thoughts and will often offer helpful details above and beyond what was requested.

A person with high awareness may not be particularly verbal or articulate, but is aware nevertheless. The therapist should help such a client articulate details that he or she might see but needs help describing with words and labels. When a therapist, through empathy, has an idea of what the client is experiencing, he or she may articulate for a client, asking for his or her modification or verification as the case may require.

The sense of certainty that accompanies this precursor manifests in the cognitive context as well. When awareness is high, the person can be certain of being uncertain. The person is easily able to identify thoughts, beliefs, conclusions, schemas, memories, perceptions, and most other cognitive phenomena. He or she will find it easy to see how cognition affects behavior and feelings and vice versa. In cases of high awareness, thoughts are generally clear, attention is focused, and the person is able to step back from a problem or complex of emotions relatively easily. This client will also be likely to identify not only the problem, but also the circumstances surrounding the problem and, perhaps, the source of a problem. He or she will likely be adept at assigning or assessing responsibility for a given situation or set of circumstances and be able to identify contributing factors in interpersonal dynamics as well. It is often helpful to observe the degree of detail, coherence, or clarity in the stories the person tells related to the presenting problem. The way a person tells such stories can give clues as to the degree of his or her awareness.

People with high awareness are not likely to get lost in feelings or emotions. With little prompting or encouragement, they are able to extract themselves from entanglement in strong emotions and return to viewing the problem or issue. Clients with a high degree of awareness may report a variety of mixed emotions, such as simultaneous love and hate or concurrent sadness, helplessness, and anger. A person with a high degree of awareness will also be likely to accurately and poignantly describe inner conflicts not only about decisions but also about opposing intentions and purposes.

Aware clients who are not verbal will not be likely to articulate what they experience, but will readily relate to reframes or reflections made by the therapist. Overall, a client with awareness is every therapist's desire. Even when change is not occurring, session time passes in a deceptively smooth way—a note of caution to not sing the praises of awareness in therapy too loudly.

How to Detect the Absence of Awareness

The absence of awareness is the one of the most frustrating conditions a therapist encounters outside of deliberate recalcitrance, deception, and obstinacy. It is a hallmark of the difficult client. Vagueness and obscurity define the client's mode of regarding both the inner and outer world. Such clients will be consistently unclear, unsure, and at worst oblivious to all that surrounds them. They typically answer the therapist's questions with brief noncommittal statements such as "I don't know" or "I guess." Blaming is common among people lacking in awareness, not so much because of an inclination toward avoidance as because of an inability to properly designate influences and causes.

It is not uncommon for a client to have acute awareness of some aspects of his or her life and be quite oblivious in others. This is sometimes referred to as "splitting" or "compartmentalizing." For example, a woman may be quite aware of her feelings and the details regarding her relationship with a man, but she may be only dimly aware of her own behavior outbursts in public when they experience conflict. A man may be sensitive to his wife's emotions and reactions to various situations, but he might have little awareness of his own behaviors and beliefs and how these affect his marriage. Another common example of lack of awareness is the employer who is convinced that he or she is loved by all but is actually widely regarded as a boor. Such people are excellent candidates for group therapy, in which getting feedback on how one comes across to others (interpersonal input) is among its greatest benefits (Yalom, 1995).

Another important manifestation of the lack of awareness is a general pattern of minimizing, which involves relegating the truly important to the realm of the insignificant and inconsequential. Minimizing typically occurs when the client claims that a problem behavior such as lying or drinking is of little or no consequence, and he or she usually accuses his or her spouse or employer, for example, as "overreacting," "blowing things out of proportion," or "barking up the wrong tree." Minimizing, or for that matter exaggerating a problem, indicates that awareness is limited.

PRECURSOR 4: CONFRONTING THE PROBLEM

As remarkable as awareness is, it is seldom sufficient to produce change. I have heard many alcohol abusers say, "Yeah, I know I'm an alcoholic. And I know that my drinking gets me into trouble. I just don't give a sh—." For such a client, awareness is present, but therapeutic change is not. Nevertheless, awareness gives rise to what may well be the core function of therapeutic change: confronting the problem.

At first these two appear to be similar, but in function they are quite different. Confronting the problem is a dramatic and radical extension of awareness. *Confronting* is the sustained awareness of a problem with the intent to penetrate and understand it. It is about actively sustaining and deepening what the awareness is addressing.

Properly implementing this precursor brings one as close as one can get to the magic in psychotherapy and counseling. There are many unexplored techniques that can be woven from it that I will detail in chapter 12. I have continually been astonished and fascinated by the raw power of confronting the problem in producing change. Not only is it powerful and direct, but it also has within its parameters some of the most laudable of human qualities. Here we find the basis of science—problem solving—and courage. This precursor is intrinsic to the desire to improve and change the human condition, individually or globally.

Definition and Description

The term *confronting*, as a precursor of change, has nothing to do with hostility, war, opposition, antagonism, or provocation. It also has nothing to do with the common therapy practice of challenging a client on an inconsistency, hesitancy, or incongruency. Like most therapy techniques, challenging a client is an attempt to implement this precursor, but the challenge itself is not the precursor.

As a precursor of change, confronting has a precise and specific definition very different from other uses of the term. *Confronting* is the function of actively observing and closely scrutinizing a problem, issue, thought, behavior, emotion, person, situation, or relationship. The person uses his or her attention and powers of viewing to look into, through, and even beyond a problem or issue. It is characterized by the active movement through a problem, instead of a skirting or dancing around it.

Confronting extends well beyond merely acknowledging a problem, as in the case of the awareness precursor. It is the attempt to enter into it looking and observing all the while, undeterred by confusion and undaunted by pain or intimidation. It differs from the willingness to experience anxiety or difficulty in that confronting is a process of seeing, looking, and observing, whereas the other is more of a feeling process.

In terms of the actual change process, confronting involves an intentional, sustained, and deliberate directing of attention or awareness toward anything that is painful, intimidating, or stultifying. It involves continuing to examine or investigate—"digging in one's heels"—in spite of fear, confusion, or the tendency toward avoiding or acting out. Almost anything at all can be confronted: mental images, memories, emotional pain, behaviors of all varieties, thoughts, thought patterns, beliefs, persons, places, objects, and relationships.

This precursor has often been cited as an important ingredient in the change process. Beutler (1983) described it well in his book on eclectic therapy. Pennebaker and Beall (1986) noted its therapeutic benefits and the importance of confronting traumatic incidents as part of resolving and alleviating their effects. Confronting also has been associated with positive physiological health benefits (Pennebaker, Kiecolt-Glaser, & Glaser, 1988). Orlinsky et al. (1994) found that focusing directly on problems in therapy was related to positive outcomes in 64% of the findings they investigated in their review.

In our study of significant moments of change, participants considered confronting the problem to be the most influential of all the precursors

(Hanna & Ritchie, 1995). Remarkably, it was rated as a definite, clear causal influence in all 20 of the 20 positive change experiences studied. Of those 20 change experiences, it was rated a necessary condition in 14 and a sufficient condition in three of the remaining six.

Confronting the problem is virtually the same essential action found in the well-researched notion of self-monitoring in behavior therapy. Goldfried (1980) noted that the mere act of examining and looking at dysfunctional cognitions may be the fundamental process active in changing them, prior to any disputing. Along these same lines, Langer (1989) used the term *mindfulness* to explain that active, intentional awareness directed at habitual thoughts and behaviors will deautomatize such patterns.

Confronting, Exposure, and Systematic Desensitization

One of the most powerful procedures in psychotherapy is systematic desensitization, a cornerstone of behavior therapy. It is based on the idea that if a person is exposed to repulsive or frightening stimuli gradually and with increasing intensity, that person's phobic reaction will eventually subside or extinguish. This procedure is well documented by research and is especially effective in treating phobias of heights, airplanes, snakes, spiders, and the like (Marks, 1978). Wolpe (1958) attributed the effectiveness of systematic desensitization to what he called *reciprocal inhibition.* Simply stated, reciprocal inhibition is the idea that a person cannot be relaxed and feel anxiety at the same time. Thus, if a person can be made to relax in the presence of noxious or repulsive objects or scenes, such as a snake or a great height, the phobic reaction will diminish and extinguish. There is little question of its effectiveness.

The process is also referred to as *exposure,* which seems to get more contemporary usage than reciprocal inhibition. It is also well documented for its potential to produce therapeutic change (Goldfried, Greenberg, & Marmar, 1990). Exposure to the object of the phobia does not have to be gradual or systematic. It is done through imagination or real life (in vivo), the latter being the more effective. Flooding and implosion therapy are two additional behavior therapies that make use of exposure.

Unfortunately, reciprocal inhibition and exposure are inadequate descriptions of this powerful change phenomenon and need a bit of help. What is neglected is the importance of the willingness to expose oneself to the object of the phobia. If one is not ready to experience anxiety, being exposed to the object of the phobia will be additional trauma. Logically, mere exposure to "noxious stimuli" is not enough to bring about therapeutic change. For example, if one were to dangle a rattlesnake silently behind a phobic person's back, so that he or she did not perceive it, there would be no reaction. This is exposure to be sure. But the person has to knowingly perceive the snake before there is a phobic reaction.

Furthermore, the snake does not have to be a snake at all to initiate the phobic reaction. It may actually be a rope coiled in the grass that is inaccurately perceived as a snake. Conversely, if a real snake is mistakenly perceived as a coiled rope, the phobic reaction does not take place. Thus, exposure must include the person's perceived understanding that they are in the presence of the object of their phobia. The phobia and its treatment are more related to perception and awareness than to the inadequate concepts of mere exposure or relaxation.

What helps the person conquer paralyzing fear is the continued, steady, and deliberate perception of the noxious object or situation. One must also be willing to experience the anxiety associated with the phobia. In an earlier article, we referred to this as "resolute perception" (Hanna & Puhakka, 1991). From a precursors perspective, procedures involving exposure and reciprocal inhibition require confronting in order to be effective. The confronting precursor is an essential change mechanism underlying exposure, reciprocal inhibition, and the procedures of systematic desensitization and flooding.

Offbeat Therapies

Confronting the problem may well be the hidden active ingredient in many offbeat therapies and may be present to some degree in the approaches that psychics and astrologers take with the mostly misguided people who seek them for help. Leister (1982) noted how astrologers and psychics function as therapists in some ways. Over the years I have conversed with many people who have engaged in quasi-therapy activities ranging from past life therapy to the "counseling" that often accompanies astrology, channeling, and readings by so-called telepaths and clairvoyants. Some people swear to have been helped by these practices and claim behavior change as well as improvement of affect (see M. T. Singer & Lalich, 1996). The puzzle, and the limitation of current research, is that the satisfied clients of fringe therapies often describe their gains with the same enthusiasm as those of mainstream therapy sessions.

To automatically dismiss these therapies because the approaches are offbeat would be easy but would be neither honest nor scientific. The precursors model shows how a person can confront a problem even if the method is indirect or bogus, as in the case of listening to a fraudulent psychic reader. The gains are due to the precursors being in place, including the person's confronting the problem, not necessarily to the channeler or psychic. If the psychic or astrologer establishes the equivalent of a therapeutic relationship, and the person talks about the problem, the therapeutic myth or rationale is there (see Frank, 1974), as well as the confronting, awareness, willingness, and social support precursors. Change happens.

But there are controversial professional practices as well. Waters (1997) suggested that resolute perception may be the ingredient behind the success of controversial therapies such as eye movement desensitization and reprocessing (EMDR), in which eye movement accompanies processing of traumatic experiences. Controversial therapies can produce change if the precursors are present.

There is a valuable lesson to be learned from the philosophy of science. Just because something works does not mean that it works because of the theory offered by its discoverer or originator. A former professor of mine once told me of a collection of accounts that he had compiled of mental disorders from a pre-19th-century source in Europe. All the descriptions of symptoms of the disorders were accurate and quite contemporary, he told me. However, the disorders themselves were explained according to the nature of the various demons that caused them.

A New Change Metaphor: The Vaccine Effect of Confronting

Confronting the problem, especially when combined with awareness and the willingness to experience anxiety or difficulty, appears to have a mental effect similar to the effect that a vaccine has on the body. With a vaccine, patients are exposed to a harmless form of a virus, such as polio, under conditions the body can control. In psychotherapy, clients are placed in conscious contact with an area of emotional pain or other difficulty, under controlled conditions, so that harm will not result. Confronting the phenomenon seems to have a healing or strengthening effect. It seems to reduce anxiety, allow for insight and personal growth, give more clarity to thought, release painful emotion, and improve interpersonal functioning. Confronting adverse conditions in a controlled setting also seems to allow a person to better adapt to and, by degrees, master his or her environment.

Metacognitive Aspects of Confronting

Confronting is metacognitive in that it involves the directing and regulating of awareness in the context of choice. We have known for a long time that attention is selective (James, 1890/1981; Wessells, 1982), that it does not randomly come to rest on various phenomena in life. It attaches to and apprehends certain objects and things for the purposes of survival, pleasure, interest, and other influences. Confronting, however, is uniquely metacognitive in that it maintains and sustains attention in spite of the impulse to avoid, give in to confusion, or act out, as I have already outlined. The precise metacognitive act is that the act of confronting involves the directing of observation and attention and does not allow attention to significantly wander, disperse, or obsess. It holds attention steady with the purpose of understanding an issue or problem.

Ancient and Philosophical Roots of Confronting

Confronting a problem or issue is intrinsic to Edmund Husserl's (1913/1982) phenomenological method and philosophy, which was also taken up by his one-time chief assistant, the renowned and controversial existential philosopher Martin Heidegger (1927/1962). Confronting is also at the basis of Indian psychology, being well expressed in the ancient text of yoga psychology, the *Yoga Sutras of Patanjali* (Aranya, 1983; Feuerstein, 1980, 1989). Patanjali's yoga is widely recognized as the chief application of the principles of various psychologies of India. *Samyama* is the name of a technique used in yoga that makes direct use of intense and highly concentrated confronting of various phenomena to arrive at deep insight and transcendence of self.

Similarly, confronting has been a cornerstone of Buddhism for 2,500 years (Rahula, 1978). Buddhist monks have been practicing a wide variety of cognitive–behavioral techniques for the same length of time (De Silva, 1984, 1985; Mikulas, 1978, 1981). Confronting is a crucial aspect of these practices (Pandita, 1991), although, in Buddhism, it is more commonly referred to as *mindfulness*. Mindfulness is fundamental to the Buddhist concept of therapeutic change and is a fascinating subject in and of itself. In many ways, this precursor can be understood as the Western equivalent.

How Confronting the Problem Leads to Therapeutic Change

Some remarkable change processes occur with the confronting of a problem. These can be considered from a number of perspectives, outlined in this section. I gathered these perspectives in phenomenological interviews with people confronting an issue or reflecting after confronting (see Moustakas, 1994; Polkinghorne, 1989).

Cutting to the Essence of a Problem

Husserl's (1913/1982, 1936/1970) philosophy of phenomenology, previously mentioned in the section on awareness, is particularly insightful when applied to the precursor of confronting and neatly explains several aspects of the process of confronting in therapy. In the early 1900s, Husserl developed a methodology of seeing and observing that was meant to free a person of his or her preconceptions. His method was probably the most fundamental, basic, rigorous discipline for observation and awareness ever developed in the Western world, as Herrnstein and Boring (1965) acknowledged.

The method was, at its core, quite simple. One puts aside as many of one's preconceptions and assumptions as possible and views the issue or object with sustained awareness. The object or issue can be any object (mental or physical) or relationship or any other worldly or mental experience or phenomenon. This is done until a person reaches or penetrates to the core or essence of that phenomenon, with the consequence of thoroughly understanding it. Husserl said that this is no mere intellectual process, nor is it a theory. It is an experiential process. Husserl called this an *eidetic reduction*. By that, he meant that one arrives at the essence of the phenomenon under investigation.

Phenomenology, in the philosophy of Husserl and others such as Sartre, Heidegger, and Merleau-Ponty, is an extraordinarily complex subject with an amazingly intricate language for describing various aspects and modes of consciousness. It also involves a method of seeing and observing that is as primary and unbiased as is possible for human beings to achieve (Herrnstein & Boring, 1965). In the phenomenological method, one observes any mental or physical phenomenon or experience openly and freely, with minimal expectations and preconceptions, with the intent of understanding it at its roots. In a therapy context, a remarkably similar method is often unwittingly applied to such problems as a cruel boss, childhood abuse, depression, anxiety, and rage. As one continues to look and purely observe, eventually the phenomenon becomes more and more clear until one begins to have insights into its nature and character. This is also a fundamental aspect of the method of scientific observation, and as Medawar (1984) noted, it is a process that seems to be as intuitive as it is intellectual; certainly, Husserl would have agreed.

Husserl's method is near to the essence of what occurs in many forms of psychotherapy. Therapists and counselors routinely and regularly ask clients to delve into an area of pain or uncertainty with the intent of coming to a more complete understanding of it. This is the case even if it means that the understanding arrived at is that the phenomenon itself is too vague to be understood, as in the case of the attempt to figure out another person's intentions. The process of continued, intense, sustained looking and observing has profound effects in terms of change. Rogers and other experiential therapists have referred to the continuous process of examining feelings and views of a problem as "peeling the onion." This is a fitting metaphor that describes the method of cutting to the essence of an issue, and it also describes the process made possible by confronting.

Cutting to the essence of a problem or issue does not have to occur verbally. It can be accomplished without putting words to the experience. Many clients do this routinely, even though they may be thought of as having "cognitive deficits." I have seen many severely emotionally disturbed teenagers able to do this. In such cases, behavior change comes with the confronting but may not be verbalized in the form of an insight. As Arkowitz (1989) wisely noted, insight often comes *after* behavior change. Once again, it is the confronting that seems to be the catalyst.

Simplicity and Complexity

Another curious phenomenon, related to the phenomenological aspects of confronting, is that the more one confronts a problem, the clearer and less mysterious it becomes. At first glance, the issue seems to become simpler, but this is misleading. What is more likely is that the problem, as it becomes more thoroughly explored, examined, and investigated, becomes less and less obscure and vague, so that its intricacies stand out in greater detail.

For example, in the case of a relationship that has gone sour, a person explores and examines all aspects of it in therapy. The relationship is quite involved and has many dynamics, outside influences and pressures, and personal and interpersonal perspectives. In therapy, the person examines the relationship in terms of empathy, love, roles, social interactions, mutual friends, parental influences, sexual relations, met and unmet needs, spiritual beliefs, and children, if any. In the process, the relationship becomes more and more crystallized, until the person achieves an overarching view of it accompanied by a more thorough understanding. The relationship is still quite complex, but now the complexities are mapped and stand out with more clarity.

Reality Testing

Another aspect of confronting as part of the change process involves differentiating reality from illusion or, in some cases, delusion. Confronting is intrinsic to the process of *reality testing*, a continuous process of verifying the accuracy of perceptions. Reality testing is related to but moves beyond simple clarification of the problem. It is the work done to test whether perceptions and beliefs hold up to the proving ground of the experiential world.

Of course, reality itself is a dubious entity. It is extremely difficult to define and identify, and it has baffled some of the greatest philosophical minds for centuries. Putting aside the current movement in constructivism, it is still important for many clients to compare what is actually present in the world and in their minds. For example, a man may be highly suspicious of his wife, wrongly believing her to be cheating on him. It can be quite important to determine whether this is true in reality, that is, whether she is cheating in fact. The man could go on constructing his own false reality forever, leading to further dysfunction, if the construction is simply not accurate.

From a pragmatic perspective, reality could be said to be what remains after all our theories, beliefs, constructions, and perceptual filters about it are stripped away. This was precisely Husserl's goal in phenomenology and often what happens in psychotherapy. It is far more functional to cope with a situation that is accurately perceived.

A Smaller Problem Space

Another curious, highly subjective phenomenon associated with confronting the problem is consistent with Lewin's (1935, 1936) conception of what he called the "life space." The life space is that part of the person's perceived world that is taken up by events, circumstances, or issues that are absorbing attention. According to Lewin, some of these issues can appear large in a spatial sense, whereas others can appear small. In everyday language, we speak of "big" problems and "little" problems.

The act of thoroughly confronting usually makes a problem or issue seem less significant. Where a problem once loomed large and foreboding, it can seem smaller and more manageable after thoroughly confronting it. The problem becomes less oppressive as it is progressively confronted. Several people I have interviewed after they directly confronted a problem mentioned that they felt "bigger" after doing so. A problem can seem smaller, or the "I" of a person can seem bigger. Either way, the implications for therapeutic change are obvious. For example, resolving a conflict with one's teenage son or daughter might initially seem quite daunting, but after confronting the problem, it appears to be more like a difficult but manageable task. When a person becomes competent at confronting, depression or anxiety can be viewed in this same fashion. This is part of developing the ability to confront as a skill of change.

Removing the Power of the Problem

When a problem or issue is ignored, resisted, or denied, it takes on what can appear to be a life of its own, influencing the person in a variety of ways. For example, I once had a client who believed that she had a lump in her breast, which she feared could be malignant. She did all that she could to divert her attention from it, to avoid talking about it, and to pretend like it was not an issue. Meanwhile, when she did think about it, she would cry, thinking that her life might be over. When I met her in therapy for another reason, she had been ignoring this problem for well over a year and a half, fully aware that things could get worse if not treated early. Little by little, as we talked about it, she realized that ignoring the problem was giving it power over her. She saw how it was intimidating her and exerting influence over her in a variety of ways. It affected how she treated her children, how she viewed her job, and how she saw herself. When she finally looked at the problem directly and thoroughly, she was, by degrees, no longer intimidated and immersed in it and acquired some overview of her life again. The mere act of deciding to see a physician gave her a sense of control, although it did not remove her fear. The lump turned out to be benign.

This aspect of confronting is related to the currently popular notion of empowerment. When the problem occupies a smaller region in the life space and begins to lose its ominous or intimidating quality, one becomes empowered to move out from under the burden of worldly or psychological oppression. It also enables one to extend one's range of influence, scope, or outlook beyond a painfully limiting set of circumstances to more comfortably deal with the challenges at hand. There is little question that such conditions contribute to the well-being of a person.

The more intensively something is confronted, the more it eventually seems to diminish in both size and power. When a problem or issue is continually contemplated, a person seems better able to endure it without becoming overwhelmed by it. This is also at the heart of the change principle of exposure. The key is to be able to look and observe even while caught up in painful emotion or profoundly confusing circumstances. Confronting is a skill that can be taught, trained, developed, and practiced.

Confronting as Holding the Problem Steady

There is another unique metacognitive aspect of confronting that is not found among any of the other precursors. It is holding the problem steady in the mind, so that it does not waver or disperse. When a person confronts an intimidating, painful, or confusing phenomenon, there is a natural tendency to turn away or avoid. Thus, whether the phenomenon is in one's mind or in the world, the person must hold it steady in conscious awareness, so that he or she can continue to contemplate it. If the person is unable or unwilling to hold the object steady, the degree and depth of confronting will be severely diminished or impaired.

As far as therapeutic change is concerned, holding the problem or issue steady in one's mind begins the fundamental shift from being at the mercy of the problem to being in control of it. There is a subtle mechanism at work here. If the person can exert control over the problem enough to hold it steady in the mind, he or she is more likely to be able to influence or affect it in the world. For example, I once worked with a 13-year-old boy, Bobby, who had developed a phobia concerning dogs. I asked him to tell me about a particular dog of which he was especially afraid. He told me that the dog belonged to a neighbor and that his name was Sam. Bobby said that this apparently ill-tempered animal was constantly trying to bite him. I asked him if he could hold a picture of Sam in his mind and "not let him get away or bite you, just look at him." He thought I was quite crazy to ask him to do this. I suggested he do it as an experiment, and he eventually did this quite well. To his amazement, as he did so, his fear began to diminish. Bobby's struggle was quite heroic and exemplifies the importance of courage in therapy (Goldberg & Simon, 1982) and how confronting is intimately related to it. Of course, the procedure was closely related to flooding, which makes abundant use of confronting. What follows is another, somewhat more dramatic, example.

A Major Change Incident Involving Confronting

John had been in therapy for 10 months attempting to resolve the loss of a relationship with a woman he had loved very deeply. During the course of therapy, feelings of depression would only slightly lift before returning. Cognitive approaches were used in an attempt to change his thinking, but change was not forthcoming. Meanwhile, he was obsessed with this woman. He thought about her continually. He also reported that he had been depressed for as long as he could remember, saying that his life had been "dominated by sadness and anxiety" and that he had been to many therapists. Therapy had "only helped slightly," he said. Then came a session in which the therapist was questioning him on what aspects of the loss of his relationship were the most difficult for him.

Suddenly, for no apparent reason, he became aware of a vivid memory from his childhood, around age 6. He "was lying in bed" and "heard an airplane flying overhead." He was "terrified" that the plane was going to drop a nuclear bomb. As he spoke of this to his therapist, he began to realize that his lifelong sadness and depression somehow stemmed from this moment. He then remembered how frightened he had been of nuclear war as a child during the Cold War, and he saw how this had negatively affected his entire outlook on the world. He almost instantly realized that the strong anxiety he felt about the woman was of the exact quality as the anxiety he felt about nuclear war as a child. He saw that his fear of nuclear war was remarkably the same as his fear of losing his romantic partner.

On seeing how silly this was, he said that his "sadness and depression disappeared and never came back." Following this, he no longer obsessed about his lost love and stopped compulsively talking about her. He said, "she wasn't the problem, this incident was." He claimed that it was this session that, as he put it, "freed up my emotions" so that he "could live a more real existence." John's story is a classic example of peeling the onion until the actual problem emerges. This pivotal session had occurred 16 years before he told me about it, and John still maintained that it was the turning point of his life.

Clinical Markers: How to Recognize Confronting

Clinical indicators of the presence of confronting are fairly straightforward and, in many cases, immediately evident. When a client is actively confronting, there is a sense of perseverance in facing up to and continuing to observe. The person displays an animated excitement or composure in meeting the challenges of life or therapy. There is a steadfastness, alternatively described as a "doggedness" or "digging in one's heels" in seeing and studying an issue to its resolution. Such a person will show a spark of determination in holding attention on a problem. The person is honest and direct, and defensiveness is overridden by the desire to overcome obstacles and barriers. He or she accepts feedback and often asks questions of the therapist that take the therapy to a deeper level.

Metacognitively, what to look for in clients confronting the problem is the ability to hold the problem steady in their minds to be inspected and explored. Such clients seem to have attention sufficiently free so that they can direct it to virtually any area of their lives or life histories. They engage in little or no deflection, aversion, or otherwise turning away from or avoiding an issue, emotion, or problem. The person is able to selectively view virtually any phenomenon.

Cognitively, there is a confidence in a confronting client that seems to say, "I can look at anything at all in my mind" without fear of being harmed, consumed, destroyed, or disintegrated. The person believes that confronting is an important act and part of the healing process and that studying a problem or issue will enable him or her to understand and be able to resolve it. This person is convinced that the way out of a problem or situation is by working one's way to the core or essence of problems, issues, emotions, beliefs, and so on. But the client does not necessarily have to articulate insights so much as be inclined toward behavioral change.

The confronting person or client is a confident person who is stable in the ability to maintain perspective. Confronting ability is a sign of high ego strength, whereby a person does not easily wallow or stew in his or her emotions, but consistently seems to be able to keep a sense of awareness and presence even in the face or threat of pain, discomfort, or deeply disturbing circumstances. This person is not intimidated by strong feelings or emotions and often displays a sense of calm, composure, or even poise in the face of adversity or hardship. From the therapist's perspective, it is common to find oneself deeply admiring such a client, appreciating and perhaps even being moved or touched by the client's courage, fortitude, and perseverance.

How to Recognize the Absence of Confronting the Problem

Clients who do not confront will protect themselves from looking at or contemplating an issue or problem in the belief that harm will result. They will be adept at deflecting challenges from the therapist by changing the subject or implying or directly telling the therapist that looking at or knowing about a problem is neither necessary nor helpful. Some of these clients may be adept at "talking around the problem" or "skirting the issue."

Such clients may wallow in their problems, becoming overwhelmed and ensnared. They hesitate or waver in the act of viewing and find it difficult to maintain focus. They also tend to offer or even prefer superficial or shallow solutions and minimize the importance of examining an issue or aspect of their lives. Such clients often need a great deal of coaxing or encouragement and may be easily intimidated by the magnitude of even small problems. Clients who seldom achieve closure on issues may be lacking in this precursor. Cognitively, a client who does not confront has not learned that confronting a problem leads to its resolution.

One of the most difficult of all difficult client styles is the intellectualizing client. This client is often highly intelligent and possibly highly educated and can simulate confronting and make it look like he or she is deeply examining issues. These clients often mistakenly believe that confronting is one of their greatest strengths and will offer a host of reasons for why the problem developed. Such clients will use sophisticated vocabulary and even therapy jargon. They may be successful at "snowing" the therapist into believing that they are well in control, when in fact they are using their intellects to protect themselves from exposure to, or in Gestalt language, "contact" with the painful emotions, difficulties, or problems present.

In such cases, the client is not confronting at all. He or she is compulsively analyzing, mulling, or thinking about an issue or problem. In an indirect way, intellectualizing can anesthetize emotional pain to a small extent, providing the secondary gain or reinforcer that perpetuates the dysfunctional behavior.

One of Perls's (1973; Perls, Hefferline, & Goodman, 1951) best known and important contributions to experiential therapy is his idea, in the context of therapy, that we "lose our minds and come to our senses." The intellectualizing client has a thinking mind so hyperactive that it has stepped beyond its boundaries and taken over the functions of being and observing. The high intelligence and compulsive thinking of such clients sabotages their ability to penetrate to the essence of a problem and achieve a viable resolution. For such clients to achieve change, they may need to learn that there is a difference between thinking and looking, and that analyzing and contemplating are not at all the same endeavor (see Heidegger, 1927/1962). Fortunately, many intellectualizers will respond to some of the approaches to enhancing this precursor offered in chapter 12.

PRECURSOR 5: EFFORT OR WILL TOWARD CHANGE

Effort or will toward change seems quite simple on the surface, but it extends deeply into an amazing network of levels of understanding that further illuminate the concept of therapeutic change. Undergoing therapy can often be such a verbal, passive, and even cerebral experience that too little action ever takes place. In a typical scenario, the therapeutic relationship becomes comfortable, and the conversation flows freely and in many ways is pleasurable and meaningful. It is extremely easy to talk to most therapists and counselors, so much so that the talking and sharing itself displaces the overarching goal of therapeutic change.

Of course, beneficial change certainly does come from having the pleasure of someone to listen and the catharsis that comes with it. But talking is not enough. A client must also make the transition to actually effect change in other areas of life. Therapy can become a kind of opiate when its purpose is only to engage in a close relationship where the therapist's chief actions are to nurture and console. This mechanism is also seen in group therapy, where a participant becomes addicted to the warmth of the group process but does not achieve change. For most clients to stabilize and improve, they must actually change the conditions of mind, behavior, and environment.

Through confronting, a person can come to feel far more comfortable and tolerant of a dirty house. One can know where every square inch of dirt and grime has accumulated, but if one does not exert effort to physically act on the dirt and remove it, the house never gets clean. Thus, it is usually not enough to be aware of, or to be open to, or to confront a problem. In so many cases, there is simply no substitute for action, and change may not take place without it.

Effort or will is the precursor that leads to multifaceted, multilevel change and ties together many of the other precursors. When it is operative, changes in thinking, feeling, and behavior enable a person to attain observable improvements in states of mind, feeling, behaviors, and relationships. This precursor marks the transition between contemplating and doing.

Definition and Description

Effort can be defined in a number of ways. For the purposes of this book, *effort* is the deliberate exertion or enacting of physical or mental energy or resources. In the broad literature of psychotherapy and counseling, it is usually discussed in the context of how much a person is "working" in therapy. Unfortunately, we still do not know enough of what actually constitutes that "working." It is likely that effort, like the variables of confronting and the willingness to experience anxiety or difficulty, is an important part of client involvement in therapy, so often associated with successful outcomes. Effort is deliberate and self-determined, and in the context of therapy it is directed toward therapeutic change in the form of self-improvement or positive changes in one's environment. It involves executing the tasks necessary to accomplish the goal of change.

Many researchers have noted that effort is vitally important to a client's progress in therapy (Axsom, 1989; Omer & London, 1989; Strupp, 1996; Yalom, 1980, 1989). Like all the precursors, effort is a common factor of change. Axsom (1989) noted that it is a "central feature of therapies" (p. 234). A. A. Lazarus (1989a) noted that the success of therapy depends to a large degree on how much effort is expended by a client and therapist. He noted that effort needs to be expended between sessions as well, and this is an important aspect of cognitive–behavioral therapy.

In our research, effort was reported to be a necessary or sufficient condition in 75% of change experiences (Hanna & Ritchie, 1995). Effort need not be seen as exhausting or draining. In its most simple aspect, it is active cooperation with a therapist, an action that Orlinsky and his associates (1994) found conducive to successful outcomes in 69% of the findings they reviewed.

The Nature of the Will

The idea of the will is a crucial, seldom mentioned, and rarely appreciated aspect of effort. It is messy and difficult to be sure, but just because a concept is ambiguous doesn't mean that it is invalid or should be ignored, especially if it has some utility.

Effort toward change is seldom, if ever, engaged without some act of will. This seemingly simple and self-evident statement is actually quite bold when viewed in the overall history of psychology. Some might say that it is better to leave out the will as being extraneous and not really contributing anything to the subject of change. Many have gone as far as to imply that the will is impotent and not worth attending to in therapy. This may be a serious error when difficult clients are concerned. Although the will is complex and even confounding, this is no excuse to avoid it.

Although Skinner (1971) surely would have been disdainful toward the subject of will, many behavior therapists currently speak of subjects like choice and intent. These terms presuppose the concept of the will and even derive their meaning from it. Even though it had been banished by behaviorism for decades as an acceptable topic in psychology, due to its "mentalistic" nature, the concept of will in general has been making a steady comeback in the wake of agency and self-determination (see, for example, Harré, 1984; G. S. Howard, 1986, 1994; G. S. Howard & Conway, 1986; G. S. Howard & Myers, 1990; Robinson, 1985; Snyder, 1994).

But what exactly is the will? David Hume (1739/1978), the 18th-century English philosopher, offered a classic definition that is as good as any I have encountered. His research revealed the will to be "*the internal impression we feel and are conscious of, when we knowingly give rise to any new motion of our body, or new perception of our mind*" (p. 399, italics in original). If we substitute *effort* in the above definition, it does not lose its descriptive power. That is, perhaps, why William James (1890/1981) noted how effort and will are intimately related—so much so that he viewed them as essentially equivalent. From this perspective, the will can be easily understood as part of the effort precursor (see Cross & Markus, 1990). It is highly metacognitive. In the end, however, the will is not all that obscure. Our research participants, for example, had no trouble recognizing it.

The will manifests whenever we act, whether that act be one of body or of mind. I have referred to the latter phenomenon as "psychological acts." Commitment is an example of the will in action. Glasser (1965) was one of the first to point out the importance of commitment to change on the part of a client as crucial in bringing about the effort needed to carry a plan through to its fruition. Commitment is a good example of a psychological act.

In our phenomenological study of therapeutic change (Hanna et al., 1995), it soon became clear that psychological acts were at the basis of the bulk of major change experiences. It was precisely these acts that brought a person to step outside of, move beyond, and transcend the confining circumstances that inhibited change. Effort or will was also perceived to be a causal influence in 100% of the change experiences we studied, and a necessary or sufficient condition in 75%.

Many clients are aware of the problem and the need to find a solution, and they can also be confronting and willing to experience anxiety or difficulty. But in spite of the (usually modest) presence of those precursors, when it comes to action toward making change, they seem to never get around to it, as though they are chained and harnessed.

Some people are actually afraid of the world, and the people in it, to the point where they seem hesitant to even have contact with it, let alone effect change within it. This is a kind existential agoraphobia. At some deep existential level, they believe that making direct contact with the world in any manner is tantamount to experiencing pain. Such people have ontological core schemas that lead to their alienation from the world (see Ottens & Hanna, 1998). Other people seem to believe that they do not have the capacity to alter either the world or their minds. Still others believe that they do not deserve the benefit of change, and through a lack of effort they deliberately deprive themselves of change. Many passive, inactive clients are in this group.

When a difficult client who seems to make little or no progress toward change seems unable to take action, it may be wise to recognize this as an affliction of the will, just as Rank (1936) noted. In fact, Rank recommended that clients have their will strengthened as part of therapy and said in no uncertain terms that this personal quality was a major aspect of a healthy human being. Low (1952) also observed that the will, as the human quality that moves beyond instincts and drives, is the key to mental health. Similarly, Assagioli (1973) saw the will as the primary element active in reaching higher stages of development.

All of these men were convinced that the will is something to be rehabilitated and restored in clients as a routine part of therapy. I do not believe, as they did, that an entire therapy should be built around the will. Nevertheless, it should not be overlooked as a point of rehabilitation in certain difficult clients, especially when a client just won't do anything. Techniques that can strengthen the will and enhance effort are provided in chapter 13.

From a slightly different perspective on will, Kanfer and Grimm (1978) found that therapeutic tasks were more efficiently completed by those who perceived that they had freedom of choice in approaching those tasks. Clients are best given options as to how to go about completing homework assignments, and their power of choice should be validated and strengthened whenever possible. In cases of antisocial personality disorder, Kierulff (1988) found therapy to be more effective when the free choice of these clients was emphasized.

In my work with young people with criminal records, I found that many choose to do anything they can get away with to gratify their desires and passions, regardless of law or convention (Hanna & Hunt, 1990; see also Samenow, 1998). In fact, the goal of "getting over on" the law or societal conventions is the challenge that often guides the choice. Rather than attempting to inhibit this twisted way of being, it occasionally helps to demonstrate the paradox that while freedom is indeed precious, exercising it unwisely can lead to a loss of that same freedom.

Effort and the Efficient Use of Time

Effort needs to be integrated into a client's everyday life before substantial change can begin to manifest. One way of looking at this is to consider that there are approximately 112 waking hours in a week. Depending on the treatment arrangement, a client sees a therapist for only one of those hours, or perhaps more if the person is hospitalized or in an outpatient format where therapy is conducted several times a week. The small number of therapy hours are often insufficient if the lessons from therapy are not converted or integrated into the client's everyday living. Effort toward change needs to be implemented by the client throughout the week for in-session lessons to merge with worldly experience. When effort is directed toward therapeutic tasks throughout the week, therapy time becomes more meaningful, productive, and valued by the client.

There is another way of viewing available time in therapy. Out of the 50 minutes of a therapy session, a therapist might find it helpful to be aware of how many of those minutes are willfully devoted toward change. This will manifest in cooperation, relationship building, and a client's proactive approach to problems in the session itself. A 50-minute session with a difficult client may have only five truly productive minutes in which the therapeutic change process is actually engaged. The other 45 minutes of session time might be spent in denial, avoidance, manipulation, or any form of circuitous communications and evasive actions. Session time is wasted if the precursors are not being implemented or utilized. A client's progress in therapy can sometimes be gauged by this measure.

How Effort or Will Leads to Therapeutic Change

How does change actually come about through effort or will? To answer this question, it is helpful to first outline two essential modalities in which effort or will initiates change: control and maneuvering. In both modalities change is implemented directly and with immediacy. Each takes place in three distinct though related contexts—the mind, the body, and the world or environment.

Control of Thoughts and Images

Control in this context refers to the psychological act of directly influencing the content and operations of the mind. Irrational beliefs are discarded and replaced with new, more reasonable beliefs. This can take place immediately, as in some cases, or it can be a psychological act that is repeated continuously until the original irrational belief is pushed to the background of the mind or deprived of its power. For example, if a client has the belief "I will not trust anyone," the act of will or effort replaces this notion with the more rational idea "I can trust some people but not just anyone."

The act of replacing the old belief may have a larger role to play in bringing about change than the content of the new belief. For example, a man learns that his idea of the perfect woman is one who is beautiful, intelligent, self-willed, and proud, and yet he also expects her to be submissive, needful of direction, and willing to sacrifice her desires and goals for his. Such a contradictory woman probably does not exist except in his mental image of the woman of his dreams. In the act of change, where effort and will are engaged, he directly alters this flawed image of womanhood in his mind, and this act may be at least as important as the image that gets put in its place.

In the case of the will directly affecting the body, an obvious example is a person who is overweight and unhealthy and finds it necessary to establish a workout routine. This person actively engages the will to get up and jog, do aerobics, climb stairs, or whatever the exercise may be. The change accompanies the engagement of the will and the effort exerted.

In the case of directly affecting the world or environment, an example is a person who is troubled by the unethical actions of the company she works for. The act of will is engaged when she commits to finding a new job and exerts the effort toward quitting the old one. If the will is not engaged, the person can be aware of the need and confront the problem itself but will talk about the need for quitting for years with no result. For the therapist, a question to ask in such cases is, What is the client really willing here? This question is addressed in chapter 13.

Maneuvering Around Problem Areas

Maneuvering involves therapeutic action around or away from troubled issues or problems that are beyond one's control. For example, in the case of depression, I have often asked clients if they "know where to find an area of pain" in their minds. I ask if they can "go there" if they so wish. I have found that many people can do this with relatively little trouble. If they know how to "go there," they also know how to stay away. This involves maneuvering within one's mind away from troubled regions of pain.

The body can also be maneuvered to avoid problem areas and difficulties. For example, a person insulted in a public meeting may need to engage the will to "hold his or her tongue," one way of maneuvering around a potentially difficult or troublesome situation in which anything said at that moment may be ill advised. This simple lesson is often helpful for defiant teenagers.

Similarly, in maneuvering around worldly or environmental dangers, a recovering alcohol abuser who is driving by one of his or her old bar hangouts and experiences a powerful urge to stop and party may need a deliberate act of will to keep the car going in a direction away from the bar and the possibility of relapse.

A Change Story of How Being Deceived Led to Effort or Will Toward Change

Mary's experience of significant change occurred in a nontherapy context 17 years before the interview. "I found out I was pregnant," she said. The man had told her that he'd had a vasectomy, and when she found out she was pregnant she was "in shock." Putting that and other information together, she admitted to herself that the man she was involved with was a "pathological liar." Her first duty was to attend to the pregnancy, as she had decided that she did not want the baby. The doctor did an abortion under a medical D & C and also performed a tubal ligation at her request. It was while she was being taken to the operating room that she realized, "I was on my way to taking control of my life." She further realized that "fate wasn't dealing me a hand, that I was responsible for my life—that I did have control. . . . I have choices." Having attended to these matters, she then "faced him" in her house. She called him a "no good lying son of a bitch" and removed him from her life permanently.

Mary reported that the same sense of control and responsibility had remained with her until the time of the interview. After telling her story, she looked at me and said that before that experience, "I always felt things happened *to* me." Then she added, "It's me." That insight seems to have been a major factor in the stability of her change.

An Experience of Effort or Will Toward Change Involving Extreme Anxiety

This remarkable story of change happened to a social worker, Ellen. A graduate student at the time of the interview, Ellen's change story took place seven years before. At that time, she had been diagnosed with ovarian cancer about a year earlier. She was experiencing a great deal of stress related to her studies, with several physiological symptoms. This stress was largely in the form of test anxiety, which included vomiting before and during examinations. An undergraduate at the time, she was working on her test anxiety with a therapist, hoping that therapeutic results would also "spill over" into helping what she called her "general anxiety." She was engaged in cognitive–behavioral therapy that included desensitization, meditation twice a day, and countering each arising "negative self-statement with two positive ones." Ellen was also reading extensively and doing aerobic exercising.

One afternoon, after about 12 weeks of this treatment approach, she had just finished meditating and was relaxing alone on the deck of her apartment. Suddenly, she felt a flood of "memories and repressed feelings and emotions" overtake her. "I think of it as a dam bursting or a wall crumbling," she said. Memories of sexual abuse rose into her awareness that took place when she was ages 4 to 6. These memories were associated with "anger, guilt, hurt, and pain."

She described this experience as both "exciting and scary." In looking back on what she realized, she reported that "up until that point I thought that people could do things to me and that I had no control over it." She had thought "that people and situations just happened to me, that I couldn't make things happen myself . . . everything felt accidental." Later on she was doing some reading on the subject of locus of control, and she had a realization: "I could wake up tomorrow and my life didn't have to be accidental, it could be intentional." This gave her insight into both her specific and general anxiety. "I now knew where the anxiety was coming from," she said. "I knew the stomachache was anxiety." Ellen's problem dramatically improved after this, and she reported that she knew that she had handled the problem after taking her comprehensive exams for her master's degree.

Clinical Markers: How to Recognize Effort or Will Toward Change

The client with a high level of effort or will is relatively easy to identify. However, one should take care to avoid mistaking a manic or hyperactive client for one with effort truly directed toward therapeutic change.

Clients with this precursor display a high degree of energy and in some cases even eagerness for completing therapeutic tasks and homework assignments. These clients seek out and ask for therapeutic exercises and activities they can perform on their own, and then proceed to carry them out to completion with attention to beneficial change. They are eager to try out new techniques, from role playing to the empty chair, and from paradox to journaling negative self-talk and disputing dysfunctional cognitions. They impress their therapists with their willingness to actually "do therapy" in the purest sense. In short, they take action dedicated to change.

In therapy sessions, these clients exert effort to actively help the therapist do a more thorough job. These clients are movers and shakers where therapeutic change is concerned. They display an experimental attitude toward change with the stated intent of improving their lives or reaching their goals or being of benefit to others. They are not hesitant to take actions to correct difficult situations in their lives, such as getting out of debt, improving a relationship with a spouse, or disciplining a defiant teenager. Energy and actions taken toward change is a chief marker, but the overlap with confronting should be obvious as well, and the two should not be confused.

When a client is endowed with this precursor, the therapist will sense an abundant determination to solve problems, accompanied by actual engagement of the body in action on the environment. Thus, such a client will actively transfer in-session learning experiences to understanding outside activities and situations. These clients may also be interested in learning not only about their own issues, but about the process and nature of therapy itself. When they are hesitant to act, they will be curious as to the nature of the hesitance, realizing that this is an issue in itself.

These clients are easily able to alter thoughts, change beliefs, and reorganize entire patterns of attitudes. They are also able to construct or deconstruct images or illusions to accomplish therapeutic tasks. I once worked with a 30-year-old client who was puzzled by his difficulties in his relationship with his fiancée. He realized after six intense, active sessions that he had harbored a false image of his fiancée functioning as his therapist. When he saw that he had a faulty or misguided image of a nurturing woman, in a matter of minutes he reorganized his beliefs about women in this regard and told me that he dissolved the image on the spot. In doing so, he realized that he had been difficult to get along with and that he had been demanding too much from the women in his life. He reported that somehow he had grown up thinking that a woman should be his "emotional servant." In a whirlwind of insight and activity, he changed his mental attitude and patched up the relationship with his now overjoyed fiancée. This is effort at its heights, attaining change remarkably quickly, deeply, and with great facility.

As one client who had a high level of this precursor once told me, "I don't need a reason to be happy, I can just go ahead and force myself to feel that way whenever I want to." The apparent fact is that feelings do not have to be binding and that one can take action to directly alter feelings (see James, 1890/1981) as well as behavior and cognitions.

How to Recognize the Absence of Effort or Will Toward Change

A client lacking in effort or will consistently takes the path of least resistance and gives up easily on projects. Such a client seems to lack energy for therapeutic tasks. Look for procrastination and making excuses. Such clients may talk about procrastination as being a problem in itself. Such a client may openly shrug his or her shoulders saying something like, "I know it is something I need to do, but I just don't seem to get around to doing it." Other clients will devote only a limited amount of energy to working in therapy and may make it appear as though great amounts are being expended. This can be the case even though his or her abilities are considerable. There are three additional styles of difficulty that a therapist may be well advised to consider in this regard: the passive–compliant client, the falsely compliant client, and the ambivalent and conflicted client.

The Passive–Compliant Client

Some clients display a puzzling style to which therapists should be alert. The "passive–compliant" client is ostensibly compliant but is so passive that real action is outside of his or her parameters. This client seems initially to be anything but difficult, coming across as admirable and compliant. Such clients are highly cooperative in session and willing to discuss and disclose even the most intimate details. They appear to have many of the other precursors, such as the willingness to experience anxiety or difficulty, high awareness, and a sense of necessity, and are even confronting the problem. They are willing to examine thoughts and beliefs. However, when the client is asked to carry out a therapeutic task or actually change anything, he or she will find excuses to avoid any direct manipulation of mind or world.

Such clients may flatter the therapist or come up with amazingly creative diversions to avoid effort. A client once told me that she could not do her homework assignment because I was "such a great therapist that all she could do was think about our sessions and how much she learned from them." She said this in our 20th session while her life was coming down around her. Another client, who was not particularly aiming to please, told me that he was so fond of his old beliefs that "it would be a shame to lose them." And I had thought he had changed them long before.

The Falsely Compliant Client

The falsely compliant client will come back to the therapist and report with great authority, "I did what you said, and it didn't work." Usually the therapist never gave direct advice and never told him or her to do anything that would make anything "work." Such clients are attempting not only to manipulate the therapist but also to avoid actual effort and prove that their situation is impossible. They almost never do the tasks assigned, and what they actually do usually leads to negative consequences. For such clients, effort expended has a way of making the problem even worse.

For example, a male client is given a homework assignment designed to deal with his tendency to get angry at his children. At the next session he tells the therapist that it didn't work and that he lost his temper. In another case, I worked with a particularly difficult client in his mid-30s who was convinced that his father hated him and was seeking to ruin his life. I had asked him, while gathering information, if he had ever talked to his mother or siblings about it. Rather than seeing this as a question, he took it as a "direct order." He came back and told me, "I did what you said, and it was a waste of time." Eventually, he confessed that he had talked to his mother, but only about whether she loved him. Then he told his father that I said he was "neurotic," a term I almost never use. His efforts were not consistent with the precursor of effort toward change.

Such falsely compliant clients may not be ready for homework assignments that require interpersonal skills. It may be more important to first implement the effort and other precursors before sending them off to do tasks in their environment. For these clients, tasks should be confined to the realm of mind in the form of cognitive rehearsals and role plays until the precursors increase and stabilize. Tasks assigned should be realistic, concrete, and clear.

The Ambivalent and Conflicted Client

Another client who is unlikely to be able to effect change is experiencing a massive infiltration of counterintentions in the mind. An example is the drug user who is desperately seeking a way to get clean but is so in love with the drug that he or she cannot act on any intention to abstain. This person wants to keep using far more than he or she wants to quit, but both intentions are clearly there nevertheless. If this is the case, the person is stymied, and effort toward change will not be expended. This type of client will be examined further in chapter 13.

PRECURSOR 6: HOPE FOR CHANGE

It is no surprise that Dante described hell as a realm bereft of hope. Without hope, life holds little in the way of inspiration or motivation. Hope could be said to be a precursor not only of change, but of possibility. It inspires both action and courage, and it paves the way for the realization of dreams, whether simple or sublime. Unfortunately, hope is widely misunderstood as something akin to longing, desiring, and especially wishing. In the professional context, wishing carries the overtones of a collapsed sense of hope, in which one has to some degree bid farewell to the real world and has become resigned to an inert fantasy that derives its power from powerless yearnings.

In recent years, the professional literature of psychotherapy and counseling has resurrected hope to its current status as the recognition of the potential and the possible. Hope is about what can occur in reality, what can truly be accomplished, even if the odds are long or daunting. The competitive athlete, for example, lives on a diet of hope. He or she must necessarily be able to envision a realistic success, or those visions of attainment amount to little more than idle fantasy.

Definition and Description

Hope for change is the realistic expectation that the future will be positive and experienceable. The only thing it shares with the aforementioned qualities of longing, wishing, or yearning is a concern for a better future. At its peak, hope involves not only seeing the future as experienceable but actually inviting or welcoming the future as preferable to the present (Hanna, 1991).

Hope is quite different from blind optimism (Snyder, 1994), which is often unrealistic and can take the form of fantasy. Hope is based on realistic vision and probability, replete with options and a plan to meet the future. Hope is intimately related to the ability to solve problems and frame problems in ways that lend themselves to solution (Snyder, 1994). What Seligman (1990) called *learned optimism* is closely related to hope. From this perspective, hope can be practiced as a skill. What may look like a fantasy future to some may actually be a calculated, realistic possibility to another who has learned that no matter how bleak things look, there may be a solution, however hidden. Without that realistic element of calculation and discernment, however, dysfunctional fantasy is always a pitfall.

Hope seems to have profound effects on the human psyche. It can inspire a person to want to survive and in the process to live more fully. It has been described as the activator of the motivational system in human beings (Korner, 1970) that leads to a personal investment in the outcome of one's actions.

Hope has been associated with enhancing a person's coping ability from a wide variety of perspectives (Snyder, 1994). Just as this book conceives of it as a precursor of change, hope has been described as a prerequisite for coping (Weisman, 1979) and a facilitator of coping skills (R. S. Lazarus, Kanner, & Folkman, 1980), as well as a mobilizing factor that organizes and inspires coping resources (Stotland, 1969).

Frank (1968; see also Frank & Frank, 1991) identified hope as the operating factor in that much-debated phenomenon of the placebo effect. Alleviation of symptoms by placebo is a rather common occurrence in studies of depression, and hope may be the active ingredient. Conversely, Frank noted that the lack of hope can delay recovery and even hasten death.

This latter observation is borne out by some classic studies on hope. Nardini's (1952) research on American soldiers in Japanese prison camps during World War II showed that those who managed to function maintained a sense of hopeful expectation that conditions could be tolerated and that eventually they would be free. Cannon's (1957) study of "voodoo death" in such places as Haiti and Australia found voodoo death to be nothing magical but rather simply the bringing about of the demise of the predisposed individual by depriving him or her of all hope. In the Nazi concentration camps of World War II, Frankl (1984) and Bettelheim (1960) noted the disastrous effects of giving up, or the absence of hope, on the survival of the prisoners under extreme conditions.

Along these same lines, both Menninger (1959) and Frank (1968) identified hope as a common factor in successful therapy regardless of the theory being utilized (see also Stiles et al., 1986). In this context, hope also includes Bandura's (1977) concept of self-efficacy, which is essentially the idea that if people believe they can perform a task, they are far more likely to be successful at it and more motivated to initiate action toward it. Of course, self-efficacy was originally formulated by Spinoza in the 17th century (Watson & Tharp, 1989), and was often discussed by Adler (1956) as well, decades before Bandura. Nevertheless, both hope and self-efficacy are often grouped together under the heading of expectancy factors (see, e.g., Grencavage & Norcross, 1990). As an expectation, it may be that hope, like a sense of necessity, is more of an indirect or subtle influence on change. Hope seems responsible more for showing or outlining the path to change rather than for precipitating the actual walking of it.

Hope and Humor

Hope also gives rise to therapeutic humor (Snyder, 1994), or humor that is insightful and uplifting and that transports a person out of a burdened mindset and into alternative perspectives that cause some degree of amusement. Humor, in this sense, functions as a therapeutic reframe of an otherwise oppressive problem. Ideally, therapeutic humor is directed at the ambiguity or quirks of life or the foibles of human nature. The kind of humor to avoid is that which is at the expense of another person, such as gloating over the misfortunes of others. Other types of destructive humor involve ridiculing another about looks, mannerisms, or lack of intelligence or skills. Humor based on stereotyping is, of course, another nontherapeutic variety. In any case, hope can give rise to humor, and using humor properly can in turn give rise to hope, reframing the problem just enough to lift the seriousness and rigidity of a problem to allow a healthy escape from an otherwise discouraging situation.

Hope and Suicide

Decades ago, Farber (1968) held that suicide is an inverse function of hope. He described it as a disease of hope that proceeds from a "no exit" belief, wherein a person believes that death is the only escape from an intolerable situation or set of conditions. This was later verified by the research of Aaron T. Beck and associates, who concluded that hopelessness is more closely associated with suicide than is depression. In other words, people who experience hopelessness are most likely to contemplate suicide (A. T. Beck, Rush, Shaw, & Emery, 1979; A. T. Beck, Weissman, Lester, & Trexler, 1974). They developed the Hopelessness Scale as a clinical instrument to measure the likelihood of suicide and found that they could then predict eventual suicide by well over 80% (A. T. Beck, Steer, Kovacs, & Garrison, 1985). Hopelessness, as a concept and as a term, soon became widely used by professional therapists.

In spite of this important discovery, the field avoided any direct mention of hope itself and focused instead on the strange double negative of "reducing hopelessness" in clients who suffered from suicidal ideation (Hanna, 1991). The obvious question was never asked due to the prevailing paradigm of logical positivism that discouraged discussion of "soft" or vague concepts (see Robinson, 1981, 1990). Why all the talk of reducing hopelessness? Why not concentrate on building hope?

Another curious research finding is that suicidal people also tend to have difficulty solving problems (Schotte & Clum, 1987). It stands to reason that a person who is suicidal has not solved the problems besetting him or her; otherwise, the future would look more desirable. If hopelessness is indeed related to a lack of problem-solving skills, problem-solving skills should not be forgotten when working with difficult clients lacking hope.

How Hope Leads to Therapeutic Change

Hope's role in change is a subtle one, without the drama of some of the other precursors such as confronting or effort. Its power is in its widespread effects on the other precursors. Hope can enhance the intensity of the major precursors, and in some cases it can be the catalyst that brings the other precursors into existence. The opposite is also true, of course, as the precursors are profoundly interdependent. Hope makes experiencing anxiety or difficulty more tolerable by indicating the positive payoff for the discomfort. It makes confronting easier through the knowledge that one will not become lost in a tangle of confusion and darkness. Hope jump-starts effort by making a positive outcome look real and viable, so that the end seems imminent and the effort expended seems well spent.

Hope can enhance a sense of necessity by bringing a person out of a state of apathy to the point of recognizing the urgency of the current predicament; hope presents a sense of possibility and plausibility of a positive outcome. A situation that once looked overwhelming and discouraging, with no solution or egress in sight, is radically altered with the introduction of hope. With hope, it still appears as a problem, but not a problem that is "tightly packed" and impenetrable. It is now "porous" with the possibility of options and alternatives, and most important, the potential for resolution.

But a sense of necessity can also inspire hope when the necessity is so urgent and so pressing that it forces a person to confront the problem and see their way clear to envisioning a solution. Thoroughly confronting a problem can give rise to hope as the problem becomes smaller relative to a person's life space. Confronting can also bring about hope by revealing the solution to a problem or situation, clearing the way for a brighter future. Social support can also inspire hope. Such interactions with hope are quite common in instances of major change.

A problem or issue can be perceived as a threat or as a challenge (Lazarus & Folkman, 1984). When a situation is seen as a threat, one is more likely to withdraw from it and to go into a defensive mode. On the other hand, when a problem or situation is viewed as a challenge, instead of withdrawing, a person is far more likely to approach the problem, and with a degree of interest and even excitement. A challenge offers opportunity and some form of benefit.

Hope, as a precursor, has the capability of transforming a threat into a challenge. For example, the loss of a job may look like a threat to one person, but another perceives it as an opportunity to improve his or her situation. In the presence of a challenge, the future is perceived as fluid rather than fixed or static, and the problem is seen as a source of potential gain rather than probable loss. Many have pointed out the remarkable way in which the word "crisis" is written in Chinese, where it is represented by two characters, one denoting danger and the other opportunity.

For example, Anthony, age 17, was six feet tall, handsome, charming, and muscular. Unfortunately, he was also a member of a gang heavily involved with drugs and violence. He was respected by his fellow gang members for his fearlessness, his ability to fight, and his loyalty. Like so many adolescents in his situation, he told me that he did indeed want to improve his life and help his little brother, who idolized him, as well as the aunt who had loved him and raised him after his mother was killed. He said that he was tired of the fighting and "all the hard-ass bullsh—." But he reported that it really didn't matter: "I'll be dead before I turn 21," he said softly and with great conviction. Then he added, "Besides, if I ever try to leave the gang, they will f--- up my world."

I told him three stories of other gang members who were able to leave their gangs and make something of their lives, and he became visibly more animated. I also promised to "hook him up" with one of those men who had made great strides in improving his life. Anthony jumped at the chance to talk to this man. The possibility that he could help himself and his family escape a desperate situation inspired him. What was once a threat had become a challenge.

Another example was Tina, age 36, who was held in psychological bondage by her husband. She was mentally immobilized by his dominance and verbal abuse. Her extreme dependence appeared to be induced by a brainwashing campaign carried out from the time they were "high school sweethearts." Having given up on her own chances for happiness and fulfillment, her chief concern was for her three children, who ranged from ages 8 to 14. During their 13 years of marriage, he had convinced her that she was incompetent, powerless, insignificant, and incapable of surviving without him. She had been in therapy for six sessions, originally for her oldest child, a highly intelligent boy who was flunking out of his freshman year in high school. She had been extremely careful to avoid any mention of her relationship with her husband.

In the seventh session, which she attended alone, she tearfully spoke of her sense of being trapped by her husband and how she needed to "get away" from him but just did not know how. She was convinced, however, that this was not easily done. "I don't think I can survive on my own," she said fearfully, but also with a strange sense of calm. She also stated with a sense of grim satisfaction, "He needs me." I will not forget the look of forlornness mixed with a desperate satisfaction on her face when she looked up at me to say that.

In time, Tina eventually achieved therapeutic change when she saw that she did not have to be dependent on her husband. Hope dawned when she learned of other women who had moved out of similar oppressive circumstances and spoke with a couple of divorced friends who had been through similar situations. As she began to see solutions to her problem, she eventually gained the confidence to move out on her own. Her husband did not allow this without a lot of anger and fuss, but she eventually reported, "It's OK. I can handle him now."

Anthony and Tina developed a sense of hope when they explored their problems with the goal of solution and when the possibility of resolution became real. Their perceived futures eventually cleared to the point of being constituted with a realistic expectation of resolution and a sense of no longer being helplessly trapped. Their futures appeared experienceable and worthy of interest and pursuit.

Clinical Markers: How to Recognize Hope for Change

The most important clinical indicator of the presence of hope is a sense of confidence that conditions will improve. Change, in the form of therapeutic goals, is seen as attainable. Even in the face of adversity, the client's outlook will be realistically positive. He or she will not become discouraged or apathetic. A hopeful client perceives a problem in terms of solutions rather than becoming entrenched in the awfulness of the problem itself. Accompanying that perception is a sense of enthusiasm or even excitement about life (Hanna, 1991; Snyder, 1994). Perhaps the ultimate in a sense of hope is when a client is thankful for the lesson learned from the problem, even when it has not yet been realized. Demoralization or distress is seen as merely temporary and transient.

The following statements are clues to the presence of hope:

- "I know things will eventually be OK, but things are really difficult right now."
- "I know I will get through this, but it is so hard and I feel so terrible."
- "I have been through tough times before, and I can get through this, too."

A therapist can also test for hope by gently probing with alternative views. For example, if a client remarks, "I have absolutely no idea how to deal with this situation," a therapist can reply, "Do you have a sense that you will eventually figure it out?" A client inclined toward hope will indeed have that sense, knowing intuitively that a way exists but has not been discovered just yet.

Another marker of hope is a client's sense of humor about himself or herself or situation (Snyder, 1994). The hope precursor can be tested through humor as well. This requires good timing, of course. For example, a male client with a verbally abusive wife once remarked to me with a sense of trepidation, "My wife said that she is going to leave me, and I don't know what I will do without her." I replied smiling and with a somewhat satirical tone, "That's quite a problem. What would you do with all of that freedom and well-being?" This client suddenly laughed, and the seriousness of the moment eased a bit. He was surprised that he did so. This hinted to me that he was hopeful enough to eventually be able to see a future without her. The timing of such moments is crucial, of course.

Hope can also be measured. J. F. Miller (1986) and Snyder (1994) developed instruments to measure the presence of hope. Either of these is helpful in assessing hope as part of the precursors assessment form.

How to Recognize the Absence of Hope for Change

A client lacking hope will display an almost palpable sense of despondency or despair, and probably a sense of apathy as well. He or she may believe that life is pointless and there is no significance in anything. Other common emotions are resentment and deep self-pity. Sometimes a hopeless person displays a pessimistic humor that conveys bitterness or biting sarcasm. Such a client will question the worthiness of life and living. A fatalism, as though all of life is out of human control, may manifest and will pervade statements and beliefs. The person may state in one way or another, "Things never turn out well for me" or "It doesn't matter what I do, it always ends in disaster."

Such a person displays little confidence in his or her ability to solve problems. Discouragement and disappointment are always just around the corner for these unfortunate people, and their inclination toward resilience in difficult experiences is low. A client low in hope may display some degree of suicidal ideation without necessarily ever intending suicide. On the other hand, suicide may be imminent, and resolving this crisis will become the first duty of therapy. The client low in hope may also harass himself or herself with self-doubt and express a general sense of protest against the seeming unfairness of life and the impossibility of ever being happy. To the truly hopeless person, life is a painful process, and staying alive means that the pain will continue. When hopelessness reaches its greatest depths, each passing moment is a kind of torment.

On the other hand, when hope is present, the vision of a bright, promising future brings with it the love of life and the joy of simply being.

When coupled with other precursors such as awareness, effort, and social support, the scenario begins to look like a poet's portrait of the undaunted human spirit. It does indeed seem to be true that where there is hope, there is life. It is simply a matter of degree.

PRECURSOR 7: SOCIAL SUPPORT FOR CHANGE

The last of the seven precursors affects almost all aspects of a person's life, including physiological health. Like hope and a sense of necessity, it is seldom if ever a sufficient condition for change in itself, but it enhances the power of all the others in both subtle and direct ways. It can be a source of motivation, inspiration, or involvement, although we found that in some cases of extraordinary human resourcefulness, it did not seem to be necessary at all. Even in those same cases, however, our research indicated that it probably would have been of great help. This precursor is well known to sociological and psychological researchers, and its importance has been noted by many in a variety of ways.

A crucial point of emphasis for this precursor is that the social support assessed must be toward beneficial, positive change. What is not always mentioned is that social support can also be neither healthy nor functional. For example, many adolescent offenders have told me that their peers have supported them in committing criminal acts. The supportive statements sound something like this: "It's OK, man, you can do it. We were scared too at first, but don't worry, you get used to it and don't even think about it after a while." This message could as easily be toward getting good grades as committing a crime. The same message is given to soldiers in the armed forces coming to grips with the fact that they may be called on to kill.

Social support is a powerful reinforcer, whether in a positive or negative context. It gratifies the primary needs of acceptance and belonging in human relationships. In effect, this precursor is rather like fire in that it can be used either positively or negatively to produce constructive or destructive results.

Definition and Description

Social support is the condition in which a person receives physical, emotional, attentional, and other resources from other human beings. From the perspective useful for understanding social support as a precursor, Arkowitz (1992a) defined it quite well: "Social support involves the person's perceived or real access to confiding relationships in which various types of help and opportunities for emotional expression are potentially available" (p. 408). A person has social support when he or she is surrounded by a network of friends or family who feel positively about the person, are empathic, and are willing to help. The ideal social support network consists of people who are available and willing to invite, receive, and accept emotional disclosures. Social support also includes a person's perception that the community or environment is conducive, and actively contributing, to his or her well-being. Social support can also include the love of pets. In assessing social support, it is important to consult with the client.

The therapeutic relationship can be considered part of the client's overall social support network. A therapist's empathy, warmth, and acts of encouragement and empowerment play an important role in social support. An empathic therapeutic relationship has been linked to positive outcomes in therapy in dozens of studies (Garfield, 1994; Goldfried et al., 1990; Orlinsky et al., 1994; Sexton & Whiston, 1994). Especially fascinating is the research showing that clients are better able to accurately rate the quality of the therapeutic relationship, including the level of empathy, than are their therapists (Orlinsky et al., 1994). Using this last bit of information is important when using the precursors assessment form. Aspects of the environment that influence a client to seek therapy, such as helpful employers or coworkers, can also be considered part of a social support network. However, in assessing the presence of social support in clients, the therapist should not consider the therapeutic relationship as part of the social support network.

Several researchers have named social support as an active ingredient in psychotherapeutic change (e.g., Beutler & Clarkin, 1990), and it has also been identified as a source of spontaneous improvement (Lambert, 1992). It can be a major influence in a person's recovery from depression (Arkowitz, 1992a), sometimes being sufficient by itself to reduce symptoms. It has also been found to be quite powerful in recovery from stress-related illness (e.g., Compas, 1987) and is positively correlated with speed of recovery in women who have had breast cancer surgery (Owen, 1990). Perhaps most remarkable is that social support seems to bring about mild improvements in physiological health by itself (Cohen, 1991; Kennedy, Kiecolt-Glaser, & Glaser, 1990).

However, social support is not always present in major change experiences. I know of at least three such experiences, all in women, where no social support was reported to be present (Hanna et al., 1995). This contradicts theories that women find their strength in the company of others. In our research, and in clinical experience as well, women seem every bit as independent and effective as men in accomplishing major change in their lives.

It is important to note that social support can exist in varying grades of quality. Even in its lowest grades, it is often seen as precious and cannot be underestimated in some clients. Probably the best perspective on understanding this phenomenon is Yalom's (1995) therapeutic factors of group therapy, which include universality, group cohesiveness, and catharsis. Such therapeutic factors can occasionally be found in street gangs, however twisted these may be. I will never forget working in an outpatient substance abuse treatment center when a Latino gang member, Lollo, came to treatment with a severe hangover and a large bruise on his forehead. He had a devastatingly sad family history and had witnessed his mother being repeatedly raped by his uncle, who also physically abused him.

That day, he defiantly told me, "Yeah, I was drunk, so what?" and refused to tell me what happened the previous night, insisting that I would "never understand." I replied that maybe I wouldn't understand, but maybe he could teach me something. He did indeed. He told me that he had gotten drunk with his gang friends the previous night. They told him that they would help him get through the treatment program (although not in a therapeutic fashion, of course) and that they would always "be there" for him. The gang leader, whom Lollo deeply admired, told him in an emotional outburst that they would always be friends. He then threw an empty beer bottle, hitting Lollo in the forehead and leaving a bruise, yelling that he loved him like his own little brother. For Lollo, this distorted declaration of affection and caring was precious and meaningful and gave him a sense of belonging and acceptance that was beyond price. It is not at all surprising that he thought I would never understand. It may well be that the service provided by support groups such as AA (Alcoholics Anonymous, 1976) is valuable because it replaces such negative social support with a social support system oriented toward positive change.

How Social Support Leads to Therapeutic Change

Social support is a primary need of human beings. A multitude of theorists in the field, ranging from Adler and Maslow to Whitaker, Bowen, and Satir, have noted the need for a sense of belonging and acceptance by fellow human beings. Social support is another term for this need. Recommending it is stating the blatantly obvious, rather like saying that eating nutritious foods would be a good idea. In the same sense that certain vitamins can cure rickets and scurvy, social support can alleviate loneliness and a sense of abandonment. It meets the need for companionship, warmth, intimacy, and communication, all of which give meaning to life (Yalom, 1980). A primary problem with difficult clients is often lack of social support, especially for positive change. Many have destroyed the possibility of positive social support through manipulation and harmful acts toward others.

I have known some difficult clients who did not change even with the help of the most compassionate and skilled therapists and well-meaning family and friends. A common example is the case of some chronic alcohol abusers who continue in their self-destructive behaviors in spite of a network of caring friends, family, and therapists. From a precursors perspective, the primary contribution of social support for change seems to be its interaction with the other precursors as a "potentiating agent." Its presence makes the other precursors more powerful.

Social support is highly influential on the other six precursors. For example, in the acquisition of hope, social support has a resounding influence (Seligman, 1990; Snyder, 1994). Change seems easier to envision when the encouragement and support of loved ones and friends is present to convince a person to contemplate new possibilities. When one has little hope for oneself, knowing that trusted family and friends are convinced of a bright future can bring about a contagion of hope. There is also evidence that when therapists believe in their clients, more positive outcomes will result (W. R. Miller, 1985).

Social support can help establish a sense of necessity simply by informing a person of the importance of a particular change. For example, if a client expresses little or no interest in change, then perhaps the advice, counsel, or concern of a friend or friends may be able to convince him or her that things are not acceptable as they are and a change is needed. Although the client may believe the specific change recommended by the friend is not important, he or she may consider the viewpoint of the friend to be highly important and in that way may become motivated to at least contemplate the change suggested.

In the presence of social support, awareness may become enhanced. People often listen to the feedback of certain friends and consider new perspectives or viewpoints but resist the same offerings by others. A batterer might listen to a friend saying, "You are being a little too hard on your wife," but he might resist the same statement by his mother-in-law or employer. Similarly, social support makes anxiety or difficulty easier to tolerate. When one knows that people are "there" to help one get through the ordeals of life, the sheer difficulty of it can be much reduced.

Social support also enhances the ability to confront the problem. When one is in an environment perceived as safe, one feels more secure in looking at threatening beliefs, mistakes, memories, or feelings. One would not readily discuss career mistakes with a prospective employer but would do so with a best friend. Likewise, when one is exploring memories of abuse, it is much easier doing so with a friend than with a person who resembles the abuser. When a person feels secure, he or she is more likely to confront more steadily and more deeply (see Hanna & Puhakka, 1991).

Effort is enhanced by social support in much the same way as the other precursors. When people have the encouragement of friends and family who believe in them, they approach tasks and duties toward therapeutic goals with more conviction and commitment. When a person is filled with self-doubt, the confidence and encouragement of family and friends can bring about the exertion of effort.

A Change Experience Involving Social Support

Alicia was in her mid-30s at the time of the interview. Her second-order change experience took place six years earlier. When I interviewed her for the study, she had since become a licensed psychologist.

Alicia was going to marry a man when he died from a chronic heart ailment. "I went nuts," she said. "I started cutting me." She showed me her arms, which still bore the extensive scars of her self-mutilation. She became "really depressed" and began to lose control of her life. "This stuff was always there" in the background, she reported, it was just that this tragedy had brought it to the forefront. She went for therapy at her university counseling center, but it was ineffective, and she eventually stopped going to school altogether.

She attempted suicide by taking an overdose of sleeping pills eight years after her fiancé's death. She was hospitalized, in critical condition, and just barely recovering. As an inpatient in a psychiatric ward, she eventually found a particularly helpful therapist, her fourth. With this man, she said, "there was some hope," and the road to her recovery began. Long after her release from the hospital, however, she was still very angry and resentful. That summer Alicia worked with kids at a Christian camp "just to give something" to people. She was also in a therapy group and was getting a lot of "positive affirmations" and support to go back to school. Her therapist soon moved out of town, and after about two months Alicia "started getting scared again."

By this time she had entered another university and eventually found her way to a counseling center. The therapist there proved to be extremely helpful and disclosed that she had once had similar problems. In Alicia's work with the new therapist, she learned more about her relationship with her mother and her mother's influence on her life. "I learned that I really did need her love and that she really did love me." This was an important insight for Alicia. At one point all of this had built to a climax, and the "therapist let me cry and held me." This experience was the focal point of change for her. It was a "letting go of anger, frustration, hurt, watching it all wash away. I learned to listen with a different heart. That was a major changing point," she said. She came to see she could "get the things I needed from other people and it's OK."

After this experience she "became less angry" and "related to people differently." She learned to "phrase things differently." She added that she learned "that you have to take control of your life and not let life control you." She also said the experience "reaffirmed my faith in God." During the six years between the change and the interview, she reported she had not engaged in self-mutilating behaviors at all. This example is typical of the excellent social support for change available through effective therapy.

Social Support and Clients of Color

Special circumstances exist concerning social support for clients of color in therapy (Garfield, 1994). Although such clients have family and friends like any other group, they perceive discrimination from society extending from the federal level down that is built into the fabric of the White-dominated culture. When a therapist or counselor fails to recognize this discrimination as real, or at the very least does not acknowledge that the client perceives it, the therapeutic relationship with that client will seldom achieve its potential.

In my experience, this key point is a benchmark clients of color use to judge the trustworthiness of the therapist. It is extremely important to acknowledge racist attitudes in society as depriving those who experience it of social support for change. This point is so important that the issue has been given a chapter of its own that includes alternative approaches to cognitive therapy for both perpetrators and victims of prejudice (see chapter 8).

Clinical Markers: How to Recognize Social Support for Change

The therapist can assess the presence of social support from information provided by the client and the nature and tone of the conversation about it. There are many signs and indicators of the presence of social support. Perhaps the easiest and most direct method consists of simply asking a client if he or she feels supported by friends and family and to what degree. Therapists can also ask if clients know of a network of friends who are supportive and helpful to each other, whether they are a part of that network, and if so, how much. It also helps to examine the client's conversation for descriptions of relationships and interactions with others.

To determine the quality of support in those relationships, one can gauge the degree of perceived empathy by asking if the client feels those people truly understand him or her, and if so, how much. Trust is another element to be assessed in gauging the quality of those relationships. It helps to ask a client if he or she actually trusts anyone and, if so, to name those people. When trust and empathy are present, the relationship will tend to be especially valued by a client, and levels of ambivalence or hostility toward the person will be low. In addition, those people described by the client should be spoken of as accessible and available in times of need.

Common references to the support of family and friends is an obvious indicator, especially when the person takes comfort in and works to maintain and develop those relationships. It is also helpful to assess religious or community involvements in terms of social support to see if those involvements are characterized by empathy and encouragement and are not critical, demeaning, or disempowering. Some difficult clients, for example, may be members of religious groups with cultlike features. Such groups can be extremely suspicious of professional therapy and will seek to sabotage apparent progress.

A client rich in social support may also demonstrate relationship skills with the therapist; this is a vital sign of the client's interaction skills. A client with this kind of skill will make the therapist feel supported in his or her work of attempting to help the client. Needless to say, this type of client is especially appreciated by a therapist. In terms of the therapeutic relationship, however, it is important to ask a client for his or her assessment of how empathic or trustworthy the therapist may be, as research clearly shows that the client's assessment is the best indicator and the therapist's generally inferior (see Orlinsky et al., 1994), unless the client is dishonest or particularly manipulative.

How to Detect the Absence of Social Support for Change

In the absence of social support, a client may complain that he or she is "all alone" or has "no one to talk to." Depressed people are also likely to report that they are without close friends or family who understand them (Arkowitz, 1992a). In some cases of personality disorders, a person may be extremely or bitterly cynical of people in general, criticizing them for being untrustworthy, selfish, or cold and uncaring. Those with interpersonal deficits will also be likely to lack social support.

In the case of a schizoid individual or a person who does not seem to need or require the company of others, there may be no complaint about a lack of friends, and the person will probably prefer to be alone in his or her private world. In other cases, the lonely person may complain that "there are so few understanding people in the world." When stated as a global declaration, the complaint should be explored in the context of social support.

As far as people of color are concerned, it is best to assume that social support is not present at the level of institutions or society in general. This may sound odd, but this approach has been extremely helpful in my experience, and African Americans and other people of color instantly respond to this empathic perspective. More will be said on this in chapter 8, dedicated to culture and gender issues.

Clients With Personality Disorders

Assessing social support in people with personality disorders is more complex. Many narcissistic clients will often boast about possessing a wide network of friends and admirers. They may boldly assert their popularity and appeal to others. The need for admiration on the part of this client is a clue to the nature of his or her relationships. Such clients do not describe so-called supportive people as those to whom they might make vulnerable self-disclosures about shame, guilt, or mistakes made in life and will abruptly cut off relationships with people who are critical. With gentle but pointed questioning, such a client may eventually admit that no one "really cares" and claims that all people are really out for their own gain.

Other difficult clients will see the support of others as a liability and will often avoid it as a potential source of pain. This is often true of borderline clients, who may interpret any gesture of help as a cause for suspicion of eventual betrayal. Many difficult clients have issues of abandonment and engulfment. Gaining social support is both a need and an admission of weakness, and while they actively seek it, they may at the same time despise the fact that they need it. Many borderline clients are unconsciously convinced that they are so worthless and undeserving that anyone who likes them must be a fool or stupid or both, and they treat potential friends with mixed neediness and contempt. Thus, to help, a therapist must be willing to be seen as an object of contempt and derision, at least for a while. The end result, of course, is that a person with borderline traits will often drive away those who seek to help. Such people deliberately sabotage help because they cannot tolerate the idea of improvement. In addition, they often punish those who try to help.

Antisocial clients also believe that needing the help of others is a sign of weakness and will manipulate those who try to help, usually by taking advantage of them in terms of money, sexual favors, gaining status or connections, or the like. Social support systems for these clients, if they can be considered that at all, are usually extremely low grade and often characterized by internal dishonesty, cheating, and betrayal of each other. The underlying belief of these people is that one can expect others to help only when they are ultimately manipulating the situation for their own gain.

Family Beliefs and Interactions

People who lack social support are likely to perceive their families with either open hostility or deep ambivalence. They are likely to see their families as a source of anxiety, emotional hurt, depression, abuse, or ridicule. They may accuse their mother or father of having ruined their lives. They describe brothers and sisters as being distant or as having so little in common

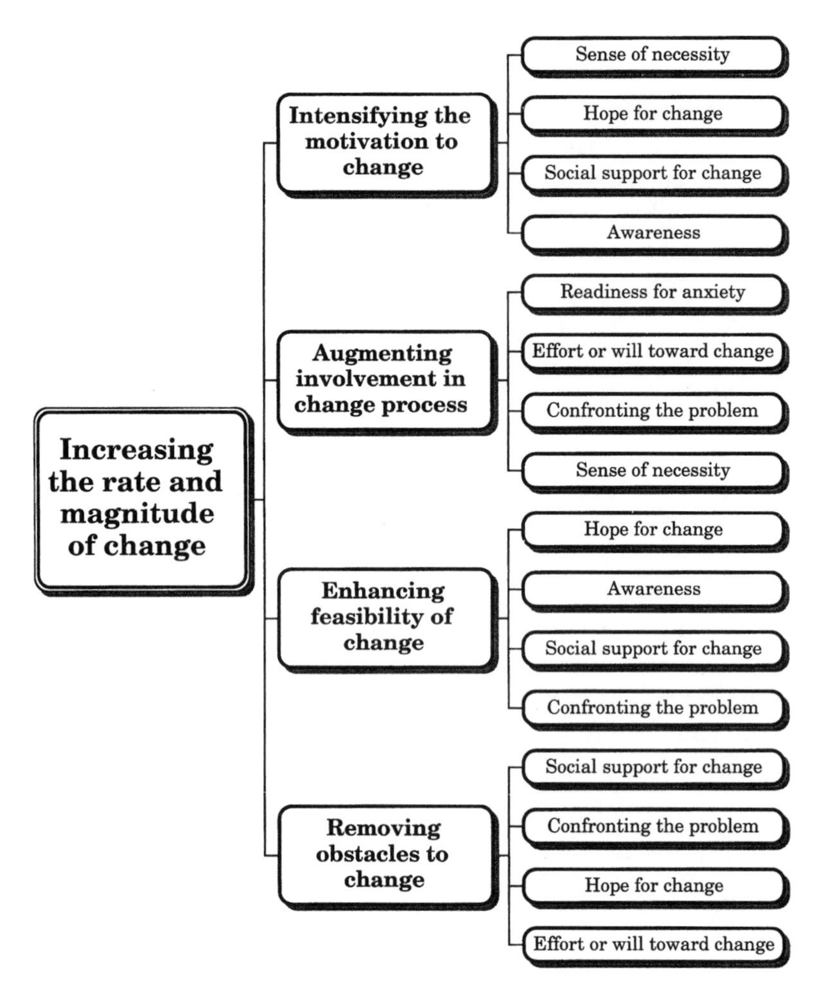

Figure 2. Increasing the rate and magnitude of change. From "Precursors of Change: Pivotal Points of Involvement and Resistance in Psychotherapy," by F.J. Hanna, 1996, *Journal of Psychotherapy Integration, 6,* p. 246. Copyright 1996 by Plenum Publishing. Reprinted with permission.

with the client that there is really no point in maintaining the relationship. All this may be true, but this does not diminish in any way the glaring fact that the person is sadly lacking a vital source of social support.

In conclusion, when a person is lacking social support, it is easier to minimize or explain away problems. Change will be viewed as an individual struggle requiring more effort than necessary, and experiencing anxiety or difficulty will look rather like torture, to be endured all alone. Further, the awareness of a problem may not crystallize with the clarity that comes with trusted feedback, and the problem may not seem quite so imminent or real to the point where confronting may actually be necessary or helpful. Clients without social support will also be inclined to more easily give up hope, lamenting that the future is an essentially lonely undertaking.

CONCLUSION

As a whole, the seven precursors delineate various modalities and means through which therapeutic change takes place. Each assists and complements the others. The model readily lends itself to pinpointing specific avenues of approach with difficult clients. Beyond that, these avenues can also be seen as lines of improvement for psychotherapy itself, at least in terms of increasing the potency of client change variables.

Based on available research, the production and enhancement of client change in psychotherapy can be seen to lie in four areas: (a) intensifying the client's motivation to change; (b) augmenting involvement in the change process; (c) enhancing the feasibility of change; and (d) removing obstacles to change. If each of these four areas of change is addressed, the rate and magnitude of client change in psychotherapy will likely increase. If the field had a variety of procedures designed to increase each of these areas for clients, the efficiency of therapy might be considerably enhanced, and psychotherapy may be able to progress beyond the state of affairs that A. A. Lazarus (1990) referred to as "the dark ages" (p. 356). Figure 2 outlines specific precursors that may play a role in enhancing each of these four areas. Of course, it is assumed that the therapeutic relationship is viable and functioning in each of the four areas.

II

ASSESSING THE POTENTIAL FOR THERAPEUTIC CHANGE

4

RATING CLIENT CHANGE POTENTIAL: USING THE PRECURSORS ASSESSMENT FORM

Some writers in the psychotherapy field have attempted to reduce change to one particular variable, such as insight or effort. Koch (1981) dubbed this mistake "single principle imperialism," or the attempt to take something enormously complex and reduce it to one basic cause or principle. For example, the major personality theories identify the following as the primary human motivation: reducing anxiety (Freud), meeting a life goal (Adler), self-actualization (Rogers), making sense of the world (Kelly), meeting needs (Murray), and reinforcement (Skinner). Even a casual study of these motivations reveals the importance of each and the liability of excluding any. As Koch noted, human beings are too complex to assign single principles to explain behaviors or motivations.

The same holds for the precursors. People who have had more than one major change experience report that different precursors accounted for varying potency at different times (Hanna et al., 1995). Therapeutic change is too profoundly complex to allow for reductionism, and the precursors model, even though it does not assume linear causation and allows for some complexity, also oversimplifies the change process.

A DYNAMIC INTERPLAY

An unfortunate characteristic of the precursors model is that the precursors seem to hang loosely together, in the same way as a patchwork quilt. However, research evidence supports the quilt metaphor. The precursors are not symmetrical, proportional, or equal in potency. They are also not consistently sequential. Many precursors can take the lead in one change experience, only to be absent in another. For example, a sense of necessity can be a dominant and driving precursor in one change experience, whereas confronting or social support can take precedence in others. The precursors model operates with a rotating form of circular causality. Instead of a static, two-dimensional patchwork quilt, the model is closer to a dynamic three-dimensional quilt where each patch changes in size, volume, area, and color in accord with the idiosyncrasies of a given client in a given situation.

The precursors undercut, include, and incorporate the major theories of therapy. They are both transtheoretical and integrative without being dependent on the major theories, even though our understanding of the precursors is enhanced by theories and vice versa. These precursors are functions or conditions that can be found in a person's mindset (in the case of hope, readiness for anxiety, and a sense of necessity), in one's environment (in the case of social support), or as metacognitive acts (in the case of awareness, effort or will toward change, and confronting).

We have known for nearly 50 years that at least a third of troubled individuals will improve on their own, with no therapy intervention at all (Eysenck, 1952). Similarly, approximately 15% of clients improve before their first session (K. I. Howard, Kopta, Krause, & Orlinsky, 1986). What are the dynamics in this improvement? The precursors model may have much explanatory power along these lines: Each person already has a configuration of waxing and waning precursors for change without ever meeting a therapist. Because the precursors are found primarily in the person, they are involved in the change process both in and out of therapy. Many clients who improve without therapy have read a book (confronting), talked to a friend (social support) who made things seem not so bad (hope), and as a result decided to work through the problem (effort or will toward change and readiness for anxiety). As Prochaska and colleagues (1994) put it, "it can be argued that all change is self-change, and that therapy is simply professionally coached self-change" (p. 17).

FURTHER AMBIGUITIES

There are many active ingredients of change in addition to the seven precursors focused upon in this book. We examined 32 variables (Hanna & Ritchie, 1995), all of which had at least some change potency. Many of the outcomes of therapy, such as finding meaning in life or a cathartic release of emotion, are also responsible for further changes. In other words, what looks like an effect of change processes can also become a cause in its own right, creating a snowball effect of more change. Kant (1787/1929) noted long ago that each effect contained within it the seeds of causality. This seems to be true in the case of psychotherapeutic change. Certain variables can be both cause and effect. An overarching insight, for example, is an effect brought about by several precursors, but the insight then can have enormous additional effects on behaviors, feelings, and cognitions.

However, insight and other variables are not listed as precursors simply because they are more of an effect than a cause.

In the case of second-order change, it appears that each change factor plays its role in combining, culminating, recombining, and then subsiding in a kind of global chain reaction. There are so many cognitive, metacognitive, physiological, affective, behavioral, interpersonal, and environmental factors operative in therapeutic change that studying it is rather like tracking and gauging the motion and influence of all the emerging bubbles in a cauldron of boiling water. Nevertheless, the seven precursors do explain a significant portion of therapeutic change—not completely, but enough to provide a manageable and workable explanation.

Thus, the precursors assessment is not offered as the true representation of the change process. It is meant to be a clinical tool for understanding and implementing change with difficult clients. The model is insufficient to explain the vastly complex change process itself. However, the seven precursors, in their nonlinear, interactive interdependence, may be enough to provide a skeletal outline that indicates the bones of change, but not the finer points of flesh, fluids, tendons, and tissues. It does seem to be the case, nevertheless, that any client who has a high degree of these seven would likely find therapeutic change both likely and welcome. Conversely, a client unlikely to move toward beneficial change would lack the critical mass that the adequate presence of these precursors would provide.

CLIENTS UNDERGOING PHARMACOTHERAPY

I am often asked how medications are related to the precursors of change. Research has of course shown that people benefit from various medications, whether antidepressants such as Prozac (fluoxetine) to anxiolytics such as BuSpar (buspirone) and Xanax (alprazolam). In terms of the precursors, medications may make it easier to develop and implement the precursors to achieve changes beyond merely those of mood. Many people who report an improvement of mood are then better able to work in therapy toward change in other aspects of their lives. A good metaphor might be weightlifting: For some clients, accomplishing therapeutic change is the equivalent of lifting a 500-pound weight. An appropriately prescribed medication can reduce that weight to something more manageable. The effects of the medications vary from person to person, of course; a medication might reduce that 500-pound burden for some people to 100 pounds but for others only to 400 pounds.

For most people, medication alone is not enough. Psychotherapy is also necessary. Several studies have shown that therapy provides more stable change over the long term after the termination of treatment. Therapy helps clients learn new coping strategies and relationship skills, something taking a medication cannot do. It is generally agreed that medication is best combined with psychotherapy, especially when a person suffers from severe depression.

VARIOUS DIAGNOSES AND THE PRECURSORS OF CHANGE

The precursors form (see Figure 3) outlines and elucidates the potential for therapeutic change across the wide range of disorders classified in the various incarnations of the *Diagnostic and Statistical Manual of Mental Disorders*, currently the *DSM-IV* (American Psychiatric Association, 1994). It is applicable to people with depression, anxiety, and personality disorders, as well as substance abuse disorders.

There are other disorders for which the model is relevant but not as directly applicable due to intrinsic deficits. Such disorders have an organic or congenital component, such as bipolar disorders or brain injury. The precursors are still applicable, even in the case of people with schizophrenia (see, e.g., North, 1987), but the model has not been applied with this population, nor has it seen more than occasional application with people with obsessive–compulsive disorders.

I am often asked how the precursors model and assessment apply to people with personality disorders, as these are often prototypical examples of difficult clients. The model seems to apply quite well and appropriately, but each personality disorder has its own style. Although that style may differ from disorder to disorder and from person to person, the different precursors apply to all at a fundamental level that lies well beyond personality traits and styles. For example, an antisocial client and a borderline client may both be low in the confronting precursor, and each will have his or her own style of avoiding confronting, but both are likely to improve if confronting is implemented.

It would be foolish to ignore a diagnosis and the information available about it, especially in the cases of antisocial, borderline, paranoid, and narcissistic personality disorders. The same general point of this book still applies. A person with a personality disorder who also has ample presence of the precursors will tend to change faster than the person with the same personality disorder who is lacking in precursors. It is the therapist's task to use strategies and techniques that will implement the precursors.

The *DSM-IV* defines a *personality disorder* as consisting, in part, of unchanging, dysfunctional personality traits. Thus, part of the essential definition of a personality disorder in general is precisely the lack of qualities and conditions described by the precursors. In one important sense, a personality disorder is a lack of therapeutic change characteristics.

Precursor & Its Markers	None (0)	Trace (1)	Small (2)	Adequate (3)	Abundant (4)
1. Sense of necessity • expresses desire for change • feels a sense of urgency					
2. Readiness for anxiety • openness to experience • likely to take risks					
3. Awareness • able to identify problems • identifies thoughts, feelings					
4. Confronting the problem • courageously faces problems • sustained attention to issues					
5. Effort or will toward change • eagerly does homework • high energy; active cooperation					
6. Hope for change • positive outlook; open to future • high coping; therapeutic humor					
7. Social support for change • wide network of friends and family • many confiding relationships					

Total Score =

Scoring guide[a]

0–6: Change unlikely. Educate client on change. Focus on precursors with lowest ratings.

7–14: Change limited or erratic. Educate client and focus on precursors with lowest ratings.

15–21: Change is steady and noticeable. Use the lowest rated precursors to stay on track.

22–28: Highly motivated to inspired client. Change occurs easily. Standard approaches work well.

[a]Scoring is intended only as a general guide to a complex process. Some precursors may be more potent.

Figure 3. Assessing the precursors of change: The Precursors Assessment Form. From "Precursors of Change: Pivotal Points of Involvement and Resistance in Psychotherapy," by F. J. Hanna, 1996, *Journal of Psychotherapy Integration, 6,* p. 248. Copyright 1996 by Plenum Publishing. Reprinted with permission.

EMPIRICAL VALIDATION OF THE ASSESSMENT

Each of the seven precursors enjoys empirical validation in the psychotherapy literature as a catalyst of change. The assessment form itself, although not empirically validated, is empirically informed. Beutler (2000) noted that it may be a mistake to exclusively insist on empirically validated treatment approaches. Rather, he suggested that practices should be empirically informed and clinically sensible. The assessment is not meant as a psychometric evaluation, nor is it meant to be a diagnostic instrument. Rather, it is a clinical guide to identifying the presence or absence of each of the seven change factors, which each have empirical support. It is a tool, a clinical heuristic, that reduces some of the mystery surrounding difficult clients and simultaneously indicates a path to change.

The assessment has been particularly useful in clinical practice in charting a course of approach to difficult clients. It has been used in various forms with many populations having difficulty with the change process or not responding to treatment. I have given the assessment form to more than 100 therapists to rate their most difficult clients. Almost without exception, those clinicians reported that the clients were severely lacking the precursors of change, and they routinely reported the assessment to be a source of hope with those clients.

The form has been helpful in putting together treatment programs for antisocial, borderline, and narcissistic clients, as well as adolescent criminal offenders, adolescent sex offenders, and alcohol and substance abusers in general. The assessment was also found to be helpful with adolescent female and male victims of sexual abuse as well as adults in general who were perceived or reported to be "resistant" to therapy. It also appears to be transcultural in its capacity and relevance to describe human change across cultures.

People who do not change tend to score lower on various developmental scales than those who do. Development, by definition, implies and assumes the process of change and simply does not or cannot take place without the change process. In the final analysis, lifespan development is therapeutic change (see Kegan, 1982; Loevinger, 1976, 1985). In my experience, people who do not change remain in an adolescent or earlier developmental stage, in spite of their chronological age. Thus, in the case of difficult clients, developmental processes are helpful to consider when assessing their situations.

USE OF THE PRECURSORS ASSESSMENT FORM

Fortunately, this assessment is among the most user-friendly assessments a clinician is likely to learn or use. The form is helpful when used both by a sole practitioner and during individual and group supervision sessions, staffings, and consultations where difficult clients are the focus of attention. The form can reveal a configuration or pattern among difficult clients in a way that makes its use in group contexts valuable. As shown in chapter 5, difficult therapists can be rated, too.

The assessment need not be applied to clients already doing well in therapy. The precursors are already amply present in such clients. To apply the precursors model with these clients might actually deter progress away from change. The assessment is of greatest help in identifying precursors that are in need of attention when a client is making slow or inconsistent progress.

Rating the Precursors

The ratings for the assessment form are based on the clinical marker sections for each precursor in chapter 3. These sections provide a guide to determining the presence or absence of each precursor for the purpose of rating it on this form. Each precursor is rated from 0 to 4. At 0 there has been no evidence of that particular precursor with the client in question. At 1, just a trace of the precursor shows itself only rarely, or perhaps a hint is given every now and then. A rating of 2 indicates an identifiable but small degree of presence of that precursor; it is not much, but it is also not as elusive as in the trace rating. With a precursor rated 2, the clinician knows there is at least something with which to work. At a rating of 3, the precursor is evident and readily apparent and, therefore, active in a person's approach to therapy, change, and resolution of problems. Precursors rated 4 are extremely evident, and the therapist often finds himself or herself spontaneously admiring these qualities in a client. Ratings of 4 are seldom found in difficult clients. Total scores range from 0 to 28, with higher scores representing greater levels of precursors for change.

As nearly as I can determine, only two of the precursors have instruments specifically designed for measuring their presence: hope (see J. F. Miller, 1986; Snyder, 1994) and social support (see Sarason, Sarason, & Pierce, 1990). These instruments are relatively easily to use, but they are not really necessary for the purpose here. For the remaining five precursors, I know of no such instruments.

I strongly recommend consulting with the client to ascertain the presence or absence of precursors. I have found that difficult clients can be quite willing to assess the presence of their precursors, as well as their own potential and ability to increase them. Of course, with highly manipulative or deceptive clients, caution is needed because the intentions of these clients are not always honest. Nevertheless, the client should be consulted whenever possible and appropriate. Consulting with clients has seemed to work well in clinical settings and is often therapeutic in itself in terms of its educational function.

In my experience clients seem to have no difficulty understanding precursors. This is the case with adolescents as well as adults. The form has not been used with children to any great extent. In addition, both trainees and experienced therapists seem to be able to rate difficult clients easily and accurately. Fortunately, clinical judgment has gained renewed respect in the literature (Shedler, Mayman, & Manis, 1993) and is obviously a vitally necessary part of gauging precursors on the assessment form.

Do Not Include the Therapist in Rating Social Support for Change

The therapist is expected to provide social support for change, but including the therapist in the rating of this precursor will confound the actual score. The focus of the assessment in this context is the amount of support in the client's environment. The therapist is viewed more as an agent of social support than a source of it in the client's living environment. This point is debatable, of course, but social support scores seem more accurate when the therapist is not included.

Rate the Actual Presence of Precursors

Rate only the actual presence of precursors as manifested in the here and now and according to the current problem or issue. One could rate the person according to his or her general ability or potential for change, but this is misleading and should be avoided.

Using myself as an example, my precursors rating would be at a respectable level concerning dealing with personal issues. However, when it comes to the particular issue of exercising and dieting, I am in need of change and am not changing at all. In the past, when younger, I was in great physical condition, having lifted weights, worked jobs requiring hard physical labor, and studied the martial arts. When rating myself on the precursors form, I would not assess myself according to my ability or potential to change but rather on the current state of precursors as regards the issue of physical condition. Of course, if I really put my mind to it, I could be in great shape, alter my diet, and slim down relatively soon. But that is not where I am at the moment on this issue. Thus, my precursor rating for getting in shape would look like this:

1. Sense of necessity	2
2. Willingness or readiness for anxiety	0
3. Awareness	3
4. Confronting the problem	0
5. Effort or will toward change	0
6. Hope for change	3

7. Social support for change	3
Total score	11

The total score is 11—quite low, but also quite accurate. This score indicates that change would be limited or erratic, and indeed it has been exactly that for several years.

If you are interested in rating the person according to his or her overall ability for change, then by all means do so. This might provide a good indicator of what expectations to have or what to aim for in a client's overall growth potential. However, when a client comes into therapy, it is important to rate the presenting problem, and have the client help you complete the rating if appropriate.

With clients who are court referred for some offense or otherwise in counseling or therapy against their wishes, therapists should rate each person not only according to the issue at hand but according to the perceived change ability as well. When rating perceived ability to change, it might help to ask if the person has ever made changes in his or her life relative to, for example, dieting or exercise, anxiety, depression, relationship problems, or work issues.

SCORING: DETERMINING THE LIKELIHOOD OF CHANGE

The scoring of the form is a general guide. Nothing is carved in stone. Part of the problem is that we do not know which of the precursors are more potent. If we did, then the scoring would be weighted, with the more potent precursors getting a higher percentage of the overall score. Also, because the form is a clinical guide and not a product of psychometrics, no claims can be made as to the precise accuracy of scoring. However, in actual practice, scoring has been remarkably sufficient as an indicator or predictor of change. In my experience doing consulting, workshops, and lectures on this subject, there is also a remarkably high degree of agreement among raters on the presence or absence of various precursors. In any case, being off by a point here or there on a precursor is insignificant, and the real purpose of the scoring is to identify the configuration of precursors for each person and find which precursors are most in need of attention.

Another source of scoring ambiguity is that precursors can wax and wane from day to day, hour to hour, or session to session. The precursors can also be far more present with one therapist than with another, as will be seen in chapter 5. Nevertheless, with difficult clients—who typically receive very low ratings—the precursors are more likely to be far less variable than with clients whose ratings are in the middle range and above. It is sometimes helpful to do a quick rating on the precursors with the same client from week to week or even from session to session. A client can be consistently low for the first five sessions and then go consistently higher as therapy continues. Change is a skill, and it is born of knowledge and work. When a client learns how to change, the precursors will naturally emerge in greater magnitude, especially when its suits his or her purpose.

Change Unlikely

When a client has a total score of 0 to 6, change is unlikely any time in the immediate future. As long as the score remains this low, standard therapy approaches may be inappropriate with this client, who might be better served by focusing on the individual precursors.

Clients who score this low should be informed—in an empowering way—about what it takes to change. Education on the precursors themselves is often helpful and important. Because no one completely understands the change process, however, clients should not be expected to either. Change can be presented as a skill to be learned. Education on the precursors and the change process is generally more effective when there is at least some sense of necessity present in that client. The sense of necessity can drive a client to learn more about what it would take to make things better.

Education about change and the precursors may help some clients, but it may be inappropriate for others, such as those with paranoid or antisocial personality disorders. For the latter, it is more important, initially at least, to go straight to work on implementing the absent precursors.

Change Limited or Erratic

A score of 7 to 14 indicates that change will take place at a rate that is slow and not noticeable. The process will be limited, erratic, and fraught with setbacks but may also yield triumphs so small they might not be noticed at all by the outside observer or even the therapist. At times, however, these small changes can seem quite large to the client. Educating the client is important at this level as well.

It may be of great help for a client to understand why his or her progress is not as fast as he or she would like. I once worked with a client, whose diagnosis was obsessive compulsive personality disorder, who complained that he was not making progress. He was relieved when I explained to him the consequences of the lack of the second precursor. Of course, it took a while for him to realize that it had anything to do with him, but it was an important educational experience when he did see it after a couple of sessions.

It can also be helpful for clients to understand why changes are being made. In addition, for clients who had lower scores earlier in therapy, increased scores may indicate it is time for education on change. The idea of change as a skill may be more readily grasped when scores reach this level, especially when a high sense of necessity is present.

Change Steady and Noticeable

A score of 15 to 21 indicates the person will make changes at a rate that is steady and noticeable, both to the therapist and to others. There is not much need for the precursors approach with many of these clients. Nevertheless, scoring can be used to determine which precursors are lowest. A person's rate of change can still be increased by focusing on the precursors with the lowest scores.

Change Highly Likely

When the total score is above 21, the client will likely achieve change with relative ease. The precursors approach is unnecessary and would probably be a waste of time. The person may respond to almost any appropriate therapeutic tool, technique, or procedure. Similarly, any theoretical approach will tend to be effective as long as the therapeutic relationship is established and the approach is matched to the client's problem and needs. Client-centered, psychodynamic, or behavior therapy, for example, will tend to work well with a client at this level.

Clients with high scores can be highly insightful and surprisingly sensitive to the approach of the therapist. These clients are not of the type that therapists become preoccupied with or worry about, simply because these people are likely to do well even on their own. In many cases, these people do not need therapy and are likely to improve with the right book or with a good friend who just listens. But when they do roll up their sleeves with an intention to change unwanted conditions, the therapeutic sparks fly.

USING THE FORM WITH STAGES OF CHANGE

I have previously mentioned the insightful and popular stages of change model of Prochaska et al. (1994). This model delineates five stages of change: precontemplation, contemplation, preparation, action, and maintenance. Each of these stages requires the presence of the precursors to make progression to the next stage possible. This is part of how the precursors model complements the stage model. The precursors are implicit and necessary not only in the beginning but during each stage of change.

Prochaska and colleagues (1992) also noted that the model is not entirely linear, being more like a spiral of progress. Part of the spiral consists of regression back to earlier stages and then forward to the later stages. In other words, progress can go back and forth. In terms of the precursors, it is likely that when a client regresses to earlier stages of change, the precursors have waned. If the therapist is also using this model and notices a regression to an earlier stage, it may be helpful to do another precursors assessment to determine which precursors are in need of attention. Doing this reassessment with the client can also serve an educational function that can help re-establish progress along the stages.

EXAMPLES OF ASSESSMENTS

In chapter 3, I described three difficult clients, Tommy, Joy, and Ricky, who did not achieve success in therapy. To illustrate the use of the form, these clients are revisited here and their configuration of precursors charted. For the sake of convenience, I will include a brief summary of each case before going on to their ratings. Again, no diagnoses are mentioned in these examples, although clinicians will recognize many of the symptoms. Diagnoses are omitted to focus on the precursors and avoid the stereotypes that can occur with dependence on diagnoses for characterizations of clients. In addition to the case descriptions, additional details are provided that were gathered by the precursors assessment.

Case Example 1: Tommy

Tommy was the charming and thoroughly self-centered man who claimed he could not stop his promiscuous behavior and who was both proud of it and ashamed about hurting his wife, Julie. He had been to three previous therapists and had fought with them all. His chief anxiety was the fear of going to hell for his immoral behavior. He was in therapy at the insistence of Julie, who had no idea of his sexual improprieties. His apparent interest in therapy amounted to an attempt to reduce his anxiety without changing his behaviors. He wanted a therapist who would tell him that he was fine, that he was a good person, and that he would not go to hell.

Therapy was at an impasse for Tommy. No progress was being made after three sessions, nor did it seem likely. The therapist soon realized that Tommy came to therapy with a purpose quite contrary to anything that could be regarded as therapeutic. His precursor profile looked like this:

1. *Sense of necessity*. When asked directly, Tommy readily admitted that something had to change. He said that he could not "go on like this" for much longer without "burning out." On the other hand, he continued all his problem behaviors with the same intensity. Rating = 2.

2. *Readiness for anxiety*. Tommy was unwilling to feel the anxiety associated with his behaviors and attitudes. He evaded or deflected any questions that led to exploring fears, feelings, or difficulty. He insisted the therapist help him feel better. Rating = 0.
3. *Awareness*. In spite of all his contradictory statements, Tommy seemed to know he was feeling bad and that something was wrong but saw his behaviors as a problem only from a religious perspective. He insisted that his infidelity was natural for a man and unrelated to the tension between him and his wife. It was fine as long as she did not find out. He seemed to have little awareness that his behavior was out of his control. In addition, he had trouble identifying specific beliefs and feelings. Rating = 1.
4. *Confronting the problem*. Tommy was doing nothing in terms of actually studying or contemplating the issues that brought him to therapy. He expected the therapist to tell him what he needed to know. Rating = 0.
5. *Effort or will toward change*. Tommy was also doing nothing in the way of resolving his problem other than going to therapy, which was a kind of effort in itself. Once in therapy, he showed little actual cooperation. Rating = 1.
6. *Hope for change*. The therapist asked if Tommy ever had thoughts of "giving up" or if "life wasn't worth living." He said no, but that sometimes he didn't think he could ever be happy. He could not envision a positive outcome. Rating = 1.
7. *Social support for change*. Tommy reported that his wife was supportive of him to get through his therapy, although she had no idea he was cheating on her. He also said that although most of his friends admired and encouraged his promiscuous behaviors, two had told him that he was making a mistake. Rating = 2.

Tommy's precursor profile, which yielded a total score of 7, accurately showed that he was not likely to change, just as his therapy history had indicated. He was lowest on precursors 2 and 4, and 3, 5, and 6 were also low.

Case Example 2: Joy

Joy was the former showgirl from the Lake Tahoe region in Nevada. She was so involved with new age pursuits that she insisted on avoiding anything that was not "positive," which meant anything associated with the slightest pain or anxiety. She also claimed that she was clairvoyant and psychically gifted and that therapy might help her to clear the blocks that stood in the way of her becoming an occult "adept." She also believed that therapy could help her forget, and cut herself off from, any negative emotions and relationships in her past. Joy reached an impasse in her therapy after eight sessions, impatiently claiming to have derived no benefit, and she often lectured to her therapist on several new age principles.

In Joy's mindset, change was clearly desired but, because of the conditions she set, almost impossible to attain. For her, achieving change was rather like insisting that a fire be started with wet logs and then becoming upset because there was no combustion.

1. *Sense of necessity*. Joy made it clear that change was important and necessary for her to reach her goal to attain a high state of being. Rating = 3.
2. *Readiness for anxiety*. Joy would not consider or allow any anxiety into her consciousness and became visibly upset at the prospect of it. Although it was clear that she was consumed with anxiety, she insisted on staying "strong." She believed she had to remain "above" all negativity. Rating = 0.
3. *Awareness*. Joy was not aware of the obvious deeper issues within which she was immersed, nor was she particularly adept at identifying beliefs and feelings. Any awareness of negativity was shunned. Rating = 1.
4. *Confronting the problem*. Caught in a fixed belief system, she was not willing to explore the painful or confusing aspects of her life and clung instead to her belief in the self she would become. She believed that to address and attend to difficult issues was a grave mistake. Rating = 0.
5. *Effort or will toward change*. Joy meditated regularly and used it as a means to ease her anxiety, but as an escape rather than as a means of dealing with it. She showed little cooperation once in therapy itself. Rating = 1.
6. *Hope for change*. Joy was expecting a future state of peace and attainment, but not without difficulty. That was realistic to her, but how to proceed was not. Rating = 2.
7. *Social support for change*. Joy reported many superficial friendships but only one friend in whom she could confide. However, she often argued with her friend, who she felt did not really understand her potential. Rating = 1.

Joy's precursor profile, with its total score of 8, presents an interesting configuration. She was relatively high in necessity for a difficult client. She also made some effort, but in this regard her effort was not particularly focused on psychotherapeutic change. She showed little or no cooperation in the therapy sessions themselves. That she had reached a therapeutic impasse is no surprise.

Case Example 3: Ricky

Ricky was the member of a street gang and a drug dealer to many children, and he had fathered at least three children with three different adolescent girls. Although never exhibiting any overt violence, he was adept at displaying nonverbal threats of intimidation. Ricky was also highly intelligent, manipulative, and spiteful toward the world and people in general.

Ricky did not disclose anything other than superficial information in six months of treatment. He viewed therapy as an intrusion into his personal life and therapists as tools of the police. For him, therapy was an attempt to make him weak and rob him of his freedom and virility. Therapists were avowed enemies, and therapy was a war that he could easily "win." Unfortunately, he was correct.

1. *Sense of necessity*. Ricky claimed to have had a great life until the "cops" interfered. There was nothing wrong with him, and nothing needed to be changed. If anything needed to be changed, it was to get out of the treatment program. Rating = 0.
2. *Readiness for anxiety*. Ricky was not willing to experience anxiety or difficulty in any way. He believed that drugs existed to relieve that sort of thing. Rating = 0.
3. *Awareness*. Ricky gave no indication that he was aware of any problems. He was certainly intelligent, but not in identifying problems, feelings, or issues. He did not see his cocaine and alcohol use as a problem. Rating = 0.
4. *Confronting the problem*. Ricky was not confronting any aspect of his life other than sex, drugs, and criminal activity. Rating = 0.
5. *Effort or will toward change*. Ricky was not putting any energy into changing. Rating = 0.
6. *Hope for change*. Ricky did not believe that he would live past the age of 21. He was certain he was going to die, having seen several members of his own and other gangs shot and killed. As far as he was concerned, the future held little or nothing for him. Rating = 0.
7. *Social support for change*. Ricky reported that he cared quite a bit for his mother and his 14-year-old sister and was extremely

protective of them both. Both loved him dearly and came to family counseling sessions, wanting to help. His gang members were also supportive. Rating = 2.

Ricky's precursor profile, with a total score of 2, presents an extraordinary challenge to therapy. I use this example because I learned a lot about change from my failure to help Ricky. With this configuration of precursors, therapeutic change was nowhere in sight. Ricky was, for me, a benchmark of the client for whom change is not likely. When I first started working with difficult clients, I would occasionally give up on people like Ricky, only to later see them make genuine changes in their lives. This taught me that therapists have a configuration of precursors for each of their clients, as we shall see in chapter 5.

USING THE PRECURSORS FORM WITH GROUPS AND FAMILIES

The precursors assessment is easily used in therapy with groups or families considered difficult or not exhibiting therapeutic change. In groups, it is helpful to rate each group member on the precursors assessment first, and then to rate the group as a whole. Clinical impressions of groups indicate that many groups have a unique character of their own. Rating a group as an entity provides insights into the precursors needed to enhance the group process toward change.

Similarly, in family therapy, each family member can be rated to determine his or her configuration of precursors. As in the case of groups, Whitaker (see Simon, 1985) pointed out that a family system has a character and personality of its own. A difficult family can also be rated as a whole to determine which precursors are missing in the family system and in need of attention.

Many of the techniques given in later chapters for implementing the precursors can be adapted for therapy with groups and families. Even when not mentioned specifically, many of the techniques described have been adapted as appropriate for use in group and family settings.

5

RATING THERAPIST PRECURSORS

Because the precursors can be configured differently for different problems even within the same person, clients can be regarded in different ways by the same, or by different, therapists. A therapist's set of precursors toward a defiant, insulting, and arrogant client can be far lower than toward a cooperative, willing, and respectful client. This difference within and between therapists can profoundly affect the change process.

This chapter deals with what is probably the most underestimated aspect of therapy with difficult clients: the therapist's disposition and reactions. It is usually referred to as countertransference and is often given lip service but is seldom given the attention it deserves. The idea of countertransference is one of the most valuable of the many contributions made by psychodynamic schools. Unfortunately, the phenomenon itself has been obscured by terminology that is not readily translatable into currently popular cognitive and behavioral language.

Transference is when a patient treats the therapist as he or she would a significant other, such as a parent. *Countertransference* is defined as a therapist's reactions to a client's transference. Freud (1910) originally described countertransference as the therapist's unconscious emotional response to the patient. Freud recognized the potential adverse effects that a therapist's emotional reactions can have on a client. Later writers in the psychodynamic field eventually broadened the concept to include both conscious and unconscious reactions to a client based on a therapist's own past relationships (e.g., Kernberg; 1965; Reich, 1951; Segal, 1977).

All, however, concur that the reactions of a therapist to a client's provocative and evocative behaviors and statements must remain under conscious control. It is further agreed that the therapist must develop a sufficient degree of maturity to avoid seeking to meet his or her needs with clients in therapy sessions. When therapy has stalled, countertransference is often the cause (Weiner, 1982). To blame treatment failure on the client's difficulty or resistance is a rationalization, and a poor one.

Unfortunately, this aspect of therapy is discussed almost exclusively by the psychodynamic schools and is too often ignored or given only passing mention by other approaches. When it comes to working with a large percentage of difficult clients, a therapist of any theoretical persuasion can get frustrated, irritated, sad, anxious, angry, and bored and can otherwise have his or her own issues, biases, or sensitivities inflamed. Fromm-Reichmann (1950) gave the example of a therapist who, as a child, was forced to listen to his elderly grandmother speak on and on in a seemingly endless chatter. As a result, he automatically detached from any long-winded communication from anyone, including clients.

Countertransference reactions are not limited to any particular diagnosis. A depressed person can provoke anger in a therapist, and so can an antisocial client (Giovacchini, 1989). As a consequence, the relationship degrades; the therapist no longer is an empathic, compassionate helper, and the effectiveness of the therapy declines.

When a therapist experiences frustration, anger, resentment, hurt, or loss of confidence with a client, the potential is there for these feelings to interfere with a client's change process. When the therapist acts on those feelings, therapy degrades into a power struggle, hurting contest, or inquiry into "who wronged whom." Therapeutic change, as a goal of therapy, is then disregarded.

DIFFICULT CLIENTS OR DIFFICULT THERAPISTS?

More than 50 years of research has shown how countertransference can interfere with the change process in even the most well-intentioned therapists (Bandura, 1956; Cutler, 1958). The client influences the therapist far more than is generally acknowledged in the psychotherapy literature (B. A. Singer & Luborsky, 1977). Countertransference is rarely taken into account in the training of therapists, however, other than in psychodynamic programs.

Countertransference is seldom controlled for in studies; the phenomenon is difficult to study because of its subjective nature. Countertransference could be occurring in a research study and, hypothetically, no one would be aware of it if they did not control for it. The methodological question is how to reliably identify it and its effects on therapy.

For the purpose of this book, the key is understanding that there is nothing pathological or disordered about a therapist experiencing countertransference feelings and attitudes. Quite the contrary, it is completely natural and is to be expected as a routine aspect of doing therapy. What is vitally important to recall is that there is a difference between merely experiencing countertransference and acting on those feelings and attitudes. The feelings evoked and provoked can be used as tools to further understand a client, as psychodynamic therapists know so well (Cashdan, 1988; Giovacchini, 1989). The lesson learned from research is that the difference between average therapists and excellent therapists seems to be how well they can manage their countertransference reactions (Van Wagoner, Gelso, Hayes, & Diemer, 1991).

Many difficult clients are expert at thwarting therapists' well-intended acts to establish relationships. They perceive help as a threat and can undermine it with great finesse—that is one of the reasons they are considered difficult. Therapists often react with great frustration; one therapist told me in supervision, "Here I am trying to help this woman, and all she does is try to block my attempts at every turn, and I am, frankly, getting sick of it." This chapter can help therapists make sense of countertransference reactions and uses the precursors assessment to show how change processes degrade in the therapist.

THERAPIST INTERFERENCE: A NEW TERM FOR A VENERABLE CONCEPT

In the past decade, a strong movement has sought to unify language in psychotherapy to make it less theory bound (S. D. Miller, Duncan, & Hubble, 1997). *Countertransference* is a limited term, representing a viable and important concept that is in desperate need of repackaging. Strean (1993) substituted the term *counterresistance* for *countertransference*. This retitling is not only more descriptive but more readily understandable by a wide range of therapists from different theoretical models of treatment. Its only drawback is that it uses another term that is becoming outmoded, and that is resistance. It does balance the scales, however, in showing that therapists can be difficult, too.

The term *therapist interference* directly conveys the idea of a therapist's hindrance of the change process, in or out of the context of countertransference. *Therapist interference* has the advantage of describing the detrimental effects of a therapist's reactions toward a client purely in terms of interpersonal interaction. It can include not only countertransference issues but other factors ranging from lack of skill to being overwhelmed by a client's complexity, difficulty, or degree of suffering and misfortune. The advantage of this perspective lies in the fact that interference can be viewed in the context of each of the precursors.

When the therapist acts on those feelings by criticizing the client under the guise of helping, making covertly hostile comments, or prematurely terminating therapy, a valuable opportunity to better know that client is lost. This is often the hidden benefit of understanding therapist interference. I have found that although many therapists know of it, few actually develop this as a skill.

ASSESSING THERAPIST INTERFERENCE ON THE PRECURSORS FORM

The precursor assessment form can be used to rate the potential of the therapist to inhibit the therapeutic change process. In this section, I list each precursor and show how a therapist with a low rating in that category can interfere with a client's progress in therapy. This tool can be helpful in supervision, or therapists working with difficult clients can use it to draw a more complete picture of their own possible contribution to an impasse in therapy.

A Sense of Necessity to Help the Client

A therapist can lack a sense of necessity to help a client, which can manifest as indifference or lack of interest and can be the result of "giving up" on a client and "giving in" to the unconscious conclusion that change is probably never going to happen. In such instances, a therapist is merely going through the motions of therapy, engaging in conversation, but without a true intent to help.

The most important characteristic for identifying a lack of this precursor is a distinct absence of the therapist's felt sense of a client's need for change. In other words, the helping instinct that may have been strong at one time in that therapist has diminished or is no longer present. The therapist may feel defeated, apathetic, or bored; he or she may be daydreaming during sessions with this client or shifting the conversation into areas more of interest to the therapist and not of any particular therapeutic value.

Another possibility contributing to a lack of a sense of necessity is if the therapist has the same or similar issue as a client that also has not been addressed, such as drinking or a failing marriage. Self-awareness is required on the part of a therapist to be able to recognize and admit that one's own apathy about an issue may be stirred up by a client.

Willingness to Experience Anxiety or Difficulty Inherent With a Client

Sometimes a therapist can be overwhelmed by disrespectful treatment by clients. Such treatment can be discouraging and daunting, especially if the client is overtly or covertly critical of the therapist. For example, some narcissistic clients find it necessary to criticize the therapist to keep their own envy and jealousy under control (Adler, 1992). The thought of wading through this kind of treatment can be disconcerting to a therapist who is not aware that this material is to be expected. The end result is that the therapist becomes unwilling to experience the anxiety or difficulty of being with the client. The same is also true of work with antisocial or borderline clients, who can be a source of considerable discomfort to a therapist.

On a different front, some therapists can become overwhelmed by the great amount of raw, painful emotion in a particular client. Similarly, when a therapist is continuously exposed to the pain of client after client, he or she might begin to avoid any further exposure to this type of painful experience; this has been referred to as *vicarious traumatization* (Saakvitne & Pearlman, 1996). As a result, a therapist will avoid any inroads into a client's case that lead to more or similar painful emotion. The therapist may have reached his or her tolerance threshold of the pain of others. If this occurs, the therapist and client may end up with an unconscious collusion that is designed to spare the client any more painful experience, even when appropriate. That willingness or readiness to undergo the anxiety of helping a client with this process is the chief aspect of this precursor.

In other cases, a therapist can be discouraged by the sheer amount of work a client has to do to change, especially when the therapist's assessment of the amount of change needed is vastly greater than what the client believes. Normally, an experienced therapist patiently prepares for the long haul, but less experienced or less patient therapists can become discouraged. I once had a supervisee say to me, "There is so much work to do here, and the client is so difficult to deal with, and she has so little awareness and insight, I don't know if I have the stamina and energy to get through it all." When the therapist no longer wants to "go through it all," this precursor is nearly gone.

Awareness of a Client's Issues and One's Own Corresponding Issues

The lack of awareness in a therapist primarily manifests as a lack of empathy and a preoccupation with one's own issues, agenda, or needs. For example, as a supervisor and consultant I have found that some therapists deeply resent some difficult clients who do not change. They do not readily admit to this, of course, but it often results from of a lack of self-esteem in the therapist. Being unaware of his or her own self-esteem needs, a therapist might be using therapy to meet these needs. Such a person needs the belief and assurance that he or she is competent and successful at doing therapy as a source of self-esteem. A difficult client can cast serious doubt on that belief, making a therapist appear or feel awkward, inept, or incompetent. That client becomes a threat to the therapist's self-esteem, and the therapist then detests and resents the client precisely because the therapist detests and resents his or her own lack of self-esteem. In supervision, this usually comes as a great insight to therapists, who quickly see the new awareness as beneficial and helpful.

Another manifestation of the lack of awareness is when a therapist does not know that a client is difficult. In some cases, this is because the degree of dysfunction is not apparent. For example, I have known a few therapists working with clients who were clearly abusing alcohol, but the therapists ignored the warning signs, and as a result addictions issues did not get addressed. When I asked if those therapists had suspected alcohol abuse, it came as a surprise, or the therapist would respond, "I wondered if something like that was going on, but I didn't know how to ask." Those symptoms would have been much clearer to those who had studied addictive behaviors. But to a therapist who is not familiar, it constitutes a lack of awareness of a problem.

Other therapist issues can be evoked when doing therapy, and if they are not managed, odd consequences can occur. I co-led a group of substance-abusing teens aged 14 to 18 with Tina, aged 35. During one group session, a female client disclosed that cocaine made her feel sexy and that she would flirt with men of all ages when she was high. At this point, Tina, my cotherapist, disclosed that while using cocaine she had had sex with man after man, never finding fulfillment. She ended by saying that she still had not found fulfillment. At that point, the entire group was intensely interested and focused their attention on her startling self-disclosure. I watched as the boys in the group looked at her, now with obvious sexual overtones.

A few weeks later one of those boys, named Timmy, spread the rumor that he had had sex with Tina over the weekend. Of course it was not true, but Tina was horrified. As nearly as I could tell, about a third of the client population in that agency believed it. Tina could not get Timmy to confess his deception and asked me to intervene. After considerable effort, Timmy finally admitted his ruse. But I do not know if Tina ever addressed her unresolved sexual issues or made the connection between her inappropriate self-disclosure and the effect it had on those boys.

The change process becomes derailed when therapists have so little awareness of their own issues that they have difficulty identifying when client issues resonate with their own. A therapist will be inclined to treat such an issue in a client the same way he or she treats it in himself or herself, or he or she may treat the client in the exact opposite way, perhaps out of guilt. For example, if a therapist has a problem communicating with his wife, he might ignore the same issue in a client. Or he might overemphasize it and even coerce a client to deal with it above and before all else. When seen through the filter of the therapist's own issues, a client's clinical issues can become obscured. Empathy becomes impaired. In short, lack of awareness of one's own issues can ruin clinical perception and empathy.

Confronting the Client's Issues

The primary clue to the lack of this precursor lies in the disposition of the therapist toward the client's issues. Just as a client can be aware of issues and not confront them, a therapist can also be daunted by a client's problem. A therapist must be able to directly identify, address, and work toward the resolution of the client's issues and to persevere in doing so in a sustained, steadfast manner. If not, the client may not be inclined to confront those issues either, and change will be mysteriously elusive.

For example, Colleen had worked in a university counseling center for seven years and had gone back to school to get a doctorate. Colleen was always well dressed, energetic, and likable. George, her client, was a graduate student in history who was in his late 20s and working on his master's thesis. He was low-key, inexpressive, and interpersonally awkward and paid little attention to his dress or appearance. He sought therapy at the university because his wife was threatening to leave him, and he was deeply troubled by the possibility. After four months, no change was occurring.

Supervision eventually revealed that Colleen had focused primarily on developing George's social skills but, for some reason, was not addressing the marital relationship itself. Colleen told her supervisor that she thought if George were more "appealing," his wife might not want to leave him. Meanwhile, it appeared that George had become quite romantically attracted to Colleen. It was a good way to forget about his troubles with his wife. He interpreted her interventions as a means for him to become more appealing to her instead of his wife. This entanglement all became clear when Colleen revealed that, in a way, George reminded her of her own husband, whom she wanted to change to become more "sensitive." Not surprisingly, she also had avoided dealing with the relationship issues in her own marriage. Colleen eventually resolved this issue both of awareness and confronting in her own therapy.

Sometimes therapists avoid confronting a client's problem when it seems foreign or bizarre. In one case, a married woman disclosed that her job was in danger and eventually revealed she was involved in encounters involving sexual dominance on the Internet. She had been meeting these men first in chat rooms, and then in person, where she was having them tie her up in ropes and chains for sexual interludes. Her therapist, although concerned, did not address the issues involved with this potentially dangerous activity. Such a therapist, lacking in the confronting precursor, may decide it is more convenient to stay on familiar territory.

Other potentially important issues that can be ignored are unethical business practices, thievery, cheating on exams, and insensitivity to others. If a therapist is uncomfortable with or avoids a client's problem, that problem may never be addressed. If it is never addressed, it may never get resolved.

Effort and Will to Work Through Issues With a Client

There is a myth that a therapist should just kick back and let the therapy process take care of itself. Some therapists believe they can just reflect the feelings and statements of the client without getting involved. Sometimes this is called "maintaining professional distance." Although important, the concept of distance is often misunderstood. Some therapists believe that to roll up one's sleeves and get involved with a client's problem is to make the mistake of becoming "enmeshed." This is also a mistake.

A. A. Lazarus (1989a) noted that success in therapy requires effort on the part of the therapist as well as the client. Simply stated, a therapist has to work hard not only at confronting the problem with the client, but also at persuading the client to work hard. Being persuasive is part of working with difficult clients, and so is modeling for a client how to exert energy toward change.

When a therapist is doing all the work and the therapy itself is going nowhere, however, it may be time for a slight withdrawal. If all that effort is not leading to change, it may be time for confrontation or even limited provocation (see chapter 9) to bring about a shift of the precursors. A therapist may be helped by the Zen state of being fully engaged in actions but not attached to the rewards; this Zen approach to doing therapy was recommended by Horney (1952/1987). Exerting effort toward helping a client is not the same as becoming enmeshed.

Hope for Client Change

If a therapist has little hope that a client will change, it is likely to be contagious through his or her nonverbal signals and cues to the client. It can show up in voice intonations and inflections and in physical gestures and postures as well. The expectations of a therapist for a client's success are an indicator of how much hope he or she has for a client. A therapist's positive expectations can have profound effects on how well substance-abusing clients do in therapy, for example (W. R. Miller, 1985).

Unreasonably positive expectations for a client, however, can amount to fantasy and are not helpful at all. Just as the precursor of hope must be realistic in a client, it helps for a therapist to be able to envision the realistic possibility of a client making changes. Hope is also encouraged by the knowledge that in work with difficult clients, a therapeutic window can open at almost any time, and change, although not evident at the moment, can nevertheless happen as a result. This is a realistic expectation born of actual experience for many therapists. This contagion of hope communicates to and affects a client in a variety of ways, one of which is showing a client that improvement, and a better future, really is possible.

A Therapist's Social Support for Facilitating Change

Some therapists are in great need of social support. If social support is lacking in the therapist's personal life, therapist and client can become so chummy and close that the therapist may inadvertently seek to keep that fuzzy feeling. Consequently, he or she may find confronting the client on sensitive issues to be threatening to the delicate security of the relationship. This most often occurs when a therapist is lonely and wants to be friends with the client or is in desperate need of empathic supervision or collegial support. To avoid this scenario, therapists must ensure that their own social support systems are adequate.

Another social support problem arises when the therapist lacks a professional support system, often the case when the therapist is in private practice. A therapist should feel, as much as possible, part of a therapeutic team. This can be accomplished by simply attending conferences and workshops, but it is much more fruitful to engage in positive and productive group, individual, or peer supervision. These latter sources of social support can alleviate feelings of isolation and bolster the presence of all the therapist's other precursors.

CASE EXAMPLES

The precursors assessment form can be helpful to therapists not only in rating clients, but also in rating themselves. Chapter 1 cited examples of therapists who had "trained" their clients to be difficult, which can happen when the therapist's interference with the change process goes unrestrained and uncorrected. I will now examine two of those examples in greater detail and an additional example involving a severe ethical violation. Following each example, the therapist will be rated according to his or her own precursors.

Rating therapists is similar to rating clients. The therapist's potential is not the focus of the rating; what is rated is his or her current attitude and actions with a particular client. Just as client precursors can vary on different issues, therapist precursors can vary widely from client to client. The focus is on the therapist's actions with a particular client in a particular moment, or with a particular client over a period of several sessions. The score serves as a general indicator of a therapist's potency as a change agent with that client at that time.

RATING KURT'S PRECURSORS

Kurt was a 39-year-old therapist working with Janey, a female university senior in her mid-20s. Janey's major complaint was that the men in her life verbally mistreated her. Although she was an engaging person in therapy, there was a certain naïveté about her and a tendency to smile even while in pain and to laugh with a shrill, almost tinny tone. After 20 therapy sessions, her current male partner continued to verbally abuse her, and she stopped showing up for sessions and then terminated by telephone.

In supervision, Kurt discovered that he harbored a hidden belief formed in high school that "girls with fake laughter" and who "smiled for no reason" were "stupid" and not likely to ever achieve any kind of significance in their lives. At a deeper level, he never took Janey seriously as a person and as a human being. He also realized that, in spite of his attitude, he was attracted to women like Janey in high school and believed they were "easy." He expressed surprise that these "old attitudes can creep into a counseling session."

Kurt's precursors could be rated as follows:

1. *Sense of necessity*. Never taking her seriously, Kurt did not see her problems as worthy of concern and solution, other than just doing his job. Rating = 1.
2. *Readiness for anxiety*. As a part of considering her at some level "stupid" and insignificant, Kurt was not really willing to experience her pain as part of an empathic process beyond a superficial devotion to duty. Rating = 1.
3. *Awareness*. Kurt was unaware of the gender issues affecting his performance as a therapist. He was also unaware of the gender issues affecting Janey's problems with her current and past partners. Rating = 1.
4. *Confronting the problem*. Kurt only superficially attempted to get Janey to confront her problem with verbally abusive men. Although he did get her to try to escape from them, part of his approach was to subtly, almost imperceptibly blame her for causing her own problems. Rating = 1.
5. *Effort or will toward change*. Kurt's exertion of effort amounted to going through the motions with no real dedication or focus. Rating = 1.
6. *Hope for change*. At the level of his core beliefs about women like Janey, he had little hope for her improvement and did not envision her empowerment. He did, however, believe in the therapy process and spoke with her as though she could improve. Rating = 2.

7. *Social support for change.* Kurt did not provide a therapeutic relationship of warmth and support toward change for Janey, but he did have the support of a supervisor and other therapists in the counseling center. Rating = 3.

With this small presence of precursors and corresponding score of 10, it is not surprising that Kurt did not act as an agent of change for Janey or that she terminated therapy prematurely. To his credit, he readily admitted that he understood why his effort was unsuccessful.

RATING NANCY'S PRECURSORS

Nancy was a 38-year-old therapist working toward her doctoral degree. Her client was Jerry, a pleasant 30-year-old man who reported feeling "lost" and lacked direction in his life. Although quite intelligent, he had no career plans, and nothing seemed to inspire him to want to do anything with his life. He was aware enough to be worried about it, however, and he sought counseling for help. Jerry was courteous and friendly and genuinely tried to cooperate with Nancy's probes and questions. He would even apologize at times for being so noncommittal about any goals or future direction. After 16 sessions, little progress was being made, and Jerry was still worried about "wasting" his life.

In supervision, Nancy reported that Jerry was so "totally passive" and so "resistant" that she could not get him to do anything at all about his problem. She also named a variety of personality disorder traits that Jerry was exhibiting, such as those of avoidant and obsessive–compulsive personality disorders. When asked to report her feelings when in the presence of Jerry, she said she found him "irritating" and "maddening" to work with. She felt badly about feeling this way about him, but also said she was not able to help and requested he be transferred to another therapist. Before doing so, she agreed to have the supervisor explore the dynamics between them.

Nancy's precursors could be rated as follows:

1. *Sense of necessity.* Nancy did recognize Jerry's predicament, in spite of her feeling irritated. Rating = 2.
2. *Readiness for anxiety.* Nancy found it difficult to empathize with Jerry and was hesitant to form a close relationship with him. She never really engaged him in a warm and genuine manner as she did her other clients. It was clear that rather than being ready for the difficulty of working with him, she was waiting to terminate. Rating = 0.
3. *Awareness.* Nancy spoke of Jerry's issues in a superficial way, occasionally speaking of him as though he were lazy and docile,

which was inaccurate. She was not aware of her own issues being stirred up by his behaviors. Rating = 0.

4. *Confronting the problem.* Nancy was unsuccessful in getting Jerry to confront anything of magnitude or substance, and she did not do so with herself in relation to him. Rating = 0.
5. *Effort or will toward change.* Although Jerry seemed cooperative and willing to work, Nancy was hesitant to apply herself to the task of working with him. Most of her session time was spent getting him to talk about various aspects of his life while she reflected and summarized. Her effort was in "doing her job." Rating = 2.
6. *Hope for change.* Nancy had not envisioned a future for Jerry that had a realistically positive outcome. Such was her frustration that the future she did envision for Jerry was referring him to another therapist, although she did believe another therapist might be able to help. Rating = 1.
7. *Social support for change.* Nancy did enjoy a fairly strong social support system. She also had several supportive friendships with other therapists and an empathic supervisor. Rating = 3.

No change is no surprise here. After the supervisor recommended that Nancy write down all the people in her life of whom Jerry reminded her, Nancy no longer associated him with her sexually abusive brother, and therapy went quite well. If the precursors assessment had been done again after Nancy's insight and her change of behavior toward Jerry, her precursors rating would have been much higher.

RATING JAMES'S PRECURSORS

A therapist who would engage in a sexual relationship with a client would, of course, be severely lacking in precursors of change. It may help, for the sake of illustration, to show how this can be. James was a 35-year-old man who took great pride in his ability to do therapy. Psychodynamic by theoretical orientation, he had 10 years of experience working as a counselor in a small, East Coast business college. He had been married for 17 years and had three children, all younger than age 15. He arranged to see me one day for peer supervision and, almost as an aside, told me he had met the woman he had "always dreamed about."

Her name was Rachel. He said that she was 24 years old, recently divorced, and "incredibly understanding and loving." He made it a point to tell me several times how attractive she was and how "perfect" they were for each other and that he was going to leave his wife Linda for his new love.

"Unfortunately," he added hesitantly, "she was my client." He then immediately emphasized with great sincerity, "But that doesn't matter." He explained that they had, just a week earlier, mutually decided to end therapy because they "knew" that their relationship was "meant" to happen, and it would have happened after termination anyway. Fate had just so arranged it, he said, that they were to meet in therapy. When I asked, he told me that the decision was made sometime during their eight sessions. Then he asked me for my viewpoint of the situation.

I decided I needed to be direct as possible. "James, she doesn't know you." He looked at me incredulously. Finally, with great frustration in his voice, he said, almost pleading, "She knows me better than anyone I have ever met!" I replied, "James, this is unethical and harmful." He pleaded with me to understand. "James," I said, "please listen. She only knows what her idealizations have projected onto you. You know this. You studied this aspect of therapy. She was your client. The sessions were all about her, right?" He nodded, and I continued. "She doesn't know you, James. She has obviously filled in all the mysteries about you with her fantasies and desires. You were her understanding, caring therapist, right? It is only natural she would feel this way. You are deceiving yourself and your client." I then informed him of the ethical code of the American Psychological Association and then of evidence that even posttermination sexual relationships with clients are harmful and told him to consult an article on this topic (Brown, 1988). Given the outcome, my approach obviously left a lot to be desired.

James told me that it was too bad I couldn't understand, that I could not see beyond the rules, and that rules don't apply 100% of the time. Realizing how entrenched he was, I acknowledged him and said, "Please do one thing regardless of what you think of what I said. Answer this question for your sake and for hers: What unmet need of yours is this client fulfilling for you?" As might have been predicted, James ignored me and other therapists whom he had also told about this affair. He promptly left his family for her.

James's precursors could be rated as follows:

1. *Sense of necessity*. James had an apparently sincere, heartfelt sense of necessity to help Rachel with her emotional issues and problems. Rating = 4.
2. *Ready for anxiety*. James, being in love, was probably more interested in helping Rachel escape from her anxiety rather than experience it. He was obviously unwilling to experience his own anxiety in terms of issues brought up in his interactions with her as a client. Rating = 0.
3. *Awareness*. It is clear that James had little or no idea of what the actual issues were that were facing Rachel. In addition,

he had no apparent awareness of his own unmet needs or unresolved marital problems. Rating = 0.

4. *Confronting the problem.* James carefully avoided any kind of direct examination of Rachel's or his own issues. Rating = 0.
5. *Effort or will toward change.* Curiously, James was going to great effort to help Rachel gain what he thought was happiness and growth. But the effort was not toward therapeutic change so much as it was toward the gratification of needs. Rating = 0.
6. *Hope for change.* James envisioned a bright future for the two of them. Was it realistic? It seemed so to him, but it seemed like fantasy to outside observers. Rating = 1.
7. *Social support for change.* James had many friends and a good deal of social support, although no one that I knew of approved of his actions. He ignored his professional and personal social support systems. Rating = 3.

This scenario involves the harmful exploitation of a client, ethical violations, and a lack of concern for a client's therapeutic change. It also shows that James was unlikely to be an agent of change. His total score of 8 diminished even further as time passed. His social support system collapsed. James was disciplined for his unethical actions. His wife divorced him. He lost his job over his affair with Rachel. Their relationship came to an end after a year and a half, leaving him severely depressed.

After going into therapy, he told me that if he had been aware of his own issues and needs, "it never would have happened." According to James, Rachel went back to therapy as well. In spite of James's training and intellectual understanding of this cardinal rule of therapy, he did not have sufficient self-awareness to recognize the harm he was doing to his client, and himself, until it was too late.

The lesson to be learned from this tragic incident is that a helper can exert great amounts of effort, feel a great sense of urgency for change, possess great affection for a client, and fail utterly in helping that client to change. This case demonstrates that change does not arise out of only two precursors on the part of the therapist. A dynamic interplay of precursors seems to be necessary for therapists as well as clients.

III

CLINICAL APPLICATIONS: FIRST STEPS

6

ORIENTING THE RELATIONSHIP AROUND CHANGE

If a client does not respect a therapist, he or she will probably terminate prematurely. That respect depends on a variety of factors, but a major factor seems to be whether the therapist truly understands the client. We have known for a long time that "feeling understood" is at or near the heart of how a person experiences empathy from another (Van Kaam, 1966). In the 1920s, Adler (1956) gave perhaps the most descriptive definition of *empathy* when he said that it is seeing with the eyes of another, hearing with the ears of another, and feeling with the heart of another. Research indicates that empathy, warmth, and compassion are related to a large percentage of the gains attained in therapy regardless of the therapist's theoretical orientation (see Garfield, 1994; Orlinsky et al., 1994). When it happens, in therapy or out, the empathic person is valued by the other. Thus, it is of central importance to respect and work from within the client's frame of reference, just as Rogers (1951, 1957) repeatedly emphasized and Duncan, Hubble, and Miller (1997) reiterated. Dozens of studies have supported the importance of empathy in therapy, and many reviews of the psychotherapy literature have come to the same conclusion (see, e.g., Garfield, 1994; Goldfried et al., 1990; Luborsky et al., 1988; Orlinsky et al., 1994; Sexton & Whiston, 1994). Empathy is indispensable in working with difficult clients (Kottler, 1992).

When a difficult client feels understood by a therapist, he or she no longer finds it easy to summarily dismiss the approaches the therapist takes or what he or she has to say. Conversely, it is likely that many people can accomplish change faster on their own than with a therapist who is not empathic and does not engage a client in a viable working relationship. A therapist can know all the most innovative and brilliant techniques, but if he or she is not adept at empathy, it is likely that he or she will lose clients (see Garfield, 1994) or have clients who do not change. I have interviewed many therapy dropouts, and a good portion of the complaints about their therapists went like this:

- "He never saw where I was coming from."
- "He made me feel stupid."
- "She kept telling me what was wrong with me and never understood me."
- "Her 'know-it-all' attitude bugged me."
- "We never connected."

These are all relationship issues, and they are all the more important to attend to when working with difficult clients.

The change process is not linear, because human beings are not linear entities. They are arguably even more complex when they are taking on the roles of clients or therapists. Thus, the therapeutic relationship is filled with complexities and subtleties that research is still limping and hobbling its way toward understanding. Many mysterious aspects remain. For starters, we do not know what empathy really is, beyond a few surface definitions (see Hanna & Shank, 1995). Is it the process of experiencing another's inner world through a real and tangible "connection"? Or is it simply constructing a conceptual model of a client from the data received, and then stepping into it and imagining what it would be like to have this person's experience? One mode is direct contact, whereas the other is inferential. Is it both, or is it neither? Each of these perspectives on empathy is based on a different set of metaphysical assumptions (Hanna & Shank, 1995). At this point we really do not know. But empathy is so crucial to successful therapy that if we did have a more complete understanding, we might be able to make therapy more effective and reduce the 40% dropout rate.

INCREASING THE PRECURSORS THROUGH THE RELATIONSHIP

Weaving change into and throughout the relationship requires a tremendous amount of skill, especially when a client views change with ambivalence. Furthermore, the interaction between client and therapist, as people, can be a tremendously complex aspect of the change process. Thus, it would be simplistic to consider the precursors as separate from the therapeutic relationship. The precursors and the relationship are interdependent.

In the context of the precursors model, the purpose of the therapeutic relationship is to provide a setting in which the precursors can be established and stabilized in a client. This is not as simple as it would initially seem. A client can have a wildly different configuration of precursors with different therapists. It is the therapist's duty to tailor the relationship to provide an environment conducive to developing such functions as hope, effort, and confronting the problem. In other words, in the precursors model of change, the enhancement of the active agency of the client takes priority; this is the purpose of the relationship.

A successful therapeutic relationship involves much more than trust. Inspiration and persuasion (see Frank & Frank, 1991) are involved as well. If a person does not feel supported and encouraged by a therapist, he or she will be more likely to drop out of therapy (Garfield, 1994) or to seek and accomplish change on his or her own or find another therapist. As far as the precursors model is concerned, if the relationship is not established as a working alliance, the precursors may never develop or stabilize. The therapist must develop and refine the relationship so that the precursors can incubate and grow to the point where the client can exit therapy in an improved state of coping, health, or functioning. What makes the therapeutic relationship therapeutic at all may well be that it develops the seven precursors, and a relationship that does not develop the precursors is not therapeutic.

Some therapists tend to ignore the relationship as the vehicle for change when working with difficult clients and tend to concentrate on techniques as the catalysts of change. I have repeatedly found that techniques only occasionally work with a guarded and defensive client who still does not trust the therapist or the therapy process. The most enthusiastic and otherwise competent therapist can try a potent therapy technique on a difficult client, only to have it land with an interpersonal "thud" to no effect at all. When this happens, it is often the relationship that is lacking. I once supervised an experienced therapist who tried the empty chair technique on a difficult client in the first session. It went nowhere. After the relationship was established, the exact same technique was effective.

It is not surprising that clients feel more comfortable and more inclined to disclose with one therapist than with another. But what exactly is that comfort? In many community agencies, clients have more than one therapist, and this allows for some interesting observations. Many clients work better with some therapists than others, and level of education and training has little to do with it. In addition, the same therapist might be preferred by one client and eschewed by another. Lyddon (1989) noted that when client and therapist share a particular worldview, they are more likely to do well in therapy. That may be part of the comfort.

A. A. Lazarus (1993) called on therapists to be an "authentic chameleon"—in other words, to provide a relationship that meets the client's needs without losing one's own genuineness or authenticity in the process. Some clients require a businesslike collaboration, whereas others need a lot of encouragement and nurturing. Either of these groups would probably find the other style unsatisfying. However, being an authentic chameleon goes beyond merely supplying the appropriate style. In the context of Lyddon's (1989) research, it also involves being able to match a client's worldview in an empathic and understanding way so there is as little "personality clash" as possible, in spite of differences.

PURPOSE OF THE RELATIONSHIP: ACHIEVING CHANGE

Linehan (1993) observed that successful relationships and interactions with difficult clients are brought about by teaching clients what kinds of behaviors lead to therapeutic change. She referred to these behaviors as "therapy enhancing" and noted that these should not be expected of clients, they should be taught. In this same vein, when a client learns that change comes about as a result of cultivating the precursors, the relationship becomes based on change principles. Therefore, a client's agreement can be procured to allow the therapist to gently or firmly point out when one or more of the precursors are being ignored or avoided. Of course, timing is crucial, but it does help in terms of keeping a client on task.

In addition, if the client knows and is reminded that the entire interaction is based on change, much less ambiguity is allowed into the relationship. There will be fewer invitations to meet outside of therapy and fewer opportunities to lead therapy astray by initiating casual conversation designed to avoid therapy involvement. The purpose of therapy is not often readily apparent to the difficult client. This is largely because the difficult client is not thinking about therapeutic change and therefore sees a relationship with a therapist in ways that often have little or nothing to do with therapy. From this perspective, it is easy to see why some difficult clients seek business dealings, friendship (see Schofield, 1964), or social interludes with their therapists.

The easiest way around this is to clearly establish that the purpose of the relationship is to achieve change, even if change is framed as the goal of happiness for the client. Anything that strays from this purpose is seen as interfering with therapy and can be named as such. So when clients suggest business dealings, casual meetings, romantic interludes, or conversation about sports, the purpose of therapy can be gently reiterated. In extreme cases, the therapist may even suggest that therapy be terminated on the grounds that the purpose of change is not being served and make a referral if appropriate.

ESTABLISHING AND USING THE THERAPEUTIC RELATIONSHIP WITH DIFFICULT CLIENTS

The next sections outline strategies for increasing empathy with a wide range of difficult clients. Although some of these may be obvious to some readers, the list forms a comprehensive overview of how to work with clients who care little for therapy, who are not interested in seeking help, or who are so fragile they are intimidated or threatened by the very prospect of change, no matter how much they might benefit from it.

There are many styles and patterns of difficult clients, so these strategies are not appropriate for all clients at all times. Therapists can refer to this list if needed when the appropriate moment arises and as appropriate for the client's needs at that time. I make no claim that any of these suggestions are original with this book; many therapists have adhered to and followed these suggestions for decades.

Being Courteous and Requesting Permission

Even though therapists and counselors are professionals, many difficult clients see routine actions by therapists as intrusive or even rude. From their perspectives, therapists are intrusive indeed, and meddling and prying as well. Courtesy can often clear the way for probes that might otherwise be rebuffed. It can be expedient to ask permission to be challenging or direct. Clients will usually agree, thus entitling and empowering the therapist to do so. I sometimes have asked a client if there is a particular way to be challenging or confrontational that would not be considered rude or intrusive. Clients often give clear instructions that make the job much easier.

Asking permission is best done before asking deeply sensitive questions, and the therapist should add that the client does not have to answer if he or she does not so desire. Clients nearly always agree to this. Asking permission has two advantages. One is that the person becomes prepared or ready for the question, which increases his or her willingness to experience the anxiety involved. The other advantage is that the client notes that the therapist is showing respect for the client's inner world. This is a form of communicating empathy in and of itself.

Part of asking permission is to be courteous about how one goes about it. This does not sound like much, but some difficult clients are going out of their way in answering such questions at all. For many, answering deeply personal questions involves quite a bit of effort in an area in which they have little practice or experience. Statements such as, "Do you mind if I ask a question you might find sensitive?" prepares the client for the question and shows respect for their dignity and right to privacy.

When a therapist begins to view a client as irritating or disgusting, he or she may be inclined to forgo courtesy or asking permission and just start firing interpretations and authoritarian pronouncements. This causes any progress to take a downturn.

Validating Positive Qualities

A client does not have to have a high IQ to be smart. If a client is perceptive, shrewd, or has street savvy, he or she can and should be validated for it. For example, I have often asked clients to use their intelligence to explain to me how a certain problem came into their life, saying, "Come on, you are very smart, you know what's going on here." Any positive quality that the client displays can be used toward therapeutic progress. Much of this approach to therapy is discovering and revealing those positive qualities and genuinely admiring them in a client. They form the platform on which the precursors rest and find stability.

However, the positive quality should be demonstrated to the client whenever possible so that the therapist does not come off as ingratiating. For example, if a client says "I am a bad person. I always hurt the people around me," simply saying, "I think you are good" is not enough. The quality of goodness is demonstrated when the therapist responds, "Sounds to me like you are actually quite a good person. Bad people don't care about whether they hurt others. They just hurt them and don't bother to think about it. I would say that you are actually a good person trying to figure out how to be better. What do you think?" The therapist then waits for an answer to the question so that the client can vocalize agreement, or otherwise engage in process.

Such validation can have extraordinary effects in terms of stabilizing a client, removing self-doubt, building the relationship, and helping him or her feel more deserving of positive changes. This practice should be done constantly in therapy to create an ever-increasing list of positive qualities. Some clients will object initially, but it can be quite humorous to all when they acquiesce.

Giving the Client the Option of Telling the Therapist to Back Off

After getting permission to intrude or confront a client, a therapist can say, "If I am bothering you, then tell me to back off, OK?" This will often ease the tension of the question or the therapist's persistence by returning a sense of control to a threatened client. This can also be effective with clients who are intimidating, some of whom, when they hear the option of telling the therapist to back off, will consider it beneath them to admit that mere questions could ever bother them.

A client who is manipulative may tell the therapist to back off indeed. When this happens, the therapist readily agrees to do so, but then asks the client if he or she was getting uncomfortable. The therapist can also ask if this discomfort occurs often, and when it does, in what kinds of situations and with what kinds of people it occurs. This must be done casually, as these moments can be delicate, requiring good timing and proper phrasing based on the needs of the client and the situation.

Attending to the Metalog and Bringing It Into Dialog

Metalog is a term I have adapted from its original use by Gregory Bateson (Bateson & Bateson, 1987) to refer to the unspoken conversation that the client may be having with a therapist. Because human beings have only one tongue but process their thoughts in parallel, that is, in many separate streams at a time (Ornstein, 1986), many of these thought streams are never given voice. For example, when a client sits down with a therapist, he or she has many thoughts in the form of silent self-statements that he or she will be unlikely to express. "I wonder if I can trust this person" is an obvious self-statement, along with, "Will this therapist like me?" and "I wonder if I can fool this guy?" All of these may be occurring simultaneously while the person is answering questions and discussing issues with the therapist.

With difficult clients, there may be a different metalog containing self-statements such as, "This therapy stuff is a bunch of crap, and I wish I didn't have to do this," or "Will I be able to control this guy?" or "I hope she doesn't say anything about my drinking." These latter statements can be clear thought content to the client, even though he or she is simultaneously making statements pledging to be cooperative with a reassuring smile.

Attending to metalog statements has two advantages. The first is that it saves valuable session time by directly addressing where a client is, focusing not only on presenting complaints but deeper, unspoken issues as well. The second is that by doing so, a client will come to respect the therapist in a way that facilitates disclosure and cooperation.

The therapist attends to the metalog through an inferential process. For example, a client reassures the therapist that he or she wants to get better, but he or she is not showing effort, confronting the problem presented, or being willing to experience anxiety. The therapist might say to the client, "Do you mind if I ask you a question?" The client will usually say something like, "Sure, go ahead." The therapist then says, "Please tell me if I am wrong, but I get the sense that you really don't want anything to do with this therapy thing. Is that right?" The therapist doesn't have to be right, but he or she may just be close enough that for the first time a real and genuine dialog takes place. By bringing the metalog into dialog, therapy becomes more vital and interesting as well. It is important to add that the therapist has a metalog as well, which is discussed in the next chapter.

Bringing Down Defense Systems From Within

When encountering a well-defended client, it sometimes helps to envision bypassing his or her walls of defense in a gentle manner and peacefully entering the city. The goal is to be given an entrance point into the city itself. It will usually be given only to someone who is perceived as a friend. A therapist is the enemy of what Masterson (1988) called the "false self." In this context, the false self is what erects those defenses and guards the walls. The therapist's purpose is to restore or establish the greatness of the client's "real self," that which is open to experience and not entrenched, bunkered down, or ready for war. Once inside, the therapist usually perceives that the outwardly forbidding ramparts and walls nearly always look delicate and fragile from the inside.

To get past the walls, it sometimes helps to present oneself as a consultant to help improve the design and engineering of the walls. Validate defenses, even hostile ones, by pointing them out and asking if they are effective and what could make them more so. For example, one could say, "I have noticed that you do not like anyone being too inquisitive toward you and that you highly value your privacy. I respect that. Do you find that you like keeping people at a distance?"

People have excellent reasons for erecting defenses. Paradoxically, if the reasons are validated and encouraged, it sometimes reduces the need for erecting them. One can also point out the energy drain that comes with keeping the defenses active so much of the time. If a person is tired, that could be reframed as due to their devoting a considerable amount of mental energy to defending instead of living.

Increasing Therapist Capacity for Empathy

If the research is correct, increasing one's capacity for empathy seems to be more of a duty than a mere suggestion. It is an idea that is seldom discussed in the literature. How much empathy is enough? Does a great therapist have a great amount of empathy? How much empathy does a client need for change to be accomplished?

There are certain exercises that can help a therapist increase empathy. One is to practice assuming the roles of other people, specifically people whom one knows or has known. It is also important to be able to assume the role of people with personality disorders such as narcissistic, borderline, or antisocial disorders. Personality disorders that have delusional aspects such as schizotypal and paranoid also make for excellent practice. A therapist can show a client that he or she is able to think in a disordered way without agreeing with that way of thinking. Clients usually know this and can use the therapist as a model.

Carl Whitaker, the renowned family therapist, often advised being able to think like schizophrenic clients to be better able to work with them. North (1987), a psychiatrist who was once diagnosed with catatonic schizophrenia, stated that this experience made her better able to help such clients because of her ability to empathize with them. Of course, being able to assume the viewpoints of people with these disorders is not the same as having had them, but it certainly can help a client to feel understood. It is also important to clients to know that the therapist is at least attempting to see things from their perspective.

It is often helpful to a therapist to do an "empathy check" by simply asking the client if he or she feels understood. This can be done in a general way or in specific ways on specific points. Statements like, "I am trying to see where you are coming from here," and adding, "Am I getting it?" serve this purpose. Simply asking, "Do you think I understand you?" is another empathy check. These serve a dual purpose. They help the therapist ensure that he or she is understanding the client, and they communicate to the client that the therapist is attempting to truly understand.

Telling the client things like, "You are ultimately the expert on you" also serves this purpose by acknowledging that the client has access to information about himself or herself that is not available to anyone else. If the client informs the therapist that he or she does not understand, this opens the door to finding out what it takes to do so and often leads to the client disclosing more information that can enhance the relationship.

Another exercise is to role play a difficult client with a colleague or supervisor by fully assuming the client's meaning and value system and answering questions while playing that client's identity. A therapist should be able to role play that client so thoroughly that he or she eventually begins to have a feel for what it is to be that person, in addition to the diagnosis or problem.

Another exercise is to assume the client's role in the presence of the client, checking with him or her to see if one is really understanding their perspective on life and living. As part of this role play, it may help to have the client assume the role of therapist. This can help raise self-awareness in the client. Although some difficult clients will eschew this kind of approach, some will take to it, and it can be quite humorous if done lightheartedly. To the degree a therapist can actually be that client, it is likely that he or she can work all the more empathically.

Reflecting Meanings Before Feelings

It is easy to plunge right into exploring a client's feelings, but this may not be appropriate with clients who are not willing to experience anxiety or any unpleasant affect at first. In such clients, feelings are not particularly accessible. It is often helpful to initially reflect meanings instead. Frank (1987) observed that "all psychotherapeutic endeavors, whatever their form, transpire entirely in the realm of meanings" (p. 293). Getting a sense of the meaning system of that client can help in accessing feelings later. Casual expressions of opinions can be extrapolated and subjected to an inductive reasoning process that leads to a person's core cognitions. This is also a way of being able to match the worldview of a client in a way that expedites the process of self-disclosure and the formation of a viable relationship.

For example, a client once made a sexist statement about women, smiling that knowing, "male-brotherhood" kind of smile and saying, "They really are only good for one thing, right?" Rather than confront the client on his sexism, the therapist found it more effective to explore and discover his attitude toward people in general. The therapist's response was, "Do you mind if I try and sort out where you are coming from?" Following the client's hesitant nod, the therapist continued: "If you figure that about women, is it fair to say that you believe in general that some people are just meant to be taken advantage of by others?" This client said, "Well, yeah, I do, sort of." The therapist then paused and said, "Well, I guess my question for you then is to which group you figure you belong, those who get used or those who do the using?"

This opened up a fruitful exploration of how this client had been used by others and how all his life he strove to become one of the users. This then led to a discussion of whether being a user was an admirable thing and who the users were in his life that he strove to be like. Of course, it turned out that the people he was striving to imitate were people that he despised. This explained a lot of the self-hate that he disclosed later.

It is often true that even casual statements on mundane subjects can allow extrapolation toward an inductive reasoning process that isolates core beliefs about self, people, problems, or life in general. With a client who is not at all forthcoming with information, it sometimes helps to evoke brief opinion statements on politics, sports, or even religion and from there move deeper toward the underlying presuppositions of the statement itself. Whether one is a conservative, a Democrat, or a Dallas Cowboy fan, such opinions can open windows into a client's deeper issues and problems. If a person says that she is a conservative because her father was, the therapist can then issue a challenge aimed at discovering whether the client ever made any independent decisions, or whether it is a good idea to be one's own person. This approach is sometimes highly valuable in easing a client toward detaching from sources of harmful or dysfunctional beliefs.

Establishing the Client's Meaning System or Worldview

This strategy is an extension of the previous one and is related to a little-known school of cognitive therapy called *philosophical psychotherapy* (Sahakian, 1976). Based on what clients tell a therapist, even casually, an entire meaning structure can be deduced and proposed to the client (see McMullin, 1986). For example, a client casually declares, "You know you have to look out for number 1 in this world." A deductive response might be, "So if you are number 1, does that mean that no one else in the entire world is as important as you?" A few clients will agree, and others may respond with a "not quite" answer. These are easy enough to handle with standard cognitive approaches. However, many difficult clients will boldly and shamelessly answer, "Of course I'm number 1; who else could be?" In this case, an entire meaning system can be structured in terms of a hierarchy.

Consider the example of William. He was around age 35, claimed to be depressed, and in the first session said that looking out for himself was indeed his primary task in life. His therapist drew a pyramid on paper, drew in various levels, and placed William's name at the apex or top level. Then the therapist asked who would be number 2 and so on down the levels. The therapist asked what kind of treatment people deserved at each level of the hierarchy. This helped to discern William's entire moral or ethical philosophy.

Like many clients of the narcissistic style, William calmly and directly said that people low in the hierarchy can be manipulated, cheated, and otherwise mistreated. The therapist asked him if he himself was ever low on someone else's pyramid. He nodded his head hesitantly and seriously. This opened an inroad into his world. The therapist inquired whether he was ever manipulated, cheated, or otherwise mistreated by that person or persons. When he nodded affirmatively, the therapist asked if it hurt or caused him anxiety or difficulty. Once again William nodded. From this point the therapist was able to construct his meaning system, which included a view of the world based on contempt for and resentment toward others.

The therapist asked permission to reflect that viewpoint back to him for verification. With William's consent, the therapist stated, "Please tell me if I am wrong, but it seems that for you, life seems to be played in terms of who outsmarts and outmaneuvers the other and is based on each person causing pain and hurt to others in the process. And whoever does it best wins. So if no one else is looking out for you, then you have to make yourself number 1 in order to survive. Is that close?" William replied, "I guess so." Because William had already admitted that he was depressed, the therapist asked if this lifestyle worked in terms of making him happy. When William said, "Not really," the therapist asked if they could use therapy to find a lifestyle that could. This empathic approach, although not productive of change on the spot, placed William on the rails toward awareness and a sense of necessity.

Operating From Within the Client's Meaning System or Framework

Once the client's worldview is somewhat defined and outlined, it can become a pivot for various interventions. Techniques can be introduced and framed from within that perspective. It is not helpful to expect a difficult client, who is minimally involved in therapy anyway, to learn a new lexicon. From the perspective of many difficult clients, a therapist's teaching terminology to a client that requires paragraphs of background knowledge and interpretation looks like an attempt to convert him or her to a new religion.

For example, the same "number 1 on the pyramid" technique was once used on a different male client who was highly self-centered and self-serving. After the therapist had gotten a good idea of his meaning system, he began to work within it. Later in therapy, the therapist seriously and solemnly reframed the client's existence as the "Unknown King," noting that because he was the most important person in the world, he should be ruling the human race and should be given anything and everything he desired. The client looked at the therapist long and hard. After a pause of several seconds, the therapist said, "If that is true, then you must be a tremendously unhappy person who is never respected, and meets frustration and disappointment at every turn in life, and believes that other people are ignorant, foolish, and petty. After all, they do not recognize that you are the king." From that point forward he began to make progress slowly toward change.

Redefining the Problem

There is always a fine balance between addressing a client's presenting complaints and resolving the almost inevitable deeper issues that underlie them. Contrary to some views on this, it can be done briefly. When a client is low in precursors, his or her explanation of the problem is usually naive and inaccurate. A sexually abused girl says it was her fault. A man with antisocial personality disorder says people do not like him because he is "too intense."

On the other hand, there is often a grain of truth in the explanation. A battered woman says that she cannot leave her husband because he needs her. Sure he does, but that is not the problem. A man who stalks a woman says that he knows that if only the woman would get to know him, she would come to love him. Well, maybe in theory, but that part of him is so hidden by pathology that the real "him" may never emerge for this woman to see. It is the kernel of truth that is the seed of the delusion.

Difficult clients should indeed be acknowledged and understood from within their meaning system, but the meaning system is probably deeply flawed. Clients in general, and especially those who are difficult, fail to account for unconscious motives and beliefs.

Respecting and Encouraging the Client's Autonomy and Freedom

Respecting and encouraging autonomy and freedom is helpful with nearly all clients, but especially with criminal or antisocial clients. Change is often a choice; at other times it is a simple matter of operant conditioning. Nevertheless, some research has shown that appealing to the prospect of change as a free choice has considerable therapeutic value (Kanfer & Grimm, 1978). In fact, this seems to be one of the few effective strategies with antisocial clients (see Kierulff, 1988; Samenow, 1998). There is a catch here, however. Criminals have learned they can violate a wide range of societal norms and dictates. They know they have the freedom to do so, and they live for it. This seems to be not so much a cognitive calculation as a palpable thrill or sensation that serves as a reinforcer. It is as important to address the thrill or sensation of freedom, and the beliefs connected with it, as it is to examine their irrational beliefs about criminality in general (see Samenow, 1998).

Perhaps the most important step toward working with the criminal mindset is to thoroughly understand two bits of information. First, the criminal seeks the admirable goal of absolute freedom of behavior—the ability to do whatever, whenever, and however. A criminal client will often combine the first goal with the contemptible goal of being able to have complete disregard for responsibility, accountability, and the well-being of others. This is often a major aspect of their flawed meaning systems.

Encouraging Uncooperativeness as a Protection of Freedom

This is paradoxical, but it is also true. If a client with a precursor rating of 8 or less steadfastly refuses to disclose anything of real substance, it might be of help to momentarily suspend the effort to get the client to self-disclose and talk about why the client likes to be uncooperative. It often turns out that some clients are so protective of their freedom and autonomy that being uncooperative is merely an attempt to retain the dignity and integrity that comes with being free. If this is the case, the therapist can offer to make an agreement with the client. "I'll make a deal with you. The minute you feel that I am taking away your freedom in any way, please tell me. I have no interest in doing anything of the sort. If anything, therapy is meant to strengthen and increase your freedom. What do you think?" Once this is done, it is surprising how much a client will allow a therapist to probe and challenge.

Answering the "What's-in-it-for-me?" Question

Difficult clients are often uninterested in therapy until they can answer the question, What's in it for me? Whenever possible, engage the client in the first session. There are many ways to do this, according to the style and disorders of clients themselves. Perhaps the best to offer is a sense of hope, even if the client does not admit to lacking it. It is not necessary to promise any resolution of problems, of course, but it often helps just to present the possibility of change or better conditions.

Many difficult clients view therapy with more than a little trepidation or suspicion anyway. They are not likely to become involved in the process until they answer the What's-in-it-for-me? question. When it appears they will gain some benefit from their participation and involvement, their interest level will pick up to that degree. In the beginning, the answer to the question might be horribly mundane, such as "to satisfy my probation officer," but it is a start.

Being Persuasive

Frank (1961) long ago made the then-radical observation that persuasion is a major feature of the therapist's role. He noted that persuasion is a common factor of all therapy approaches, operating in different ways but present in some form nonetheless. Persuasion is a crucial aspect of working with such clients. It is part of the different set of therapy skills that are necessary for working with difficult clients.

Frank and Frank (1991; see also Frank, 1987) also identified rhetoric, closely related to persuasion, as another common factor of therapy. The style of language and the force of its delivery often influence how clients view problems, situations, or events. Corsini (1989), editor of a major psychotherapy textbook, observed that much of psychotherapy is a sales job, promoting and "selling" the benefits of mental health to clients who are not convinced of its value.

Frank (1974) also noted that our ideal of living in a democratic society tends to discourage us from considering the idea that therapists are indeed persuasive and influential of clients. It is also contrary to some notions of psychotherapy as a science. Nevertheless, in 1996, Dr. Frank told me himself that persuasion not only is inseparable from therapy, but its methods should be improved in psychotherapy training programs.

To implement precursors and help clients to advance along stages of change, persuasion is a powerful variable in the psychotherapeutic relationship. To be able to facilitate a client's movement toward change without impinging on freedom of thought, identity, or autonomy is a fine art indeed, but nevertheless often necessary. The art of persuasion is different from following a therapy formula or manual and is implicit in virtually all schools. It involves promoting the idea of personal growth, mental health, and well-being.

Another aspect of being persuasive is to establish a teaching environment within the therapeutic relationship. Much of therapy, depending on the theoretical approach, is a teaching enterprise (G. S. Howard, Nance, & Meyers, 1987). Therapists relay information to clients with the intention of helping them cope with various aspects of their lives. However, with many difficult clients, any one-up position taken by the therapist that conveys the unspoken message of "I know and you don't" is likely to produce needless power struggles. Suggestions for how to avoid this are provided in the next chapter.

Displaying Compassion and Caring

Compassion may be the most underrated element in all of therapy (Lewin, 1936). Many clients have told me that the only thing that kept them going was knowing that someone cared about what was going to happen to them. One client taught me, many years ago, a lesson I will not forget. He was rigid, opinionated, and stubborn when I first met him. After working with him for 15 months he had made remarkable changes in his life, and I asked what helped the most during that time. I was expecting to hear of a particular technique or intervention. Instead he said unhesitatingly, "Just knowing that somebody cared." I remember feeling disappointed at the time, because I really wanted to hear how great my techniques were.

If a client knows someone genuinely cares about him or her, this functions as a kind of ticket or sanction to improve and get better. When someone else cares, it allows a person to feel deserving of improvement. So many human beings believe that if they are not loved, they are not worthy of happiness or joy. Thus, when someone cares, this is an indication of the person's significance. Simple, perhaps, but it was a valuable lesson for me. This could be one explanation for why people with borderline and narcissistic disorders are so obsessed with obtaining the love and admiration of others.

Some difficult clients are extremely adept at getting people to hate them. It serves the inverse purpose of the false self further solidifying the core belief of unworthiness and insignificance (see Masterson, 1988). A therapist must be on the lookout for this unconscious tactic, as it can stop the change process immediately. It helps to remember that it is merely a coping mechanism.

Moderating Compassion With Antisocial Clients

With clients diagnosed as antisocial, compassion and caring require a slightly different approach. These people are often accustomed to manipulating people who care about them. Many believe that to show love or caring is a sign of weakness, and thus they tend to peg the warm, caring therapist as someone who is easily manipulable and not worthy of respect. For a therapist to openly display warmth and caring can be a mistake with some of these clients. With others it is a wise and important approach indeed. Clinical judgment needs to be exercised, but a fairly reliable indicator is to show some genuine warmth and watch to see how the client responds.

Addressing Problems in Chunks

It took me a while to learn a lesson that others probably have well in hand or for whom it was never a problem. If too much contradictory, destabilizing, or painful material is opened too soon for a client, he or she will tend to withdraw and feel disempowered and threatened by the depth and extent of the problems. It gives the "rug-out-from-under" feeling, and one's inner world appears to be poised at the brink of a void. The problem then no longer seems manageable and is a cause of reduced hope.

I finally learned to define and address things in "chunks." The aim is to handle only what the client can confront without being overwhelmed. Sometimes a client is difficult precisely because his or her tolerance of pain is so low. I remember a couple of clients I "trained" to be difficult because I wanted them to confront more than they could. A client can feel degraded or demeaned by a therapist who outlines a vast map of psychopathology. The relationship can be severely damaged, and a premature termination may be imminent. Leading a client to confront too much material actually reduces the confronting precursor.

Expecting Some Hesitance After Great Effort

I have made this mistake a few times as well: A great session finally occurs with a difficult client. I become very pleased that a "breakthrough" has taken place. Then, in the very next session, the client is belligerent, uncooperative, and even defiant. In some cases, especially with people diagnosed as borderline, there may be extreme hostility and defiance toward the therapist for "tricking" him or her into disclosing or working. This can be upsetting to a therapist who does not know that such behaviors should be expected.

Thus, after a session in which a client does much confronting and exerts great effort, do not plunge further ahead, but assess where the client stands with what was done. Enjoy the plateau. He or she may not be ready for more just yet. Pacing in such situations is of the utmost importance.

Setting Boundaries

Each therapist has his or her own limits on what they will accept from clients in terms of middle-of-the-night telephone calls and the like. It is important to define limits that neither impede nor threaten therapeutic change. The therapist should instruct clients that he or she will not always have time to talk, that taking "no" for an answer is sometimes necessary, and that keeping agreements and agreeing to cancel rather than skipping sessions is desirable behavior (see Linehan, 1993).

Threats of physical harm from a client, whether thinly or thickly veiled, in those extremely rare occasions when they occur should not be tolerated under any circumstances. If the client is already on probation or parole, therapists should inform the police of any threats (the therapist should be in contact with the probation or parole officer anyway). It should be made firmly clear to the client that in spite of compassion, empathy, caring, and the like, no boundary violations of this variety will be tolerated, especially those of security.

It is equally important for female therapists to make it clear that sexual comments or innuendoes will not be tolerated. Some difficult male clients are adept at using graphic sexual language in a session to give themselves a cheap thrill and make the therapist uncomfortable. Any actions like this require immediate attention, and if it continues, termination may be necessary. For female therapists who have trouble dealing with this kind of behavior and language, I have found that the best approach is to learn from other female therapists who have become experts in dealing with this client style: another of those therapy skills that is seldom taught in universities.

Grounds for termination should be made clear ahead of time with some difficult clients. With borderline clients especially, the range of acceptable and unacceptable behaviors needs to be set clearly and concisely so the client can be reminded, with as little ambiguity as possible, when he or she has gone too far (Linehan, 1993). At the same time, it is important to soothe a client's feelings about observing limits while not compromising the limits themselves.

Matching the Client's Emotional State

Match the client's emotional state, but with one vital additive—interest. For example, if a client is sad or dejected, the therapist does not have to be melancholy and helpless along with the client. However, if empathic contact is present, the therapist will resonate with the client's emotions enough to reflect back that sadness. This empathic resonance helps the client accept the therapist and his or her input.

The danger is that it is possible for the therapist to sink into sympathy and lose the empathic contact. After all, some difficult clients have backgrounds so devastating and tragic that a therapist's empathy can easily degrade into sympathy. One route of escape from this is through the element of interest. I have found that a strong and powerful sense of genuine interest on the part of a therapist, focused on a client and his or her condition, can be contagious. A therapist's interest can stimulate a client to also be interested, without any verbal persuasion. In many cases, especially when coupled with humor, a therapist's contagious interest can help a client to be lifted, or at least dislodged, from entrenched emotions or mindsets.

Opening a Therapeutic Window

Much of working with difficult clients is probing here and there, trying this approach and that, searching for an entrance point, an inroad, or a window to open that makes the client accessible. This is a difficult phenomenon to describe, as it is highly subjective. In any case, in working with difficult clients, one becomes familiar with canned responses, disingenuous behaviors, and flat, feigned, or exaggerated affect. Many clients have become hardened to any external inspection and have a response for just about any kind of potential intrusion. But every now and then, a probe or a confrontation will bring a hesitance, a response that reveals a soft spot in the armor. A client may look at you with a sensitivity or genuineness that was not present and indeed may not have ever been there before.

When a therapeutic window is opened, a therapist must enter through it soon, for the client may close it with a new defense formed in a matter of moments. For example, when working with angry, defiant male and female teenagers, I have noticed that they are often proud of their anger. Although anger management strategies can get them to talk about their anger, many such clients will change little if anything about it. The teenager will often brag about his or her anger as though it is a prized possession. An example of opening a therapeutic window with this type of client is to ask, "Have you ever been hurt?" The answer is typically yes. This makes the client pause. The window can then be further opened by asking, "Is that hurt related to your anger?" and then, "If you didn't have the hurt, what would happen to the anger?" This approach will often open a window that allows entrance beyond anger into the inner world of the client. It changes the relationship and initiates the change process (see Hanna & Hunt, 1999). Opening the window and entering smoothly are part of bringing down defenses from within.

Looking for and Connecting With the "I Behind the Eye"

In instances where a therapist has experienced a sense of "connection" with a client, it is quite revealing to ask oneself what got connected. Was it two brains? Two worldviews? Two selves? Two multigenerational family systems? Phenomenologically, the therapist may perceive something in a client that forms the basis for a relational exchange. It may appear as though one has "located" this client within a maze of swirling, turbulent thought patterns, raging emotions, and destructive behaviors.

Thinking too much in terms of clinical labels sometimes risks obscuring the actual person behind a series of professional templates and categories. When it comes to establishing relationships, it is probably better to suspend the labels and templates so that one can get a sense of connection with the person. Gendlin (1992) described the person as the "I who looks at you from behind the eyes" (p. 453). That "I"—the real person—can be accepted unconditionally, even though negative behaviors and thoughts are seen as needing change. Unfortunately, sometimes it takes a year or so for that "I behind the eye" to show up in a therapy session, and sometimes it may not happen at all, especially with antisocial clients. But for the therapist who knows how to locate that "I," it may be likely to happen sooner.

Developing Perspicacity as a Wisdom Characteristic

Clients with antisocial or conduct disorders often respect therapists who are suspicious. "Bull----" is a common term in casual conversation in this culture. Its use is ubiquitous among antisocial clients. Most learn at an early age to deal it out. Their peers ridicule them when they are susceptible to it, saying, "You idiot, you believed that bull----?!" They will test therapists by tossing out falsehoods to see how sharp or how gullible he or she may be. A degree of tacit respect is given to a person who can recognize it. One of the characteristics of an effective therapist, especially with this population, is what Sternberg (1986, 1990) called "perspicacity," or the capacity to see beyond appearances, to not be easily deceived or fooled (see Appendix).

Antisocial clients will be forced to respect a therapist who has a well-functioning, reasonably accurate "bull---- detector." This may not be sufficient by itself to get such a client to be compliant or to work in therapy, but it is essential to establishing a relationship and cannot be underestimated. The same is true in working with clients who abuse alcohol and drugs, another population notorious for dishonesty and deception concerning drug use and behaviors. It is difficult to teach, but I have observed that even initially naive therapists can cultivate it through experience.

Matching the Therapist With the Client

One of the intangibles that is still largely unaccounted for by research is that some clients seem to do better with particular therapists. This is often a matter of class, gender, and culture. But it often has little to do with these at all. Much of it seems to be related to shared worldviews (Lyddon, 1989); when clients and therapists share general outlooks on the world and life, they seem to do better together in therapy. Of course, the therapist's personal responses and issues also play an important role as well and will be explored in the next chapter.

I found in my first experience in a community agency that even though I had worked very hard with a particular client, there were times when the counselor in the next office seemed to develop a natural and spontaneous rapport with that client that I had not accomplished in spite of my best efforts. In other cases the reverse was true. In consulting in community agency settings, I often recommend switching therapists for the sake of the client, if it will help bring about change sooner.

Using the Concentric Circle Technique

When working with difficult clients, a therapist often wonders how close he or she is to a particular client and how far clients are allowing the therapist into their confidence. In other words, it is helpful to know the level or degree of a client's self-disclosure. A. A. Lazarus (1989b) described a remarkably helpful and effective technique for finding out how far a client has "let one in." This adaptation is done by drawing five concentric circles and labeling them circle 1 at the core, or innermost circle, to circle 5 in the circle at the outermost perimeter. The therapist then asks the client to conceive of the core self as being in the center at circle 1, where his or her most private and personal information is held. Circle 5, at the outer perimeter, is where the most superficial and insignificant information about the person is—that which everyone knows. The therapist can ask the client directly, "Into which circle have you allowed me?" After finding out, he or she can further ask, "What would it take for me to get into the next circle?" or "Whom have you allowed into circle 1?" or "For a person to get into circle 1 with you, what do they have to do or be like?" Clients can be surprisingly honest in using this technique. It takes little effort but can be highly productive.

Using All Three Therapy Modalities

The three major therapy modes are individual, group, and family therapies. Each has its own particular and peculiar set of benefits not readily available from the others. Many difficult clients need all three, if and when appropriate.

Individual therapy may not be the mode that a particular difficult client needs most. For example, an alcohol abuser may be more in need of a group with similar issues and problems than an individual setting. Chances are he or she may need both—and family therapy as well. Children and adolescents can greatly benefit from family therapy, not to mention parents. Each modality provides a unique opportunity to build relationships with a therapist, with peers, and with family members. These skills can then be taken into everyday life to build a social support network, possibly leading to a logarithmic effect on change.

7

REDUCING THERAPIST INTERFERENCE AND INCREASING THERAPEUTIC WISDOM

In this chapter I present a series of strategies to help therapists in dealing with their own issues as they arise while working with difficult clients to minimize therapist interference with the change process. I use *therapist interference* in place of *countertransference* because it is more descriptive and applicable to a greater range of therapies. Therapists can use these strategies in developing self-awareness and using that self-awareness for the client's benefit.

WISDOM AND THERAPY

Manuals and formulas for doing therapy tend to be of limited utility when working with difficult clients. A client's skills in averting and avoiding can be far more competent than a therapist's skills in awareness and confronting. Remarkably, it is in work with difficult clients that a therapist's skills become honed and refined and knowledge of human beings becomes deepened and seasoned. Mere theories, techniques, and even empathy are often not enough. Influencing difficult clients to change often calls for therapeutic wisdom, a set of abilities that include and transcend classical or formal therapy training.

Wisdom is not the same as intelligence (Sternberg, 1986, 1990). It involves abilities and kinds of understanding that will not be assessed by an IQ test. Such abilities involve dialectical thinking, self-awareness, self-transcendence, impeccable timing, and the ability to formulate reframes and metaphors that can easily transfer into and out of a client's worldview (Hanna & Ottens, 1995). The characteristics of wisdom are listed in the Appendix. Karasu (1992) also provided an excellent set of tips under the heading of wisdom, and the book is highly recommended to therapists working with difficult clients.

The primary starting point for a therapist working with a difficult and challenging client can be conceptualized as being fully attentive, centered, genuine, engaged, empathic, and committed to helping that client increase precursors so he or she can confront and experience issues that lead to therapeutic change. The therapist is present, both intellectually and intuitively, for whatever the client offers, both verbally and nonverbally, and is open to any kind of difficulty that may interpose itself into the relationship.

Difficulty for the therapist arises when a client displays behaviors that compromise this starting point. A client may do or say something that has the effect of introverting and collapsing the therapist into his or her own issues, knocking him or her off center, breaking contact between client and therapist, and compromising the therapist's empathy. Wisdom helps a therapist to maintain empathy and poise in spite of inclinations to the contrary. Once established, a therapist should be alert to the breakdown of this essential state, and when the breakdown is apparent, the warning flags should begin to wave.

HOW TO HANDLE POTENTIAL SOURCES OF THERAPIST INTERFERENCE

A personal state of equanimity is invaluable when working with difficult clients. To learn how to develop it, I highly recommend a book called *Everyday Zen*, by C. J. Beck (1989), which has remarkable implications for therapists. The following suggestions may also be helpful in reducing therapist interference and maintaining one's therapeutic presence. The basis of most of the following suggestions depends on the self-awareness or mindfulness of the therapist, carefully monitoring and gauging his or her own reactions to a client who is perceived as difficult.

Nonattachment to the Fruits of One's Actions

Horney (1952/1987) noted that the lesson Zen can teach therapists is to be wholeheartedly and fully present. This is not a matter of being a cold observer, she said. The therapist should not have any "personal axe to grind and no neurotic craving" (p. 31) attached to the outcome of therapy. The therapist must pay full attention to the client without any involvement in self. This means having, as she put it, "the highest presence and the highest absence" (p. 34). In her advice to therapists, she recommended being so totally absorbed in the practice of therapy that one is putting "all of yourself in what you do" (p. 31).

Some difficult clients are extremely alert to a therapist's desire that they improve and will react to that desire by attempting to frustrate the therapist and sabotage therapy in a wide variety of ways. Such clients learned such skills long before meeting the therapist, perhaps as a result of their interactions with those who oppressed them or denied them in their families, schools, neighborhoods, and other environments. If a therapist is open and not egotistically craving a particular outcome, or if he or she is not defending his or her ego or competence, a difficult client has no "hook" or "tug" on a therapist that can draw the change process off course.

Empathy as an Act of Will

Empathy does not always occur naturally and automatically. If it did, the entire human race and the living of life would likely be qualitatively and radically different. A rule of thumb: Empathy will tend to break down to the degree that one's own unresolved issues begin to emerge. Another rule is that empathy breaks down to the degree the other person presents with viewpoints or perspectives that seem strange or foreign. Thus, when either of these conditions manifest, empathy requires an act of will to be maintained (Margulies, 1989).

In addition, some clients are uncomfortable with empathy and are adept at discouraging it in a therapist. Mindfulness of this phenomenon in the moment the client is making the attempt is extraordinarily helpful in recognizing how and why one's empathy begins to dissipate. Once again, at that point, empathy must be recalled, re-established, and maintained through a conscious act of will (Margulies, 1989).

Avoid Asserting One's Credentials or Degrees

When a client is particularly difficult, it is easy for one to "pull rank" and begin to assert one's college degrees, license, credentials, or years of experience as "proof" that one knows what one is doing. This is usually a symptom of the therapist's frustration and a sign of burnout and is seldom effective. It is also a possible indicator of a power struggle the therapist is losing. An apparent attempt to one-up the client will create barriers that prevent genuine interaction and hinder the therapeutic process. It is often a last ditch attempt on the part of the therapist to gain respect, but unfortunately respect usually has to be earned in other ways.

Many difficult clients will take an adolescent "whatever" attitude toward this display and become resentful and rebellious. Some privately ridicule, as part of their metalog, people with degrees and see the assertion of one's degrees or education as similar to boasting about one's wealth or property. The therapist should be aware of any inclinations to do so and note carefully when the urge arises, which often signals the arrival of an impasse.

Be Aware of When One Becomes Either Too Rigid or Too "Flexible"

When a therapist has become adversely affected by working with a difficult client, he or she may begin to become rigid in his or her dealings with that client. This is usually a last ditch effort to gain control. When one notices this tendency in oneself, it is important to take a step back and check out when it began and what was said or done that led to the rigidity.

On the other hand, sometimes clients are adept at persuading a therapist to take a break from all the "hard work" and to soften his or her efforts toward change. The client may say something like, "Do we have to do this now? I'm not really in the mood." Because most therapists are truly nice people and not taskmasters, they do not want to be controlling or dominating. Once again, when one notices oneself becoming loose or lackadaisical in one's efforts toward client change, the tendency should be explored with attention to when and how it started. Chances are there is a lesson to be learned in reflection on that moment. Either extreme is a potential move away from therapeutic change.

Humor Can Be Both Disarming and Engaging

The value of humor in therapy cannot be overestimated. If a difficult client can be helped to see the humor in his or her situation or behaviors, the aura of seriousness and tragedy can diminish and make it easier to confront. It is important, of course, to avoid humor that delights in the pain or misfortune of others.

Humor must always be sensitive to the needs and condition of the client in the moment. Empathy rules. The therapist should avoid any humor that has traces of residual anger or resentment toward a client. In my own case, I look for an inclination toward sarcasm as an indicator of my own unresolved issues being stirred up by a client. When my own humor is healthy, I tend toward existential irony. When I am tempted to use sarcasm or cynicism, I know that I must be careful with the use of humor. I consider it my duty at that point to resolve any of my own issues related to or evoked by a client so that my healthier sense of humor can return.

Meet Hostility With Equanimity and Humor

If a client knows that a therapist will shrink away from open hostility, the client may use it as a controlling mechanism. Clients tend to respect therapists who genuinely show no negative or fearful reaction in the face of hostility. Equanimity serves a dual purpose. It shows the client that the therapist will not act out, and it models how to respond to hostility. If the hostility continues, it needs to be discussed empathically with the client. If it still continues, termination may be necessary, but this is rare.

Defiance and hostility may present an opportunity to use humor. A therapist can occasionally use self-deprecating humor to place himself or herself on an even status with the client. This is especially helpful with aggressive adolescents who use profane and obscene language. If I can insult myself more severely than the client can, it diminishes the momentum, and, paradoxically garners respect. Of course, the humor must be natural and not strained.

For example, if a client calls me an "ass----," my reply might be "Have you been talking to my friends?" If I am called stupid, my reply might be, "Yeah, and that wouldn't be so bad if I weren't so ugly, too." Another reply to being called stupid is, "I wish I was smart enough to see that." These cannot be canned lines, however. They must be spontaneously delivered in the moment to be fully effective. The purpose is to lessen the client's impression of the therapist as a symbol of authority or as a bundle of predictable responses. Role playing such situations with a supervisor or with another therapist can be extremely helpful along these lines.

It Is More Important to Be Respected Than Liked

Many therapists believe that difficult clients will be more likely to work in therapy if they like their therapists. Although there is evidence to support this (see Orlinsky et al., 1994), it can be a mistake to place too much emphasis on it. If a therapist has a neurotic craving to be liked by clients, the client may only validate and reinforce certain actions by a therapist that lead to being liked but do not lead to client change. It is more important to be respected than liked. If a client respects a therapist, this is a tacit permission for the therapist to operate as a change agent.

Do Not Allow Caring to Interfere With Empathy

Caring and empathy are not the same. In fact, a therapist can show caring toward a client and still cause the client to deteriorate (Lambert, Bergin, & Collins, 1977). For example, when a therapist genuinely cares for the client but lacks empathy and is authoritarian and intrusive, not only is change unlikely, but such attitudes disempower a client. Empathy can also degrade when a therapist is deeply emotionally affected by a client's stories of abuse and tragedy. Therapists can get caught up in feelings of protest, sympathy, protectiveness, and righteous anger toward those who hurt the client, which can interfere with the therapist's ability to empathically see the world from a client's perspective. The therapeutic process can stop at this point if one is not aware.

When You Cannot Focus, You Have Lost Your Locus

When the therapist's thoughts are swirling and feelings and emotions are in turmoil in the presence of a client, the therapist has likely lost the sense of being centered and should seek consultation. This is a danger especially when one works with many difficult clients during the same day or week. A former supervisor taught me that difficulty focusing on a client may be a sign that one has taken on oneself the baggage of clients' unresolved issues, a burden that impairs one's ability to do therapy. I am quite sure there is no research to support this, but this insight helped me at the time. Regardless of why, when one loses focus, it is time to get centered; list the unresolved problems, behaviors, and attitudes of clients that are taking up one's attention; and consciously let them go, one by one.

Therapists Defend Against Clients, Too

There are times when an overworked therapist is so weary from working with difficult clients that he or she might create artificial distance from clients, unconsciously perceiving them as a threat to his or her own sanity or peace of mind. This can be a sign of burnout, or it may result from the fear of becoming somehow "polluted" by the negative attitudes and problems of unsavory clients. An indicator that this may be happening is a reluctance to form a relationship, perhaps coupled with a sense of bitterness, sadness, or helplessness. Several therapists have told me they erect mental walls to maintain their own space that a difficult client cannot touch or violate. The problem with walls is that they also incarcerate therapists, keeping them from making empathic contact with clients. When this kind of distancing occurs, it is time to seek help.

The Discouragement or Disgust You Feel May Not Be Your Own

When working with difficult clients, it is common to feel discouraged, disgusted, or hopeless. Such feelings may actually be an empathic "borrowing" of how that client habitually feels toward himself or herself. To test this, it is sometimes possible to describe to the client the feeling of disgust or discouragement or hopelessness that one is experiencing as a therapist and to inquire whether this is, in fact, what the client is experiencing. It is often accurate to some degree. Clients can sometimes be so surprised by this revelation that trust may be deepened. This is also true of anger and resentment as well. Phrasing is important; one would never tell a client that he or she is disgusting or hopeless.

Be Firm About What Is Tolerable and Acceptable

Some clients have a way of making a therapist feel silly about not being willing to discuss their own personal lives or fantasies, or not being willing to meet outside the office, or not being able to "take a joke." Too many of these clients on one's caseload can eventually cause a therapist to begin to doubt his or her sanity. The only course of action is to be sensitive to one's own sense of propriety, personal space, privacy, and limits. These must be communicated to the client clearly and unhesitatingly for the sake of the change process. It is also important to stay in contact with colleagues or a supervisor to maintain one's own social support system.

Avoid Accusing the Client of Being Defensive

Some therapists directly say to a client, "You are being defensive" or "You are in denial." This might work on some occasions but more often makes clients resentful and recalcitrant. To many difficult clients, such a statement appears to be an accusation. Such "in-your-face" confrontation tactics are outmoded and have been shown to be largely ineffective (Hester & Miller, 1989; W. R. Miller, 1983).

Rather than accuse the client of being defensive, ask the client if he or she does not like someone trying to get inside his or her head. Also, using the term *protective* can be helpful. Saying, "Are you trying to protect yourself by not answering my question?" may be far more to the point. One might also say, "Did you notice how you did not answer my question just then? Do you think it is too much of a hassle to deal with?" This latter question addresses the readiness precursor.

Confrontations Should Be Made Without Rancor or Impatience

Therapists and counselors in some community-based treatment programs I have seen continue to confront clients in a hostile way. Such confrontation, replete with accusations of denial and dishonesty, also are still used in the addictions field. Defenders of this approach have described it to me as "tear 'em down and build 'em up." Unfortunately, the people are ignoring the excellent work on motivational interviewing (Hester & Miller, 1989; W. R. Miller, 1983). Heavy confrontation tactics are a mistake of considerable magnitude made by people who have neglected to resolve their own hostilities and frustrations or who are tormented by their own unresolved issues. Being so tormented, they also torment clients.

Confrontation can be an extremely effective tool when it is done with curiosity, empathy, compassion, serenity, and the intention to help. When done in anger, it can create a power struggle with the client, who may become defiant or hostile or, conversely, submissive and docile, or it may only produce premature termination. Either way, change is not likely. Therapy with difficult clients is not the same as training soldiers or disciplining inmates.

Confrontations Should Be Done With Compassion and Empathy

Confronting with compassion and empathy is hard to do if they are not genuinely felt. It can be extremely difficult to care about some difficult clients, such as those who are cruel or insulting or who make sexist or racist comments. Some difficult clients deny anything, no matter how obvious or plain. Then, when it would be useful to confront such a client, the agitated therapist may feel so much hostility or disgust, he or she is afraid it will be revealed and as a result avoids confronting altogether or does so ineffectively.

Confrontation can be an effective tool if done with care and respect. If a therapist does not honestly like a client and a confrontation is necessary, the therapist should be respectful and courteous to that individual in spite of his or her feelings. Ideally, a therapist would work through any negative feelings in therapy or peer supervision. If this is not possible, a therapist can suspend or bracket those feelings, leaving the mind clear to go ahead with the confrontation, knowing that his or her negative reactions to a client are natural and to some degree expected. Suspending or bracketing negative feelings is a skill that one is well advised to develop. It allows one's natural helping instincts to come to the fore and take over the process. One should never ignore such feelings, but rather suspend them with full awareness of what one is doing.

Hooking and Unhooking

When working with difficult clients, the temptation to confront and challenge can come too soon, and therapists who yield can actually contribute to their clients' uncooperativeness. Before engaging in confrontation, the therapist must thoroughly convince the client that he or she is understood through empathic reflections of meaning and feelings to the point where the client has little choice but to believe the therapist understands. Then and only then can challenges and confrontations be made that will be respected and not dismissed out of hand. Kiesler (1988) called this approach "hooking and unhooking," and it is quite effective with difficult clients.

Warm, Cozy Relationships Can Serve as Detours to Change

The warm feeling that often accompanies a therapeutic relationship, while no doubt therapeutic, is threatened every time a confrontation is made. This threat can cause a therapist to retreat from any confrontation of a client, compromising progress toward change. This is perhaps why a client can keep coming back to a warm, supportive therapist for years but not make any progress toward therapeutic change.

Be Alert to Projective Identifications

Projective identifications is another term that is too vague and loosely defined, but it represents something of great value to therapists. A functional definition of this concept is any feeling produced in a therapist by a client that does not originate with the therapist (Cashdan, 1988). For example, if a client stimulates sexual feelings in a therapist for no apparent reason, it could be the client's projection of sexuality. If a therapist experiences feelings of intimidation by a client, it could be the client's projection of power. If a therapist feels indebted to a client, or as though he or she owes something to a client, it could be a projection of ingratiation. If a therapist is disgusted by a client, it could be a projection of repugnance. All of these reactions can be used in therapy to further empathy with the client through the recognition that this is also how people in this person's environment feel in his or her presence.

Projective identifications can be approached passively or actively. For example, in the case of an intimidating client, one may feel afraid, powerless, or weak. Although it is not a good idea to admit when one is afraid of a client, one can ask, "Do you find that people in your life are scared of you?" A client will often respond to this in the affirmative in some manner. The therapist can then ask how he or she came to be that way. One can also ask if it works for him or her in life, in terms of advantages and disadvantages. In addition, one can find out who the client's models were who were also intimidating. If the client can describe the models, the therapist can re-examine them and ask if identifying with those models was a good idea. Each of these approaches can be fruitful.

Long-Winded Explanations Interfere With the Change Process

Karasu (1992) said it best: "Anything that cannot be said concisely is best not said at all" (p. 150). This is especially true of difficult clients, and even more so with difficult adolescents, whose interest in therapy tends to wane easily (see Hanna, Hanna, & Keys, 1999; Hanna & Hunt, 1999). Packing a lot of meaning into a single sentence is an art form that is seldom appreciated. It gets easier with practice. If a therapist finds himself or herself fumbling for words in an explanation, the verbiage can actually hinder the therapeutic process. For example, instead of a long-winded explanation about drug use to an addicted client, one could say instead, "So you figure you are your own physician and you are prescribing illegal medicine to heal your pain. Am I getting it?" The client will usually correct the therapist with a better description or approximation, leading the conversation in the direction of further awareness and confronting.

Have Empathy for Yourself

Working with difficult clients can make one feel foolish and inept. Margulies (1989) noted that empathy for oneself is an important aspect of mental health and happiness. If one is understanding with and of oneself, it is easier to recover from the inevitable mistakes one makes with difficult clients. This has the added benefit of indirectly serving as modeling for the client as well. No therapist needs a critical, invalidative stream of negative self-talk sabotaging his or her spontaneity in therapy; this can be handled through standard cognitive approaches (see, e.g., Burns, 1980). Seeking therapy of one's own is a good idea if empathy for oneself wanes.

Attend to One's Own Metalog

Like clients, each therapist has a metalog. It is sometimes extremely revealing to listen attentively to the several thought streams that run through one's mind when doing therapy, especially when a therapist is listening to a difficult client tell a story or describe a problem. One thought stream might think the client is being deceptive, while another wants to believe the client. Simultaneously, another reaction could be disgust, yet another sympathy, and still another a desire to console the client. Accompanying all this may be the thought that it may take years for this client to change, while another stream is considering various approaches and strategies that may be of help. Still another stream may be wondering all the while if the current approach is having any beneficial effect. As if this were not enough, the therapist may also be experiencing both approach and avoidance impulses (see Townsend & Busemeyer, 1989) with regard to several aspects of what the client presents.

These reactions can be extremely revealing to a therapist who is unsure where to go with a certain client or what to believe about what he or she says. The more these parallel processes are present in one's mind at a given time, the more concerned the therapist should be about the success of the therapy. Noting all these thought streams may be helpful in the case of difficult clients who are confusing, misleading, or extraordinarily complex. Of course, one must be able to do this while still maintaining active contact in terms of the relationship. It takes some practice, but attending to one's own metalog can be quite helpful.

Closely Monitor Visceral Reactions

That "queasy" feeling in the pit of one's stomach may be communicating something of inestimable value. One may be going along listening and reflecting a client's statements, not suspecting anything amiss at the intellectual level, yet one's "gut" may be churning in a way that says something is wrong. The gut feeling may be a nearly imperceptible tightness in the stomach, or an empty feeling, or another indication of anxiety. It is easy to ignore.

The gut feeling is often a sign that something is going on at the level of one's own metalog that needs to be examined. When the therapist recognizes these feelings, he or she can then suspend them and explore how and why they arose. Often there is much more to such a client than meets the intellectual eye. Perhaps this client is intimidating or threatening in a way that is easy to ignore, and the therapist wants to give him or her the benefit of the doubt. On the other hand, perhaps the therapist is feeling nervous, self-conscious, or worried or wants to escape. Or it could be a projective identification on the part of the client. Whatever the case, monitoring and attending to gut reactions reap rewards in terms of greater learning and insight.

Attend to Differences in Socioeconomic Status

Sometimes clients make sarcastic jokes—thinly veiling bitterness, resentment, or contempt—about the gap in socioeconomic status between client and therapist. Clients with low socioeconomic status can ridicule well-dressed, "proper" therapists, just as clients from higher classes can look down on therapists with lower socioeconomic status (see Sennett & Cobb, 1972). Therapists may also be bothered by the gap, even if they do not show it in any outward way. Such differences can be part of the metalog. It is sometimes helpful in relationship building to put such differences on the table and talk about them openly to see if they are interfering with forming a therapeutic relationship.

Avoid Power Struggles

Many difficult clients expect a power struggle with a therapist, just as they would with any person who has a potential influence on their lives. A way to avoid power struggles is to call or identify any agenda or "game" the client is playing, whether it involve sex, intimidation, or simple evasiveness. To win the struggle, the client must keep his or her game a secret. For the change process to occur, the therapist must bring the game into the open and call it faster than the client can reset it. Empathy is key and is indispensable in identifying the client's power agenda. Calling the game is superior to winning the struggle, especially when the client admits to the game being called.

I once worked as a consultant with a 16-year-old girl who had steadfastly refused to disclose anything for more than 90 days in an agency for adolescent criminal offenders. The director of the agency was concerned that she had made no change at all. In a meeting, the therapy team described her to me as a "classic borderline." When I met with her, I told her that she must be remarkably intelligent and powerful to be able to resist all the highly educated people with master's and doctoral degrees in that agency. I told her it was about time someone gave her credit for being so smart. "You have won," I told her. "You have proved that you can stop these people from ever affecting your life." I then told her she was so smart that she might be outsmarting herself by not letting these people help her. That acknowledgement was all she needed, and her change process began with the knowing smile she radiated, in spite of herself.

Power-seeking clients will sometimes respond to an appeal to the human need for admiration. A therapist could say, "From what you have told me, I am willing to bet you have learned some pretty remarkable lessons about life and people. Do you ever share any of that knowledge? I'll bet there is a lot I could learn from you." A simple rule: Treat a client who does not change not as a failure but as an opportunity for valuable learning. There are times when it is helpful to inform a client that he or she is functioning as a teacher. This approach can produce a shift in how the client regards the therapist in a way that reduces power struggles and promotes the genuineness of the relationship.

Some therapists feel a need to be in continuous control of a session and feel threatened by a client who rebels against that control (see Herron & Rouslin, 1982). In many cases, if the therapist was not enforcing the control, then the client would not be so likely to rebel against it, creating a power struggle. It is sometimes helpful to reverse the interaction by first getting a rebellious client to admit he or she hates being told what to do, even by a therapist. I have done role reversals along these lines with defiant teenagers and have told them to "boss me around for a while," within reason, of course. It was helpful for both client and therapist. If done in a group, it can be quite entertaining.

Clients Are Often Disliked Because They Do Not Change

In consulting and supervision, therapists reveal that they simply dislike certain clients. Exploring this issue reveals that the client will not respond to the therapist's interventions and strategies or attempts at forming a relationship. The client is a threat to the therapist's self-esteem; if the client does not change, then the therapist fears he or she is ineffective. If the therapist believes himself or herself to be ineffective, then self-esteem becomes diminished. From that point forward, the client becomes a symbol of the therapist's low self-esteem.

A Client Who Is Irritating or Bothersome Functions as a Teacher

Storr (1989) said that what we most dislike in other people is something we have not accepted in ourselves. He recommended therapy for the purpose of doing away with these dislikes, which he referred to as *prejudices*. From a different perspective, a client who evokes such strong reactions of dislike or criticism from a therapist also functions as the therapist's teacher. Such situations provide a rare and wonderful opportunity for therapists to learn more about their own issues and deeper self. It is an added benefit of therapy that is seldom mentioned, an aspect that enhances one's own personal growth.

Ask Therapy Veterans How They Have Managed to Defeat Therapists

Occasionally, a therapist will run into a client with a history of confounding and defeating therapists. Some even seem to have made it a hobby. Many enjoy being so complex and mysterious that no one can understand or reach them. In a convoluted twist, many clients believe that to be understood is to be humiliated. I have directly asked therapy veterans how they managed to foil the attempts of so many intelligent people. I praise their intelligence and credit them for a job successfully accomplished. It can be helpful to reframe their "failure" as a client as a "success" in defeating a therapist, which should be noted as a skill born of intelligence, craftiness, or shrewdness.

I also tell them that they will, no doubt, defeat me as well. I make no pretense about being better than any other therapist. I tell them I just want to learn from them, if they do not mind teaching me, how to defeat therapists. It might even help to suggest the client could probably give lectures on therapy if they were so inclined. But I also point out they really haven't tried therapy yet at all, and that maybe they could give it a try for the first time. If the client can be persuaded to teach his or her skills, a therapeutic window may open. It often turns out that many of these clients are secretly convinced that they are empty inside, devoid of soul or self. If a therapist, or anyone, were to discover their true nature, it would result in a kind of mortal disintegration.

CONCLUSION

Kottler (1992) provided six techniques that are of great help in dealing with therapist interference. When no progress is being made in working with a difficult client, therapists can easily and readily do the following exercises:

1. List what one is doing to exacerbate the situation.
2. List the therapist's "buttons" that are being pushed by the client.
3. List the people from the therapist's past with behaviors similar to the client.
4. List the ways the therapist's impatience is acted out.
5. List the therapist's expectations of the client and if they are being met.
6. List the therapist's needs that are not being met by the client.

8

MULTICULTURAL AND GENDER CONSIDERATIONS: A NEW ADAPTATION OF COGNITIVE THERAPY AND A FRAMEWORK FOR EMPOWERMENT

I have sometimes heard the following curious statement made by well-intended therapists: "When I look into someone's eyes, I don't see color." Although admirable on the surface, the statement masks many deeper issues that are in great need of attention. To people of color, such "color-blind" people may be kind and caring enough but do not understand life from the perspective of someone who has suffered from racial discrimination (Close, 1997). In fact, many African Americans have told me that this statement is insulting. A color-blind therapist probably does not possess the necessary empathy to be effective with people of oppressed groups.

The past decade has seen a remarkable increase in awareness of the need for multicultural understanding in counseling and psychotherapy. It is widely accepted that clients from cultures different from those of their therapists need to be understood from their own unique perspectives. This is a function of empathy, although it takes into account an added dimension of cultural understanding that can be gained by studying the customs and beliefs of various cultures.

However, there is another, pervasive dimension of culture and gender that must be acknowledged in practice: the phenomenon of oppression. If not for oppression, gender and cultural issues would have far less significance and controversy. Oppression has much to do with the situations and difficulties of many difficult clients.

THE NATURE OF OPPRESSION

Most of the difficult clients encountered in therapy have had difficult lives, often filled with pain and suffering inflicted on them by others. Many difficult clients cause similar pain and suffering to those around them, continuing a cycle of anguish and misfortune. That many of these people's problems are a result of being oppressed by an individual or group is a relatively new perspective on therapy and psychopathology with important implications for therapy (Lord & Dufort, 1996). Jacobs (1994) pointed out that oppression is the primary source of all psychopathology that does not have its basis in disease or genetics. *Oppression* is defined as the abuse of power at the expense of the well-being of others. It occurs through two modalities, force and deprivation (Hanna, Talley, & Guindon, 2000). Both modalities negatively affect the precursors of change.

Oppression by Force

Oppression by force, coercion, or duress is the act of imposing an object, label, role, experience, or set of living conditions on another or others that is unwanted, brings needless pain, or detracts from physical or psychological well-being. An imposed object, in the context of oppression, can be a bullet, a bomb, shackles, a bludgeon, a fist, a penis, unhealthy food, or abusive messages designed to degrade or reduce the self-determination of the person in question. Other examples of oppression by force can be coerced labor, enforced religion, degrading jobs, and negative media images and messages that foster distorted, negative beliefs.

Oppression by Deprivation

Oppression also includes depriving another or others of an object, role, experience, or set of living conditions that is desirable and conducive to physical or psychological well-being. It also includes the deprivation of respect, dignity, or loved ones. Neglect is another form of oppression by deprivation; essentials such as love, social support, or parental bonding can be deprived, as well as the basic needs of food, shelter, or clothing. Objects deprived can be a house, a plot of land in a desirable neighborhood, various forms of wealth, or gainful employment. Oppression can deprive one of one's children, parents, friends, freedom, or even one's childhood. Religious practice can also be deprived, as was the case from 1890 to 1940 when the United States banned certain practices of the Sioux tribes (Brown, 1970).

Roles and labels can be both imposed and deprived. For example, people can be deprived of jobs that are desirable and forced to take those that are limited in range and pay because of the dominant majority's insistence on the inferiority of the person's culture, gender, or sexual preference.

These modalities are not mutually exclusive. Throughout history they have commonly occurred in combination or in tandem. If one examines the wide range of problems encountered in psychotherapy from this perspective, it quickly becomes apparent that oppression is an active ingredient in the formation of psychological and emotional problems. But there is a curious and widely overlooked benefit that comes with it as well, and this benefit has remarkable implications for cognitive therapy and empowerment with difficult clients.

THE POWER OF PERCEPTION

In 1887, Lord Acton offered an often-quoted observation: "Power tends to corrupt and absolute power corrupts absolutely." Because oppression is commonly defined as the misuse of power, those who are denied power must nevertheless cope somehow in order to survive. The urge toward survival begins by developing a greater degree of perception of the oppressor as a necessary survival mechanism (J. B. Miller, 1986). Perception has to do with cognizance, recognition, or noticing, closely related to the awareness precursor. In this context, it is also related to what Sternberg (1990) called "perspicacity," that aspect of wisdom that is the ability to see beyond appearances, to "see through" situations, or to "read between the lines." Although oppressed people are largely unaware of any hidden benefit, it is within this dynamic that we find the mechanism of empowerment. This mechanism operates in members of oppressed groups and in oppressed people who have been abused by an individual.

The phenomenon is transcultural. I have directly observed and interacted with members of many culturally oppressed groups, such as the Tamils of Sri Lanka, the Uighurs of northwest China, the untouchables of India, and the Bataks of Sumatra in Indonesia (Hanna, 1998), and also have interviewed dozens of African Americans at all levels of education and socioeconomic status. In nearly all cases, members of the oppressed groups were able to make accurate, detailed observations about the behavior and attitudes of their oppressors. Conversely, members of the oppressive groups described members of subordinate groups to me in ways that justified their own possession and superiority. In both remote and well-traveled parts of the world, I heard the usual stereotypes; the subordinate groups were called "lazy," "dirty," and "stupid" and accused of not caring about their children. Even a cursory examination of descriptions of oppressors by members of oppressed groups reveals remarkable perception. For example, the writings of Frederick Douglass (1855) or Viktor Frankl (1984) are far more detailed and accurate than any of the bankrupt accounts and descriptions by Nazis and slaveowners.

Solomon Northup (1853/1968) was a free African American who was kidnapped from New York state and sold into slavery in Louisiana. He had no education and no status, but he was highly intelligent and wise. The following clinical analysis of slaveowners was worthy of any of the systems thinkers of the next 15 decades:

> It is not the fault of the slaveholder that he is cruel, so much as it is the fault of the system under which he lives. He cannot withstand the influence of habit and associations that surround him. Taught from earliest childhood, by all that he sees and hears, that the rod is for the slave's back, he will not be apt to change his opinions in maturer years. (pp. 157–158)

During the years of Northup's bondage, he observed how being an oppressor hardens a person, turning men and women alike into callous and cold beings:

> The existence of Slavery in its most cruel form . . . has a tendency to brutalize the humane and finer feelings of their [the slaveholders'] nature. Daily witnesses of human suffering—listening to the agonizing screeches of the slave—beholding him writhing beneath the merciless lash—bitten and torn by dogs—dying without attention, and buried without shroud or coffin—it cannot otherwise be expected, than that they should become brutified and reckless of human life. (p. 157)

Whether within cultures or between cultures or among individuals of the same or differing cultures, this phenomenon of perception has the paradoxical and altogether remarkable advantage of keeping the oppressed person or group alive and aware. It is unfortunate that the price is pain and suffering. In contrast, the oppressive group or person becomes progressively more oblivious, unempathic, and unaware of the oppressed, as well as of his or her own psychological state. Power corrupts, whether it is abused in the context of a country, culture, workplace, family, or marriage. What is almost never mentioned is that being deprived of power often awakens perception in many people (J. B. Miller, 1986), and if one learns from the experience, character tends to awaken as well. It seems that when a person is rejected from a group or excluded from its benefits, it inspires that person to notice and study the oppressive group. This seems to be the case with overweight people, alienated teenagers, gay men and lesbians, people of color, and people with disabilities. They can be highly perceptive of therapists as well.

A body of research literature on a phenomenon called *depressive realism* sheds indirect light on this topic (Alloy & Abramson, 1979). Alloy and Abramson (1988), in their review of the literature, found that depressed people may be more sad but are often more accurate in their perceptions than are nondepressed people. This led them to conclude that depressed people more often have accurate judgments, whereas nondepressed people are likely to err in the direction of being overly, and unrealistically, optimistic. In this way, nondepressed people are often more "irrational" in their assessments than those who are depressed.

In a review of 14 studies on depressive realism by Alloy, Albright, Abramson, and Dykman (1990), "eight found that the severely depressed subjects' perceptions and judgments were completely unbiased or accurate and another four found severe depressives' inferences to be accurate for some of the experimental tasks or conditions" (p. 73). Unfortunately, this same body of research seems to indicate that depressed people are not so capable of assessing themselves. It is there that the perception becomes confused.

Being depressed and oppressed is not exactly the same, of course. Many oppressed people are not depressed. Nevertheless, depressed people often are so because of real and genuine oppression. In this light, their accurate perception can be reframed in therapy as a strength, not only in perceiving their current situation, but as a way out of it as well. Thus, oppressed people need not be looked on as helpless victims. Although they have experienced hardship, the admirable ability of perception emerges in so many, even though they may not be aware of it. Although their lives have been ruled by harsh realities, their therapeutic ticket is the raw and penetrating perception that develops out of that painful experience. Conversely, the road to healing for oppressors is through recovering the empathy and awareness lost through abuse of power, with the goal of bringing them out of the obliviousness that develops as a result of their corruption.

COGNITIVE THERAPY FOR OPPRESSED CLIENTS

Many difficult clients seem to have difficulty isolating and identifying distorted cognitions or beliefs. However, there is an alternative that may make it easier for some clients who have been oppressed. It involves using clients' perception to identify the beliefs of those who have hurt them and forced dysfunctional beliefs on them. Because of oppressed people's perceptive capabilities, they may be better able to identify the oppressors' irrational beliefs and messages of their oppressors, which they consequently absorbed. This approach is based on Heidegger's (1927/1962) classic descriptions of how a person loses his or her authenticity.

One of the few criticisms of cognitive therapy is its lack of recognition of environmental or interpersonal factors (Coyne, 1989). From the perspective of oppression, an oppressed person's negative beliefs are heavily influenced by the oppressor, whether a group or an individual. Part of this oppression is a series of beliefs that the oppressor "inflicts" on the victim, in addition to emotional or physical pain. For example, the belief that one is stupid, worthless, incompetent, or unlovable can be seen as inflicted rather than formed. Typically, the standard cognitive approach would be to help a client identify their irrational or dysfunctional beliefs as though he or she generated these beliefs. In the context of oppression, this is a well-intended form of blaming the victim. The client is all too often not the origin of these beliefs; the oppressor is. The client's mistake is to agree with the beliefs that were inflicted or forced on him or her, creating the typically negative array of feelings and dysfunctional behaviors. The goal is to end the agreement and replace the dysfunctional beliefs with those that are accurate and real.

If a client is having difficulty identifying dysfunctional beliefs, the therapist can try a cognitive approach that loosely consists of four steps. Before taking these four steps, the therapist must help the client identify the oppressive person or people in his or her life.

Following identification of the oppressor and oppressive beliefs, the first step is to ask the client, "What did [the oppressive group or person] want you to believe about yourself?" For example, if a man was oppressed by his father, his father may have given him beliefs that he was a mistake or that he was worthless or ugly. African Americans could identify the dominant group as the White society that passed on messages that Black people are stupid, ugly, lazy, or incompetent. Specific people, such as teachers, neighbors, or employers, can be cited as oppressors as well.

Women are inundated with messages of their inferiority (Daly, 1992), especially with regard to beauty and thinness, from the time of puberty and earlier. Sexually abused women can also benefit from this approach. With women, the focus would be on listing dysfunctional beliefs received from men, boys, and the media, citing actual sources when possible, such as specific movies, musical groups, brothers, or fathers. For example, when she was asked, a severely battered woman once listed these beliefs as those that her abusive husband forced on her:

- "I am stupid."
- "I am immoral."
- "I am a terrible mother."
- "I am fat and ugly."
- "I cannot make it without him."
- "I am a chronic liar."

She was easily able to recognize how much she had agreed with the beliefs and how he wanted her, and in fact needed her, to believe all these things so that she would not leave him. It is relatively easy for perceptive clients to spot the beliefs and tactics of others, but more difficult when those beliefs are treated as uniquely their own.

The therapist can help clients identify oppressive beliefs inflicted by others. If a lesbian, for example, were asked to list the beliefs forced on her by a rigidly heterosexual society, it is possible that she might omit certain beliefs, such as "All gays are immoral." The therapist could help by submitting that belief for the client's verification, and then see if she agreed with it and to what extent. Alternatively, if a woman reports a negative belief about herself, she can be asked if there was a person or group in her life who wanted her to believe it. It may turn out that the belief was inflicted on her by boys or men, and that her only mistake was agreeing with something that was false. Such sources are usually easy to discredit.

After isolating the beliefs that were enforced, inflicted, or otherwise fed to the client, the second step is to ask the client how much he or she agreed with the message. A little? A lot? It might be rated on a scale from 1 to 10, with 10 being the most that one could ever believe anything and 1 being just a tiny bit. The belief will have its most damaging effect, of course, if the client still heavily agrees with it. At this point, one examines the consequences of agreeing with the belief and the purpose for which the oppressor wanted or demanded the agreement. For example, a woman's agreement with the negative belief, "I am not attractive because I am not skinny," serves the purpose of always having her doubt herself and never feeling worthy enough to challenge her husband on possible sexual manipulations or power schemes. Part of this step is also to examine how one feels and acts as a result of agreeing with this belief.

The third step involves the client's consciously and actively terminating his or her agreement with any or all of these enforced beliefs. It is best to disagree with the least damaging beliefs first. If the client does not readily see the benefit of terminating agreement, the therapist can ask that he or she try it just as an experiment to see how the act of disagreeing with the belief feels. The Jamesian device (see chapter 14) can also be used here to determine the truth or falsehood of an enforced belief. This approach is not about clients cutting themselves off from or ending all ties with the oppressor; that is another decision entirely.

The fourth step comes if or when the belief is not readily or easily terminated. It can also occur after the second step. It consists of disputing the dysfunctional belief in standard cognitive therapy fashion. Once the harmful or dysfunctional aspects of the belief are revealed through disputation, the client can then go ahead and disagree with it and replace it with more accurate beliefs or self-talk. This approach can be easily adapted to group therapy.

Empowerment Through Perception

I have found a twist on cognitive therapy to be a highly useful approach to empowering clients: It consists of pointing out, and clients realizing, that they possess a hard-won and valuable ability. This acknowledgment does much to stimulate the precursor of hope. The aim is to get a client to describe the oppressive group or person. The therapist should get as many details as possible. Abused women, for example, typically can give highly descriptive accounts of the batterer's triggers, behaviors, attitudes, and emotions, complete with predictions of when and under what circumstances the abuse will occur. They seldom see any evidence of this being a skill, however. When told that this same perceptive ability can be used to read people in a variety of settings, from the workplace to romantic relationships, they are often surprised to learn that they possess a valuable ability. The same is true for children and adolescents who have been sexually or physically abused.

Empowerment From the Gender Perspective

I have run groups for teenage girls with gender as the main theme. The themes of such groups are guided by such questions as, "How do men want women to be, or think, or behave?" These are designed to further refine and clarify their perception. Other fruitful questions for groups for women and girls are the following:

- "What kinds of behavior by women get rewarded in this society?"
- "How do men and society treat women who are considered overweight?"
- "How do men treat women who are not considered 'feminine'?"
- "How are women's bodies portrayed in magazines and movies?"
- "What does a man gain from having a woman with low self-esteem?"
- "Do any men want a woman to be independent or powerful?"
- "Why are women more often depressed than men?"
- "What kind of partner is a man who has little or no empathy?"
- "What kind of man is likely to physically abuse women or girls?"
- "How do women benefit, or suffer from, being dependent on men?"

To survive in this society, girls and women become highly adept at answering such questions, even if they do not like the answers (see Greenspan, 1983; Laidlaw & Malmo, 1990). Part of the discussion of such questions can be aimed at isolating the beliefs inflicted and then terminating agreement.

Once again, it is the client's perception that needs to be validated. It is not always perfectly accurate, of course, and like any skill, that perception often needs to be honed. In any case, the approach is based on the idea that low self-esteem in women can be due as much to mistaken agreement as faulty thinking. Women need not be blamed for having negative beliefs about self; it is often a result of a patriarchal mindset.

Empowerment From a Multicultural Perspective

The effective multicultural therapist will not fail to recognize the depth of tension, anger, and resentment felt by African Americans, Native Americans, Asian Americans, and Latinos toward the dominant White society. It has been my experience that these clients will want a therapist who can empathize with this anger and resentment. They will be disappointed if the therapist defends or makes excuses for White society. Just as in any client, it is the therapist's duty to validate feelings and perceptions and not to discourage the anger so many feel. It all begins with seeing the dominant culture from the client's perspective. The quality of the therapeutic relationship hangs in the balance.

What can therapists do with the anger that oppressed people feel? The key is not to invalidate the anger, but to help clients express it, manage it, and redirect it toward worthy goals, such as education and community involvement. In groups that I have run with African American adolescents, I have often made anger at White society a focus in many sessions. In some cases, it is helpful to suggest that the clients make their anger their "friend," so as to become acquainted with it and use it to supply energy toward positive goals. However, this anger is usually of such a destructive nature that only acknowledging it, validating it, and reflecting its intensity and meaning can take oppressed clients beyond it. Anger management strategies, in my estimation, risk failure with oppressed groups when they do not acknowledge that oppression causes justifiable anger.

Finding hope and social support for oppressed clients is also very important. Therapists can tell stories of, and help clients connect with, people who have escaped difficult conditions, such as gang involvement, and achieved a degree of happiness or fulfillment. They can also link clients directly with community resources or organizations that offer help to people in need. Churches often perform this function.

The following questions can be discussed, and then the answers disagreed with or disputed, in therapy sessions. At the least, these questions, even if pursued only briefly, can be helpful in relationship building.

- "What beliefs does the dominant society have about the client's group?"
- "How does the dominant society hold its control over people of color?"
- "How does the dominant society want people of color to be, think, and behave?"

- "What messages about the client's group are in movies and television?"
- "How are Black males treated in this society?"
- "How are people with heavy accents (Black or otherwise) treated?"
- "What behaviors by the client's group are rewarded in this society?"
- "What attitudes by the client's group are rewarded in this society?"

The purpose of this approach is not to build resentment or fan the flames of anger, but to produce a sense of liberation (see Hanna et al., 2000) from negative beliefs about self and one's group. This liberation aids the person in implementing the precursors, the bulk of which are inhibited by the negative messages of racism and discrimination. To merely adjust or adapt to a society that does not work toward the best interests of some of its members is to reduce the integrity of that client. The goal of liberation releases a person to transcend cultural differences rather than trade one culture for another. Clients who are members of more than one oppressed culture, such as lesbians or African American women, are doubly oppressed.

Mixed Oppression

A client can be oppressed in one context and an oppressor in another. For example, a woman may be oppressed at the workplace but be abusing her children at home. In these not uncommon cases, the client needs to be helped to restore empathy for those he or she oppresses and to be liberated from his or her oppressors through the cognitive approach described above.

Beliefs that are conducive to the abuse of others can be agreed with just as easily as the beliefs inflicted on the abused. This occurred among the children in Mao's Red Guard during the Cultural Revolution in China and among so many German people during Hitler's regime. In this same way, boys come to believe that women are sex objects to be abused and deceived; heterosexuals believe that gays are immoral; and whole societies become convinced that minority groups are dirty, lazy, stupid, and do not care about their children. To be immersed in a culture is to be immersed in its context, and that context, at its core, is made up of beliefs (Scharfstein, 1989). Liberation is the process of being freed from limiting beliefs.

Avoid "Benign Stereotyping"

There is considerable variation in the attitudes of members of oppressed groups toward their oppressors. Some may not have experienced the intensity of oppression that other members of their groups have. Assuming that all Latino Americans, for example, have had the same experiences or attitudes is a mistake and could be called "benign stereotyping." As an issue, racism may not be of the same magnitude for all clients from oppressed groups.

SUSPEND EUROPEAN AMERICAN ASSUMPTIONS

In terms of therapist interference (see chapter 7), certain assumptions commonly made by White, middle-class therapists can impede the progress of the relationship and therapy (Cullare, 1996). Examples of such assumptions are "America is the land of opportunity" with "freedom and justice for all," and "America is the greatest country in the world." To an African American who is even dimly aware of the history of oppression of his or her people in the United States, there are many both subtle and overtly racist aspects of such assumptions that go unnoticed by members of the dominant group (see Asante, 1987; hooks, 1995).

Evidence that such assumptions have real consequences is the fact that dozens of African American and Latino teenagers kill each other in each of the major cities in America every year, but what gets the headlines is when White kids do the same thing in schools in rural or suburban areas (see Hanna et al., 2000). To clients of color, this is evidence of racist thinking, and it is indeed. But it is also more than that; it is simple insensitivity and lack of empathy for teenagers of color. I daresay that if White teenagers were killing each other in the same numbers in cities like New York, Baltimore, Miami, and Los Angeles, federal, city, and state governments would be spending billions of dollars to alleviate the problem.

Many difficult issues are still unresolved among oppressed groups. Rape, for instance, although condemned by all, is seldom acknowledged as having been institutionalized during slavery, when Black women were legally and routinely raped (Genovese, 1974; McLaurin, 1991). This has tremendous implications for African American female clients. It helps to bear in mind that slavery is not dead but is alive and well in the hearts and minds of African Americans and Whites who have yet to achieve closure with this issue (Akbar, 1984), and it is carried forward through what systems thinkers call *multigenerational transmission*. A similar term, *historical trauma*, has been used in discussing the Holocaust, slavery, and the many massacres that Native Americans suffered at the hands of U.S. government soldiers. The therapist who can connect with these and similar issues in members of oppressed groups will form relationships both faster and deeper. And carefully mixing humor with empathy and understanding cannot be overestimated.

IV

CLINICAL APPLICATIONS: IMPLEMENTING AND ENHANCING THE PRECURSORS

9

INSTILLING A SENSE OF NECESSITY

This chapter begins the discussion of techniques and strategies for implementing each of the seven precursors. These therapy techniques will work on some clients some of the time, but they will not work with all clients all of the time. They also will not work with the same client at all times. It is important that therapists not be bound by a manual or formula when working with difficult clients. The therapist's spontaneity is crucial. One's therapeutic toolbox should be filled with options and ready for a wide variety of clients and situations.

Knowing as many approaches as possible is optimum, as is being able to deliver them with timing, finesse, wisdom, and the proper amount of indifference or enthusiasm, according to the needs and dictates of the moment. Of course, any and all reasonable techniques from the major psychotherapy theories are called for if and when they can be of service to a client.

CLIENTS WITH LITTLE SENSE OF NECESSITY

Some therapists like to set goals for therapy with a client in the first or second session. The general wisdom for setting these goals is that both the client and the therapist agree on their worthiness and importance. Unfortunately, without a sense of necessity, goal setting is not likely to have its desired effect. In fact, it may be premature. Any goals initially set with a difficult client may not be genuine or realistic to that client. He or she may just be going through the motions. Perhaps a more fruitful approach in the beginning stages of therapy is to instill a sense of necessity to at least get the person motivated in the general direction of change. Among the tremendously wide range of styles and patterns of difficult clients, a considerable number are low in this precursor.

There is also a wide variation of styles within and among clients who are low in this precursor. Many are indifferent. Some believe that the only real necessity is to show up for therapy, and once they get there a sense of tedium takes over as they wait for the therapist to change their lives as though with a magic wand. In other cases, a person has been court-ordered into counseling because of an alcohol or drug problem or spouse abuse or similar offense. These clients are often compliant because of their desire to graduate from treatment programs but have little or no sense of necessity for change. Other clients claim they neither care what the problem is nor believe that anything needs to be done about it, whatever it may be.

People who have experienced abuse and suffering often equate it with change that is negative and destructive. They may unconsciously associate the prospect of any kind of change, positive or negative, with that same pain. They have had enough of change and will not consider it worthy of pursuit, positive or negative. They express no desire for change. Others feel they are undeserving of anything better in their lives. They may be filled with guilt or regret about things they have done. They may hold core beliefs that consider that if they got better they could be dangerous to loved ones or others around them, and the only solution is to stay inhibited and miserable, and innocuous. It is twisted proof of their goodness and worthiness.

Other clients appear uninterested in change simply because they have not envisioned what the benefits of it might be. These clients often have low levels of the hope precursor. They may be so dejected and discouraged with life that they hold core beliefs that any interest shown in positive change merely sets them up for more disappointment. They have "learned" that any prospect of change is threatening and that familiar misery is better than strange change.

A variety of techniques, strategies, and approaches can be derived from these possible scenarios. The remainder of this chapter will be devoted to listing them. To apply these techniques, the therapeutic relationship must be viable and functioning and the therapist must not be engaging in any interference.

RATE THE NECESSITY FOR CHANGE FROM 1 TO 10

Once a behavior or feeling that needs change is decided on, the therapist can ask the client in a straightforward, simple, and direct fashion where on a scale from 1 to 10, with 10 representing the most important and urgent thing in one's life and 1 the least important, he or she would rate the importance of personal change or solving the presenting problem. The response will indicate the level of urgency the client feels with regard to the problem. This quick, simple rating is helpful in determining how important therapy is to the client and provides a clue to his or her degree of motivation. If someone else says the client has a problem—for example, a judge or a spouse—he or she should rate the problem in the same way.

If the client gives a low rating, which is to be expected, the therapist can ask him or her what it would take to get the rating up to, say, 7 on the scale. Do not imply that it should be 7; only ask what would have to happen to get it there. Answers to this question might be, "If I knew I was hurting someone" or "If I thought I would get in trouble." Such answers provide insights into what motivates the client and what he or she considers important. The next step is to connect the problem to those evaluations of importance, so as to increase the level of necessity.

FIND OUT IF CHANGE IS IMPORTANT TO THE CLIENT

For some clients, rating something on a scale of 1 to 10 is not particularly interesting or appealing. The problem may seem too vague, or the person may blame someone else for causing the problem or issue and want the blamed person to solve it. Rating may also seem too much like a game the therapist is making him or her play, and the client may not be interested in what looks like jumping through a hoop.

If the client is involuntary or has no presenting problem or issue, it can help for the therapist to suggest a few possible examples of changes to determine the kinds of change in which a client may be interested. These suggestions can be as mundane as getting in better physical shape to as abstract as being better able to solve problems or make friends. Once a client hints at a change that might be desirable, the therapist can ask if it would be nice to have that particular change actually happen. If a change is seen as desirable, the therapist can ask if it is a little important, highly important, or urgent. This is a more casual alternative to the 10-point scale and usually takes little time. In any case, therapy should be aligned to or associated with being able to help bring about the desired change.

FIND SOMETHING IMPORTANT TO THE CLIENT AND ALIGN IT WITH THERAPY

For some clients, going after direct change is still asking too much. In these cases, it is better to simply find out what is important to a client in their overall worldview. Reflecting meanings can help here (see chapter 6). The therapist can then instill a sense of necessity by aligning to therapy whatever is most important.

The Story of Carl

For example, Carl was a difficult client who was suspicious of therapy and lacking in verbal and articulation skills. He sat with his arms crossed and slouched far back in his chair. Carl was 36 years old and had two children with his wife, Ginger. He had worked in an automobile textile factory for 21 years. He claimed to have problems with his marriage. It was clear for the first half hour of the first session that Carl was rigid and unbending in his thinking and convinced he did not have a problem. He was especially low in the necessity and willingness precursors. The dialog begins with addressing the metalog.

Therapist: Tell me if I'm wrong, but we have been talking for a while now, and it seems you don't care much for any of this therapy stuff?
Client: Yeah, you're right about that.
Therapist: I see. So here we are, doing something that you really don't give a damn about, and it's all supposed to be about you anyway. That must be a pretty strange position to be in.
Client: Right again. No offense, but this doesn't interest me much.
Therapist: Yeah . . . Let me get this straight. You originally said you are here to save your marriage, but really you're just here because your wife demanded it. You really don't expect anything to actually happen.
Client: Well, I guess. She said that I really needed it, and here I am talking to you.
Therapist: But you really don't expect much to change.
Client (looking at the therapist intently but briefly): To be honest, no, I don't.
Therapist: So as far as you see it, you think you are pretty much OK.
Client: Yeah. I mean, I ain't perfect, but she makes a big deal about lots of things that ain't important.
Therapist: Like what?
Client: Like I said, it ain't important.
Therapist: You don't feel like talking about it.
Client: You got it. *(Adds a smug smile.)*
Therapist: OK. I get the message. But it's part of my job to ask questions. And we have to fill up the time somehow. Do you mind if I ask you a question now and then? You obviously know you don't have to answer anything if you don't feel like it.
Client (with a wave of his hand): Go ahead, I don't give a sh--.
Therapist: You seem to be a guy who is pretty sure of himself. There must be something wrong in your life, or you wouldn't be here talking to somebody like me. I have to think that if you didn't care about your marriage, you wouldn't be here at all. Am I wrong?
Client: No. You ain't wrong there.
Therapist: So the marriage is important to you. *(Client nods.)* My guess is, you think your wife is the one with the problems, and that she's the one that should be here.
Client: Yep.
Therapist: OK. But before we get into all that, can I ask you a question, Carl? *(Client nods.)* How important is it for you to save your marriage? A little? A lot? Give me an idea.

Client: I guess it's pretty important. I don't want to get divorced. I don't want to go through all that bullsh-- again.
Therapist: So you have done it before, and it was pretty rough.
Client: Yeah.
Therapist: Carl, I will make you a deal. Tell me what you think. You and I will work on saving your marriage. I can see you went through a pretty rough time before, and you don't want to get divorced again. I might be able to help. Is it worth giving it a shot?
Client (nodding slowly and deliberately): OK.

Carl's interest was now sparked and, with it, an alignment of purposes—his to the therapist's and the therapist's to his. What was important to him was now directly connected to and aligned with therapy.

The Story of Nick

Another example of this approach was in the case of Nick, a 22-year-old client who said that obtaining sex was the most important thing in his life. He'd had a few relationships and dozens of one-night stands and said that sex made him feel "great." He was in therapy because of a problem with alcohol but was not interested in working on that at all, even though it was recommended by his employer. When asked if he ever felt empty after any of those one-night stands, Nick genuinely and openly laughed at the therapist. From his perspective, he had good reason. He was already so empty that sex was one of the few things that could occupy the void in his life. In his narcissism and lack of empathy, he was aware of little else other than his own needs.

Cautiously, the therapist advanced the idea that therapy could help him understand women better. For the first time, his interest was kindled. He had no idea, of course, that the therapist's intent was to help him gain understanding through acquiring empathy for women as opposed to exploiting them. He eventually admitted that many women thought he was, in his words, "a jerk," and the therapist helped him to see why. This single inroad led to working on many of Nick's issues, including his alcohol abuse.

ADDRESSING AND USING SUBPERSONALITIES

In cases of a trace or nonexistent sense of necessity, a client might deny any need to work on a problem and display outright apathy about resolving it. If a therapist were to point out that a particular problem or situation was negatively affecting his or her life, he or she might shrug and say, "So what?" A classic problem in psychotherapy is how to motivate such a client.

An approach that is often successful in motivating indifferent and apathetic clients has to do with addressing and using subpersonalities. This approach is based on some century-old ideas in psychotherapy that have again become popular. The approach assumes that the human personality is made up of many separate parts, each containing different attitudes, purposes, and interests. It is not at all the same as multiple personality or dissociative identity disorder. This phenomenon has been described in various ways and can be found in the writings of Jung (1934/1969), Assagioli (1965), and James (1890/1981), and more recently in Goulding and Schwartz (1995), Ornstein (1986), Rowan (1990), Puhakka and Hanna (1988), and Schwartz (1995). One of the most effective ways of dealing with apathy is to acknowledge it, fully accepting its presence. This helps build empathy and avoid power struggles. From there, using a "subpersonality" can be helpful. The following story illustrates the technique.

Tracey was a slim, attractive, 17-year-old young woman who displayed a majority of the characteristics of borderline personality disorder. She engaged in self-mutilation (cutting and scratching designs into her wrists and forearms with various sharp implements) and reported that it made her feel better. She often stated that life was too depressing to be worth living. She had a history of sexual abuse perpetrated by an uncle and was promiscuous with men and boys who were clearly interested only in using her. She also regularly abused drugs and alcohol and occasionally engaged in binging and purging. She was extremely vigilant for the slightest sign of a lack of caring or presence by the therapist and engaged in intense emotional outbursts at such times. A phrase she used several times to describe her perceived lack of affect was that she felt "empty inside," and it was clear she had little or no sense of self, being almost totally dependent on others for any sense of identity. At the time of the critical session, Tracey was failing three subjects.

There were clearly a host of issues on which to focus with Tracey. Unfortunately, she was deeply apathetic about doing anything for herself, typical among women and girls with these traits. Whenever it was suggested to her that she do something for herself or that she might take better care of herself, she merely shrugged her shoulders and said, "Whatever." When asked if she was concerned that her boyfriends might be taking advantage of her desire to be liked, she admitted that she thought this was true and that she hated men, but she showed no sense of necessity for change. The "whatever" response appeared again when Tracey was asked if she cared about her failing grades, and yet again when she was asked if she ever worried about what was going to happen to her. This did not seem to be a game or a power struggle on her part. It was as though her necessity for change was frozen or paralyzed, as if something vital and dynamic in her personality makeup was missing or absent—a characteristic often seen in personality disorders.

When the critical session occurred, she had had 15 previous therapy sessions. By this time a fairly strong relationship had been established and a reasonable amount of trust.

After seeing no change, and knowing the pain these clients routinely experience, the therapist decided to use a different approach. Being met by indifference and apparent apathy at every turn, the therapist decided to believe this girl was not as dedicated to being as miserable as she appeared. Her wall of apathy was still imposed on the therapist, who struggled to find a way to get around, past, or through it. The therapist decided to try the subpersonality approach.

The therapist said, "Tracey, from what you have told me, it seems that you know that things are not quite right in your life and could be much better, but you don't seem to really want to change anything. Is that right?" She smiled helplessly and said, "Yeah, I guess so." "Well, can I ask you another question, and if it's OK, I would really like you to think about this one before you answer." She looked at the therapist steadily and said, "OK." The therapist continued. "Tell me, Tracey, is there a part of you, some tiny little part of you, that worries about what is going to happen to you?" She looked interested but asked for clarification, saying, "What do you mean?" The therapist replied, "Maybe it's a little voice in the back of your mind, or some part of you that you don't pay any attention to, but I just wonder if there is that part of yourself that is worried about what is going on in your life."

She looked at the therapist, somewhat unsure of this new territory, and said, "Yes, there are times when I hear a little voice that says things like 'you shouldn't do that' or 'you have to study,' things like that." The therapist was cautiously enthusiastic; it seemed some progress might be occurring. Even her tone was different. "How much of the total you is that part that cares?" Many clients can give percentages—for example, 20% or the like—but this was not her style. She was noncommittal. The therapist took out a piece of paper, drew a circle, and said, "Pretend this circle is like a pie that represents all of your personality. Can you draw a slice of it that shows me how big that part of you is that cares about what will happen to you?"

She drew a wedge that was about 25% of the total. This was, surprisingly, quite a bit, as many clients draw 10% or less, although other clients judged as difficult can estimate up to 40%. "Can I talk to that part of you, Tracey?" She thought about it briefly and said willingly, "Sure." Sensing that a therapeutic window was opening, the therapist immediately asked this newly identified part of Tracey, "I understand that you are worried about what's going to happen to you; is that true?" She looked at the therapist steadily again, and her face seemed a touch softer than before. "I am very worried. I think I do a lot of things that are wrong and get myself into trouble. And like, I know better, but I don't stop it."

"Like what do you do that's wrong?" She paused and said, "Like what I do with boys, for one thing, and I drink too much and smoke too much weed." This was a brand new side of Tracey coming out now. "Is it like your life is out of your control?" She looked quite sad as she said, "For sure." Once again, the therapist tried to see if she was interested in change. "Would you be interested in changing the things that get you in trouble and get more control over your life?" She immediately answered, "Yes."

"How about if we work together on this in counseling?" She nodded and the therapist, gathering momentum, forged ahead. "Just help me understand something, Tracey. Remember the pie?" She nodded. "If the part of you that wants to change is 25% of the whole pie, is it fair to say that the other 75% of you is out of your control?" She said softly, "I never thought about it like that, but I guess that's about right." The stage was finally set. "How much control would you like to have?" She thought about it for a while, then took the pen and paper and drew another pie circle. This time she shaded in about 75%. "That's how much," she said and looked up at the therapist. "So you want 75% control, instead of the 25% control over yourself that you have now?" She looked at the therapist almost longingly and asked, "Can I do that?" The therapist replied, "It is definitely possible, and we can give it our best shot. Are you willing to give it a try?" She looked like she was preparing for a fight. Finally, she said again, "Yes."

For the first time, Tracey was a motivated client with a sense of necessity for change. The apathetic Tracey would often emerge, but it was now identified as such. When it did happen, it was relatively easy to access the part of her that she eventually came to call "the real me," which grew in size relative to the rest of the pie. As far as the precursors were concerned, she was now on the rails toward change and was responsive to established therapy approaches. Although she never achieved change in leaps and bounds, she did manage to make steady progress.

THE USE OF COGNITIVE DISSONANCE

We have known for more than 40 years that cognitive dissonance leads to change (Axsom, 1989; Festinger, 1957). It begins with the presentation of incongruent, inconsistent, or contradictory information concerning the self, beliefs, behaviors, or lifestyle. This then produces a sense of anxiety in a person that is followed by a desire to resolve the incongruency and anxiety. This desire is closely related to a sense of necessity. There are a variety of ways of producing cognitive dissonance; some are innocuous and simple, whereas others are provocative and require more skill and finesse.

One method for producing cognitive dissonance can be borrowed from reality therapy (Glasser, 1965). It is a three-stage process that begins with asking a client the general question, "What do you want in your life?" This may or may not be related to the presenting problem, if there is one named at all. The answer to this question should not be superficial, such as getting a Ferrari or winning the lottery. For this approach to work, it is important to concentrate on getting a proper reply from the client, that is, one that is somehow related to cognition, affect, behavior, or relationships. A client may volunteer that he or she wants to be happy, to be in love, to find work, or to have more friends.

Once this is established, the second step is to find out what the person is doing in his or her life relative to the want or desire. For example, a 15-year-old young man may say he wants to have more friends. Some exploration reveals that he is angry at many people, including teachers, family members, and peers. Further inquiry reveals he is suspicious, untrusting, critical, and abrasive toward those around him and given to temper outbursts as well. It is not surprising that he lacks friends when what he is actually doing is alienating and antagonizing people.

With this information, the final question is posed to the client in this way: "You have told me how you interact with people—saying mean things and losing your temper. Is what you are doing getting you more friends? Is it working for you?" When the client admits that it is not working, the therapist can then ask if the client is willing to explore different ways of making friends that may be more efficient than what he has already tried. On the other hand, if the client is hesitant to say that it is not working, it can be effective to present the problem in a single sentence and wait for a response: "Explain to me how you can make friends by driving people away from you." Assuming that the client really does want to make friends, this approach can be effective in many cases. Once again, producing cognitive dissonance produces the discomfort or anxiety, and then allows the therapist to point out a way to alleviate the anxiety—therapy.

WHAT WOULD HAPPEN IF NOTHING CHANGED?

Another way of producing cognitive dissonance is by asking a client what would happen if nothing changed at all, that is, if the client continued to do little or nothing about the issue or problem. This approach assumes the client has some rudimentary awareness that there is a situation in his or her life that is not desirable. The question is whether the problem would stay the same or get worse. Typically, a difficult client will assert that a problem stays the same if unattended. However, if a therapist can establish a pattern of decline or progressive worsening of the problem over time, this may lead to an increased sense of necessity for change. For example, if a client consistently blames others for problems that are mostly due to his or her own actions, ask if the blaming has served to resolve the problem. One can also ask if the blaming makes the client feel better, and if so, how much and for how long. The answer is usually something on the order of "Not much."

CAREFULLY INCREASE ANXIETY LEVELS

There is another strategy for increasing the level of necessity that involves increasing anxiety levels and bringing about some cognitive dissonance. Garfield (1994) noted several research studies that indicated that preliminary discomfort was an indicator of eventual positive outcome. This was also consistent in our research (Hanna et al., 1995; Hanna & Ritchie, 1995). Carefully increasing anxiety levels in clients has been described by several therapists such as Whitaker (Whitaker & Bumberry, 1988) and Kiesler (1988). Freeman, Pretzer, Fleming, and Simon (1990) noted that anxiety in moderate amounts can motivate and mobilize clients to change.

This approach requires a considerable degree of skill and a dispassionate, casual, almost aloof demeanor that remains empathic and compassionate. To be successful, the therapist's voice must be free of even the slightest inflections or intonations that hint at resentment, impatience, condemnation, or moral judgment. Because many difficult clients are extremely sensitive to being judged as a bad or wicked person, the therapist's voice must remain, even, steady, curious, and caring. If even the slightest trace of the therapist's personal issues are evident, many clients will pick up on it and immediately initiate a power struggle.

Having done anxiety-inducing techniques many times, I have noticed again and again how clients, on hearing a provocative question or statement, visibly and noticeably open their eyes and take my measure to see where I am coming from. I freely let them do so and then calmly repeat the question or statement, varying it from different angles.

Spitting in the Client's Soup

A technique called *spitting in the client's soup* is a way of increasing anxiety levels in the interest of change. Adler (see Dinkmeyer, Dinkmeyer, & Sperry, 1987) originated this version of raising anxiety levels and gave it its name. This technique is especially useful with a client who is boasting about some form of disorder or destructive behavior. There are many situations worthy of this technique—for example, a woman who boasted about her ability to destroy her coworkers' reputations, a woman who reported how much she enjoyed using her looks to entice her friends' husbands into affairs, or a man who loved competition to the point of saying that he always tried to outdo his friends.

Spitting in the client's soup requires a considerable amount of skill to be done smoothly and effectively. It is important to bear in mind that at no time is the client actually discouraged from or told not to engage in the questionable behavior. The purpose is to make the behavior less attractive without interfering with the person's choice to continue. The following is a case example depicting Jason, a 27-year-old factory worker presenting with depression about his marriage and his life in general.

In the first session it was clear that Jason was only toying with therapy and minimizing his problem. His rating for the necessity precursor was 1. In the third session, he disclosed that he was often unfaithful to his wife. When asked to be more specific, he reported with great certainty that his many affairs were necessary to his "self-confidence" and that it was the only thing that could get him out of his depression. He was convinced that his affairs had nothing to do with the difficulties with his marriage and that the failing marriage was really all his wife's fault.

Client: I have to admit I am really good at bedding women. What can I say, they love me. My wife doesn't love me anymore, but what the hell does she know. If you're good at something, you might as well pursue it, right? It really makes me feel good—better than anything else in the world.

Therapist: So having these affairs is really important to you. Almost like a lifesaver for your ego.

Client: Exactly.

Therapist: Just curious, Jason; do these women know you are married?

Client: Of course not.

Therapist: What would they say if they knew?

Client: They wouldn't like it, so I don't tell them. C'mon! How can I bed all these women if I tell them I'm married?

Therapist: So all these women that you seduce are just like your wife. They want loyalty and faithfulness just like she does.

Client: Yeah *(smiling)*, women are all the same, you know. They all want me to be faithful to them and have a relationship *(the last word pronounced with added sarcasm)*. But what they don't know won't hurt 'em.

Therapist: I see. Am I right in saying that the pleasure in your life depends on your hurting people?

Client (visibly stiffens at the statement): Well, I wouldn't put it that way. I make 'em feel real good, you know.

Therapist: Jason, I have to believe that you are a good person who doesn't want to hurt anybody.

Client: Yeah. That's right.

Therapist: But I am also tempted to believe that feeling good is so important to you that you are willing to hurt some nice, decent people just so you can feel good yourself.

Client: I never thought of it like that.

Therapist: Can I say something else, and you tell me what you think?

Client: I suppose so. You're going to tell me anyway.

Therapist: If I was mean and uncaring toward the feelings of people who cared about me the way you are toward your wife and the women you have told me about, I would be depressed, same as you are.

Client: But it's the only thing that makes me happy.

Therapist: I'm not telling you to stop, Jason. I am only wondering if the thing that makes you happy in one way makes you unhappy in a bigger way.

Client (mixed anger and sadness): So I am doomed to be depressed for the rest of my life?

Therapist: Not at all. It's kind of like a man who is stuck on a steady diet of beef jerky. He has a great need for a good steak, but he doesn't even know there is such a thing. He knows there has to be something better, but all he ever gets is beef jerky. That might be the case with you. Maybe you never learned and don't know how close relationships can make you much happier than sex.

Client: But bedding women makes me feel better.

Therapist: I understand what you are saying. Maybe all you know is beef jerky and have never known the real pleasures of porterhouse or filet mignon.

Client (with a tone of protest): So you think that I need better relationships.

Therapist: I am only asking if any of this makes sense to you, and if so, whether you are willing to give it a try and see if it helps with your depression. I also would like your permission to find out some of your beliefs about women, people, and relationships. These attitudes might also be part of your depression. Does it seem worth a try?

Client: Yeah. I guess I see what you're saying. We can try it.

With this approach, the therapist instilled a sense of necessity in Jason through spitting in his soup and using a metaphor relevant to his situation. He was more willing to discuss his depression and no longer minimized the affairs to the same degree. The remainder of that session, and the next several, were spent discussing the notion of viable and satisfying relationships and how not having them in one's life can lead to depression. Jason's beliefs about women and people were also examined and linked to his depression and his failing marriage. Eventually, he engaged in couples therapy with his wife.

The Story of Charles

Charles was a handsome, highly intelligent, manipulative 17-year-old African American young man who often complained of racism and unfair treatment at his school and in trying to find jobs. His complaints about White people were about not only his own negative experiences but those of other African Americans as well. He was court-ordered to a day treatment center for adolescent criminal offenders and had not been responding to treatment. His initial precursors rating was around 5. Fortunately, I had established a fairly good rapport with him.

His complaints with regard to racism were justified. I did not question them and, in fact, validated them as well as his acute perception on that count (see chapter 8). However, after about five sessions, he revealed to me that he was selling crack cocaine and making large sums of money at it. When I asked him who his customers were, he looked at me as if to forgive my ignorance and said with a sneer, "the fiends." This is a term many crack cocaine dealers use to refer to addicts. I asked him the usual questions about whether he thought it was hurting people and so on, but he was so attached to the high income that nothing I said had any impact. He often said with great pleasure, "I go shopping all the time now. It's great."

Anyone who has worked with clients in this situation knows of the incredible difficulty involved in achieving therapeutic change. There was a time when I would feel frustrated by my ineffectiveness in reaching young men in this situation, but by the time this story took place, I knew how to increase anxiety levels with some degree of control. I asked Charles what color his customers were. He said some were White. When I pushed, he said most were Black. I said to him calmly, flatly, and in a matter-of-fact tone, "No offense, Charles, but you are agreeing with and backing up all those prejudiced, racist, White people that you complain about." He said, "What?"

I leaned toward him and said, "Tell me if I am wrong. But your customers are slaves. The [crack] pipe's got 'em all, and you are contributing to their slavery. You are a smart man, intelligent and sharp, and you are using your intelligence to make slaves and keep slaves. No disrespect intended, Charles, but you are just like a lot of those White people who believe that Black people are worthless and stupid. You benefit from keeping Black people down, just like they do. And what really worries me is that if you had your way, you would be making a lot more of your brothers and sisters worthless and stupid by selling them more of that poison and turning them into fiends."

Charles sat there looking at me incredulously and silently. I could see him trying to formulate a defense against these serious charges. He could not ignore what I said. It was too close to home. He looked at me hard and with great intensity, taking my measure to see if I was being hostile or judging or superior in any way. I was clean. He could find nothing to hook into or grab onto in my demeanor or presence. He finally answered in frustration and anger, "Hey. What the f--- do you know about what I do? You don't know sh-- about me or my life."

I expected him to be angry. I deserved it, and I told him so. I had spit in his soup, and I was giving it as nasty a taste as possible. However, I knew I was finally reaching him, and I was not going to back down. Remaining both compassionate and dispassionate, I replied, "You have told me quite a bit about yourself, Charles, and I'm sure I don't know everything. But you still have not answered me. I am still sitting here trying to figure out the difference between what you do and what the slaveowners did to Black people. Sure, it's a different kind of slavery, but it's still slavery. Talk to me, man. Is there a difference?"

Charles couldn't answer. After about 30 emotionally charged seconds, he slowly began to express his regrets and, amazingly, his guilt over what he was doing. His voice now crackled with emotion. It was a pivotal point in his treatment. One moment he was a smooth, arrogant crack dealer, outwardly convinced he was exactly who he wanted to be. The next moment he was a confused teenager struck by the foolishness of his own ignorance and false bravado. A sense of necessity for change had been established through carefully generating high anxiety levels, which produced considerable cognitive dissonance. Working in tandem with the other therapists in the agency, we eventually got him to see not only the destructiveness of drugs, but the need to be aware of and empathize with the "fiends" as his brothers and sisters. He soon became an asset to the treatment program, helping other clients in group sessions who were also using and dealing.

IDENTIFY SECONDARY GAINS OR CROSS-PURPOSES

For many clients, therapeutic change is in direct conflict and at cross purposes with other goals. A sense of necessity for change will not emerge if there is a greater necessity to remain the same. It is part of the self-protectiveness Mahoney (1991) described so well. The problem, disorder, or issue is retained because it is serving a purpose that the client has deemed important, usually referred to as *secondary gain*. Take, for example, the case of a person who is receiving worker's compensation for a painful back injury. The person is referred to a clinic that includes therapy for the emotional and psychological aspects of managing the pain. Some of these clients are highly difficult to work with simply because any decrease in pain threatens their eventual financial settlement. Thus, the client will resist any decrease in perceived pain in order to eventually gain financial reward, usually through a lawsuit.

Another example of secondary gain is in the case of a man with explosive anger outbursts. The man knows that others will more readily bend to his will if they can avoid a confrontation. Thus, it pays to hold on to and use the angry attitude to maintain control over others. Illness being used to gather attention and caring from others is another example of secondary gain.

It is often tricky to determine what purpose the problem, disorder, or issue is serving, and many clients find it difficult to identify and discuss secondary gain as well. It is sometimes up to the therapist to suggest it as such. But when it can be done, it is often rewarding and fruitful work. The benefits of change can be weighed against the benefits of not changing at all. It helps to rate the benefits of change and of remaining the same. It also helps, if possible, to find a solution that will bring the benefits of both. When a client sees the irrationality of keeping a disorder or problem, a sense of necessity will likely arise that can motivate the person toward change.

ACKNOWLEDGE THE AMBIVALENCE

Some difficult clients believe that change is tantamount to an admission of defeat and a loss of pride. This belief interferes dramatically with a sense of necessity. Such clients may find themselves in competition with the therapist to prove they are smart and savvy. There is not necessarily a power struggle here, but there is a double bind. On the one hand, to admit to the need for change brings about a feeling of being stupid and wrong. On the other, to deny the need for change leads to feelings of hopelessness and apathy. It is extremely important for such clients to see any move toward change as their own idea and as brought about under their own power. If a therapist has any need to be acknowledged for his or her great therapeutic ideas or interventions, he or she runs a strong chance of failure with this type of client. These clients often have a lot of pride in the way they have lived their lives and in the way they have survived difficulties and hard times. It is difficult for them to admit to making mistakes. The bottom line is that they must feel like change is their own brilliant choice—and so it is.

USE FEELING GOOD AS A MOTIVATING FORCE

It is amazing what people will do to feel better. It is one of the major reinforcers in all of life. Going to therapy is just one of the things that people will do to bring desirable feelings into their lives. Taking illegal drugs is another. One of the hidden promises of therapy has to do with holding out the possibility of feeling good. In itself it is a rather crude enticement, but it certainly can be persuasive to clients who think in hedonistic terms. If a client can be convinced that therapy may actually make him or her feel better, a sense of necessity may well emerge out of dark emotions and bitter attitudes. No promises should be made, of course, but it is certainly fair to mention feeling good as a possible outcome.

IDENTIFY CORE BELIEFS

In most clients, specific core beliefs, ontological or otherwise, inhibit a sense of necessity. Many clients have never verbalized such beliefs. Knowing this, it is sometimes helpful to infer the belief and submit it to the client, awaiting his or her comment. For example, a therapist could say, "I sometimes get the sense from you that, deep down, you believe that nobody ever gets any better, so why bother. Is this true for you?" Once identified and disputed in classical cognitive therapy fashion, the doors to change, including second-order change, can be opened. Examples of core beliefs that can inhibit or prevent a sense of necessity are

- "I don't care about anything."
- "I am just fine the way I am."
- "I don't care what happens to me."
- "Change is a source of great anxiety."
- "If I change, I will feel terrible."
- "I don't deserve anything good, so why even think about it?"
- "Only fools think they can better themselves."
- "There is nothing worth trying for in this world."
- "Nobody ever really gets better, so why bother?"
- "If the problem were to change, it would only get worse."
- "If I changed, it would only mean that [a specific disliked person] was right."
- "Everybody is screwed up, so why should I be any different?"

INCREASE THE LEVEL OF HOPE

Hope is closely tied to the necessity precursor. A sense of necessity will sometimes spontaneously arise when hope is established. When nothing else is working, it may be fruitful to attend to discovering and increasing hope (see chapter 14).

10

ESTABLISHING THE WILLINGNESS OR READINESS TO EXPERIENCE ANXIETY OR DIFFICULTY

A client with a high sense of necessity but no willingness to experience anxiety or difficulty will probably want the therapist to do the work. This chapter describes how to help clients prepare for the work that only they can do. Some clients need preparation for therapy and change, much like athletes need to warm up and mentally prepare for meets, tournaments, and games. Therapy can involve something akin to hardship, and working through issues requires some degree of getting in shape to deal with it. Dealing with difficult people, marital turmoil, and emotional pain requires a certain amount of determination and readiness. It is in promoting the willingness or readiness to experience anxiety or difficulty that doing therapy most closely resembles coaching.

An effective therapist can inspire a client, through persuasion, to work through difficult, painful, anxiety-ridden problems. Through the empathic connection, therapists can promote this precursor without being coercive; surpassing the tolerance limits or threshold of anxiety can be harmful and discourages a person from further work in therapy. This chapter catalogs techniques and strategies that can inspire a person to recognize and be willing to tolerate and experience the anxiety and difficulty that come with therapeutic change. The use of metaphors is a major approach to increasing this precursor.

EDUCATIONAL METAPHORS

There are many possible metaphors or reframes that can stimulate this precursor. Because it is probably the most difficult to immediately understand, metaphors are helpful in pointing out how important the willingness to experience anxiety or difficulty is to the therapeutic process. All too often, difficult clients simply do not know that this precursor is helpful or that it can be articulated. Some may see this precursor as threatening. Thus, education is often an essential aspect of the implementation of the willingness or readiness to experience anxiety or difficulty.

No Pain No Gain: The Workout Metaphor

The workout metaphor communicates well to some clients. It essentially states that one gets out of therapy what one puts into it. In the world of physical conditioning, weight lifting, and bodybuilding, a common phrase is, "No pain, no gain." It is often advised that the muscles have to "burn" or be sufficiently stressed to grow and develop. Many clients can readily understand and relate to this perspective. One example was a 20-year-old bulimic woman who was regularly binging and purging. Like many women with this problem, she worked out furiously for two to four hours a day in an effort to lose weight. She knew and operated on the "no pain no gain" principle.

However, when it came to looking at psychological issues, she was unwilling to tolerate anxiety to any marked degree. In fact, it was soon established that whenever she felt the anxiety or edge of her emotional pain, she was off to the gym or binging on junk food. She was able to see this relatively easily (see Levenkron, 1991). Her understanding of therapy and the therapeutic process was enhanced when it was explained to her that "no pain, no gain" also applied to therapy. The muscles burn in physical exercise, she was told, just like anxiety "burns" in mental therapy. In either case, the burn is important and necessary for growth, but it should not be overdone. In her case, it was further promised that she would not be deliberately thrown into painful memories or feelings unless she was willing and ready.

Workout Machines

Along these same lines, many people buy abdominal exercisers or various other workout machines knowing they have to change some part of their body or health. Unfortunately, in so many cases those machines do not get used, simply because many people are not willing to experience the difficulty that comes with actually exercising. As a result, the machines are bought with the best of intentions but collect dust because of the person's lack of willingness to actually experience the discomfort that accompanies exercise. Similarly, people can pay for therapy and "have it around" for years, but they may not ever really use it to make changes in their lives. Thus, therapy gets wasted and "collects dust," just like those workout machines.

The Stuffed Closet

The stuffed closet is somewhat similar to the cleaning house metaphor. Clients who report that they do not like to think about their problems have the classic symptom of people lacking a willingness to experience anxiety or difficulty. The problem can be likened to a closet that gets packed full of "stuff": Every time the person does not want to deal with something, he or she just throws it into a mental closet. Eventually the closet gets so full that the door will not close properly, and the person is constantly trying to keep the door shut. It is OK to "stuff" a few things in there, and one might get away with it, but at some point the closet begins to overflow and spills painful material into the rest of the house.

Alternately, the mind can be likened to a house with several rooms and closets. Some people stuff one mental room after another full of painful issues and difficult problems. They continue to ignore them until there are so many rooms full that the person has only a fraction of his or her mind left in which it is comfortable to live. Guests are also kept out of those rooms. For some people, the bulk of their mental life is spent keeping the doors to those rooms closed so that they do not have to think about what is in there. Anxiety builds, and whatever peace of mind or contentedness the person may have had begins to fade progressively. As the metaphor goes, if a person were to take the time to sort out all the stuff, he or she would eventually be able to breathe easier and be more comfortable. The willingness to experience anxiety or difficulty has to do with being willing to go through and clean out all the junk and get the house in order.

Driving With the Brakes On

Another metaphor illustrates how some people want change to occur but inhibit themselves in various ways. A therapist can inform a client that research shows that experiencing emotions and anxiety is conducive to the change process. But being willing only to talk about things and not to actually experience the anxiety connected with those issues is rather like driving with the brakes on. The car might move along in jerky motions, or it might not move at all. Furthermore, after a while the brakes begin to wear out from overuse. Similarly, a person who resists the pain while talking about it might go through years of therapy but may not ever arrive at any viable or lasting change, ending up exhausted after fighting the anxiety over the years.

Washing Hands With Gloves On

Talking about issues in therapy without ever getting into the experiential aspects is rather like washing one's hands while wearing gloves. The washing is good, but the hands never get clean. The problem never gets contacted or worked through, because it is never really experienced. Eventually, it becomes time to take the gloves off.

To Properly Clean, You Have to Get Dirty

When one cleans, if the job is challenging, one is bound to come into contact with dirt and grime. The paradox is that cleaning up requires looking for, exposing, stirring up, and scrubbing away dirt and dust. To clean you have to get dirty, and the same is often true in therapy. Therapy can be viewed as a cleansing of the mind, feelings, and behaviors. Things can get messy with emotions and beliefs, but that is part of any cleaning process. One can hire someone to clean the house and yard, but in therapy only the person can do the work; no else has direct access to another's mind, feelings, and behaviors.

Old Pipes and Dirty Water

For a person who is hesitant to touch or come into contact with what phenomenologically appears as messy—painful emotions and feelings—a metaphor of old, rusty pipes can be used. When the pipes have not been used for a long time and the faucet is turned on, the water will flow a dirty brown color, but if the water is allowed to flow, eventually it will turn clear and clean. The same is true for those "messy" emotions and feelings once they begin to be experienced, processed, and discussed.

It Takes Guts

The guts metaphor speaks especially well to men, although it has helped with women as well. It is ideally suited to many defiant adolescents who are suspicious of and ridicule the idea of counseling and therapy. With this metaphor, therapy is represented as an exercise in courage. Many difficult clients might respond to a statement like, "Anyone can ignore their own thoughts and feelings, but it takes guts to be honest about them and not back off from what you are really about." A variation designed to increase this precursor with defiant, aggressive adolescent young men and some young women might be, "Anybody can go off and pop [hit] somebody that pisses them off, but the real guts and courage is in facing up to the feelings of anger and hurt."

FRAMING A TECHNIQUE AS AN EXPERIMENT

There are times when a client is uncertain about whether to follow the therapist in the direction in which he or she is headed. A technique from Gestalt therapy called "the experiment" (Polster & Polster, 1973) allows the therapist free access to his or her creativity based on the needs of the client, the status of the relationship, and the climate of that particular moment. The technique is framed as an "experiment" to the client, and the client will nearly always be willing to try it out, even though he or she may not engage it with full commitment. Any technique in this chapter, or in this book, can be thus framed to encourage a client's willingness, readiness, and involvement. Part of framing the experiment is to inform the client that he or she may end it at any time. An example of an experiment is given in the section on the use of paradox later in this chapter.

IDENTIFY THE INTERNAL DIALOG THAT AVOIDS ANXIETY

This cognitive–behavioral strategy can be effective in removing obstacles to being open to experience. If the therapist knows a possible issue for change, the therapist can ask the client to just consider making the change in question, and then to describe for the therapist his or her automatic thoughts or self-talk associated with the thought of the change. If the client is especially difficult, he or she can be first told, "Please do not make the change; I just want to ask you something related to it." Usually the client will agree to this quasi-paradoxical approach. Also, when clients are hesitant to experience anxiety or difficulty, they are prone to deflect questions and change topics. It is often necessary to repeat questions and, if necessary, get prior permission to interrupt a client's rambling on other less disturbing topics.

For example, Tony, a man in his late 40s, admitted that he liked to fight with his wife, Sara, to get her agitated and upset. He knew that this was mean and even cruel, but he said that he enjoyed it and did not know why. Sara, meanwhile, was extremely angry with him and knew all too well that he enjoyed it. She told him she would not take this kind of treatment any longer. This client had not responded to any approach to changing this behavior, and the precursors assessment indicated a rating of 0 or 1 in the willingness precursor.

> *Therapist:* I am going to ask you only to think about changing your "agitating behavior" with your wife. Please do not change it or stop it. Then, once you are considering the change, I want to ask you a question or two about it. Is this OK with you?
> *Client:* OK.
> *Therapist:* Get the idea of supporting your wife's peace of mind and happiness, and tell me when you have it. *(Client nods.)*
> *Therapist:* What do you feel like at this moment as you think about it?
> *Client:* It's OK with me.

Therapist: Didn't you just tell me that you like to get her agitated and upset?

Client: Yeah, I guess I did, but it's not like I don't want her to be happy.

Therapist: Of course. Do you ever start a fight with her when she is sad?

Client: No.

Therapist: Do you ever start a fight with her when she is angry about something?

Client: No.

Therapist: Let me bounce something off you, and tell me if I am wrong. When Sara is happy, does it kind of bug you in a way? Does it sort of get under your skin, and you have this urge to mess with it?

Client: Well, yeah. It's like I get kind of mischievous. *(smiling and looking for agreement)*

Therapist: I am going to say something very direct to you, and I want your permission to do so. If you want me to sugar coat it, I will.

Client: Go on, tell me straight.

Therapist: It sounds like one of the roles you play in your marriage is to keep your wife from ever knowing happiness and joy. What do you think?

Client: You make me sound like a real ass----.

Therapist: I am not saying that at all. I am trying to understand your role in the marriage.

Client (irritated): I work hard, long hours and lots of overtime. I keep the house and yard together.

Therapist: No doubt, and I bet you are good at what you do.

Client: Damn right.

Therapist: Tony, I am just trying to understand what is going on here between you and Sara, and pardon me for saying so, but it sounds like you don't want to answer me about not wanting her to be happy. Do you want me to repeat it?

Client: I know what you said. *(Pauses . . . silence)* I feel kind of ashamed about it, you know.

Therapist: Did that feeling of shame get in the way when I earlier asked you to tell me your thoughts about your wife and your marriage?

Client: But you don't know how much she bugs me. She is all the time acting like she knows everything, and she drives me nuts. *(Client continues in this vein for two or three minutes.)*

Therapist: Can this be one of those times when I can interrupt you?

Client (mildly surprised): OK.

Therapist: I noticed that when I brought up that feeling of shame, you started talking about Sara instead of your feelings. Do you find it uncomfortable to talk about that feeling of shame?

Client (shifting in the chair): Can we talk about something else?

Therapist: Sure, for now, though if you just give me a yes or no, it would help me understand where you are coming from. Do you not like to talk about those kinds of feelings?

Client: Yeah. It's like I just don't want to think about it or have to bother with it.

Therapist: And it's easier to complain about her?

Client: I suppose so.

Therapist: What do you think would happen if you got into that feeling of shame?

Client: I would end up feeling down and depressed, and I don't feel like getting into all that.

Therapist: So you believe that if you ever come into contact with or get into your feelings, you will end up getting depressed?

Client: Well, yeah, wouldn't you?

At this point a dysfunctional core belief was isolated that obviously interfered with the therapeutic process and specifically the willingness precursor. Tony believed that contacting or experiencing his feelings would result in depression. The therapist disputed the belief and used the "old pipes and dirty water" metaphor to help Tony understand that contacting feelings is not a formula for depression, but can actually be part of a way to alleviate his depression.

In addition, the therapist asked Tony if he had a habitual pattern of avoiding any kind of difficult feelings, as he had just displayed in therapy. He said that he did indeed, all his life, and when asked, he said he thought this was what one "was supposed to do" with such feelings. The stuffed closet metaphor was then used to advantage with Tony to illustrate how he had stuffed so many aspects of his life into a mental closet that the door could no longer be locked shut, and "material" was seeping out from the cracks around the door. It took one session to establish this precursor with Tony, moving him from a rating of 0 to 2 on the scale. He was more open to emotional experience after this and much less avoidant.

Typically, when clients become ready to experience anxiety or difficulty, they find therapy to be a much more smooth and tolerable endeavor, with many more rewards or reinforcers. In Tony's case, he did eventually explore his preventing Sara from being happy. Therapy went relatively smoothly after he was willing to experience the obvious anxiety that came with his having to face the incongruence between his self-image as a fun-loving, nice guy and his behavior of interfering with the happiness of the woman he married.

THE USE OF PARADOX

Research findings on paradoxical techniques have shown them to be highly effective (Orlinsky et al., 1994). Paradox can be helpful in developing several of the precursors, including the willingness to experience anxiety or difficulty. For example, Cindy was a woman in her mid-40s who was extremely sensitive to emotional pain. She would consistently deflect attempts to discuss anything unpleasant or anxiety provoking. Her conversation seemed geared more toward making the therapist like her and think that she was acceptable as a human being than it was toward alleviating her presenting problem of depression.

The therapist attempted to validate and reassure her of her value and intelligence in many ways. After the initial relationship was formed, the therapist explained to her that therapy sometimes required difficult topics be addressed and discussed. She said she knew this, but that it was "really hard" for her. The therapist then asked her what was so hard about doing so. She said simply, "I don't want to hurt anymore." Using the old pipes and dirty water metaphor helped a bit, but she was still extremely sensitive to any further pain, even though she was intellectually aware that she would eventually need to deal with it. Sensing her fragility in this regard, it was clear that to expose her to painful emotions at this point in therapy would be premature. The therapist decided to introduce a paradoxical technique.

Therapist: Cindy, I understand that you just don't want to hurt any more, and that is why you don't want to talk about anything uncomfortable.
Client: It's just so hard, and I just don't have the energy anymore.
Therapist: What would you prefer to talk about?
Client: You mean, anything?
Therapist: Yes.
Client: I like to talk about the novels I read. I also like to talk about stores and sales.
Therapist: Would you like to try an experiment?
Client: What is it?
Therapist: Let's talk about any of those things you mentioned, but with one added ingredient.
Client: What's that?
Therapist: How about if you talk about what you find enjoyable and during the entire time, deliberately avoid talking about anything painful or uncomfortable. Are you willing to try it?
Client: Sure.
Therapist: Please remember, you can stop this at any time if you want.

Cindy was soon talking about books, and then her friends and neighbors, and a variety of other topics. This went on for about 10 minutes with the therapist listening, acknowledging, and asking an occasional question. At two points in the conversation, the therapist interjected a question verifying that Cindy was still deliberately avoiding anything painful or uncomfortable. She said that she was.

Therapist: OK, Cindy, you have been telling me about all kinds of things for about 10 minutes now. Did you notice anything while you were deliberately not talking about anything painful or uncomfortable?
Client: Yes *(speaking softly)*. It's the same thing that I do all the time anyway. I have been through so much in my life that it seems whenever I talk about anything, I am trying to not think about the bad things that have happened to me. *(Begins to cry.)* I don't know if I can ever feel better.
Therapist: So what you are saying, Cindy, is that your emotional hurt is so close to the surface that it's always there to some degree, even when you try to forget about it.
Client: (Softly crying.) Yes. It's always been like that. A lot of the things I enjoy doing I am really doing because I am trying to forget about the bad things that have happened to me.
Therapist: Has it worked for you?
Client: What do you mean?
Therapist: Have you been able to forget about the bad things by avoiding them in your actions and behaviors?
Client: Not really.
Therapist: Would you be willing to try a different approach? Therapy exists so that feelings of hurt and pain can be diminished to the point of not having them on your mind all the time.
Client: I guess I knew that.
Therapist: True, but it didn't seem you were willing to give it a try. Am I wrong here?
Client: No. It's just that it's so hard.
Therapist: What if we only go a little bit at a time, and you tell me when it's getting too intense and then I will back off as soon as you tell me.
Client: That would be OK. I just don't want to cry all the time. I have done so much of that, and I am afraid it's what you want me to do.
Therapist: I think it's cruel to ask a person to go swimming in all their pain if they can end up drowning in it. What I am asking you to do is to go wading little by little, toes and ankles first, until you feel comfortable in the water.
Client: You know there's a lot that has happened to me . . . .

Therapy was conducted very carefully at first, checking with her to see if she was feeling overwhelmed at any time. Eventually she disclosed several traumatic experiences and was able to work through these to her satisfaction. In this case, the paradoxical injunction to avoid anything painful showed her that it was what she was already doing. Cindy further realized that she had been fighting and resisting painful memories and emotions throughout her life. She eventually reported that she had become so accustomed to keeping those feelings at bay that the thought of not doing so was intimidating and disorienting.

TAKING OWNERSHIP AND STOPPING BLAME

In chapter 3, owning the problem was mentioned as an aspect of a person who is willing to experience anxiety or difficulty. In many ways owning the problem is the opposite of blaming, or compulsively attributing responsibility for a problem to another or others. Difficult clients typically blame others for their problems and issues. Getting a difficult client to take ownership of a problem can be demanding work, but when successful it is rewarding for all concerned.

A key to bringing about a sense of ownership is, of course, to help a person see that he or she has some contributing influence on the problem. Even if the person is truly blameless or not at all responsible for what happened, as in cases of sexual abuse, the person is still responsible for how they think about that problem (see Frankl, 1984). A person's attitude toward a situation or problem can still come under his or her control. Blaming, and its close associate, hating, is often the result of a decision.

As a result of his experience at Auschwitz, Viktor Frankl (1984) learned a lesson that therapists can present to clients. He said that although he had no control over what the Nazis did to him and the other people there, he did have control over his attitude toward what they did to him and others. This story and lesson can be used to advantage with people who blame, complain, or detach from events that have affected them. I have found that recommending his book is quite helpful, if the client will read it.

The following list of questions and statements may be of help to those who habitually complain or blame others for a problem or a particular issue:

- "How is this problem controlling you?"
- "Has complaining about the problem helped any?"
- "Do you feel better when blaming [a person or situation] for the problem?"
- "Has blaming [the person or situation] helped to ease the difficulty?"
- "Perhaps you don't give yourself enough credit for your own influence."
- "Have you set this problem up so that you would be helpless over it?"
- "Have you set yourself up to be the slave of this problem?"
- "Is having someone to blame important to you?"
- "How has this problem robbed you of your freedom?"
- "Is this problem worth giving up your freedom for?"
- "Sure you didn't cause the problem, but can you control your reaction to it?"

Some of these questions are highly confrontative, whereas others are meant to induce processing. They are meant to be used appropriately to match different clients' situations at different times. All are questions that many difficult clients will seek to avoid, and therefore they need to be pursued. If asked curiously and openly, each has the potential to open a therapeutic window. The questions or statements, and variations of the same, will need to be repeated in many instances to achieve some depth of processing.

Processing these questions and statements can help a client understand that blaming involves the avoidance of anxiety that comes with responsibility (see Yalom, 1980). The goal is for a client to learn that blame brings neither solutions nor joy, whereas responsibility can bring both. Generally, responsibility is merely the willingness to take charge of the circumstances that make up the problem or issue. Clients can be taught that *responsibility* is not a word that weighs 500 pounds and sits on one's shoulders. It has often been described as the ability to respond, or "response-ability." Blaming inhibits the ability to respond by placing all control in the hands of the blamed person. In many cases, this lack of ownership of a problem or issue comes from never having accepted the problem. Acceptance can be a powerful change factor in a small number of instances of therapeutic change (Hanna & Ritchie, 1995).

THE CONTROL OR FREEDOM CHALLENGE

Therapists can use a specific technique to help clients stop blaming others as a means of avoiding anxiety or difficulty. The focus of the technique is a mechanism used by difficult clients of all ages. An example might be the sixth grader who says, "He made me do it," and another the wife batterer who says, "If she didn't make me angry, I wouldn't have hit her." The proper response to these statements is to indicate somehow that the person himself or herself has given up control of his or her life to the person being blamed. This is not at all the same as indicating to a client that he or she lacks self-control, which is a familiar song to these clients, and such a strategy will usually end up being uneventful.

The therapist must point out that the person has given up control over behaviors and thoughts to the person who is being blamed, as this is in most cases a more accurate representation (see Hanna & Hunt, 1999). For example, when a sophomore in high school says, "Joey made me do it," the response could be, "So Joey now controls your life?" Similarly, when an abusive husband says, "She nagged and nagged and got me so mad I just hit her," a proper response could be, "So you have no control over your emotions and behaviors?"

These statements can be followed up by saying, "It's too bad you don't have any freedom." This is a distinctly provocative statement, and the therapist must recognize it as such and be aware of the consequence of increased anxiety. Another statement that can be made in response might be, "It's too bad you no longer have any say over your own life." The therapist can then offer to help the client get his or her life back.

This approach is especially effective with defiant and conduct-disordered adolescents (Hanna & Hunt, 1999). Because it is provocative, this technique will usually evoke self-righteous protest and even defiance by clients prone to blaming others. The therapist responds to the increased anxiety levels by saying, "I mean you no disrespect. I am only wondering if you know that you give up your life and your freedom to other people every time you blame them." After the anxiety level reduces a bit, the therapist can say something on the order of, "Tell me if I am wrong, but it seems like [the person] is controlling your emotions and behaviors with his or her words and attitudes. Do you have any freedom left, or have you given it all away?" At this point the therapist can again offer to help the person take back that freedom. This is initially done by having the client observe and reflect on times when he or she blindly acted out in response to a stressful situation. For this technique to work, the therapist must be both compassionate and dispassionate in using it.

Once again, the therapeutic strategy is to show that whenever people blame others for their own actions, they have given their self-control or freedom away to the person blamed, and even their thoughts are now controlled by the blamed person. This approach is especially effective if the person blamed is someone the client dislikes, does not respect, or is competing against in some way. It brings about considerable cognitive dissonance and will often influence a client to be willing to experience anxiety or difficulty in seeking to regain freedom or control over behaviors. The technique is a classic example of a difficult situation that produces a moment of great therapeutic potential. It is unwise to use the term *freedom* with children under 14 year of age, as they do not seem to respond to it. The use of *control* is much better with that age group.

SELF-MONITORING THE WAXING AND WANING OF ANXIETY

Self-monitoring, a behavioral technique adapted from Meichenbaum (1977), can be used to show some difficult clients that they have a low tolerance of anxiety and that they may resort to avoidant behaviors rather than face it. The technique consists of pointing out moments in which a client shrinks from, deflects, or otherwise avoids anxiety. Many defiant adolescents, for example, have a low tolerance of anxiety, even though they may assert that they can handle any kind of confrontation or difficult situation. Pointing out the low tolerance is best done in vivo, there in the session, with the therapist asking permission to do so.

For example, Marie was a teenager who seldom studied, being more interested in entertainment of various kinds. She was, nevertheless, highly sensitive about her low grades and would get irritated or annoyed at the mere mention of them. Her therapist used this, in combination with a strategy for increasing a sense of necessity, as an opportunity for her to learn about anxiety.

> *Therapist:* Have you noticed that some people can deal with things without getting upset, and they just seem to be very cool and not let things get to them?
> *Client:* Yeah.
> *Therapist:* Would you want to be more like that?
> *Client (protesting):* I am like that. Don't you think I am?
> *Therapist:* In many ways you are. But you also know that many people know exactly what to say to get you annoyed and irritated, right?
> *Client:* Yeah.
> *Therapist:* How would you like to get less annoyed and irritated and be more on top of things?
> *Client:* I can do that?
> *Therapist:* Yes. Can I explain to you about a thing called anxiety?
> *Client:* I guess so.
> *Therapist:* Anxiety is an agitated feeling that we all get when something happens that we don't want to happen or we feel sensitive about. It's like an itch you can't scratch.
> *Client:* Yeah, so?
> *Therapist:* Well, I am going to deliberately say something about your grades, but I don't mean what I say, I just want you to watch the feeling you get. Is that OK with you?
> *Client:* So now you are going to tell me to get good grades, too?
> *Therapist:* Do you have that agitated feeling right now, Marie? The itch you can't scratch?
> *Client (protesting):* I thought you said that you didn't care about my grades.
> *Therapist:* I said that I cared more about you than your grades. But this is not about grades. Can I go on?
> *Client:* OK, I just am so tired of people bothering me about my grades.
> *Therapist:* I understand. Marie, have you noticed that any time someone mentions your grades, like right now, that you get irritated with them and say things like "Whatever," or "I don't care," or "Leave me alone"?
> *Client:* Yeah.
> *Therapist:* Well, I am going to say it deliberately again, so that you can watch the feeling rather than give in to it and get all irritated and angry. Is it OK if I do that?

Client: OK.
Therapist (playing the role with a stern voice): Marie, your grades are terrible, and you can do a lot better. What happened when I said that?
Client: I wanted to strangle you.
Therapist: Fair enough. But what did you feel the moment I said that?
Client: I felt like I was going crazy . . . like I can't stand it.
Therapist: Right. That "can't stand it" feeling is the anxiety I am talking about. How often do you feel that feeling?
Client: A lot.
Therapist: If that didn't bother you so much, would your life be different?
Client: Well, yeah, a lot different.
Therapist: How?
Client: I wouldn't, like, be going off on people and yelling at them to leave me alone all the time.
Therapist: Would you like to learn how to handle that anxiety feeling so it doesn't bother you as much? You can, you know. And it might help you to feel better.
Client: Sure. What do I do?

The therapist then explained to Marie the idea of self-monitoring. In this case, it involved just watching her anxiety levels at school, at home, and with her friends. She was told to watch what she did whenever she felt it and to "look, don't think." She did this quite well and soon was paying attention to it with relatively little effort. Once she was willing to experience the anxiety, she began to use the stress management techniques she had previously ignored. Her progress in therapy was enhanced as well. With difficult clients, merely speaking of anxiety usually will not communicate the point, but demonstrating it to a client can do so quite well. Unfortunately, the anxiety sometimes needs to be induced in the session.

IDENTIFY CORE BELIEFS

There are several core beliefs that can interfere with establishing the willingness or readiness to experience anxiety or difficulty. If these beliefs can be isolated, identified, and successfully disputed, therapy is likely to progress more quickly. It may be helpful to recall that many of these beliefs are ontological (Ottens & Hanna, 1998); that is, they involve implicit learning (Dowd & Courchaine, 1996) and may have been formed preverbally. Thus, when attempting to isolate such a belief, the exact wording is not as important as the concept of the belief itself. Some of the core beliefs related to this precursor are

- "Experiencing emotional pain is self-torture."
- "Experiencing emotional pain makes me weak."
- "Experiencing anxiety drains my energy."
- "Anything unpleasant is a sign of impending pain."
- "Only fools immerse themselves in emotions."
- "To open oneself up to emotional pain threatens the integrity of the self."
- "If I begin to feel, I will begin to fall apart."
- "There is always a way to avoid anything difficult."
- "I can avoid anything."
- "If I have no feelings, I have no pain."

When one of these statements is presented, the client will often amend it and, with the help of the therapist, give the concept the proper wording. Once identified, disputing an ontological core belief can bring about second-order change in some cases.

William James (1904/1977) wrote a brilliant series of articles in the first decade of the 20th century called *Essays in Radical Empiricism*. Both Bertrand Russell (1972) and Alfred North Whitehead (1925) believed that in those essays, James had found the long-awaited solution to the centuries-old Cartesian dualism of mind versus matter. Essentially, James showed how all of life, space, time, relationships, objects, and even awareness boil down to pure experience. For our purposes and on a much more mundane level, this means that pain is experience, and so is joy—just experience—merely experience—no more, and no less, than experience. People who have learned this lesson and apply it in everyday life are well-endowed with the willingness to experience anxiety or difficulty.

11

CULTIVATING AWARENESS

The aware client can be among the trickiest of all difficult clients. When working with a client high in awareness, therapists are likely to believe that change is imminent. However, I have seen aware clients who are highly articulate, self-disclosing, and insightful, but who do not take any steps toward change. This is the case when certain precursors, such as hope, confronting, effort, or readiness for anxiety, are missing.

Many such clients are remarkably skilled at pointing out their issues and explaining their maladies. Such clients seem like gifts to the inexperienced therapist—until it becomes apparent that change is nowhere in sight and may never occur. In some cases, these clients may have been reinforced and validated by previous therapists for having awareness but not for making changes in their lives. Awareness, like the other precursors, is merely a necessary and not a sufficient condition for change.

On the other hand, the lack of awareness is a serious deficiency indeed. A client can be laden with an amazing array of issues and problems and have little or no awareness of the issues negatively affecting his or her life. To these clients, both the mind and the world are shrouded in haze and obscurity. An example is the obsessive–compulsive client who repeats and checks behaviors, knowing only that it has to be done. Another example is the criminal who has spent his life learning to victimize others. His behaviors have been validated and reinforced repeatedly by peers and the environment, to the point where he believes the only improvement needed in his life is in his skills at deception and intimidation. Clients lack awareness in different ways, but in each the pattern is similar: Confusion, ignorance, or rigidly blind beliefs dominate. Another indicator that awareness is low is when what looks like a problem to the therapist is judged as an asset by the client. This is evident when the client takes an "ignorance is bliss" kind of stance.

Without awareness present and operative to some degree, the other precursors will lack focus and power in producing change. Therefore, the therapeutic task when working with clients low in this precursor is to build or cultivate awareness so that confronting and effort resources can be brought to bear on a known problem or concern. Bringing about awareness in clients who receive low ratings in this precursor can be quite challenging and demands considerable creativity on the part of the therapist. This chapter contains several approaches to cultivating awareness in the form of metaphors, reframes, and techniques.

METAPHORS THAT ILLUSTRATE THE LACK OF AWARENESS

As with the willingness precursor, metaphors can help a therapist educate a client toward understanding that he or she may have a problem or an area of life that is in need of attention, even though he or she may not know that it is there. Some of the metaphors that follow are rather graphic, even off color, but if used appropriately they will illustrate to a client how he or she has overlooked or ignored important issues.

The metaphors are meant to normalize the lack of awareness so that the client does not feel criticized. Difficult clients usually perceive a direct statement that he or she lacks awareness as an insult delivered by an arrogant therapist. I have made that mistake a few times. Metaphors can help therapists avoid this pitfall when used with wisdom, tact, and timing and within the proper context.

The use of metaphor is one of those abilities that is limited only by the therapist's wisdom and imagination. I have seen many memorable cases in which therapeutic change emerged through the use of a simple but powerful metaphor. To produce metaphors with great change potential, understanding the client's frame of reference is essential. Often clients provide the best metaphors, knowingly or unknowingly.

Blind Spots in the Rearview Mirror

This metaphor is helpful for any client who has a driver's license. The therapist tells the client that people do not see everything on the road, and that is why we have rearview mirrors, so we can be more aware of what traffic is surrounding us. Unfortunately, rearview mirrors have blind spots. Relying only on the mirrors will not reveal a nearby vehicle at certain angles. Sometimes we have to turn around and look at the road directly.

Awareness also has blind spots, and to compensate for them we sometimes have to turn around and look, that is, inspect our minds for thoughts, intentions, and feelings, as well as our environment for what is going on with us and to us. This metaphor is effective in getting a client to see that there may be things he or she is doing or thinking that have negative consequences and that it is time to check things out.

Bad Breath

For some clients, this graphic albeit crude metaphor can be highly effective in communicating how a person can have issues or problems that he or she is not aware of at all. The therapist can ask the client if he or she ever knew someone with bad breath who had no idea of it and needed to be told. The point can be made that all people have their blind spots. The therapist can then seek permission to point out a possible blind spot for the client's consideration. If the relationship is reasonably stable, the client will usually give permission, even though he or she may not agree that they have the issue. But by that point the door has been opened for discussion through the further use of the metaphor. Another point the therapist can make is that all of us at certain times in our lives rely on someone else for feedback. In the context of therapy, a therapist's function is to provide that feedback in a trusting, confidential climate.

Body Odor

This metaphor serves the same purpose as the bad breath metaphor and can be used if and when appropriate with clients for whom it is suitable. It can be quite effective in conveying the idea of how a person can have a problem but lack awareness of it, especially if it affects relationships with others. Body odor can be used as a metaphor to explain a "behavior odor," that is, a behavior such as being obnoxious or arrogant that can get a person into difficulty, but the person is so used to it that he or she can no longer "smell it" or be aware of it. It is a primitive but often useful metaphor.

The Mountain Overlook

Part of attaining awareness is to step back to gain a more global view of the situation or problem. A. T. Beck (1976) referred to this psychological act as *distancing*. It is often needed when a client is so immersed in a particular viewpoint that he or she will not budge from it. Stepping back can be suggested in therapy with the help of the mountain overlook metaphor. It is easier to understand a city by looking down on it from the top of a mountain than by walking a single street or alley. The therapist can ask the client to step back and provide what can be called "the big picture" of his or her situation. This process can be enhanced by outlining, mapping, or diagramming the problem to get a more complete perspective. The therapist can sometimes add new aspects to the map or diagram for the client's consideration as part of attaining an overarching view of the problem or issue.

FINDING AN EXAMPLE OF AN UNAWARE PERSON

Almost everyone knows someone who has quirks, odd habits, or idiosyncrasies of which, it seems, the person is completely unaware. It is sometimes helpful to use this observation as a transition or pivot point to create an opening through which clients low in awareness can take a fresh look at themselves. The first step is to get a person to recall someone in his or her own environment who had strange, harmful, or otherwise eccentric habits. Once recalled, it can be pointed out that virtually all of us have quirks of which we are unaware. At that point, the therapist can respectfully ask if it is possible that the client might have some habits or actions of which he or she may not be aware. The therapist then asks permission to point one out for the client's comment. This will often help initiate the process of enhancing the awareness precursor.

REFRAMES THAT RAISE AWARENESS

A primary and invaluable strategy for building awareness in clients of individual problems and issues is the use of reframes. As a technique, the use of reframes has been praised in many theories and schools of psychotherapy. When formulated according to the client's language, experience, and understanding, these can be quite powerful. The most effective reframes are a result of a good deal of empathy.

Reframing Negative Behaviors in a Positive Frame

Marvin, age 17, was court-ordered into an outpatient treatment program for adolescent criminal offenders after a theft conviction. After being in the program for a month, he had already acquired the reputation of being difficult and incorrigible. He was described to the consulting therapist as a "compulsive thief and liar." Marvin had little regard for boundaries and felt entitled to own any object that he perceived. This client's father, apparently a career criminal, was currently serving time in prison, and his mother's whereabouts were unknown. He was being raised by his favorite uncle, who also appeared to be a habitual criminal offender. Marvin had little or no awareness of the consequences of his actions and would not tolerate even broaching the subject of theft or stealing.

Eventually, it became clear that when Marvin was a child, his father, mother, and uncle consistently validated and encouraged him whenever he came home with something he had stolen. Stealing made his parents proud of him, and it became a source of pride and self-esteem for Marvin. Because of the heavy reinforcement of this behavior, the therapist promptly reframed his stealing as "being a good boy." Marvin found this quite amusing and often laughed out loud when the therapist said it. The therapist asked Marvin if he could use that phrase in place of the word "stealing." Marvin agreed. From his perspective, the reframe was much closer to reality. The reframe also greatly contributed to the fast formation of a therapeutic relationship.

Eventually, awareness of his problem emerged as he explored the contradictory messages he had received from his parents, schools, courts, and society and the consequences of those contradictions. He also developed awareness of the problem as a multigenerational family issue. Marvin's story is continued in the next chapter, where the confronting precursor is the focus.

Awareness as Savoir Faire

For many adolescents and adults, awareness is a largely foreign term. A worthy goal in educating clients on the benefits of awareness is to help them regard it as desirable and worth pursuing. It can help to point out that many of the people whom the client admires already possess awareness in some form or another, even if it is in terms of knowing what people want or knowing "what's cool." Reframing awareness as knowing "what's happening" or "what's going down" puts it in a more desirable light for many clients. Eventually, the client learns that awareness is related to therapeutic change and leads to better coping strategies and success in life. When awareness can be aligned with the client's personal goals, a greater level of hope develops as the future is perceived with increased clarity. The trick is to help the client see that greater awareness is what he or she really desired all the time anyway.

A Situation Rather Than a Problem

Some difficult clients respond negatively at even the hint that their issue is a "problem." Some boldly proclaim, "This is not a problem!" It can be a mistake to assert that a client has a problem, and a typical response is for the client to stiffen or become somewhat or outright defiant or indignant. Although many clients with a lack of awareness will not admit to a problem, they may be amenable to reframing it as "a situation that is in need of attention." Thus, terms like *situation*, *challenge*, or *puzzle* can substitute for *problem* quite nicely. One can introduce the idea by questioning and probing into the consequences of the situation if it were to continue unchecked. Of course, the initial response would be a superficial denial, but this will usually diminish to the degree the "situation" is defined.

Getting Lost in the Thought Stream

People who are subject to compulsive behaviors such as excessive shopping, sexual acting out, checking, and substance abuse often find themselves caught up in the escalating desires and thoughts that lead to repetition of the unwanted behavior. Therapists can help clients enhance their awareness of the phenomenon by reframing these automatic thoughts as being "lost in the thought stream." This can be combined with a metaphor of being caught up in the river rapids of the mind, which carry one away helplessly. The metaphor can then be extended by introducing the idea that it is possible to swim to the shore and to remain on the shore of the river observing the rapids from a safe, calm vantage point.

I have often used this metaphor with adolescent sex offenders. The client can be helped to identify the pattern of cascading thoughts, desires, and emotions that consume him or her, sweeping him or her away in the stream. It also helps for the client to observe and identify the environmental triggers that bring on the onslaught of desires, emotions, and thoughts. The therapist can also, in a controlled fashion, recreate the cascade in the session and help the client swim to the shore. The metaphor of keeping one's head above water can symbolize not getting submerged by the rapids of desires and thoughts until one reaches the stability of the shore, which is, of course, sustained awareness.

CONFRONTATION

Confrontation is perhaps as old as therapy itself and needs no further explanation here. (It is, of course, completely different from the confronting precursor.) Virtually every school has a version of it, except perhaps pure Rogerian therapy, although even there confrontation takes place in its own fashion. It remains a classically effective way to bring a client to awareness. The key to confrontation is that it be done compassionately and with empathy. When not done in this way, needless power struggles are often the result.

ISOLATING AUTOMATIC THOUGHTS

Automatic thoughts are habitual and are repeated in a kind of thought stream, with no conscious decision to actively form them (A. T. Beck, 1976). The phenomenon carries a slightly different label for Meichenbaum (1977; Meichenbaum & Cameron, 1974), who referred to it as *negative self-talk*, another commonly used term in therapy. For all practical purposes, *automatic thoughts* and *self-talk* are the same phenomenon and can be treated in the same fashion.

With regard to the awareness precursor, automatic thoughts to be alert for are related to denial of the existence or severity of a problem or issue. One method of access to automatic thoughts can be done in two ways. The first is to have a client repeat a dysfunctional statement to the therapist, doing so out loud and with conviction. The other is for the therapist to make the same statement directly to the client, with the same conviction. Then the client reports what thoughts were stimulated when the statement was made. The therapist writes the thoughts down, if the client agrees, so that they can be examined and disputed later.

In the case of a client with a drinking problem, a therapist might choose the second method. He or she can say to a client, "I am going to make a statement to you. Please understand that I am not trying to convince you of anything; I just want to know what your immediate reaction is in your mind when I say it. The statement will be, 'You have a drinking problem.' Please remember that I am not trying to argue or force anything on you. Just tell me what thoughts go through your mind when I say it. Is this OK?" The client, presumably, gives consent. The therapist then repeats the statement with deep conviction and says, "OK, what happened there?"

In the many times I have done this with clients, the typical self-talk reported was, "My drinking is under control," "I don't have a problem," "I am doing just fine," "Nobody understands," and "I don't want to think about this." Defiant statements mixed with obscenities were also common. Such self-statements are more or less designed to reduce awareness of the problem or issue. Awareness can be increased by focusing on these statements, examining their function in terms of reducing awareness, and then disputing them in the cognitive behavioral fashion. Self-monitoring can be recommended to clients so that they can observe the operation of these thoughts in everyday life. If the therapist attempts to convince the client that there is a problem, however, the exercise can degrade into an argument.

LOCALIZING FEELINGS AS SENSATIONS IN THE BODY

Many difficult clients have difficulty verbalizing or differentiating feelings. Indeed, many such clients are not developmentally advanced enough to differentiate feelings and feel almost harassed by therapists who insist on working with feelings. According to Loevinger (1976) and other developmentalists, it is easier for clients in lower developmental stages to identify sensations as opposed to emotions and feelings.

Quite often clients can identify feelings by pointing to the location in the body where they feel "tensions" associated with the problem. This is taken from Gendlin's (1981) focusing technique. Goldman and Morrison (1984) reported that they had used this technique with thousands of clients. I have found it to be highly effective in enabling clients to eventually identify and verbalize feelings. For example, Joe was a firefighter in his late 20s who sought therapy to resolve his shyness around women. When it became apparent that he had great difficulty identifying feelings, his therapist asked, "Joe, as you talk to me about your shyness, do you feel any sensations or tensions in your body?" Joe immediately pointed to his chest just under the sternum and said, "Yeah, I get really tight right here, and it's like I can't say anything."

Other clients report a feeling of tightness or heaviness in the pit of the stomach, or in the chest or throat. Although a client may not be up to saying he is sad, he might have no trouble saying that he feels "choked up" in the throat. Once the area of the body is identified, the client can then physically outline with the index finger how large the area is in which the sensation is felt. The sensation can then be used in self-monitoring, rather than focusing on a feeling of sadness or fear that may still be too vague. From there, it is a natural progression to eventually identify actual emotions, although even then they may only be felt and articulated in a primitive form.

ROLE PLAYS OF OTHERS

Role playing is part of a great many theories and schools of therapy and probably originated in the psychodrama school in the first decade of the 20th century (see Moreno, 1946). The adaptation of this old therapy technique is based on the idea of stepping back or distancing and is designed to initiate this fundamental psychological act. Role plays can be highly effective with difficult clients when they are willing to engage in the procedure. Many difficult clients do not like role plays and will not do so until a relationship is well established. Others do not seem to have much difficulty with it.

Awareness of a situation or problem can sometimes be enhanced by having a client do role plays of people who know him or her well, such as current or former friends; current or former husbands, wives, or romantic partners; and family members. A trusted person is usually the best choice. Speaking as the person who cares about and knows the client well, the client can become aware of how others view him or her. This technique can have the benefit of revealing aspects of self or behavior that have not been previously considered.

The role playing approach is especially helpful for clients who tend to be self-centered to the point of not knowing what effect they have on those around them. Following the role play, the therapist can play the role of the trusted person and have the client respond to the earlier statements and observations that were given when the client played that same role.

THE EMPTY CHAIR

The empty chair technique can be used as an alternative to role plays. Typically listed in the category of experiential techniques, it is powerful in building awareness with some clients. It is another old technique that probably originated with psychodrama in the early part of the 20th century, although it is commonly associated with Gestalt therapy. Unfortunately, many difficult clients will eschew this approach, steadfastly asserting that they will not talk to "a chair with nothing in it." Nevertheless, other clients will respond to this technique remarkably well in the context of a therapeutic relationship. It is one of those techniques that is best framed as an experiment (Polster & Polster, 1973).

Four modalities of roles qualify as candidates for "sitting" in the empty chair. The first is people currently available and accessible in a client's life. The second is people who have died or are otherwise no longer available. The third modality is subpersonalities or different parts of the self that have not been given voice. The fourth modality is the client and consists of the current self, the past self (as in childhood), and the future self.

When doing the empty chair, it is important to the interaction that the client actually move to the other chair, assuming the identity that has been projected in it and communicating from that perspective. The process is continued until increased awareness results. The technique can result in the resolution of inner conflicts, the coming to terms with parents both dead and alive, and enhanced empathy for others.

SELF-MONITORING

Both behavior and existential therapies use forms of self-monitoring to heighten awareness. Many difficult clients, for example, are not interested in homework assignments and simply will not do them. However, the therapist can issue a challenge to them to make use of awareness gained from a previous therapy session to apply in a self-monitoring context. If the client is not told to actually do anything but observe, such homework might have more compliance.

For example, Peter, a passive–aggressive client in his late 40s, was sarcastic, bitter, and defiant toward authority figures, especially in the work-place. He almost immediately displayed similar behaviors toward his therapist. Even though many of his complaints about his superiors were partially valid, his hostility made his interactions with them difficult.

During a role play of a work situation, Peter was made aware of the intensity of his hostility toward authority. The therapist repeated the statement, "I need this by Friday" to him in the same condescending manner as his supervisor and processed it between repetitions. Before this role play, Peter had firmly denied feeling any anger and resentment toward his supervisor, but he found it emerging through this process. The therapist asked him to observe and monitor his feelings when in the general vicinity of his boss.

Peter soon reported that he had not suspected how much resentment he showed toward even the most benign directives from people in authority positions. Issues that arose between him and the therapist were used as opportunities to study his transference reactions based on his childhood spent with a verbally abusive father. As with many difficult clients, giving Peter homework tasks other than awareness would have been premature.

THE USE OF PARADOX

There are times when instructing a person to continue their lack of awareness can bring about awareness. For example, a 15-year-old girl in treatment for cocaine abuse was perceived as compulsively manufacturing lies by a treatment team and her fellow group members as well. She would not, however, admit to having such a problem and repeatedly and loudly declared that she was being unfairly accused. After some discussion, her therapist contracted with her the paradoxical directive that she was not to tell the truth in group. The therapist explained to her that she had to lie about her past, her beliefs, her behaviors, her family, and so on. After she agreed to try this experiment, her fellow group members were also (necessarily) informed and were glad to help by going along with whatever she said, even asking her questions that required further lying on her part.

The intent of this intervention was for her to achieve an initial awareness of telling lies by consciously and constantly differentiating truth from falsehood as required by the intervention. In other words, to be a successful liar, she also had to know what was true. Eventually, she asked the therapist if she could start telling the truth, because she was "getting tired of lying." She articulated no specific insight, but after six of these group sessions she reported that her lying was indeed a problem. Subsequently, it was much easier for her to address it as part of her treatment, and her mother enthusiastically reported improvement in following up on the intervention's apparent success. It was also a classic example of how insight can both follow, and precede, behavior change (see Arkowitz, 1989).

SETTING AND CONTRASTING CONTEXTS

A problem will seem so only in the context of other factors (Bateson, 1979). Alcohol abuse is a perfect example. It does not seem a problem at all in the context of the bar and its inhabitants. In the context of the family and the workplace, however, alcohol abuse is profoundly problematic. Similarly, some people justify in the context of "business" actions that are questionable in other contexts, such as friendships. If directed toward friends, "business" behaviors and attitudes are cruel and cold. The most obvious comparison of contexts is the killing of human beings in the context of war and in the context of murder. Both are killing, but the former is societally sanctioned.

A client can come to understand that a problem, issue, or concern is acceptable in a particular context but does not transfer to others. The task of the therapist in this strategy is to describe the contexts and then make the dialectical switch. By pointing out that the problem behavior is acceptable and fine in one context, the therapist can then switch the context so that the negative aspects of that behavior stand in stark contrast. This approach often results in an increase of awareness, accompanied by an increase in cognitive dissonance.

In working with substance-abusing teenagers who insisted that they did not have a problem, I would run groups based on setting contexts. For example, I would have members take turns and name the three most important things in their lives. Typically, they would name friends, family, freedom, and love as the most important. I would then have them explain how the use of drugs and alcohol affected each one of those important aspects. This contrasting of contexts draws out many dysfunctional beliefs and behaviors and makes for spirited, animated group sessions and interesting insights. It can be done individually as well.

ACTING-OUT THEATER

Acting-out theater is an awareness approach for groups and is not unlike what might be done in psychodrama. The technique involves designating a stage that the group can observe as an audience. One group member portrays another member's negative attitudes or acting out behaviors, without saying who it is. The group's challenge is to guess which member is the one whose behavior is being portrayed. Group members must be reasonably familiar with the behaviors and attitudes of their fellows, or the approach is likely to fail. The approach is especially effective with children and adolescents in inpatient settings or outpatient settings where there is sufficient contact between members. One of the most interesting aspects of this kind of approach is to observe how the person being portrayed protests as the other group members loudly assert that the portrayal was indeed accurate. It has considerable potential to build awareness in these clients.

HANDLING INTENTIONAL UNAWARENESS

Some difficult clients seem to deliberately reduce or diminish awareness in order to maintain a problem behavior. Such clients are highly unlikely to change without addressing this deliberate reduction. Clients whose presenting problems arise directly from treating others poorly or without compassion or empathy are often unwilling to admit they are unfeeling, insensitive, or uncompassionate. Many have deliberately dulled their awareness so they can remain convinced that they are good, decent people. These clients directly cause their presenting problems but typically blame them on others. In many clients who are harming those around them, a carefully considered choice seems to take place just outside of their awareness. The choice is never to inspect or evaluate the harmful behavior or attitude. People who make this choice can thus be "antisocial" without the criminal elements that would normally qualify them for a personality disorder diagnosis.

People who have made this choice believe, usually without being aware of the belief, that if they are not aware of harming others, then their selfish behaviors can continue unchecked. They deliberately and even passionately keep their continuous harmful behaviors out of awareness. I have found that many of these clients simply will not improve until this mechanism is exposed or until they admit that their own selfishness or self-centeredness is harming others. The executive who believes that he does what is best for the business or company and that he has to be "brutally honest" and direct with employees is one such example. Another is the harsh father who believes that he must be "stern" with his children and wife so he can keep them "disciplined," when in fact he is abusing them. The employee who embezzles property or company funds while rationalizing and complaining of management and how badly she is mistreated at work is another. Such people are unlikely to change simply because they are dedicated to remaining oblivious.

Getting a client to be cognizant of harmful or insensitive behaviors is difficult in part because the ignorance is intentional. A helpful strategy for reversing this ignorance is the use of paradox. A client can be told that, for one day each week, he or she is to be "deliberately unaware." The therapeutic task is to avoid observing how those around them—family, friends, coworkers, employers, and employees—respond to their actions. In some cases, this will actually spark awareness. In other cases, the therapist can directly challenge the client, courteously and empathically, about whether or not the client really wants to know how he or she is affecting others.

EMPATHY AS A REMEDY

In the precursors model, empathy is viewed not only as a necessary characteristic for an effective therapist but as a mark of mental health and well-being for people in general. Cautela (1996) observed that developing empathy in clients should be a routine aspect of therapy. He referred to the insensitivity of people who regularly harm others as *empathy immunization* (p. 341). Perhaps *empathy inurement* is more descriptive.

Many clients who harm others lack empathy. These clients do not necessarily meet the criteria for antisocial or narcissistic personality disorders, as many have no criminal involvement, but they are similarly cold, callous, and unempathic. They are found in many walks of life, but that empathy deficit is a shared characteristic.

The idea of social interest or community feeling, Adler's most important concept (Adler, 1979; O'Connell, 1991), is based on the idea that a healthy person is one who is sensitive to and identifies with others, extending ultimately to all of humanity. The concept is built around empathy (see Adler, 1956; Ansbacher, 1992). People lacking in empathy, because they do not feel the pain of others, find it easier to perpetrate selfish acts on those around them. Nonempathic people may be so self-absorbed and limited in the awareness of others that they may be deeply and continuously upsetting those around them without a clue they are doing so. Such a person's road to change is built on becoming aware of how they contribute to so many of their problems. Rehabilitating empathy is one approach to such clients.

Perhaps the best approach for helping a person see how they affect others is the feedback received in group therapy. Yalom (1995) called this *interpersonal input*, and his research indicated that of all the therapeutic factors provided by group therapy, this was the most important and provided the greatest benefit. The feedback provided by group members concerning how the unempathic member affects them is invaluable, and the effective group therapist will take advantage of this at every opportunity. Such feedback can also occur in family and couples therapy as well. It can also be done in individual therapy, but it lacks the dramatic impact of having one's insensitivity exposed by a group of one's peers.

BUILDING TOLERANCE OF CONFUSION

Another clinical observation of difficult clients lacking in the awareness precursor is that some seem to have a low tolerance of confusion, which inhibits or shuts down the development of awareness. These people seem to withdraw from or avoid any kind of complexity, disarray, or disorganization, and in that act of withdrawal, they abandon awareness. When the thoughts and events in their minds are in disarray, they are unwilling to explore the mess. For these people, it is helpful to outline, diagram, or draw problem situations, reactions, impulses, and anything else that may be excessively complex or confusing.

IDENTIFY CORE BELIEFS ABOUT AWARENESS

Several core beliefs interfere with cultivating awareness. If these can be isolated, identified, and successfully disputed, there may be fewer obstacles to prevent the client from developing awareness. These beliefs are so fundamental that clients cannot be expected to mention them, except perhaps in blurting one out unwittingly. The therapist would need to present each belief to a client for comment to see if he or she agrees with the statement. In addition, the belief should be stated using language that is familiar to the client. Disputation and replacement are the best means for handling these beliefs, which the client may never have articulated before. The following statements indicate core beliefs about awareness:

- "To be aware is to feel pain."
- "Awareness only makes pain more intense."
- "If I am not aware of something, it can't hurt me."
- "Awareness interferes with my fun."
- "If there is no awareness, there is no suffering."
- "Awareness is a risk and a liability."
- "Awareness only reveals how bad I am."
- "Awareness reveals how empty I am."
- "To be aware is to know that I am unlovable."
- "Awareness exposes all my faults."
- "Awareness will make me feel ashamed or guilty."

Masterson (1988) noted that the authentic self can engage and experience the full range of human emotions and feelings. Just as the shunning of awareness is the essence of defensiveness, the strengthening and enhancing of awareness open the doors to exquisite feelings of vitality and aliveness. The key to that vitality seems to be the belief that even the awareness of pain is better than no awareness at all.

12

ENHANCING CONFRONTING

Virtually all of the techniques used in psychotherapy, with the exception of medications and pure operant conditioning, make use of the confronting precursor in some way (Hanna & Puhakka, 1991). The vast array of procedures, such as identifying and disputing dysfunctional beliefs, role playing, the empty chair, social skills and assertiveness training, working through transference, interpretation, paradox, reframing, and the use of metaphor, as well as the "talking cure" itself, all require the problem to be confronted either directly or indirectly. In essence, any approach that calls for sustained, continuous, and deliberate viewing of a situation, whether to talk about it or to cope with it, makes use of the confronting precursor. The techniques provided in this chapter are specifically for developing confronting in difficult clients.

There are some important points to bear in mind regarding confronting. Forcing a person to confront too much, too soon, is traumatic by definition. Bringing a client to contact painful phenomena must be done with care and attention to the person's level of tolerance. Overwhelming a client with mental, emotional, or environmental material that is too much to confront will not only bring about early termination, it will cause harm. Thus, exposure to sensitive memories, feelings, or beliefs should be done gradually so the client will be successful and not view therapy as a source of failure and pain. The techniques and strategies in this chapter are designed to encourage, implement, and strengthen the confronting precursor.

Confronting is not only a psychological act, it is also an ability, and like muscles with weight lifting, it becomes stronger with practice and discipline. Of course, the chief task with difficult clients is to initiate confronting, if only in its most bare and fundamental form. That is the focus of the strategies that follow.

THE STRENGTH METAPHOR

Some clients seem to find confronting their problems not only difficult but abhorrent and repulsive. For many, the act itself is painful. This is especially the case with clients with personality disorders. Although such clients are often almost vilified as being uncooperative, manipulative, malicious, and intrinsically flawed, the truth may be that, at the core, they are lacking in the skill and ability to confront such things as unpleasant thoughts, feelings, behaviors, and events. These people are often in need of education concerning this and other precursors. Many may have never learned that it is through confronting problems that problems resolve and that the act of confronting, rather than being harmful, is in fact the beginning of healing and a source of exhilaration.

Thus, the metaphor of strength can be used to show clients that the more one confronts issues, the better at it one gets. Although some people can confront a vast range of psychopathology in one grand sweep of consciousness, others can take in only small bits and portions at a time, and even then with great difficulty. The difference, as in lifting weights or exercising, lies in understanding that the more confronting one does, the more capable one is of doing more of it, and the more stamina and strength one develops.

CONFRONTING THE HESITANCY TO CONFRONT

Often clients are aware of a problem area such as alcoholism, depression, anxiety, or some compulsive behavior but are unwilling to confront anything about it. In such cases, the therapist can offer an approach framed as an experiment. The therapist can openly inform the client that confronting the problem is not necessary. He or she then asks the client simply to "think about" the problem and to report all the thoughts and feelings that arise. The therapist again informs the client that he or she should not talk about the problem itself, only what springs to mind as he or she thinks about it. The client will typically report that he or she dislikes the subject and just does not feel like thinking about it or any other problems. These statements can then be fully acknowledged and reflected.

The purpose of this technique is to identify the automatic thoughts, beliefs, and feelings that stand in the way of confronting. Then go with the diversion. Get the client to talk about not wanting to talk about or explore anything. Fully understand and reflect everything said. Eventually, he or she may be more likely to confront the problem or issues and may do so spontaneously.

CONFRONTING THE IDEA OF CHANGE ITSELF

The above technique can also be applied to difficult clients who find the idea of change itself uncomfortable or objectionable. The client can be asked simply, "Get the idea of making changes [or one particular change] in your life." Then he or she can be asked what kinds of thoughts and feelings rise to awareness, including thought streams and even unspoken verbal responses such as, "Go to hell" or "That's a load of bull----" or similar statements. It will often turn out that therapeutic change is something that appears to insult the person's character or dignity and that the mere suggestion of its need is a kind of criticism. Furthermore, the contemplation of change by a difficult client can bring up a variety of beliefs about change, such as "to change is to fail" or "to change is an admission of being wrong" or "to change is to give up." When disputed, some fascinating clinical material is often encountered that accompanies these beliefs.

IN VIVO CONFRONTING

Talking in therapy does not always lead to the "talking cure." Talk can be used to circumvent and even avoid problems and issues, resulting in the illusion of progress but never any real resolution. In many cases, the emotions, passions, and desires involved with dysfunctional behaviors must be aroused so they can be addressed in the present moment. Talk therapy does not always accomplish this. In vivo confronting is a variation of the well-tested and venerable techniques derived from the behavioral principles of exposure and reciprocal inhibition, which also recognize the limits of the talking cure. This technique is equally well explained by the concept of the resolute perception of particular issues and problems. The problem can be recreated in the therapy room in real time with therapeutic benefit, invoking the vaccine effect.

In vivo confronting is an adaptation of the classical behavioral techniques of flooding and systematic desensitization, as well as resolute perception. Of course, the classical application of these techniques is with phobias, and it is so well documented there is no need for elaboration here. However, these principles, all based on the confronting precursor, can be applied to compulsive behaviors such as stealing, substance abuse, and compulsive sexual behaviors. In applying this approach, it is wise to inform the client of the procedure and frame it as an experiment he or she can back out of at any time.

Marvin: The Rest of the Story

Marvin was the difficult, conduct-disordered teenager introduced in chapter 11 who had been convicted of theft and placed in an outpatient program for adolescent criminal offenders. After the development of awareness through the metaphor of the "good boy," the door was opened to full-scale confronting. Because stealing was the problem that landed Marvin in the outpatient treatment program, the consulting therapist decided to use a technique designed to get Marvin to confront his compulsive stealing behaviors, which he was now willing to discuss in both individual therapy and in group.

The therapist asked Marvin if he was willing to try an experiment regarding his urge to take things that belonged to others. Marvin readily agreed. At that point the therapist pulled out a $20 bill and placed it in front of the client, turned his back on him (he was sitting between the client and the door, of course), and then asked him to report his thoughts and feelings as he looked at the money. Marvin immediately said, "I want to take it, man." The therapist asked him, "What are you feeling in your body right now, Marvin?" He replied that he was feeling excited and pointed to his stomach. When asked, he added that this was associated with the challenge of getting away with something, as well as doing something at which he felt competent (stealing).

The therapist asked him, "Marvin, is this the same feeling you get when you are in the street or in a store and you think about stealing something?" He replied simply, but somewhat contemplatively now, "Yeah, it's the same feeling." The therapist then asked him, "When you have this feeling, are you also feeling pretty good about yourself?" Marvin looked at the therapist and said, "Yeah, it's like I feel really cool, and I can take anything." A discussion then ensued concerning the relationship between stealing and his sense of self-esteem and self-worth and how his parents and his uncle had tied these together. Marvin recognized this and was by now capable of elaborating on it. The therapist then asked if this was how he gained respect from his peers. Marvin also replied affirmatively to this, saying that among his friends, he was acknowledged as "the best."

The term *stealing* was now being used directly. There was no more use of the good boy reframe. Importantly, it soon became clear that to Marvin, the most appealing aspect of stealing was the feeling, the excitement, and the challenge of taking something not his own. He reported that the biggest obstacle to quitting stealing was not the value of the item stolen, but the appeal of the thrill and excitement that came with the mere prospect of stealing it. The therapist directly asked him, "Marvin, do you feel more alive when you are thinking about stealing something?" He quietly said, "Yeah." As a result of this experiment, the therapist asked if it would be OK to get a little more serious about producing that feeling, to which Marvin agreed.

The therapist then placed a credit card in front of him (turned upside down and face down, of course) and once again turned to the door. With his back to the client, the therapist asked if the feeling of excitement was there again. Marvin replied that it was indeed, and even stronger this time. He was then asked to describe the feeling in detail, outlining where in his stomach he felt the feeling. Marvin did so. The therapist then asked Marvin, "When you have the feeling, do you feel like you *have* to take something?" He thought a minute and said, "Yeah, it's like it's there, and I gotta do it." The therapist then asked if he could feel good by not giving in and being ruled by the feeling. Marvin had never considered this.

The therapist took Marvin to a local store, walked around with him, and asked if he felt the excitement feeling in his stomach. Marvin reported that, like always, he did. There was a pocketknife that appealed to him. Marvin was asked to describe the feeling and what it was like to watch the feeling and not be taken in by it or drawn into it. "Weird" was the word he first used to describe this new feeling. "Good weird or bad weird?" asked the therapist. "Kinda good," he said, "Like I don't have to give in to it just because I feel it." The therapist then asked if part of this new feeling was a sense of strength. Marvin responded positively, and the therapist pointed out that perhaps the real strength was not in the guts to steal but in the strength to resist. He had already proved that he had the former but not the latter.

This was the beginning of Marvin's rehabilitation. In his case, it was not only his thinking but his need for sensation that needed attention. The success of this technique in Marvin's case was through establishing the confronting precursor by getting him accustomed to looking at and examining issues. After this, he responded to group and individual therapy. When dealing with people who engage in criminal behaviors, therapy is probably incomplete without addressing the sensations and feelings that accompany the acts (Samenow, 1998).

The Story of Rusty

Rusty, age 16, was addicted to crack cocaine. He had previously been arrested several times for possession. He had just spent six months in a youth detention center for dealing crack. He had also been expelled from three schools for behavior problems. His father was an angry man who weighed nearly 500 pounds. He was habitually abusive, physically and verbally, to Rusty; was on disability; and rarely left the house in their poor neighborhood.

In treatment Rusty said simply and often that he loved crack, could do nothing about quitting, and did not want to quit. The director of the program described Rusty to the consulting therapist as a noncompliant "borderline" client for whom the treatment program had been so far ineffective. He had already been in treatment in this outpatient substance abuse program for about four months, and his urine screens had consistently indicated the use of both cocaine and marijuana. Rusty sometimes acquired money by mugging people and taking purses and wallets.

In the first session, the consulting therapist asked Rusty if he was willing to try an experiment. Rusty agreed to this, probably because of the novelty of having a new therapist and because of the chance to get out of group. After establishing an initial rapport, the therapist then offered him a small piece of chalk and asked him to pretend that it was a "rock." Rusty was quite surprised at this, but he was excited to get the chance to talk about using crack. "When you look at this rock, Rusty, what are you thinking?" Rusty unhesitatingly answered, "I want some right now, man, you have no idea how bad." The therapist acknowledged this and said, "So you are craving the high at this very moment?" Once again the immediate answer was, "Yeah, really bad."

"Is there a place in your body that you feel the craving, Rusty?" Rusty considered the question for a moment, looked up, and said, "Yeah, right here," and pointed to the area in the upper part of his stomach. "When you look at that part of your body, Rusty, what kind of feeling is in there?" Once again, he considered the question for a moment and said in one word, "Emptiness." The therapist was quite encouraged by this answer, which indicated an unexpected degree of awareness. He asked, "Is that emptiness a good feeling?" Rusty replied, "No. I don't like it." The therapist went on, "And when you are high, what does the cocaine do to that emptiness feeling?" Rusty said, "It's like it fills it up." The therapist then asked, "So is it fair to say that you use crack to fill up that feeling of emptiness you don't like?" Rusty thought about it momentarily, looked up deep in thought, and said, "Yeah, I guess I do." Continuing, the therapist asked, "How much does smoking crack actually fill up the emptiness feeling? All of it, or only part?" "Only part of it" was Rusty's honest reply. "So you always have some emptiness inside you, and it really bothers you. Is that fair to say?" Rusty responded, "Yeah."

The therapist went on, "You know, Rusty, counseling can show you how to fill up the emptiness in ways that won't land you in jail or in programs like this one, and there are no cravings like the ones you have right now. All you have to do is keep looking at and talking about your problems just like what you just did here. You interested?" Rusty, still deep in thought, said, "Yeah."

This was the beginning of Rusty's road to recovery from his use of crack cocaine. His urine screens were clean from that session onward. His continued abstinence was documented for two years after his graduation from the program, which occurred 90 days after that session. Of course, there is more to this story. This conversation was just the beginning, and many other precursors needed to be established in Rusty before his recovery strengthened and stabilized. However, the establishing of the confronting precursor in this session was what placed him on the road to recovery and was the key to all of his successful treatment. This case example shows how it is possible for confronting to be used to advantage even with clients noted for being difficult.

THE ONION PEELER

The onion peeler, a powerful technique that makes use of direct confronting, is derived from Husserl's (1913/1982) phenomenological method and from various applications of existential and Gestalt therapies (Perls et al., 1951). It can be quite intense and should be used only with a client who has a rating of at least 2 for awareness on the assessment form, and the willingness precursor also contributes to its success. It is also powerful in enhancing the change process in clients who are not difficult at all. It is called the onion peeler because it strips away automatic thoughts, self-talk, beliefs, defenses, and feelings and helps a client arrive at the heart of the problem or issue. It evokes deep emotions and can produce insights that are central to the nature of the problem.

The onion peeler is a cyclical question that is repeated over and over again after getting an answer to each cycle. The central question is, "How does [fill in the blank with whatever the problem is] appear to you now?" Variations such as "How does it look to you at this point?" or "What seems most obvious about it now?" can also be used occasionally. Another variation is, "How are you experiencing [the problem] now?" These questions require the client to observe in order to answer the question. Remarkably, the problem will appear to change after several cycles, and possibly it will change again and again until what appears to be the core of the onion is reached.

Before beginning the technique, it is important to identify or name the problem or issue with the client's agreement that this indeed characterizes the problem itself. This is where awareness is established. Once the problem has been identified, then the characterization can be inserted into the body of the cyclical question. The client should be fully informed of the nature of the procedure, its purpose, and what to expect in terms of how it is done.

The problem itself can be almost anything. For example, the problem could be a person, such as an ex-spouse, current spouse, son, daughter, employer, probation officer, teacher, betraying friend, or abusive parent or relative. It can be also be a condition or feeling such as depression, anxiety, loneliness, or helplessness, or it can be a situation such as a lack of romance, homelessness, or an unpleasant marital or work situation. One can also fill in the blank with alcohol, cocaine, or other drug of choice. "How does your body appear to you now?" can be used with some people with eating disorders.

For clients who are on probation or parole, "How does [the particular crime] appear to you now?" can be used. Of course, therapeutic judgment should be exercised about the proper timing of these techniques.

As the onion peels, the question can be further refined as the problem appears to change or become reshaped, allowing for more focus. For example, after asking, "How does your depression appear to you now?" 15 times or so, the problem reshapes itself, and the question becomes, "How does being alone appear to you now?" or "How does being a failure appear to you now?" With the client's approval, the refined version is then used. The technique itself can be used at many levels. At much higher developmental levels, well beyond the focus of this book, the sentence can be filled in with such items as the ego, life, meaning, god, or the world in general.

Every now and then, in between the cycling questions, the therapist is advised to add a processing question, such as "What's happening?" or "What are you experiencing?" or "How are you feeling about the problem?" This helps maintain the communication link between therapist and client and is often where the client will report insights, progress, or how the problem seems different.

The initial responses to the onion peeler question are usually defensive, with typical answers ranging from "Who cares?" to "It sucks." The therapist simply acknowledges these responses, saying "OK" or "alright," and perhaps reflecting on the meaning or feeling involved. However, to be effective, the question should be returned to as soon as possible to continue peeling the onion. Later answers tend to be characterized by more intense feelings, such as deep concern or feelings of helplessness.

In the case of a highly defensive male alcohol abuser, for example, his initial answers to "How does drinking appear to you now?" were along the lines of not having a problem or not needing to drink. After about 20 repetitions, answers revolved around his loving to drink, and after about 60 or 70 questions, he was worried that he could not quit. Obviously, the technique can last several sessions, and if done smoothly, it should not be a grinding or abrasive process. It is always important to check with the client to make sure his or her interest in continuing the procedure is still present or if the client feels like progress is being made. If the client is not interested, the therapist should not continue.

HOW COULD THE PROBLEM BE WORSE?

In this book, I have focused on clients who deny their problem behaviors or attitudes and who avoid awareness or confronting by minimizing their dysfunctionality and presenting it as normal or even advantageous. However, there are clients at the other end of the scale who will not confront an issue or problem simply because it is deemed so terrible or horrible that it is unconfrontable and beyond their capacity to view, explore, or otherwise tolerate. With these clients, a technique can be used that works at developing the confronting precursor indirectly through imagining something even worse. By talking about how things could have been worse, the client is more or less forced to see the event or situation in context, and in seeing how things could have turned out worse than they did, the client begins to tolerate the condition as it is.

This is, of course, delicate work, and appropriate only in particular situations where the client will not think his or her problem is being invalidated as insignificant. Thus, while fully and rightfully respecting the severity of the problem, the therapist can ask the client, "As terrible as this is, it seems you were fortunate that [a worse circumstance] did not occur." This can sometimes be appropriate for clients who have suffered a disability or family tragedy.

However, this technique is not recommended with victims of rape. Rape has been minimized throughout history and across cultures (Daly, 1978). To lessen or dismiss the tragedy of rape by finding something worse would be destructive and harmful and would only serve to perpetuate the ill-founded, ignorant, patriarchal tradition that contributes to violence against women. Thus, it is better to avoid this technique rather than to inadvertently do harm with it.

MIRRORING

Mahoney (1991) described a valuable technique that can be used with some difficult clients. The technique consists of presenting a mirror to a client and asking him or her to dialog with it or to comment on what he or she perceives in it. Although its potential might not be immediately accessible with difficult clients, it can be used as a means to get a client to begin to confront the self and how he or she regards it. It has the advantage of showing a client how little actual confronting of his or her life has actually taken place. If done correctly, it can get a client to begin to confront dysfunctional traits or aspects of the self that are a source of shame, self-blame, guilt, or regret. It also helps a person take stock of his or her life and goals and can also be used to assess degrees of self-loathing.

REPRESENTATIONAL OR CONCRETIZED CONFRONTING

Some difficult clients find the prospect of confronting thoughts or problems to be too abstract. There are times when it is easier to treat problems and emotions as concretely as possible using objects or props to represent thoughts and images with the purpose of enhancing a client's understanding of confronting. This is often helpful with children but can be highly effective with adults as well. It is especially helpful for clients who are not adept at holding a problem steady in their minds (see the confronting section in chapter 3) so that it can be more readily and fully studied or examined. For example, with a client who tends to deflect or avoid issues and problems, the therapist can point this out to them. Then the therapist represents the thought, idea, or image as a physical object to be used as a prop.

For example, Elizabeth, age 45, was wealthy and unhappy and blamed a wide variety of people for her "unhappiness," including her children and her parents. In her descriptions of the people in her life, she perceived them as wanting her to be unhappy and treating her in a way that was disrespectful and insensitive to her needs. Her depression was "their fault," and attempts to isolate beliefs related to her unhappiness had failed. Unfortunately, she also repeatedly avoided her therapist's attempts to get her to confront her own actions as part of her situation. Other approaches to blaming had also been ineffective. Rather than pursuing this line further, the therapist pointed out her avoidance and then attempted to concretize the problem in an effort to help her hold the problem steady.

> *Therapist:* I've noticed that as soon as I bring up the possibility of how your attitude might play some small part in your unhappiness, you immediately change the subject or blame someone, like your husband or your children. Please tell me if I am wrong.
> *Client:* You don't understand—they are all mean and cruel to me. They hurt me over and over again.
> *Therapist:* Yes, you feel that all they cared about was making you hurt and that you did nothing to bring this on, it just wasn't your fault at all.
> *Client:* Yes, that's it. I don't deserve this!
> *Therapist:* I don't blame you for feeling that way. Isn't it interesting, though, that every time I mention the possibility that your own attitude might have some part in your unhappiness, you immediately change the subject?
> *Client:* But they were the ones . . .
> *Therapist:* Please pardon me for interrupting you, but do you see, you are doing it again. You don't have to agree with me, just tell me if I am wrong.
> *Client:* About what?
> *Therapist:* Do you change the subject every time I ask if your own attitude might play a part in your unhappiness?
> *Client:* Because it's not true.
> *Therapist:* Fair enough. Can I have your permission to go on with this just a bit more?

Client: I suppose.

Therapist: Please tell me if I am wrong. Is it fair to say you don't like the idea that at least part of your unhappiness has to do with how you might be thinking and acting at times?

Client: I don't like that idea at all.

Therapist: I understand. Would you mind trying an experiment?

Client: I guess so.

Therapist (offering client a pen): Let's pretend for just a moment, Elizabeth, that this pen is the thought that your attitude might have some role in your own unhappiness, OK?

Client: OK . . .

Therapist: I am going to hand the pen to you as though I were saying that thought to you again. As I do, please show me, with the pen, what you do with that thought.

Client (Throws that pen to the side of the room and looks at the therapist.)

Therapist: Is it like you don't want anything to do with that thought at all?

Client: Nothing.

Therapist (retrieving the pen and handing it back to her): Would you mind just holding it in your hand and telling me what feelings and thoughts you have?

Client (looking at the pen and then beginning to cry): Sure, I have made mistakes, but they are mean to me, and then I do things that I know aren't right, but I just can't help it.

In this fashion, the technique did its job of breaking through some of Elizabeth's strong deflections to the point of opening a productive dialog about mistakes she had made and her regrets and guilt about them. She slowly progressed toward examining and changing her beliefs and behaviors.

CONCENTRATION THERAPY

Concentration therapy, as with representational confronting, also helps a client hold the problem steady in the mind. This technique is another adapted from Gestalt therapy (Perls et al., 1951) and is also a form of exposure. It consists of asking the client to hold a thought, image, feeling, emotion, problem, or situation in the mind. As with concretized confronting, the therapist then asks the client to continue to look at the object in the mind, holding it steady and reporting on what occurs as he or she does so. The image of a boss, parent, or coworker would be examples.

Such moments call for communicating empathy and understanding to clients, because holding a problem steady in the mind can seem contrary to common sense. As a defense, some clients believe that unconsciously jettisoning a thought or image from the mind is exactly what will relieve them of anxiety. They believe that if it does not stay in the mind, it won't hurt. Clients, especially those diagnosed with attention deficit hyperactivity disorder, often need to do these therapy techniques while walking around or otherwise being active. This technique also works well with the concretized confronting.

THE MIRACLE QUESTION

The miracle question technique originated with solution focused brief therapy (de Shazer, 1985) but was actually used by Adler (1956) many decades before. Assuming that the person has a small degree of awareness of a problem, this technique can be a bridge to greater confronting. The "miracle question" goes like this: "Suppose one night, while you were asleep, there was a miracle and this problem was solved. How would you know? What would be different?" To be answered, this well-crafted question requires the act of confronting and clarifies the problem even further by requiring the client to look at the problem itself, and then look through it and beyond it. It can also build the hope precursor.

ESTABLISHING THE "OBSERVER" OR "WISE MIND"

Another confronting tool is helping a difficult client establish the "observer," or what Linehan (1993) called the "wise mind." Her use of the technique was effective with borderline clients. It is a step beyond self-monitoring or self-observation. This technique awakens the "central self" (Ornstein, 1986), or the "observing self" (Deikman, 1982), that center of consciousness that is aware of and observes one's own emotions and behaviors even in the midst of acting out or giving into needs or demands. It often is present during or just after times of crisis or obsessive compulsive behaviors. It is also present during times when one sees the truth of a particular situation or when one "knows" the right thing to do in spite of temptations to the contrary and even when making mistakes in life.

The first step of this approach is to educate the client, letting him or her know that virtually every person has this capacity and that it is present and can be accessed at almost any moment. The second step is to point out a time when he or she was cognizant or "used the observer" in various situations. The third step is to actively access the observer in the therapy session so that its manifestation is by choice and not by circumstance. Homework assignments can then be issued in which the client uses the observer in various situations in his or her current environment. If a client learns this skill, the confronting and awareness precursors can be greatly enhanced.

A CLOSING NOTE ON CONFRONTING

Virtually every therapy technique makes use of the confronting precursor. Techniques and adaptations that can establish confronting enable standard techniques to work more efficiently and smoothly. When therapy techniques in general are understood from the viewpoint of confronting, new techniques can be generated and added to this list.

13

INCREASING EFFORT OR WILL TOWARD CHANGE

The precursor of effort or will toward change is where the work of change actually gets done. The amount of effort expended, however, seems to be a function of the presence of other precursors. Conversely, expending effort spontaneously increases the other precursors. Confronting is often enhanced when exerting effort toward the resolution of a problem or situation, whether environmental or psychological. However, without confronting, effort might never be engaged at all. Although confronting overlaps with effort, the essence of the latter involves the actual doing and action that reshape, alter, and implement old or new cognitions, feelings, behaviors, relationships, situations, and problems.

Hope is another precursor with a strong influence on effort. If a person can see no realistic, desirable outcome for an expenditure of effort, he or she is not likely to attempt it (Bandura, 1977). A therapist attempting to increase the effort precursor cannot lose sight of the importance of hope. A sufficient degree of a sense of necessity can be enough to spring a person into effort and action, even when neither hope nor self-efficacy is present.

Effort is fundamental and essential for change. Even when it spontaneously arises out of insight and the resulting change appears "effortless," the client may have expended great amounts of energy. Where there is great interest, great effort appears effortless. Whenever possible, a sound approach is to increase the client's interest in the task, thereby increasing the degree of effort expended toward change. This chapter lists ways to encourage the client to expend effort in doing homework assignments and to increase the client's interest in exerting effort. These are methods to inspire a person to get off their fence, couch, or behind, as the case may be.

CLARIFYING THE GOAL

Many clients display a lack of effort when it is not clear to them what exactly it is they are striving to achieve. Sometimes busy therapists inadvertently assume that a client understands why a particular task is being recommended. Few clients will carry out a task when it seems pointless. To a lesser extent, there are times when a client knows the goal but does not have a sufficiently detailed image or conception of it. People tend to display effort toward change when they believe that the effort is of their own choice (Kanfer & Grimm, 1978). When difficult clients clearly see how the task relates to the "what's-in-it-for-me" question, compliance is likely to result. Thus, the client must believe that the effort is being exerted by free choice toward a realistic, clear, and desirable outcome or result.

SELF-OBSERVATION

Some difficult clients simply will not do homework assignments. Nor will they make any sort of effort to change whether inside or outside of the therapy room. For these clients, the most appropriate form of homework assignment is that of self-observation or self-monitoring, which can be done in and out of therapy. Rather than issuing a homework assignment, the therapist can ask the client to not actually change anything, but only to watch or be aware of a particular behavior or situation in everyday life, and then to report on it in the next session. Although this paradoxical approach is suitable as a technique for building awareness, it is also a good preparation for exerting effort and energy toward change. A client can also do role plays in which he or she is not expected to do anything other than observe what happens in terms of behavior, self-talk, or emotions. Once the client has done some self-observation, it is then possible for him or her to engage in tasks requiring specific acts. Resistance to self-observation could mean the client made a decision to dull or diminish his or her awareness, and that is the issue that needs to be addressed (see chapter 11).

ASSIGNING GRADUATED TASKS

Assigning graduated tasks is a fundamental aspect of behavior therapy that is also related to the self-observation technique. Some clients are not up to performing complex tasks. It is relatively easy in some cases to overestimate what a client is capable of doing. There is a threefold requisite to assigning graduated tasks. First, the therapist should check with the client to establish that the task is realistic. Second, he or she should make sure the client is interested, understands the rationale, and agrees it is necessary. Finally, the therapist should assign only those tasks that the client is capable of performing successfully, because to do otherwise is to set the client up for a failure, which could lead to premature termination. Once simple tasks are done successfully, the client can move on to those that are more difficult or challenging.

METAPHORS FOR IMPLEMENTING EFFORT AND ACTION

Like so many other precursors, the idea of exerting effort lends itself well to the use of apt therapeutic metaphors. Many clichés also apply, such as "Nothing ventured, nothing gained" and "You don't know unless you try." The following metaphors may help clients understand the importance of effort or will.

The Finger Technique

I have found that some clients do not understand the act of will that moves a person into action and can be helped with a bit of education. The finger technique is a thought experiment that illustrates the act of will through a simple demonstration. It is especially helpful with procrastinating clients, and the therapist should demonstrate it first and then ask the client to try it. Ideally, the client does the exercise along with the therapist.

The technique begins with the therapist holding up an index finger. The therapist explains to the client that exerting effort begins with an act of will. Holding the finger in front of his or her face, the therapist shows different ways of trying to bend it. The therapist first explains that he or she is thinking about bending the finger. Of course, the finger does not move. The therapist then shouts at the finger to bend, and still it does not move. Then the therapist begs and pleads with the finger to move, with no effect. The therapist then says in a procrastinating way, "Don't worry, I am going to bend it tomorrow." The finger does not move. The therapist then says that he or she is forming a mental image of bending it, and the finger almost moves, but not really. Then the therapist actually exerts the will to move the finger, explaining that this is the only thing that will get it to move and that it is the act of will that actually accomplishes the task. It can be explained that virtually all human actions that are not on some automatic or autonomic routine are accomplished in this way.

The therapist then asks the client to bend his or her finger several times and to closely observe the act of will that brings the motion about. Performing this simple act of willing, a person can often come to understand what procrastination is as well as what it takes to actually engage effort toward a task. If the will is not exerted, effort is not expended. Once the exercise has been done, if a client does not do a homework assignment, the therapist can make use of the metaphor by saying, "So you didn't move the finger?" In this way, the client will readily understand the metaphor as it relates to therapeutic goals and tasks and to the fundamental act of achievement and accomplishment.

The House Cleaning Metaphor

The house cleaning metaphor is appropriate for some clients in communicating the importance of effort. The person's mind or life can be likened to a house in need of cleaning. One can even be acutely aware of how dirty the house is, and even confront every detail of the dirt and grime, but it will not get cleaned by awareness or confronting. It will also not get cleaned by talking about how much it needs to be cleaned. At some point, a person actually has to sweep the carpets, do the dishes, scrub the floors, and disinfect the bathroom. That is the effort precursor in essence. If a person is not willing to go through the actions, the house accumulates more and more dirt until it begins to become unhealthy. The same is true for the effort needed to change the conditions of one's mind, behavior, or environment.

IMMEDIACY

Clients who are not in therapy because of their own decision are unlikely to exert effort toward change. They may even string the therapist along, making excuses or only pretending to be cooperative as a means to graduate from a treatment program. Of course, these clients are likely to lack a sense of necessity.

Immediacy is a technique whose purpose is to communicate the therapist's complete acceptance of and empathy with the client's current goals or attitudes toward therapy. Rather than push a therapeutic agenda and a series of corresponding activities, it is more important for the therapist to deal with clients exactly where they are at in terms of how they are feeling and thinking about treatment itself. These clients need the freedom to admit, and the therapist to acknowledge, that they do not give a damn about and have no use for therapy, the therapist, or any connected program. The therapist must make it clear that he or she completely understands. The therapist should acknowledge that the client probably feels that his or her rights to freedom as a citizen are being violated. This acknowledgment will bring involuntary clients closer to a viable relationship and will encourage a willingness to self-disclose to a therapist. No one will exert much effort toward a goal without it resonating with some sense of meaning or purpose.

SUBPERSONALITY APPROACH TO EFFORT: MODE 1

Once the immediacy approach has helped to establish a therapeutic relationship, a subpersonality approach (see chapter 9) may be used to address a part of the unwilling client that does indeed want to work toward change but has heretofore gone unacknowledged. The therapist can ask the client if there is a part of him or her that does indeed want to work toward change. Although this might take some discussion, most clients will eventually admit that they do. The therapist can then ask if he or she can talk to that part. Once a subpersonality has been identified, then it can be directly addressed, with the permission of the client, so as to give it voice. Thus, from his or her own mouth, the client "hears" that he or she does indeed have inclinations toward change. The subpersonality of the person that was uninterested in change can then eventually be disidentified with, and treated as being well intended but ultimately detrimental to, the person's well-being.

SUBPERSONALITY APPROACH TO EFFORT: MODE 2

Some clients will say that they do want to exert effort toward change, but they never get around to it. Many of these difficult clients appear to have a strong sense of lethargy, being unable to expend energy largely because they do not seem to have any. They might report that they wanted to change, but that it all seemed so difficult. Sometimes this problem is related to a lack of willingness to experience anxiety or difficulty, but in other cases the willingness precursor may be adequately present, but effort is rated at trace or nonexistent. For such clients, the subpersonality approach can be of occasional service. In this application, a subpersonality may be actively though silently opposing intentions or goals.

For addressing this brand of lethargy, the therapist can ask the client if he or she wants to complete the task. If the client replies in the affirmative, the therapist can validate the client and suggest that there is probably a good reason why he or she did not carry out the homework assignment. The therapist can ask if the client is willing to explore this possibility and then ask any of the following subpersonality questions as appropriate:

- "Is there a part of you that does not want to do anything to change?"
- "Is there a part of you that does not want to do anything in therapy?"
- "Is there a part of you that does not want to do the homework assignment?"

- "Is there a part of you that is stopping you from completing the task?"
- "Is there a part of you that believes something bad will happen if you do this?"
- "Is there a part of you that feels nervous or hesitant about the task?"

The therapist then asks if he or she can talk to that part of the client. In carrying on an empathic dialog with the subpersonality, much information is gained that can then be addressed using other techniques offered in this chapter. Several approaches can then follow. For example, the empty chair can be used if the client is up to it, or perhaps a role play in which the therapist plays the client or the subpersonality so that a dialog can ensue that will lead to some integration with the lethargic self. The purpose of the technique is to increase effort expended by reducing the lethargy produced by being at cross-purposes with different aspects of the self. When the client's counter-effort reduces, there is more energy available to devote to effort toward therapeutic goals, without the previous inhibition or hesitancy.

MAPPING INTENTIONS

Once again, if the client genuinely states a desire for change but is not actually doing anything to achieve it, it is sometimes a good idea to indicate that there must be a good reason. At one level, perhaps the client truly wants change, but at another, less conscious level, change is threatening. It is often the case that a client "knows" change to be a liability and works to sabotage all efforts even while consciously attempting it. A diagram of intentions oriented around and in relation to a therapeutic goal can reveal why effort is stalled.

The therapeutic task with such clients is to understand what the intentions and purposes are in the client's mind and to map or diagram them in terms of intentions and counterintentions or purposes and counterpurposes. The therapist records on the map both intentions that are conducive to achieving the goal and intentions that are directly counter to it.

This technique is not at all the same as listing pros and cons for a particular activity or goal, which in my experience is largely unproductive. The mapping intentions approach is different because it lists not reasons but active intentions. A counterintention is not listed in negative terms and judged as a "con," but is recorded as a purpose in and of itself that simply runs in a different direction. In mapping these, it is important to state each intention in an active context, avoiding terms such as "not" or "don't" or "should" or "must." After all, a counterintention is nothing more than a conflicting intention. The intention "to travel the world" is an intention, but it can be a counterintention when juxtaposed with "to get a doctorate." Each is active, and each mostly excludes the other, at least in the same time period.

Naming each intention properly is important, and the client must agree that the wording is accurate. After the intentions and counterintentions are mapped, the therapist then gets the client to examine each intention and determine if it should be supported, altered, suspended, or eliminated. The goal is to allow the person to see these currents of intentions and to be released from them so that effort can be freed up to pursue change.

For example, Carla, a woman in her mid-30s, was in great distress over the verbal abuse her husband heaped on her and her two children. He was a rather charming fellow who was often apologetic after a particularly cruel outburst. Carla had decided to leave him. She set a task for herself of calling a lawyer to initiate divorce proceedings, but she could not bring herself to actually do so. Her progress in therapy was stalled, and she was low in the precursors of effort and confronting.

With the help of the therapist, she mapped her intentions and counterintentions. Her intentions were to be happy, protect her children, be free, and grow as a person. Her counterintentions to the goal of seeking a divorce were to have financial security, help her husband, be true to her marriage, show her children that marriage can work, and prove to her parents and friends that she had good judgment in men.

In therapy, each intention and counterintention, as revealed and identified, was newly evaluated, with Carla deciding whether to support, alter, suspend, or eliminate each. She supported all of her intentions. With her counterintentions, she suspended temporarily her goal to have financial security, knowing she would be facing hardship through the divorce. She also suspended (with considerable relief) her goal to be true to her marriage and eliminated her intention to prove to her parents and friends that she had good judgment in men. As a result, she finally went into motion and took action on the divorce proceedings.

FACILITATING THE DECISION TO CHANGE

Therapeutic change often comes as a result of a specific decision, which is often a necessary condition for change to take place (Hanna & Ritchie, 1995). Such a decision often manifests as a firm commitment. Many factors combine to culminate in a pervasive, integral decision. Unfortunately, I know of no easy way to facilitate such a decision; many precursors seem to weave together in such cases. It seems that confronting and a sense of necessity are especially involved. At times a client can be asked, straightforwardly, if he or she has made a decision to change. If no change has been forthcoming, the client is likely to admit that he or she has not made such a decision. The therapist can then ask the client what it would take to make such a decision. He or she can also ask the client, in the tradition of the Adlerian "as if," to go ahead and pretend to make the decision, to try it on for size and see if it "feels right." This can sometimes influence a decision and a commitment.

IDENTIFYING AND DISPUTING AUTOMATIC THOUGHTS OR NEGATIVE SELF-TALK

This approach consists of asking a person to perform a therapeutic task, preferably in the session, and then having him or her immediately watch for and report any opposing, contrary, or negating thoughts that arise. Such automatic thoughts can sabotage effort. For example, Wendy, a client in her early 20s, had a male employer who was verbally abusive but veiled his hostility with biting jokes and laughter. Wendy found it extremely difficult to ask her employer if he would stop and could not bring herself to do even graduated tasks based on role plays. To discover possible automatic thoughts, the therapist and client agreed to set up a role play in which Wendy was to address the therapist playing the role of her verbally abusive employer. The variation was that instead of going through with the role play and being concerned with what to say to her boss, Wendy was to report any opposing thoughts in the way of doubts, criticisms of self, negative expectations, and distorted images associated with speaking to her boss. Once these were addressed and disputed, Wendy found it much easier to do more realistic role plays and actually did confront her employer. Her strategy was to avoid any accusations of him while still being assertive. In their meeting, she informed him that even though he meant no harm, telling her that she was "dumb" and "silly" was hurtful to her and did not help her perform better on the job. What was more helpful, she told him, was when she was given details and instruction on how to do better. She was pleasantly surprised when her employer quietly agreed to her request.

IDENTIFYING AND DISPUTING CORE BELIEFS ABOUT EFFORT

When other precursors are present but effort is not manifesting, a host of core beliefs could be inhibiting a person from moving toward change. The following are possible core beliefs that can inhibit effort and the exertion of the will:

- "I don't deserve to get better and will not do anything toward it."
- "I have hurt too many people to deserve to devote effort to myself."
- "I screw everything up anyway, so why try?"
- "I cannot be trusted to succeed."
- "Becoming effective will only make me capable of hurting people more."
- "I know that if I try, I will fail."
- "I am afraid of making more mistakes."
- "I feel guilty if I try to help myself."
- "Someone else should do the work for me."
- "I am waiting for someone to rescue me from all this."
- "God will take care of me."

When these core beliefs are disputed, the person may spring into motion and make effort toward therapeutic tasks and goals.

ATTENDING TO THE METALOG

It is easy to hand out homework assignments to uncooperative clients. It is just as easy for clients to listen to them. The question is whether the client will actually execute the assignments or make self-initiated actions toward change. In many of these cases, a cognitive approach may be enhanced by attending to the metalog between client and therapist. The concept of the metalog was introduced in chapter 6. The client may be engaged in a metalog that is inhibiting therapeutic progress. For example, many difficult clients have told me that as soon as their therapist suggested a task to be completed outside of therapy, they immediately responded with an unvoiced statement such as, "I know I ain't gonna do this," or "I don't care about this," or simply, "No way." The client may be only dimly aware of this response until asked about it. Curiously, while engaging in this self-talk, the clients were readily agreeing to do the tasks assigned. Addressing and vocalizing the metalog can reduce interference with the effort precursor. Once the metalog is identified and articulated, it can be handily treated by using the subpersonality approach, mapping intentions, or finding core beliefs. As long as the metalog is not addressed, however, the therapist runs the risk of the client's continued ambivalence and lack of cooperation both within and outside of therapy sessions.

14

BUILDING HOPE FOR CHANGE

If a client leaves his or her first session with a sense of hope, the odds of his or her attending another session are likely to be much higher. Building hope involves directly empowering a person, helping him or her to become more capable and confident as part of perceiving a favorable, realistic future. The enterprise is largely dedicated to helping a client become more stable in the face of adversity and better able to focus on positive outcomes with the realistic expectation that problems and situations will turn out well. The client who is hopeful has sufficient coping skills to deal with problems and issues, as well as that fascinating quality that psychodynamic therapists refer to as ego strength. The hopeful person also has the capacity to see beyond problems toward a bright future.

The techniques and strategies in this chapter are designed to instill hope as a precursor to change by strengthening and empowering the person. When a client has hope, the other precursors can be positively affected by its pervasive influence throughout the range of that person's life. The gift of hope is the gift of a desirable future. Thus, hope building is done through any approach that can make the future more tolerable. The following techniques can help the therapist build the hope precursor in clients.

REFLECTING THE HOPELESSNESS

It is often a mistake for a therapist to refuse to accept the client's conviction of the hopelessness of a situation or condition. To work with a client who is bereft of hope, it is often of vital importance for the therapist to reflect that hopelessness, conveying that it is fully understood and why. A client may be more inclined to listen to messages of hope when it appears that the therapist truly understands the grimness of the situation. Many hopeless clients seem to demand that their therapists see the hopelessness and feel it as well. To meet this demand, it is helpful to empathically paraphrase and summarize exactly why things cannot and will not improve. The therapist then invites the client to comment on the degree of the therapist's understanding.

For example, a therapist might say to such a client, "Please tell me if I am tracking with you here. You figure that no matter what you do, things are going to be a disaster, and you will end up being a failure. There is no point in trying, and the only way out is by ending your life. Am I close to understanding how you see all this?" When the client is convinced that the therapist truly understands the depths and degree of his or her hopelessness and the internal logic of that hopelessness, he or she may be more inclined to explore or consider alternatives or options.

ALTERNATIVE THERAPY

Alternative therapy (A. T. Beck et al., 1979) is an approach in which options for dealing with various situations or problems are generated and formulated. The options can be rehearsed or role played. The purpose is not to find the perfect solution, but to start generating a variety of solutions to choose from. When a client sees that he or she can come up with various options in the face of hard times, it builds a positive outlook. This technique was originally designed for clients with suicidal ideation, and it can be adapted to many situations in which a client believes that he or she is stuck, stymied, or trapped. The purpose is to show that if there are many ways to solve a problem, the problem is much less threatening.

THE JAMESIAN DEVICE

William James (1907) developed a theory of truth that is suited to personal knowing that does not rely only on objective criteria. This has an application in therapy that can be of great help to some clients. Many difficult clients are remarkably hesitant to believe that anything positive about them may be true. The definition of truth that James established can provide clients with an internal measuring device that can indicate whether or not a particular belief or statement has any truth value. The therapist explains to the client that when a statement or belief is true for a person, it produces positive feelings and a sense of well-being and resonates and harmonizes within oneself. Even if the statement is negative, that resonance will take place, producing a feeling of peaceful acceptance "deep down inside." Many clients, on hearing this idea, immediately discount it as wishful thinking. However, when told it was originated by America's greatest psychologist (Korn, Davis, & Davis, 1991), it is then easier to accept, or at least less easy to dismiss.

For example, Michelle, a woman in her early 20s, was depressed and lacking in self-efficacy. She found it exceedingly difficult to accept any positive statements about herself from her therapist and would not engage in disputing negative beliefs. She told her therapist several times that it was nice to suggest such nice things, but she knew they simply were not true and for that reason she would not believe any of them. "I know," she said, "that there is nothing positive about me, and that all the people who have hurt me were right."

At that point the therapist introduced James's theory of truth and explained it in language that was real to Michelle. The therapist then asked her if she would like to try an experiment. Michelle agreed with a sigh. The therapist said, "I am going to give you a statement to repeat to yourself out loud. When you repeat it, rather than think about whether it is true or false, I would like you just to watch and see how the statement makes you feel inside." Michelle agreed, and the therapist gave her the self-statement, "I am a good person," a statement she would not even consider previously. Michelle repeated it to herself a couple of times and then looked up at the therapist hesitantly and said, "It makes me feel kind of good to say that, but I am just kidding myself." The therapist asked, "Did it feel good deep down and give you a sense of inner peace?" Michelle, now on new territory, only nodded. "Well, Michelle," said the therapist matter-of-factly, "according to William James, you may very well be a good person." Michelle was forced to consider this and in the following sessions tried out many other self-statements to measure using her new internal measuring device. The therapist also told her she could use this tool in everyday life when someone criticized her or forced a belief on her. Such affirmations and positive self-statements had not worked before. This experiential technique bypassed the difficulty she was having disputing her cognitive distortions.

This internal measuring device gauges the validity only of self-evaluative statements, and not of environmental conditions or other people. Otherwise, this device would convince paranoid or narcissistic clients, for example, that their ideas of reference are correct, making such clients even more difficult to treat. Examples of statements that should not be used in this technique are, "They really are out to destroy my life," "I am going to win the lottery," or "Mary, the girl I have dreamed about, is in love with me."

EMPOWERMENT STRATEGIES

In the enterprise of hope building, it is wise to take every opportunity to help a client feel capable and empowered to make changes. Many therapists have told me they sometimes do not know how to empower dysfunctional clients who seem to have little going for them. As part of empowerment, it helps to recall that even the most dysfunctional people occasionally do something functional and to concentrate on reinforcing that fact, rather than implying that they lack skills and have to learn new skills. In many cases, new skills do need to be learned, but it is easier to do so when these can be built on a foundation of acknowledged skills. Two modes of empowerment are especially helpful in this regard: reframing negative behaviors as skills and converting a threat into a challenge.

Reframing Negative Behaviors as Skills

One of the most helpful ways of empowering clients is to demonstrate to them that their dysfunctional, negative behaviors can be reframed into positive skills, available to them through their own choosing. All too often, the message received by people who have negative behaviors is that the behaviors are "bad" and are something that no good or worthy person would ever do. The key is to reframe negative behaviors as skills. For example, rather than inform a manipulative client that his or her behavior is destructive, the therapist can reframe it as a kind of skill that involves accurate perception and persuasiveness in getting people to do what they want.

Clients are far more willing to talk about their being manipulative when it is framed as a skill. The therapist can admire it as a skill, hard earned and well practiced. Then he or she can suggest that the skill is actually underused and can be used in other, more positive ways. If one is a selfish manipulator, one can redirect or reverse that very same skill and become a helper. The same perception that is used to exploit a person can also be used to help. The same is true of the skill of counseling: If that skill were reversed or redirected, an effective therapist would become an extraordinarily effective verbal abuser.

Thus, the therapist can inform the client that up until now, that skill at manipulation was being used for selfish purposes, but if the client so wished, he or she could use the same skill in a positive way to become a corporate manager, salesperson, or counselor. When the client realizes that he or she already has the blueprint of positive skills, it builds hope by making the refinement of those skills seem a realistic possibility. This technique can also be used with other "skills." Lying, for example, presupposes a creative ability to reshape and reformulate information. The negative behavior of verbal abuse, when reversed, is validative, encouraging, and even inspirational. The blueprint is there. The challenge is to use it.

Converting a Threat Into a Challenge

When a person is threatened by a set of circumstances, problems, or general conditions, hope can be adversely and sometimes seriously affected. The greater the perceived threat, the lower the level of hope will be for a positive outcome. The key to this strategy is to reframe that perceived threat into what looks more like a challenge, thus rendering it more likely to be successfully handled (R. S. Lazarus & Folkman, 1984). If a threatening problem is perceived as a challenge, hope will not only remain intact, it may also be enhanced.

The procedure comprises two steps. The first is to find and identify the client's skills, of which he or she may not even be aware. If the person was a victim of oppression, for example, he or she may be highly perceptive of others, even if easily exploited. Similarly, being a survivor of abuse can be reframed as an ability to endure hardship as part of solving a problem. Ingratiating or "people-pleasing" behaviors require the skill of perception as part of knowing what people want. A host of skills can be recognized in clients ranging from patience and strength to assertiveness and intelligence. A skill is a skill, no matter how little or well developed it may be. If a client recognizes it as a skill, hope may be enhanced.

After skills are identified, the problem itself can be addressed. The therapist suggests that the client's skills are especially suited to the problem at hand and are what is needed to solve it. When clients see that the skills they possess in other domains can be transferred to the current problem, hope can be increased, and the effort precursor may be enhanced as well.

The Story of Gwen

Gwen, age 38, was a salesperson for a major pharmaceutical company. She presented with what appeared to be a career issue of being bored with her work, and she was no longer willing to continue her career. She referred to her job as "drug pusher" and said that it was not in harmony with her true nature. In spite of her depression, she had an inauthentic way of smiling through it and saying that everything was as it should be. In the second session, she hesitantly though enthusiastically revealed that she was studying with a group whose guru had magical powers over her well-being and spiritual development. She also revealed that the real reason she was in therapy was that her husband, Bill, had insisted on it. Bill believed that the guru was crazy and was convinced Gwen had fallen prey to his manipulations and that it was ruining their marriage. The guru himself, she said, was opposed to her receiving therapy and was not happy with it.

Gwen maintained a schizotypal belief system based on and reinforced by her guru, who had convinced her that even her dreams and moods were a result of his control over her mind. Part of this belief system was that the guru was putting her through uncertainty and depression for the purpose of spiritual "testing" and "cleansing" for her eventual enlightenment. Gwen had little self-efficacy and almost no faith in her own ability to achieve happiness and fulfillment. Her faith in the magical powers of the guru was a way of bypassing her own helplessness so he could achieve happiness for her. Only he could do it. She vigorously defended against any perceived criticism of the guru.

In the third session Gwen admitted that even though she had great faith in her guru, he was not making her as happy as she would have liked. However, she anxiously added that this was a "test" of her loyalty and resolve, and that in due time she would be rewarded with a mystical experience of supreme peace and tranquility.

In the next session, the therapist recognized and reframed her resolve and her faith as skills. Taking great care not to threaten or attack her delusional system, the therapist reframed Gwen's belief in the guru and her presenting problem of wanting to quit her job as related to the deeper, more pervasive, and admirable goal of attaining self-knowledge and self-mastery. Gwen agreed that this was indeed her ultimate goal. The guru's test that had caused her so much distress was reframed as part of the challenge for her to come to know herself.

Gwen accepted the reframe, as it fit rather easily and comfortably into her delusional system. The therapist further informed Gwen that therapy was another path to self-knowledge and self-mastery that did not have to conflict with her spiritual beliefs, and that therapy had the capacity to help her be happy and find fulfillment. The therapist did not challenge her spiritual beliefs, in the recognition that her beliefs were from ancient sources and were not dependent on the guru for their validity. The therapist took great care not to invalidate the guru himself, because it was clear that Gwen would likely terminate therapy if this were to happen.

This approach was consistent with her beliefs and delusions about her guru and allowed an egress from her attachment to the guru and the cult in which she was entrenched. The basis of hope provided to Gwen early in the therapeutic relationship was the prospect that therapy could lead to self-knowledge and self-mastery. Crucial to her liberation from the guru was the recognition that the vast power she had attributed to him was evidence of her own power of belief and that she could begin to use some of it now instead of waiting. This was another great source of hope for her.

In time, she began to see that the intense dislike of her job was a source of self-knowledge in itself, and she no longer linked it with her guru's ridicule of such "lowly" occupations. She also took heart in her absolute faith in the guru, having reframed it as an insight into her own admirable quality of faithfulness, loyalty, and friendship. Most important, she began to see the guru's narcissistic needs for admiration and control. Her faith in him began to progressively weaken as she regarded him in this realistic fashion. After about 15 months, she had left her job and entered law school full-time, and she gradually ended her involvement with the guru and his circle of admirers. Gwen attributed her change to the promise of hope, the various reframes, and the relationship that kept her engaged in therapy in spite of her guru's admonitions to terminate.

HOPE AS A CONTAGION

We know that a therapist's positive expectations of a client can be highly influential on the client's success in therapy (W. R. Miller, 1985). The therapist's confidence can be contagious. When working with a client to build hope through empowerment, just believing a client can indeed get through an issue or successfully solve a problem will indirectly affect the client. This belief is communicated through the therapist's metalog and dialog; of course, it also helps for the therapist to directly and often voice his or her belief in a client's skills or ability to deal with an issue. Many clients have told their therapists that they successfully handled a problem because of the faith or confidence the therapist had in them. In this way hope is contagious.

CREATIVE NARRATIVES: RELATING AND REWRITING

In some cases, therapists can begin work on the hope precursor by asking a client to tell the story of his or her life. There is no need to focus on tragedy or trauma, only to get the view of his or her life that the client conceives. If the story is told tragically, the therapist can help the client reconstruct the story to retell it with a sense of hope, empathy, and understanding—as a story still in the making. If the story is told in a narcissistic fashion, complete with fantasies of brilliance or superiority, the story can be retold to show how difficult it must have been for others to appreciate such a great person, and how important the development of empathy and compassion for others might have been, so that the other people in the client's life would have been more communicative and appreciative. The purpose, again, is to open a therapeutic window.

The retelling of a life story can be quite powerful for some clients. It allows a client to become liberated from a stuck or fixed pattern of conceiving the self and its surrounding context. When creatively and therapeutically retold, the story can allow therapeutic change to become part of the story itself, allowing the emergence of other precursors such as willingness, awareness, and necessity.

TELLING STORIES OF RECOVERY

Many difficult clients have great difficulty conceiving the possibility of change. Telling stories of clients and people with similar problems who made positive changes in their lives can be helpful. Clients will often inquire about the person or client mentioned by the therapist, sometimes bringing them up months or weeks after the story was told. Stories can be introduced by saying, "You know, I once knew someone who was similar to you," or "You remind me of someone who was in a predicament similar to yours." Clients have sometimes told me later that a particular story about a person with a similar dilemma was what kept them going during difficult times.

EXPOSURE TO OTHERS WHO SOLVED THE SAME PROBLEM

Whenever possible, group therapy can be remarkably powerful in its ability to build hope. This therapy modality has benefits not found in individual or family therapy. Yalom (1995) accurately pointed out that when clients observe their peers making changes, hope is instilled, and the possibility of change becomes clearly and realistically possible for themselves. Group therapy can communicate a client's potential for change in a way that goes far beyond encouraging messages from a therapist. In addition to groups, hearing speakers, seeing films, or reading books that contain stories of change can also be a powerful source of hope. In treatment programs for adults or adolescents, bringing in people who have worked on similar issues to tell their stories of change is another effective strategy. I have observed several instances in which a sense of necessity arose in a client when a person inspired hope by relating a personal story. This is especially helpful, for example, with adolescent gang members who believe they have no future and no escape from their circumstances. It is also helpful for substance abusers.

EXAMINING CORE BELIEFS ABOUT THE FUTURE

Because hope is intimately intertwined with the future (Hanna, 1991), hope building can take the form of examining core beliefs about the future itself and the context of those beliefs. If a person is habitually inclined to regard the future with suspicion, fear, apprehension, and anxiety, that person's capacity for hope is severely diminished. In many cases, if these core beliefs are not addressed and disputed, the techniques mentioned in this chapter and this book may not bear fruit. Distorted views and beliefs about the future can affect the smooth implementation of any program of therapeutic change, regardless of theoretical approach. Like other ontological core beliefs, those that interfere with hope may never have been previously stated as such in words and language. It is the therapist's job to help identify and properly phrase these beliefs with the client's assurance of accuracy before disputing them. The following are examples of core beliefs about the future:

- "The future holds nothing for me."
- "Only bad things are waiting for me."
- "The world is a cruel place to live."
- "No matter what you do, things will never really get better."
- "Life is a process of failing to realize one's dreams."
- "The future holds only what others want."
- "Other people dictate my future."
- "The passing of time is painful."
- "The future provides nothing but anxiety."
- "The future is filled with continuous disappointment."
- "The future is filled with unforeseen catastrophes."
- "I am unable to affect the future."
- "The future is a continuous threat to my well-being."
- "Hope is for fools."
- "Nobody has any idea of the future."
- "My life has been disappointing, and the future will be more of the same."

When these beliefs are disputed and reconstituted, a person will likely be far more willing to experience anxiety or difficulty, invest effort, and confront a problem. The new acquisition of hope may also increase his or her sense of necessity by moving a desired set of positive conditions from the realm of the unreachable to the realm of the plausible and possible.

HUMOR

Unfortunately, humor cannot be taught to therapists in any consistent way. But therapists can be encouraged to use it to lighten a heavy load or brighten a dark outlook. When a client can laugh at a problem in an existential way, things begin to look less serious and more cheerful. Humor at another's expense should be avoided, of course. In general, proper timing and appropriateness are the keys. In some cases, therapeutic humor can be conducive to an increase of awareness.

A therapist who is genuinely lighthearted and who can relay it somehow has a valuable talent. Generally, clients look forward to sessions where the work is hard but fun and done in a setting that combines lightheartedness and learning. Of course, it is extremely important to fit the humor into a framework acceptable to the client. As for training therapists to be humorous with clients, modeling it in supervision may be a good approach.

15

DEVELOPING SOCIAL SUPPORT FOR CHANGE

Social support paves the road to therapeutic change. It fills some potholes, evens a few bumps, and turns gravel and dirt into asphalt. It does not do the entire job, but it does make traversing the road smoother and easier. In some cases, social support seems to alleviate depression all by itself (Arkowitz, 1992a). Without social support, a person will be less resilient, less confident, and less hopeful. This precursor affects all the others in ways that are both subtle and direct.

Helping difficult clients develop social support networks consists of three separate but related modalities. The first is to diminish or minimize contact with people who are harmful, abusive, negative, exploitative, or otherwise oppressive to the client. If uncorrected or undeterred, such people can discourage the presence of the precursors of change just as surely as a good therapist can encourage them. In general, of course, it is usually futile to attempt to change people who are not supportive.

The second modality for increasing social support is to increase the presence of people who do encourage the precursors of change. These people are generally empathic and helpful and serve as sources of understanding, trust, and active support. Increasing this kind of social support involves teaching a client social skills and communication skills.

The third modality is important for some clients who have lost valuable friendships. Therapy can help clients rebuild once-supportive relationships that have deteriorated. This goal is often unrealistic, of course. Many clients with personality disorders or alcohol or drug abuse problems tend to exploit people who trust them and make a habit of wasting relationships. They often regret having done so, and therapy can sometimes help clients recover those friendships, although it can be delicate work because of the intense emotions and feelings, including betrayal, on both sides.

A CAUTIONARY NOTE

Therapists should use caution in teaching empathy, reflection of feelings, and other communicative skills to clients who will use them in harmful ways. For example, male sex offenders may use social support skills to victimize women, taking them into their confidence only to betray them. Criminal offenders may use these skills to exploit people with the end result of doing harm. The clinician must use careful judgment to ensure that irresponsible clients do not use newly learned social support skills to exploit, betray, and otherwise hurt the people around them. In my experience, empathy and responsibility need to be rehabilitated in these clients before they can be trusted with skills that engender the trust of innocent people.

TEACHING A CLIENT TO RECOGNIZE EMPATHY IN ANOTHER

Many clients get themselves into trouble by trusting or becoming attached to people who are harmful and exploitative. This often happens in romantic relationships; a person marries or otherwise becomes attached to a partner who is not empathic. A battering husband does indeed love and care for his wife, just as an abusive father cares for his children. However, these men have little or no empathy for the people they love.

Clients can benefit from learning to recognize the presence of empathy in another person. The telltale sign is whether the client feels understood by the other person, as if the person understands the client "from the inside out." Many clients need to be taught this fundamental phenomenon because they are simply not familiar with it.

Recognizing empathy is a skill that can be used throughout one's life. Teaching a client to recognize empathy or the lack of it in another person and to avoid confiding in nonempathic people can help him or her avoid many difficult situations and be able to recognize a vital aspect of friendship. Perhaps the best standard of measurement for empathy is the therapeutic relationship. Clients can use it as a model, especially in those who lack empathic relationships in the rest of their life and have no way to compare the quality of relationships.

IDENTIFYING SOURCES OF SOCIAL SUPPORT FOR CHANGE

Once able to recognize empathy, the therapist should help the client identify sources of social support in his or her environment. In determining whether to discourage or increase a continued association, the therapist can explore with the client the idea of the confiding relationship (Arkowitz, 1992a) or the presence of empathy in the person or group. It also helps to assess whether the person or group contributes to the presence of the precursors of change. Social skills training can be used to strengthen and reinforce positive relationships.

THE CONCENTRIC-CIRCLE TECHNIQUE

In chapter 6, I described A. A. Lazarus's (1989b) concentric-circle technique as an excellent means of gauging the closeness of the therapeutic relationship and the level or degree of the client's self-disclosure to the therapist. As part of developing social support, this same technique can be used to gauge the client's closeness to the people in his or her current environment. Once this is done, the client can discuss whether the person in question contributes to his or her social support toward change or whether the person is harmful to it or merely tangential.

The technique is useful in several ways. If a client has a habit of taking people into his or her confidence who then betray or abandon the person, the technique can be used as a tool to help delineate and establish boundaries. In other words, clients who have such boundary problems can begin to establish criteria for allowing a person entrance to each inner circle. For clients who have experienced pain from unwisely disclosing personal information to inappropriate people, this technique helps to determine who is a worthy candidate of this precious trust. If a client associates pain with allowing a person into the two innermost circles, this is an indication that he or she needs to be more perceptive and discreet. Another use for this technique is to count the number of people the client has allowed into the two inner circles. The therapist can ask the client how it feels to have so many people with intimate knowledge of him or her.

At the opposite polarity, some clients have allowed and plan to allow no one into the two innermost circles. This has consequences and a set of corresponding feelings. People who have shut out virtually everyone from emotional intimacy may feel alienated, lonely, sad, or resentful. The approach would be, once again, to determine what it would take to allow someone into those two inner circles. A client's criteria may be quite irrational, from too rigid on the one hand to too demanding on the other. A therapist can help clients formulate more realistic beliefs with the intent of easing the negative feelings associated with being disengaged from one's fellow human beings.

IDENTIFYING PEOPLE WHO ARE OPPOSED TO THERAPEUTIC CHANGE

Curiously, in almost every difficult client's life there are people who oppose the client's therapeutic change. In such cases, beneficial change runs at cross-purposes to that person's intentions for the client. Some clients are needed by others to remain exactly the way they are. Dysfunctional families also tend to resist the improvement of one of its members because of systemic influences, called *homeostasis*. Virtually all therapists have encountered these extremely difficult situations. Many difficult clients swear that the people who are in fact most harmful to them are also the most important people in their lives. Thus, helping clients identify the harmful or negative influences of these people is often a major therapeutic task.

The therapist should assess, either directly by asking a client or indirectly, whether people in the client's life encourage therapeutic change. The client must be able to answer specific questions. For example, do the people in question tend to quell the sense of necessity, discourage confronting, or destroy hope? Do they seek to undermine effort toward change? In the case of enabling, does a caring family member or spouse actively discourage the willingness to experience anxiety? Such questions can be formulated easily enough, and the therapist can then present the evidence to the client for his or her consideration. The therapist can also ask some clients how they "feel" about themselves or their lives in the presence of the person to get a kind of visceral assessment. Another approach is to ask what the person wants the client to believe about himself or herself (see chapter 8). The overall goal is to help a client be able to gauge who is not supportive of his or her growth; in this way a difficult client can recognize the consequences of associating with difficult people and avoid this source of needless anxiety and trouble.

RECOVERING LOST SOURCES OF SOCIAL SUPPORT

Many clients live with the hidden regret of having lost relationships with close friends or family members that once provided social support. The relationship may have been lost due to the client's acting out, betrayal, manipulations, or dishonesty. Clients can feel considerable shame and guilt at the mere thought of these lost relationships. The client may try to convince himself or herself that the relationship was not important or that the other person was at fault. Many clients also use the excuse that the person in question "never really understood" them anyway, so there is really no loss, when in fact such people may have understood a bit too well.

In a few cases, social support can be rehabilitated with those relationships. Of course, in many other instances, the residual distrust is so great that the relationship is for all practical purposes beyond repair. Nevertheless, therapy can help determine how and why such relationships fell apart to begin with so the client can avoid making the same mistakes with new relationships. Help in recovering relationships is not recommended for clients who are criminal or extremely manipulative. In such cases, they may only again victimize people who were happy to be free of them. Protecting others from such clients is often the primary concern until they are no longer destructive in relationships.

EXPLORING TRUST

For many difficult clients, the issue of trust is surrounded by irrational beliefs and a sense of righteous indignation. These clients must learn that trust must be earned and that it is not a birthright. Many clients exploit and betray others, only to later complain that no one trusts them, as if they have been deeply wronged. Such blaming behavior can be addressed by setting up scenarios, role plays, role reversals, and dialog, in which such clients can experience the effects of their own manipulations. The purpose is to produce empathy in the client toward those who no longer trust them. In a role play, the therapist can assume the role of the client, displaying the same behaviors that led to a loss of trust, followed by a role reversal. Responses and feelings can then be explored that may lead to an understanding of how the relationship broke down.

STANDARD SOCIAL SKILLS TECHNIQUES

Standard therapy techniques and approaches can be used to help clients develop social support networks. These are described in introductory textbooks on counseling and psychotherapy and are not described in detail here. Each is valuable in teaching clients how to go about finding, building, and maintaining empathic relationships based on empathy and caring.

GROUP THERAPY

Group therapy provides a context and format that are highly conducive to developing social support. A well-run group can be tremendously powerful in teaching clients the power of empathy and compassion. The amount of empathy generated in a group that has achieved the working stage is exponentially more powerful than that of a single therapist. In group a person can come to experience empathic, supportive friendships that if provided by an individual therapist would violate ethical codes on dual relationships.

For a group to achieve the working stage, the members need to have progressed through the early-stage disagreements, personality conflicts, and the like and proceed to provide high-quality help to each other (see Corey, 1996). This is a standard aspect of group process. The group therapist is only minimally active at the working stage, unless carrying out a specific set of therapeutic techniques. In this regard, group therapy has far more utility than individual therapy. Ideally, group and individual therapy can be done concurrently. They need not interfere with each other, and in fact, each can enhance the progress of the other. When done well, it is a model of empathic relationships. An additional benefit of group therapy that is not found in individual therapy is the opportunity the client has to learn helping skills and apply them in a therapeutic setting (Yalom, 1995). Unfortunately, in my consulting practice, I have seen many group therapists who have not experienced a group at the working stage due to limited training or poor treatment plans by agencies.

EXAMINING CORE BELIEFS ABOUT PEOPLE AND RELATIONSHIPS

Difficult clients can possess an amazing array of dysfunctional core beliefs about people and relationships. These can have a profound influence on the kinds of people with whom they associate and the kinds of relationships they form and keep. Dysfunctional core beliefs about relationships and people in general, when firmly held, can influence a person to become attached to people who are exploitative and self-serving. These beliefs can also influence a person to engage in and develop behaviors of their own that will subvert, undermine, and eventually damage potentially valuable relationships.

Many dysfunctional core beliefs seem essentially sound at first glance but have a logical flaw in them that, when acted on, can sabotage relationships. If a therapist is adept at identifying and extrapolating core beliefs, much work can be accomplished with clients who lack social support for change. As with other ontological core beliefs, clients may require the therapist's assistance in giving the following beliefs content, context, and language:

- "People are sources of anxiety and pain."
- "I cannot live without love."

- "I am only alive when others are paying attention to me."
- "If I can please people, then they will like me."
- "I need other people to tell me how to be."
- "I need other people to tell me who I am."
- "I must have a person to whom I can give up control of myself."
- "A friend is someone who will rescue me from my problems."
- "Even cruel attention from others is better than no attention at all."
- "I am secure only when others are around me."
- "Only fools would be interested in supporting me."
- "The people stupid enough to support me cannot be trusted for that reason."
- "Nobody ever really cares about anybody."
- "People really only care about themselves."
- "I am intrinsically unlovable."
- "The presence of others threatens my survival."
- "The pain of others is mine to inflict or control."
- "People are tolerable only when they are under my control."
- "If I stay away from the company of others, they cannot hurt me."
- "I am not as good as anyone else and thus deserve to be treated badly."
- "If I am in conflict with someone, it is better to end the relationship."
- "If a relationship requires work, it is not worth keeping."
- "If I run into difficulty with one person, I can always find someone else."

Identifying, disputing, and changing these core beliefs can have an amazing effect on a person's willingness to engage in intimate relationships and choose relationships that are healthy and stable rather than painful and destructive.

Finally, clients will respond to therapy when they feel their therapists like and accept them (Orlinsky et al., 1994) and when they experience their therapists as having positive expectations for them (W. R. Miller, 1985). All these are vital aspects of social support generated by the therapist.

V

CONCLUSION

16

AT THE HORIZON OF CHANGE

For more than a decade, researchers have been calling for a compilation and better understanding of therapeutic change processes (Beutler, 2000; Wolfe & Goldfried, 1988). There have been relatively few answers to the call. There is no doubt that valuable research has been done on the effectiveness of therapy, the effectiveness of various techniques and approaches, the therapeutic relationship, and especially the effectiveness of therapy with specific diagnoses and specific populations. However, considerable research remains to be done on discovering active change processes and principles.

The precursors model is an example of how specific change processes can be identified in a context that owes allegiance to no particular theory. It is an example of how a therapy approach can focus on change itself and orient techniques, theories, procedures, and stages around specific change functions. The seven precursors are so fundamental that they lie at the core of theories, manuals, approaches, and procedures. This is not a global model of therapy, nor is it meant to be. But I hope that it has served as an example of how techniques and manuals can be oriented around change rather than treated as ends in themselves.

If psychotherapy is to advance as a discipline and as a science, it must be able to achieve therapeutic change more quickly, deeply, and efficiently. The advancement of theory and technique, although important, must be accompanied by a clearer and more complete understanding of the actual functions and factors that bring about change. From a precursors perspective, a fundamental duty of therapy is to know why a client is not changing. It must also be able to identify and establish missing change functions in a client, and then proceed to prescribe the appropriate theory, strategy, or technique. Hypothetically, this can take place with many clients. The precursors model, however, seems most valuable with clients who are difficult. The precursors are so fundamental to change that it would be difficult to imagine how therapeutic change could take place in therapy without them. I hope I have been able to make that clear.

Psychotherapy as a discipline has several problems that are often mentioned in the literature. The precursors model may be able to shed some light on a couple of these. One is the problem of the hundreds of theories of psychotherapy. The precursors model reveals how the metaphysical characteristics of those theories preclude any real solution. If therapy is oriented around change, the theories themselves become a menu of pragmatic solutions rather than the independent and conflicting sets of metaphysical dogma that we have now. However, there is another problem that has vexed the field for many years that can be examined from a precursors perspective.

THE PROFESSIONAL VERSUS PARAPROFESSIONAL DILEMMA

Research has shown that paraprofessional therapists seem to be as effective as or only slightly less effective than professionals, in spite of the professionals' added years of training and education. The evidence first became apparent more than 20 years ago in a study by Durlak (1979). Around the same time, Strupp and Hadley (1979) found that college professors untrained in psychotherapy were just as effective as experienced professional therapists. Many of the clients in this study had challenging disorders, and yet there were no appreciable differences in effectiveness.

Five years later, a meta-analysis by Hattie, Sharpley, and Rogers (1984) compared paraprofessionals to professionals (psychologists, psychiatrists, and social workers). Their conclusion, based on 154 effect sizes, was that "paraprofessionals are at least as effective, and in many instances more effective" (p. 540) than professionals. Level of education and years of professional experience were not significant in determining effectiveness. This classic study has withstood the expected criticism, and its results remain important and relevant. What this means is that people who have only 20 or so clock hours of therapy training are as effective, or at least nearly as effective, as professionals with doctoral or master's degrees, hundreds of hours of training, and many years of experience.

Years later, Stein and Lambert (1995) further investigated this controversial area in a carefully controlled and well-conducted study. They did find differences between professionals and paraprofessionals, with professionals faring slightly better than paraprofessionals. "However," they concluded, "given the enormous, national investment of physical and human resources in graduate programs, it is quite remarkable that more compelling evidence is not available that demonstrates that graduate training directly relates to enhanced therapy outcomes" (p. 194). This is, once again, a sobering conclusion.

In the substance abuse treatment arena, another interesting comparison was made between professional cognitive–behavioral therapy and the paraprofessional 12-step approach of Alcoholics Anonymous. Ouimette, Finney, and Moos (1997) found that the effectiveness of the two approaches was essentially the same. The authors concluded that this was more evidence of the equivalency of effectiveness among therapy approaches in general.

Related to these controversial findings is evidence that the number of years of experience a therapist has accrued does not seem to be an indicator of therapeutic effectiveness (Dawes, 1994; Dumont, 1991; Hattie et al., 1984; Smith & Glass, 1977). At first glance, it would seem likely that lessons learned during many years of experience would add to overall effectiveness and even contribute to a sense of therapeutic know-how. On the whole, however, it does not appear that therapists actually get more effective over time. One of the findings of the meta-analysis by Hattie et al. showed that recently graduated students are as effective as doctoral-level professionals with 20 years of experience.

What do such studies really tell us? Howarth (1989), after contemplating the complexities and mysteries cited above, said, "Psychotherapists do not know what they are doing and cannot train others to do it, whatever it is" (p. 152). Howarth's comment has often been quoted in the psychotherapy literature by those concerned about its development. But Howarth's comment is overstated and need not be the case.

THE PRECURSORS SOLUTION

From a precursors perspective, the dilemma boils down to two essential points. The first is that some people are more capable of helping another to change, regardless of education. In other words, professional training seems limited in its capacity to train some people to be more effective change agents. The second point is that if we more fully understand therapeutic change, we can then better understand what therapists are supposed to do to help make it happen. The effectiveness of therapists is not dependent on the university attended or the type of training program (Peterson, 1995), but rather on the personal characteristics of the therapist (Goldfried, Greenberg, & Marmar, 1990).

Thus, it is not the theory that therapists use, nor the university or type of training program they graduated from, so much as the skillfulness of the individual therapist (Whiston & Sexton, 1993). In other words, being an effective therapist has little to do with GRE scores, as Sternberg and Williams (1997) so clearly showed, or high grade point averages, number of publications, research skills, or the ability to pass exams or write dissertations. The real question is what it actually takes to facilitate change and to train and graduate facilitators of change who are effective at it.

A. A. Lazarus (1989b) noted that great therapists are not unique to any single profession. He observed that formal education and training in psychotherapy and counseling can take a person's natural therapeutic warmth, wisdom, genuineness, and empathy and degrade them into a stylized professionalism that is detrimental to a would-be therapist's natural skills (A. A. Lazarus, 1990). Lazarus (1990) used the metaphor of "taking a can of spray paint to an artistic masterpiece" (p. 352) to describe how academic training can spoil a student's natural helping skills. Lazarus also suggested that much of what is taught to graduate students of all professional persuasions about doing therapy amounts to "deadwood, superstition, and plain rubbish" (p. 352) rather than useful knowledge about what is actually effective.

From the perspective of the precursors model, graduates of training programs learn professional language; an array of theories, research findings, research methods, and ethical principles and behaviors; and a carefully cultivated professional demeanor, but they are not necessarily taught how to facilitate change itself. I have seen therapists at all levels who, for example, do not use session time in ways that are conducive to actually arriving at solutions or strengthening therapeutic relationships with the goal of change.

Stein and Lambert (1995) concluded that what matters is the trainer, not the school attended or the theory being taught: "Training can be for better or for worse and, as in therapy, the trainer may be even more important than the manual or technique itself" (p. 194). It just may be that people who are change agents learn from others who are change agents, and these are in all probability randomly distributed across universities and therapy training programs.

While consulting, I have observed several people working in community agencies who were clearly gifted and talented therapists who did not hold even a bachelor's degree. They just had a knack, a natural understanding and ability of the type that Lazarus noted, that helped clients actually change. They had wonderful relationship skills, did the right things with a sense of timing and precision, and tailored their interventions to the needs of each particular client. Yet most of them routinely berated their skills as being deficient because of a lack of education and formal training. I have also seen many formally trained therapists with the same expertise. If Lazarus, the research, and my observations are correct, then level of education is not the answer. In the final analysis, it seems that what is ultimately important is quite simple: The therapist must have the skills for helping to bring about change, regardless of degree, training, or theory.

From a precursors perspective, the skillfulness of a therapist may be little more than the ability to inspire, engage, and enhance the presence of precursors in clients. He or she can orchestrate and implement change ingredients with a client through empathy, warmth, persuasiveness, techniques, reframes, metaphors, and general wisdom about human beings and life. The therapist could be the family doctor or the professional therapist in private practice. It could be the school counselor at the local high school or the recovering alcoholic who works for near minimum wage at the local community substance abuse treatment center. Professional or paraprofessional, when these characteristics are present in a person, he or she has the capability to be an agent of change and a fine therapist.

Let's be brutally honest: There are a certain number of fairly well-off people who can be helped by almost any well-intended therapist using almost any sound approach (Lambert, 1992). Bartenders and hairdressers routinely perform this function. Some astrologers, psychics, and channelers act as therapists as well (Leister, 1982). If all that is needed, according to Frank (1974), is a myth to explain the healing, astrology and channeling certainly provide that. People claim to gain benefit from these offbeat, at best, and at worst harmful therapies (M. T. Singer & Lalich, 1996). Why? That is the point of this book. If the precursors of change are present in a person, he or she is likely to change. If the precursors are not present, change is unlikely. The skill of the therapist boils down to the skill in establishing and facilitating the precursors. The question remains as to what that skill is.

WISDOM AND THE WISE THERAPIST

There is a concept that accounts for the mostly unspoken and largely unspecified skills that differentiate the average therapist from the highly effective therapist. The concept is called *wisdom* (see Hanna & Ottens, 1995; Sternberg, 1990). This ancient concept is imported from research in developmental psychology and has great explanatory power. Researchers (see Sternberg, 1990) generally describe wisdom as a high degree of knowledge and expertise regarding the living of life itself. It is not the same as intelligence, although the two complement each other quite well. The characteristics of wisdom include empathy, compassion, metacognitive skills, perspicacity, self-awareness, and self-transcendence, among many others (see the appendix).

It may well be that the lack of wisdom is at the core of the puzzle concerning why the number of years of therapy experience does not seem to influence effectiveness. According to Sternberg (1990), one of the characteristics of wisdom is to resist habit in or automatization of thought and behavior routines. Take two therapists with 20 years of experience. One person continued to learn and improve therapy skills for a full, rich 20 years of experience, whereas the other had one year of therapy experience that was then automatized and repeated 20 times. In the latter case, the therapist more or less went through the motions of therapy on autopilot, with the net result of no longer improving his or her skills (Dumont, 1991).

The effective therapist tends to be a wise therapist. Of course, intelligence is certainly handy and helpful, but when it comes to the skills necessary to be effective, the characteristics and thinking styles that make up wisdom seem more relevant than those of intelligence. Yet we accept people into graduate training programs with criteria based on intelligence rather than wisdom. My point is that therapists need both. I would go a bit further, however, and submit that the characteristics of wisdom may also be the characteristics possessed by the master therapist.

When comparing the characteristics of wisdom to the characteristics of an effective therapist, one comes to a remarkable conclusion concerning the professional and paraprofessional issue. Could it be that graduate level trainees end up with the same general level of wisdom as paraprofessionals because wisdom is not taught in graduate schools? After all, wisdom is also not taught in elementary and secondary schools either, and it is probably randomly distributed across the population. Thus, it would be rather evenly distributed among professional and paraprofessional therapist samples as well (see Hanna & Ottens, 1995).

From a precursors perspective, a wise therapist may well be the most capable of inspiring and implementing the precursors of change. Pure intelligence is not oriented around skills such as listening, empathy, and interpersonal expertise (Sternberg, 1990). Thus, the crucial difference on which to place a research focus may not be the professional and paraprofessional, but the wise and not so wise. The difference may well lie in the ability to facilitate the precursors. With regard to research, it may be time to explore some research avenues implied or indicated by the precursors model.

SUGGESTIONS FOR FURTHER RESEARCH

Having made the case for the precursors and for wisdom, and having stated that the precursors model is by no means the final or best example of a therapy model oriented around change, what would be necessary to develop such a model? The answer, of course, lies in further research. I am persuaded that an important dimension of psychotherapeutic change can be explored through research on the role of metacognition. I defined metacognition in chapter 2 and have referred to it in various places in this book. There is much to learn in this regard that may make the difference between change and premature termination in a significant number of clients. In the introduction to this book, I gave several examples of change processes that might occur in difficult clients, posed in the form of questions. I would like to examine the examples one by one and show how further research may be able to increase success with such clients. I believe that both qualitative and quantitative research is necessary for enhanced understanding.

The first question concerned how a callous and cruel man would move from nearly exclusive self-centeredness toward opening to the feelings and views of others from their perspective. There are some very subtle decision processes that involve stepping out of a closed mindset and opening to new vantage points outside the self. We know far too little about these subtleties. This is an area that would be difficult for most quantitative research methods to access. I would recommend qualitative research methods, at least initially, that can study examples where this exact scenario occurred. Conversely, people can also be studied who do not seem to be able or likely to make the transition from exclusive awareness of self to others, a problem found in many difficult clients.

Another question concerned the dynamics that make an involuntary, defiant, court-ordered client wake up to become aware of a problem and involved in therapy. The precursors model would indicate that the awareness precursor has been stimulated, and this would be accurate. But knowledge of the process of coming to awareness is still remarkably incomplete. It involves the mystery of denial, or removal, or holding things out of awareness, without knowing that one is doing so. What are these psychological acts, and how can they be better addressed in clients so as to interfere with their obstruction of change? Perhaps studies can be done with populations of involuntary clients such as drug and alcohol abusers or batterers to find those who have come to awareness and those who have not. Phenomenological research methods are difficult to do well, but the key would be to pinpoint any exact moment where awareness dawned and find out more about the process that led to it, specifically the metacognitive, attentional processes involved.

I also gave the example of a hopelessly depressed person who realizes that his or her chronic depression is something that can be influenced and altered toward improvement. What brings a client from reactivity to proactivity, from a sense of helplessness to a sense of control? According to the precursors perspective, it may have to do with ontological core beliefs or a sense of necessity. Perhaps, but I believe that there is much more that we need to understand here. Chronic depression is a difficult problem in therapy, and we need to know how to help clients more quickly believe that they can influence it in a positive way. Why not ask people who have made the transition? Then with enough qualitative data, quantitative studies can be done that measure the process and find out who is likely to make the transition and who is not. It is not enough to assume that our therapy techniques and theories connected with them sufficiently explain the change process involved here.

Finally, I asked about the client who is sitting on the fence between responsibility and blaming. What nudges the person toward responsibility?

Once again, this is a central question concerning difficult clients in general, but especially the criminal mindset. If we could come to understand the metacognitive processes of these clients, the results would likely have implications for all of society.

In addition to the above examples, research that could increase our knowledge about the subtle decision-making process involved in change would be valuable. Another, far more abstract, research area might be the study of the formation of meaning itself and how meaning comes to be altered at the ontological level. This may seem too abstract, but I believe that to truly understand the change process, we may end up heading in that direction.

ADVANTAGES OF THE PRECURSORS MODEL

Even though the precursors model is not a final solution, it may well be a small step in the direction of isolating change principles that are not bound by jargon, techniques, theory, stages, or personality traits. The model moves in a direction that cuts to the essence of therapy in attempting to isolate the functions and conditions of change. This approach has a number of advantages.

The first advantage arises when a difficult, perplexing client seems unlikely to change. Rating him or her on the precursors assessment form may be helpful in formulating approaches to achieving therapeutic change. Using the techniques provided in this book may help in implementing the missing precursors. There are, of course, many techniques and strategies that can be developed for each precursor beyond what I have listed. I leave it to the reader to add new approaches and techniques. When one understands the nature of the precursors, suitable techniques for each tend to spontaneously develop. Indeed, many therapists do this already.

A second advantage is gained through rating the precursors of a therapist. Possibly for the first time, a gauge is provided that supervisors and trainers can use to take some measure of a therapist's potential as a change agent with specific clients. Similarly, when having difficulty with a client, the assessment form can help practicing therapists rate themselves and pinpoint their own missing precursors. The aim in this context is to bolster or increase those missing precursors to help therapists maximize their efforts to help difficult clients. It can also be of assistance in rehabilitating impaired therapists or those suffering from burnout.

A third advantage is that the precursors model can help a therapist or counselor better understand the process of therapist interference. When a therapist can recognize that his or her actions or attitudes are diminishing the presence of specific precursors in a client, he or she can make corrections to increase rather than reduce those precursors. For example, sometimes therapists make the mistake of thinking that certain actions or attitudes that were helpful with one client may be helpful with others. This can actually impede the emergence of precursors in some clients. Thus, awareness of therapist interference is an important aspect of a therapist's process of developing wisdom in the form of self-awareness and self-correction. It also helps therapists avoid automatizing their therapy approach with difficult clients.

A fourth advantage is that a focus on precursors may help in training therapists and counselors in client-specific change processes and variables. When trainees are taught to think in terms of therapeutic change, including what causes it and what discourages it, the psychotherapy enterprise is seen as a process of removing the obstacles to change and implementing elements that expedite its progress (see Figure 2; page 108). Manuals and treatment procedures should be the second priority after change itself. In fact, the most effective therapists are the ones who occasionally violate manual guidelines for the sake of therapeutic change (Anderson & Strupp, 1996).

When trained in the precursor model, students can recognize that resistance and difficulty are spontaneously removed by increasing the precursors. A resistant or difficult client, then, is not to be thought of as a rigid diagnostic category, nor is he or she any kind of stereotypical entity. A person who is difficult to work with may simply be a person who is missing precursors at that time. Because the precursors wax and wane from day to day or week to week, almost everyone is bound to be difficult now and then.

A strength of the precursors model lies in the fact that it uses and applies change principles backed by research, while incorporating all the major theories, strategies, approaches, and techniques of psychotherapy. In view of the evidence that 40% of clients drop out of therapy prematurely, establishing the precursors in the initial stages of therapy may be just enough to keep a client involved and motivated to show up for the next session.

THE PRECURSORS IN BUSINESS

Just as the precursors can be used to rate the change potential of groups and families, they can also be used to rate corporate departments, sections, and divisions. A particularly rigid, compulsive, or driven executive, for example, may be clearly lacking in certain precursors and thus may be decreasing the precursors of the employees under his or her charge. The precursors assessment seems to have the potential for helping executives, as well as rank-and-file employees, to think in terms of generating, tolerating, and working toward positive change. After learning this model, many people who have had difficulty with a particular employer or employee are often immediately able to point out which precursors were missing in that person.

HELPING THE POOR TO GET RICHER

A curious phenomenon has been noted by several researchers and clinicians: People who are already in a good state of mental health seem to make the greatest gains in psychotherapy. O'Malley, Suh, and Strupp (1983) borrowed a concept from sociology described as the *rich get richer* phenomenon, or Matthew effect. The paradox, and the tragedy, is that clients who need change the most tend to be the ones who are least capable of achieving it.

What are the assets of the rich who get richer in therapy? It may well be that the precursors of change are the mental and emotional equivalent of wealth and resources needed to achieve and maintain mental health. Even a cursory analysis indicates that a person with an ample supply of mental health would also have an abundance of these seven, or more, precursors. If the rich really do get richer, time invested in establishing and increasing the presence of the precursors in people who find change to be a struggle may pay healthy dividends in terms of the amount of productivity per session.

APPENDIX: CHARACTERISTICS OF WISDOM

The following is a table of the characteristics of wisdom and, perhaps, of a master therapist (see Hanna, Bemak, & Chung, 1999; Hanna & Ottens, 1995; Sternberg, 1990).

Characteristic	Definitional Elements
Empathy	Strong sense of the feelings and outlooks of others Understanding of others from their subjective point of view and from a perspective that is not self-centered
Concern	Compassion for others Caring for the welfare of living beings and the environment
Recognition of affect	Recognition of the interdependence of cognition and affect Awareness of emotions and feeling states
Deautomatization	Resistance of tendencies toward habitual, automatic behavior and thinking patterns Emphasis on awareness of actions and responsible choice
Sagacity	Listening skills Deep insight and awareness of human beings and relationships Self-knowledge and capability of self-transcendence Ability to learn from mistakes

(Continued)

Characteristic	Definitional Elements
Dialectical reasoning	Recognition of context, interdependence of phenomena, situations, and the interplay of opposing views Fluid and intuitive reasoning Ability to consider all sides of an issue Orientation toward beneficial change
Efficient coping skills	High level of ability to cope smoothly and efficiently with a wide range of people and life situations in an optimum fashion Ability to find fulfillment and meaning in life
Tolerance of ambiguity	Recognition of ambiguity as intrinsic to the nature of human beings and their interactions with others and world Ability to perceive, appreciate, integrate, and use shades of gray
Perspicacity	Ability to "see through" situations Capacity to avoid being fooled or deceived Ability to intuitively understand and accurately interpret the environment Ability to look beyond appearances
Problem finding and solving	Ability to identify and properly frame a problem so that the solution is efficient and does not lead to more problems Capacity to reframe problems and situations Expertise in the use of transferable metaphors
Metacognitive perspective	Ability to recognize presuppositions and assumptions Awareness of awareness; knowing about knowing; thinking about thinking Capacity to direct awareness, behavior, and emotion toward change

Note: From "Toward a New Paradigm for Multicultural Counseling," by F. J. Hanna, F. Bemak, and R. C. Chung, 1999, *Journal of Counseling and Development, 77,* pp. 127–128. Copyright 1999 by American Counseling Association. Adapted with permission.

REFERENCES

Adler, A. (1956). *The individual psychology of Alfred Adler* (H. L. Ansbacher & R. R. Ansbacher, Eds.). New York: Harper & Row.

Adler, A. (1979). *Superiority and social interest* (H. L. Ansbacher & R. R. Ansbacher, Eds.). New York: W. W. Norton.

Adler, G. (1992). Psychotherapy of the narcissistic personality disorder patient: Two contrasting approaches. In N. G. Hamilton (Ed.), *From inner sources: New directions in object relations psychotherapy* (pp. 195–212). Northvale, NJ: Jason Aronson.

Akbar, N. (1984). *Chains and images of psychological slavery*. Jersey City, NJ: New Mind Productions.

Alcoholics Anonymous. (1976). *Alcoholics Anonymous*. New York: Alcoholics World Services.

Alexander, F., & French, T. M. (1974). *Psychoanalytic therapy: Principles and application*. Lincoln: University of Nebraska.

Alloy, L. B., & Abramson, L. Y. (1979). Judgment of contingency in depressed and nondepressed students: Sadder but wiser? *Journal of Experimental Psychology: General, 108*, 441–485.

Alloy, L. B., & Abramson, L. Y. (1988). Depressive realism: Four theoretical perspectives. In L. B. Alloy (Ed.), *Cognitive processes in depression* (pp. 223–265). Evanston, IL: Guilford Press.

Alloy, L. B., Albright, J. S., Abramson, L. Y., & Dykman, B. M. (1990). Depressive realism and nondepressive optimistic illusions: The role of the self. In R. E. Ingram (Ed.), *Contemporary psychological approaches to depression: Theory, research, and treatment* (pp. 71–86). New York: Plenum Press.

American Psychiatric Association. (1994). *Diagnostic and statistical manual of mental disorders* (4th ed.). Washington, DC: American Psychiatric Association.

Anderson, T., & Strupp, H. H. (1996). The ecology of psychotherapeutic research. *Journal of Consulting and Clinical Psychology*, *64*, 776–782.

Ansbacher, H. L. (1992). Alfred Adler's concepts of community feeling and of social interest and the relevance of community feeling for old age. *Individual Psychology, 48*, 402–412.

Aranya, H. (Trans.). (1983). *Yoga philosophy of Patanjali*. Albany: State University of New York Press.

Arkowitz, H. (1989). From behavior change to insight. *Journal of Eclectic and Integrative Psychotherapy, 8*, 222–232.

Arkowitz, H. (1992a). A common factors therapy for depression. In J. C. Norcross & M. R. Goldfried (Eds.), *Handbook of psychotherapy integration* (pp. 402–432). New York: Basic Books.

Arkowitz, H. (1992b). Integrative theories of therapy. In D. Freedheim (Ed.), *History of psychotherapy: A century of change* (pp. 261–303). Washington, DC: American Psychological Association.

Asante, M. K. (1987). *The Afrocentric idea*. Philadelphia: Temple University.

Assagioli, R. (1965). *Psychosynthesis: A manual of principles and techniques*. New York: Penguin.

Assagioli, R. (1973). *The act of will*. Baltimore: Penguin.

Axsom, D. (1989). Cognitive dissonance and behavior change in psychotherapy. *Journal of Experimental Social Psychology, 25*, 234–252.

Bandura, A. (1956). Psychotherapists' anxiety level, self insight, and psychotherapeutic competence. *Journal of Abnormal and Social Psychology, 52*, 333–337.

Bandura, A. (1977). Self-efficacy: Toward a unifying theory of behavioral change. *Psychological Review, 84*, 191–215.

Bateson, G. (1979). *Mind and nature*. New York: Bantam Books.

Bateson, G., & Bateson, C. G. (1987). *Angels fear: Toward an epistemology of the sacred*. New York: Bantam.

Beck, A. T. (1976). *Cognitive therapy and the emotional disorders*. New York: New American Library.

Beck, A. T., Rush, A. J., Shaw, B. F., & Emery, G. (1979). *Cognitive therapy of depression*. New York: Guilford Press.

Beck, A. T., Steer, R. A., Kovacs, M., & Garrison, B. (1985). Hopelessness and eventual suicide: A 10-year prospective study of patients hospitalized with suicidal ideation. *American Journal of Psychiatry, 142*, 559–563.

Beck, A. T., Weissman, A., Lester, D., & Trexler, L. (1974). The measurement of pessimism: The hopelessness scale. *Journal of Consulting and Clinical Psychology, 42*, 861–865.

Beck, C. J. (1989). *Everyday Zen: Love and work*. San Francisco: HarperCollins.

Bergin, A. E., & Garfield, S. L. (1994). Overviews, trends, and future issues. In A. E. Bergin & S. L. Garfield (Eds.), *Handbook of psychotherapy and behavior change* (4th ed., pp. 821–830). New York: Wiley.

Bergin, A. E., & Lambert, M. J. (1978). The evaluation of therapeutic outcomes. In S. L. Garfield & A. E. Bergin (Eds.), *Handbook of psychotherapy and behavior change: An empirical analysis* (2nd ed., pp. 139–189). New York: Wiley.

Bettelheim, B. (1960). *The informed heart*. Glencoe, IL: Free Press.

Beutler, L. E. (1983). *Eclectic psychotherapy: A systematic approach*. New York: Pergamon Press.

Beutler, L. E. (2000). David and Goliath: When empirical and clinical standards of practice meet. *American Psychologist, 55*, 997–1007.

Beutler, L. E., & Clarkin, J. F. (1990). *Systematic treatment selection: Toward targeted therapeutic interventions*. New York: Brunner/Mazel.

Blum, L. H. (1988). Motivation: Escape to freedom, the important ingredient in short-term psychotherapy. *Psychological Reports, 63*, 381–382.

Bohart, A. C., & Tallman, K. (1999). *How clients make therapy work: The process of active self-healing*. Washington, DC: American Psychological Association.

Brogan, M. M., Prochaska, J. O., & Prochaska, J. M. (1999). Predicting termination and continuation status in psychotherapy using the transtheoretical model. *Psychotherapy, 36*, 105–113.

Brown, D. (1970). *Bury my heart at wounded knee*. New York: Bantam.

Brown, L. S. (1988). Harmful effects of posttermination sexual and romantic relationships between therapists and their former clients. *Psychotherapy, 25*, 249–255.

Bugental, J. F. T., & Bugental, E. K. (1984). A fate worse than death: The fear of change. *Psychotherapy, 21*, 543–549.

Burnett, P. C. (1999, April 16). *Assessing what clients learn from counselling*. Presentation at the World Conference of the American Counseling Association, San Diego, CA.

Burns, D. D. (1980). *Feeling good: The new mood therapy*. New York: Avon Books.

Cannon, W. B. (1957). Voodoo death. *Psychosomatic Medicine, 19*, 182–190.

Cashdan, S. (1988). *Object relations therapy: Using the relationship*. New York: W. W. Norton.

Cautela, J. R. (1996). Training the client to be empathetic. In J. R. Cautela & W. Ishaq (Eds.), *Contemporary issues in behavior therapy* (pp. 337–353). New York: Plenum.

Christensen, A., & Jacobson, N. S. (1994). Who (or what) can do psychotherapy: The status and challenge of nonprofessional therapies. *Psychological Science*, 5(1), 8–14.

Close, E. (1997). *Color-blind: Seeing beyond race in a race-obsessed world*. New York: HarperCollins.

Cohen, S. (1991). Social supports and physical health: Symptoms, health behaviors, and infectious disease. In E. M. Cummings, A. L. Greene, & K. H. Karraker (Eds.), *Life-span developmental psychology: Perspectives on stress and coping* (pp. 213–234). Hillsdale, NJ: Erlbaum.

Compas, B. E. (1987). Coping with stress during childhood and adolescence. *Psychological Bulletin, 101*, 393–403.

Corey, G. (1996). *Theory and practice of counseling and psychotherapy*. Pacific Grove, CA: Brooks/Cole.

Corsini, R. J. (1989). Introduction. In R. J. Corsini & D. Wedding (Eds.), *Current psychotherapies* (4th ed., pp. 1–16). Itasca, IL: F. E. Peacock.

Coyne, J. C. (1989). Thinking postcognitively about depression. In A. Freeman, K. M. Simon, L. B. Beutler, & H. Arkowitz (Eds.), *Comprehensive handbook of cognitive therapy* (pp. 227–244). New York: Plenum Press.

Cross, S. E., & Markus, H. R. (1990). The willful self. *Personality and Social Psychology Bulletin, 16*, 726–742.

Cullare, S. (1996). *Treatment resistance: A guide for practitioners*. Boston: Allyn and Bacon.

Cutler, R. L. (1958). Countertransference effects in psychotherapy. *Journal of Consulting Psychology, 22*, 349–356.

Daly, M. (1978). *Gyn/ecology: The metaethics of radical feminism*. Boston: Beacon Press.

Daly, M. (1992). *Outercourse: The be-dazzling voyage*. New York: Harper.

Davison, G. C. (1998). Being bolder with the Boulder model: The challenge of education and training in empirically supported treatments. *Journal of Consulting and Clinical Psychology, 66*, 163–167.

Dawes, R. M. (1994). *House of cards: Psychology and psychotherapy built on myth*. New York: Free Press.

Deikman, A. (1982). *The observing self: Mysticism and psychotherapy*. Boston: Beacon Press.

de Shazer, S. (1985). *Keys to solutions in brief therapy*. New York: Norton.

De Silva, P. (1984). Buddhism and behaviour modification. *Behaviour Research and Therapy, 22*, 661–678.

De Silva, P. (1985). Early Buddhist and modern behavioral strategies for the control of unwanted intrusive cognitions. *Psychological Record, 35*, 437–443.

Dinkmeyer, D. C., Dinkmeyer, D. C., Jr., & Sperry, L. (1987). *Adlerian counseling and therapy*. Columbus, OH: Merrill.

Douglass, F. (1855). *My bondage and my freedom*. New York: Dover.

Dowd, E. T., & Courchaine, K. E. (1996). Implicit learning, tacit knowledge, and implications for stasis and change in cognitive psychotherapy. *Journal of Cognitive Psychotherapy, 10*, 163–180.

Drozd, J. F., & Goldfried, M. R. (1996). A critical evaluation of the state-of-the-art in psychotherapy outcome research. *Psychotherapy, 33*, 171–180.

Dumont, F. (1991). Expertise in psychotherapy: Inherent liabilities of becoming experienced. *Psychotherapy, 28*, 422–428.

Duncan, B. L., Hubble, M. A., & Miller, S. D. (1997). *Psychotherapy with impossible clients: The efficient treatment of therapy veterans*. New York: W. W. Norton.

Durlak, J. A. (1979). Comparative effectiveness of paraprofessional and professional helpers. *Psychological Bulletin, 86*(1), 80–92.

Elliott, R., Llewelyn, S. P., Firth-Cozens, J. A., Margison, F. R., Shapiro, D. A., & Hardy, G. (1990). Assimilation of problematic experiences by clients in psychotherapy. *Psychotherapy, 27,* 411–420.

Epictetus. (1944). *Epictetus: Discourses and Enchiridion.* New York: Walter J. Black. (Original work published circa 130)

Eysenck, H. (1952). The effects of psychotherapy: An evaluation. *Journal of Consulting Psychology, 16,* 319–324.

Farber, M. (1968). *Theory of suicide.* New York: Funk & Wagnalls.

Festinger, L. (1957). *A theory of cognitive dissonance.* Stanford, CA: Stanford University Press.

Feuerstein, G. (1980). *The philosophy of classical yoga.* New York: St. Martin's Press.

Feuerstein, G. (1989). *The yoga-sutra of Patanjali.* Rochester, VT: Inner Traditions International.

Flavell, J. H. (1979). Metacognition and cognitive monitoring: A new area of cognitive developmental inquiry. *American Psychologist, 34,* 906–911.

Frank, J. (1961). *Persuasion and healing.* Baltimore: Johns Hopkins Press.

Frank, J. (1968). The role of hope in psychotherapy. *International Journal of Psychiatry, 5,* 383–395.

Frank, J. D. (1974). Therapeutic components of psychotherapy: A 25-year progress report of research. *Journal of Nervous and Mental Disease, 159,* 325–342.

Frank, J. D. (1987). Psychotherapy, rhetoric, and hermeneutics: Implications for practice and research. *Psychotherapy, 24,* 293–302.

Frank, J. D., & Frank, J. B. (1991). *Persuasion and healing* (3rd ed.). Baltimore: Johns Hopkins Press.

Frankl, V. E. (1984). *Man's search for meaning: An introduction to logotherapy.* New York: Washington Square Press. (Original work published 1959)

Freeman, A., Pretzer, J., Fleming, B., & Simon, K. M. (1990). *Clinical applications of cognitive therapy.* New York: Plenum.

Freud, S. (1910). The future prospects of psychoanalytic therapy. In J. Strachey (Ed.), *The complete psychological works of Sigmund Freud* (Standard ed.). London: Hogarth.

Fromm-Reichmann, F. (1950). *Principles of intensive psychotherapy.* Chicago: University of Chicago Press.

Garfield, S. L. (1994). Research on client variables in psychotherapy. In A. E. Bergin & S. L. Garfield (Eds.), *Handbook of psychotherapy and behavior change* (4th ed., pp. 190–228). New York: Wiley.

Garfield, S. L. (1998). Some comments on empirically supported treatments. *Journal of Consulting and Clinical Psychology, 66,* 121–125.

Gendlin, E. (1981). *Focusing.* New York: Bantam Books.

Gendlin, E. (1986). What comes after traditional psychotherapy research? *American Psychologist, 41,* 131–135.

Gendlin, E. (1992). Celebrations and problems of humanistic psychology. *Humanistic Psychologist, 20,* 447–460.

Genovese, E. D. (1974). *Roll, Jordan, roll: The world the slaves made.* New York: Pantheon.

Gilligan, C. (1982). *In a different voice: Psychological theory and women's development.* Cambridge, MA: Harvard University Press.

Giovacchini, P. L. (1989). *Countertransference: Triumphs and catastrophes.* Northvale, NJ: Jason Aronson.

Glasser, W. (1965). *Reality therapy.* New York: Harper & Row.

Goldberg, C., & Simon, J. (1982). Toward a psychology of courage: Implications for the change (healing) process. *Journal of Contemporary Psychotherapy, 13,* 107–128.

Goldfried, M. R. (1980). Toward the delineation of therapeutic change principles. *American Psychologist, 35,* 991–999.

Goldfried, M. R. (1995). Toward a common language for case formulation. *Journal of Psychotherapy Integration, 5,* 221–244.

Goldfried, M. R., Castonguay, L. G., & Safran, J. D. (1992). Core issues and future directions in psychotherapy integration. In J. C. Norcross & M. R. Goldfried (Eds.), *Handbook of psychotherapy integration* (pp. 593–616). New York: Basic Books.

Goldfried, M. R., Greenberg, L. S., & Marmar, C. (1990). Individual psychotherapy: Process and outcome. *Annual Review of Psychology, 41,* 659–688.

Goldman, E. E., & Morrison, D. S. (1984). *Psychodrama: Experience and process.* Dubuque, IA: Kendall/Hunt.

Gomes-Schwartz, B. (1978). Effective ingredients in psychotherapy: Prediction of outcome from process variables. *Journal of Consulting and Clinical Psychology, 51,* 581–586.

Goulding, R. A., & Schwartz, R. C. (1995). *The mosaic mind: Empowering the tormented selves of child abuse survivors.* New York: W. W. Norton.

Greenspan, M. (1983). *A new approach to women and therapy.* New York: McGraw-Hill.

Grencavage, L. M., & Norcross, J. C. (1990). Where are the commonalities among the therapeutic common factors? *Professional Psychology: Research and Practice, 21,* 372–378.

Gupta, B. (1998). *The disinterested witness: A fragment of Advaita Vedanta phenomenology.* Evanston, IL: Northwestern University Press.

Hanna, F. J. (1991). Suicide and hope: The common ground. *Journal of Mental Health Counseling, 13,* 459–472.

Hanna, F. J. (1992). Reframing spirituality: AA, the 12 steps, and the mental health counselor. *Journal of Mental Health Counseling, 14,* 166–179.

Hanna, F. J. (1993). The transpersonal consequences of Husserl's phenomenological method. *Humanistic Psychologist, 21,* 41–57.

Hanna, F. J. (1994). A dialectic of experience: A radical empiricist approach to conflicting theories in psychotherapy. *Psychotherapy, 31*, 124–136.

Hanna, F. J. (1995). Husserl on the teachings of the Buddha. *Humanistic Psychologist, 23*, 365–372.

Hanna, F. J. (1996). Precursors of change: Pivotal points of involvement and resistance in psychotherapy. *Journal of Psychotherapy Integration, 6*, 227–264.

Hanna, F. J. (1998). A transcultural view of prejudice, racism, and community feeling: The desire and striving for status. *Journal of Individual Psychology, 54*, 336–345.

Hanna, F. J., Bemak, F., & Chung, R. C. (1999). Toward a new paradigm for multicultural counseling. *Journal of Counseling and Development, 77*, 125–134.

Hanna, F. J., Giordano, F., Dupuy, P., & Puhakka, K. (1995). Agency and transcendence: The experience of therapeutic change. *Humanistic Psychologist, 23*, 139–160.

Hanna, F. J., Hanna, C. A., & Keys, S. G. (1999). Fifty strategies for counseling defiant and aggressive adolescents: Reaching, accepting, and relating. *Journal of Counseling and Development, 77*, 395–404.

Hanna, F. J., & Hunt, W. P. (1999). Techniques for psychotherapy with defiant, aggressive adolescents. *Psychotherapy, 36*, 56–68.

Hanna, F. J., & Ottens, A. J. (1995). The role of wisdom in psychotherapy. *Journal of Psychotherapy Integration, 5*(3), 195–219.

Hanna, F. J., & Puhakka, K. (1991). When psychotherapy works: Pinpointing an element of change. *Psychotherapy, 28*, 598–607.

Hanna, F. J., & Ritchie, M. H. (1995). Seeking the active ingredients of psychotherapeutic change: Within and outside the context of therapy. *Professional Psychology: Research and Practice, 26*, 176–183.

Hanna, F. J., & Shank, G. (1995). The specter of metaphysics in counseling research and practice: The qualitative challenge. *Journal of Counseling and Development, 74*(5), 53–59.

Hanna, F. J., Talley, W. B., & Guindon, M. H. (2000). The power of perception: Toward a model of cultural oppression and liberation. *Journal of Counseling and Development, 78*, 430–441.

Harré, R. (1984). *Personal being: A theory for individual psychology*. Cambridge, MA: Harvard University Press.

Hattie, J. A., Sharpley, C. E., & Rogers, H. J. (1984). Comparative effectiveness of professional and paraprofessional helpers. *Psychological Bulletin, 95*(3), 534–541.

Heidegger, M. (1962). *Being and time*. New York: Harper and Row. (Original work published 1927)

Hergenhahn, B. R. (1996). *An introduction to the history of psychology*. Belmont, CA: Wadsworth.

Herrnstein, R. J., & Boring, E. G. (Eds.). (1965). *A sourcebook in the history of psychology*. Cambridge, MA: Harvard University Press.

Herron, W. G., & Rouslin, S. (1982). *Issues in psychotherapy*. Bowie, MD: Prentice-Hall.

Hester, R. K., & Miller, W. R. (Eds.). (1989). *Handbook of alcoholism treatment approaches: Effective alternatives*. New York: Pergamon Press.

hooks, b. (1995). *Killing rage: Ending racism*. New York: Henry Holt.

Horney, K. (1987). *Final lectures*. New York: W. W. Norton. (Original lectures given in 1952)

Howard, G. S. (1986). *Dare we develop a human science?* Notre Dame, IN: Academic.

Howard, G. S. (Ed.). (1994). Free will and psychology. *Journal of Theoretical and Philosophical Psychology, 14*(1, Special Issue).

Howard, G. S., & Conway, C. G. (1986). Can there be an empirical science of volitional action? *American Psychologist, 41*, 1241–1251.

Howard, G. S., & Myers, P. R. (1990). Predicting human behavior: Comparing idiographic, nomothetic, and agentic methodologies. *Journal of Counseling Psychology, 37*, 227–233.

Howard, G. S., Nance, D. W., Meyers, P. (1987). *Adaptive counseling and therapy: A systematic approach to selecting effective treatments*. San Francisco: Jossey-Bass.

Howard, K. I., Kopta, S. M., Krause, M. S., & Orlinsky, D. E. (1986). The dose-effect relationship in psychotherapy. *American Psychologist, 41*, 159–164.

Howarth, I. (1989). Psychotherapy: Who benefits? *Psychologist, 2*, 150–152.

Hume, D. (1978). *A treatise of human nature*. Oxford: Oxford University Press. (Original work published 1739)

Husserl, E. (1970). *The crisis of European sciences and transcendental phenomenology*. Evanston, IL: Northwestern University Press. (Original work published 1936)

Husserl, E. (1982). *Ideas pertaining to a pure phenomenology and to a phenomenological philosophy: First book*. The Hague: Martinus Nijhoff. (Original work published 1913)

Jacobs, D. H. (1994). Environmental failure: Oppression is the only cause of psychopathology. *Journal of Mind and Behavior, 15*(1–2), 1–18.

James, W. (1907). *Pragmatism and four essays from the meaning of truth*. New York: New American Library.

James, W. (1977). Does consciousness exist? In J. J. McDermott (Ed.), *The writings of William James: A comprehensive edition* (pp. 169–183). Chicago: University of Chicago Press. (Original work published 1904)

James, W. (1981). *The principles of psychology*. Cambridge, MA: Harvard University Press. (Original work published 1890)

Janosik, E. H. (1986). *Crisis counseling: A contemporary approach*. Monterey, CA: Jones and Bartlett.

Jung, C. G. (1969). *Collected works: Vol. 8. The structure and dynamics of the psyche*. Princeton, NJ: Princeton University Press. (Original work published 1934)

Kanfer, F. H., & Grimm, L. G. (1978). Freedom of choice and behavior change. *Journal of Consulting and Clinical Psychology, 46*, 873–878.

Kant, I. (1929). *Critique of pure reason*. New York: St. Martin's Press. (Original work published 1787)

Karasu, T. B. (1992). *Wisdom in the practice of psychotherapy*. New York: Basic Books.

Karr-Morse, R., & Wiley, M. S. (1997). *Ghosts from the nursery: Tracing the roots of violence*. New York: Atlantic Monthly Press.

Kegan, R. (1982). *The evolving self: Problem and process in human development*. Cambridge, MA: Harvard University.

Kennedy, S., Kiecolt-Glaser, J. K., & Glaser, R. (1990). Social support, stress, and the immune system. In B. R. Sarason, I. G. Sarason, & G. R. Pierce (Eds.), *Social support: An interactional view* (pp. 253–266). New York: Wiley.

Kernberg, O. (1965). Notes on countertransference. *Journal of the American Psychoanalytic Association, 13*, 25–31.

Kierulff, S. (1988). Sheep in the midst of wolves: Personal-responsibility therapy with criminal personalities. *Professional Psychology: Research and Practice, 19*, 436–440.

Kiesler, D. J. (1988). *Therapeutic metacommunication*. Palo Alto, CA: Consulting Psychologists Press.

Koch, S. (1981). The nature and limits of psychological knowledge: Lessons of a century qua "science." *American Psychologist, 36*, 257–269.

Kolb, D. L., Beutler, L. E., Davis, C. S., Crago, M., & Shanfield, S. B. (1985). Patient and therapy process variables relating to dropout and change in psychotherapy. *Psychotherapy, 22*, 702–710.

Korn, J. H., Davis, R., & Davis, S. F. (1991). Historians' and chairpersons' judgments of eminence among psychologists. *American Psychologist, 46*, 789–792.

Korner, I. N. (1970). Hope as a method of coping. *Journal of Consulting and Clinical Psychology, 34*, 134–139.

Kottler, J. A. (1991). *The compleat therapist*. San Francisco: Jossey-Bass.

Kottler, J. A. (1992). *Compassionate therapy: Working with difficult clients*. San Francisco: Jossey-Bass.

Kuhl, J. (1984a). Volitional aspects of achievement motivations and learned helplessness: Toward a comprehensive theory of action control. In B. A. Maher (Ed.), *Progress in experimental personality research* (Vol. 13, pp. 99–171). New York: Academic Press.

Kuhl, J. (1984b). Volitional mediators of cognitive behavior consistency: Self-regulatory processes and action vs. state orientation. In J. Kuhl & J. Beckman (Eds.), *Action control: From cognition to behavior* (pp. 101–128). New York: Springer-Verlag.

Laidlaw, T. A., & Malmo, C. (Eds.). (1990). *Healing voices: Feminist approaches to therapy with women*. San Francisco: Jossey-Bass.

Lambert, M. J. (1992). Psychotherapy outcome research: Implications for integrative and eclectic therapists. In J. C. Norcross & M. R. Goldfried (Eds.), *Handbook of psychotherapy integration* (pp. 94–129). New York: Basic Books.

Lambert, M. J., Bergin, A. E., & Collins, J. L. (1977). Therapist-induced deterioration in psychotherapy. In A. S. Gurman & A. M. Razin (Eds.), *Effective psychotherapy: A handbook of research* (pp. 452–481). New York: Pergamon.

Langer, E. J. (1989). *Mindfulness*. New York: Addison-Wesley.

Lazarus, A. A. (1976). *Multimodal behavior therapy*. New York: Springer.

Lazarus, A. A. (1989a). Multimodal therapy. In R. J. Corsini & D. Wedding (Eds.), *Current psychotherapies* (4th ed., pp. 503–544). Itasca, IL: F. E. Peacock.

Lazarus, A. A. (1989b). *The practice of multimodal therapy*. Baltimore: Johns Hopkins University Press.

Lazarus, A. A. (1990). Can psychotherapists transcend the shackles of their training and superstitions? *Journal of Clinical Psychology, 46*, 351–358.

Lazarus, A. A. (1993). Tailoring the therapeutic relationship, or being an authentic chameleon. *Psychotherapy, 30*, 404–407.

Lazarus, A. A. (1996). The utility and futility of combining treatments in psychotherapy. *Clinical Psychology: Science and Practice, 3*, 59–68.

Lazarus, R. S., & Folkman, S. (1984). *Stress, appraisal, and coping*. New York: Springer.

Lazarus, R. S., Kanner, A. D., & Folkman, S. (1980). Emotions: A cognitive-phenomenological analysis. In R. Plutchik & H. Kellerman (Eds.), *Emotion: Theory, research and experience* (pp. 189–217). New York: Academic Press.

Leister, D. (1982). Astrologers and psychics as psychotherapists. *American Journal of Psychotherapy, 36*, 56–66.

Levenkron, S. (1991). *Obsessive-compulsive disorders: Treating and understanding crippling habits*. New York: Warner Books.

Lewin, K. (1935). *A dynamic theory of personality*. New York: McGraw-Hill.

Lewin, K. (1936). *Principles of topological psychology*. New York: McGraw-Hill.

Linehan, M. M. (1993). *Cognitive-behavioral treatment of borderline personality disorder*. New York: Guilford Press.

Loevinger, J. (1976). *Ego development*. San Francisco: Jossey-Bass.

Loevinger, J. (1985). Revision of the sentence completion test for ego development. *Journal of Personality and Social Psychology, 48*, 420–427.

Lord, J., & Dufort, F. (1996). Power and oppression in mental health. *Canadian Journal of Community Mental Health, 15*(2), 5–11.

Low, A. A. (1952). *Mental health through will training*. Boston: Christopher.

Luborsky, L., Crits-Christoph, P., Mintz, J., & Auerbach., A. (1988). *Who will benefit from psychotherapy? Predicting therapeutic outcomes*. New York: Basic Books.

Lyddon, W. J. (1989). Personal epistemology and preference for counseling. *Journal of Counseling Psychology, 36*, 423–429.

Lyddon, W. J. (1990). First- and second-order change: Implications for rationalist and constructivist cognitive therapies. *Journal of Counseling and Development, 69*(6), 122–127.

Mahoney, M. J. (1989). Scientific psychology and radical behaviorism: Important distinctions based in scientism and objectivism. *American Psychologist, 44*, 1372–1377.

Mahoney, M. J. (1991). *Human change processes: The scientific foundations of psychotherapy*. New York: Basic Books.

Mahoney, M. J., & Lyddon, W. J. (1988). Recent developments in cognitive approaches to counseling and psychotherapy. *Counseling Psychologist, 16*, 190–234.

Mahrer, A. R. (1985). *Psychotherapeutic change: An alternative to meaning and measurement*. New York: W. W. Norton.

Mahrer, A. R. (1986). *Therapeutic experiencing: The process of change*. New York: W. W. Norton.

Mahrer, A. R. (1989). *How to do experiential psychotherapy*. Ottawa, Ontario, Canada: University of Ottawa.

Margulies, A. (1989). *The empathic imagination*. New York: W. W. Norton.

Marks, I. M. (1978). Behavioral psychotherapy of adult neurosis. In S. L. Garfield & A. E. Bergin (Eds.), *Handbook of psychotherapy and behavior change: An empirical analysis* (pp. 493–547). New York: Wiley.

Maslow, A. H. (1970). *Motivation and personality*. New York: Harper & Row.

Masterson, J. F. (1988). *The search for the real self: Unmasking the personality disorders of our time*. New York: Free Press.

McLaurin, M. A. (1991). *Celia, a slave*. New York: Avon.

McMullin, R. E. (1986). *Handbook of cognitive therapy techniques*. New York: W. W. Norton.

Medawar, P. B. (1984). *The limits of science*. New York: Harper & Row.

Meichenbaum, D. B. (1977). *Cognitive–behavior modification: An integrative approach*. New York: Plenum Press.

Meichenbaum, D., & Asarnow, J. (1979). Cognitive-behavioral modification and metacognitive development: Implications for the classroom. In P. C. Kendall & S. D. Hollon (Eds.), *Cognitive-behavioral interventions: Theory, research and procedures* (pp. 11–35). New York: Academic Press.

Meichenbaum, D., & Cameron, R. (1974). The clinical potential of modifying what clients say to themselves. *Psychotherapy: Theory, Research and Practice, 2*, 103–117.

Menninger, K. (1959). Hope. *American Journal of Psychiatry, 116*, 481–491.

Merleau-Ponty, M. (1962). *The phenomenology of perception*. New York: Humanities Press.

Mikulas, W. L. (1978). Four noble truths of Buddhism related to behavior therapy. *Psychological Record, 28*, 59–67.

Mikulas, W. L. (1981). Buddhism and behavior modification. *Psychological Record, 31*, 331–342.

Miller, J. B. (1986). *Toward a new psychology of women*. Boston: Beacon Press.

Miller, J. F. (1986). Development of an instrument to measure hope. (Doctoral dissertation, Health Sciences Center, University of Chicago, 1986). *Dissertation Abstracts International, 47* (University Microfilms No. DA8705572).

Miller, R. B. (1983). A call to armchairs. *Psychotherapy: Theory, Research and Practice, 20,* 208–219.

Miller, S. D., Duncan, B. L., & Hubble, M. A. (1997). *Escape from Babel: Toward a unifying language for psychotherapy practice.* New York: W. W. Norton.

Miller, W. R. (1983). Motivational interviewing with problem drinkers. *Behavioral Psychotherapy, 11,* 147–172.

Miller, W. R. (1985). Motivation for treatment: A review with special emphasis on alcoholism. *Psychological Bulletin, 98,* 84–107.

Moreno, J. L. (1946). *Psychodrama: First volume.* Beacon, NY: Beacon House.

Moustakas, C. (1994). *Phenomenological research methods.* Thousand Oaks, CA: Sage.

Nardini, J. E. (1952). Survival factors in American prisoners of war of the Japanese. *American Journal of Psychiatry, 109,* 242–248.

Nikhilananda, S. (1963). *The Upanishads.* (Trans.). New York: Harper & Row.

Norcross, J. C. (1990). Commentary: Eclecticism misrepresented and integration misunderstood. *Psychotherapy, 27*(2), pp. 297–300.

Norcross, J. C., & Prochaska, J. O. (1986a). Psychotherapist heal thyself: I. The psychological distress and self-change of psychologists, counselors and laypersons. *Psychotherapy, 23,* 102–114.

Norcross, J. C., & Prochaska, J. O. (1986b). Psychotherapist heal thyself: II. The self-initiated and therapy facilitated change of psychological distress. *Psychotherapy, 23,* 345–356.

North, C. (1987). *Welcome, silence: My triumph over schizophrenia.* New York: Simon & Schuster.

Northup, S. (1968). *Twelve years a slave.* Baton Rouge: Louisiana State University Press. (Original work published 1853)

O'Connell, W. E. (1991). Humanistic identification: A new translation for Gemeinschaftsgefühl. *Individual Psychology, 47*(1), 26–27. (Original work published 1965)

O'Donohue, W. (1989). The (even) bolder model: The clinical psychologist as metaphysician-scientist-practitioner. *American Psychologist, 44,* 1460–1468.

O'Malley, S. S., Suh, C. S., & Strupp, H. H. (1983). The Vanderbilt psychotherapy process scale: A report on the scale development and a process-outcome study. *Journal of Consulting and Clinical Psychology, 51,* 581–586.

Omer, H., & London, P. (1988). Metamorphosis in psychotherapy: End of the systems era. *Psychotherapy, 25,* 171–180.

Omer, H., & London, P. (1989). Signal and noise in psychotherapy: The role and control of nonspecific factors. *British Journal of Psychiatry, 155,* 239–245.

Orlinsky, D. E., Grawe, K., & Parks, B. K. (1994). Process and outcome in psychotherapy: Noch einmal. In A. E. Bergin & S. L. Garfield (Eds.), *Handbook of psychotherapy and behavior change* (4th ed., pp. 270–376). New York: Wiley.

Ornstein, R. (1986). *Multimind: A new way of looking at human behavior*. London: Macmillan.

Ottens, A. J., & Hanna, F. J. (1998). Cognitive and existential therapies: Toward an integration. *Psychotherapy, 35*, 312–324.

Ouimette, P. C., Finney, J. W., & Moos, R. H. (1997). Twelve-step and cognitive-behavioral treatment for substance abuse: A comparison of treatment effectiveness. *Journal of Consulting and Clinical Psychology, 65*, 230–240.

Owen, C. (1990). *The relationship of selected variables to level of hope in women with breast cancer*. Unpublished doctoral dissertation, University of Toledo, Toledo, OH.

Pandita, S. U. (1991). *In this very life: The liberation teachings of the Buddha*. Boston: Wisdom Publications.

Pennebaker, J. W., & Beall, S. K. (1986). Confronting a traumatic event: Toward an understanding of inhibition and disease. *Journal of Abnormal Psychology, 95*, 274–281.

Pennebaker, J. W., Kiecolt-Glaser, J. K., & Glaser, R. (1988). Disclosure of traumas and immune function: Health implications for psychotherapy. *Journal of Consulting and Clinical Psychology, 56*, 239–245.

Perls, F. S. (1973). *The gestalt approach & eyewitness to therapy*. Palo Alto, CA: Science and Behavior Books.

Perls, F. S., Hefferline, R. F., & Goodman, P. (1951). *Gestalt therapy*. New York: Dell.

Persons, J. B. (1991). Psychotherapy outcome studies do not accurately represent current models of psychotherapy. *American Psychologist, 46*, 99–106.

Pesut, D. J. (1990). Creative thinking as a self-regulatory metacognitive process: A model for education, training, and further research. *Journal of Creative Behavior, 24*, 105–110.

Peterson, D. R. (1995). The reflective educator. *American Psychologist, 50*, 975–983.

Polkinghorne, D. E. (1989). Phenomenological research methods. In R. S. Valle & S. Halling (Eds.), *Existential-phenomenological perspectives in psychology* (pp. 41–60). New York: Plenum Press.

Polster, I., & Polster, M. (1973). *Gestalt therapy integrated: Contours of theory and practice*. New York: Vintage Books.

Popper, K. (1963). *Conjectures and refutations*. New York: Basic Books.

Power, R. N. (1981). On the process and practice of psychotherapy: Some reflections. *British Journal of Medical Psychology, 54*, 15–23.

Powers, W. T. (1973). *Behavior: The control of perception*. Chicago: Aldine.

Prochaska, J. O., & DiClemente, C. C. (1982). Transtheoretical therapy: Toward a more integrative model of change. *Psychotherapy: Theory, Research and Practice, 19*, 276–288.

Prochaska, J. O., DiClemente, C. C., & Norcross, J. C. (1992). In search of how people change: Applications to addictive behaviors. *American Psychologist, 47*, 1102–1114.

Prochaska, J. O., Norcross, J. C., & DiClemente, C. C. (1994). *Changing for good*. New York: Avon Books.

Puhakka, K., & Hanna, F. J. (1988). Opening the pod: A therapeutic application of Husserl's phenomenology. *Psychotherapy, 25*, 582–592.

Rahula, W. (1978). *What the Buddha taught*. London: Gordon Fraser.

Rank, O. (1936). *Will therapy*. New York: W. W. Norton.

Reandeau, S. G., & Wampold, B. E. (1991). Relationship of power and involvement to working alliance: A multiple-case sequential analysis of brief therapy. *Journal of Counseling Psychology, 38*, 107–114.

Reich, A. (1951). On countertransference. *International Journal of Psychoanalysis, 32*, 25–31.

Rholes, W. S., Michas, L., & Shroff, J. (1989). Action control as a vulnerability factor in dysphoria. *Cognitive Therapy and Research, 13*, 263–274.

Robinson, D. N. (1981). *An intellectual history of psychology*. New York: Macmillan.

Robinson, D. N. (1985). *Philosophy of psychology*. New York: Columbia University Press.

Robinson, D. N. (1990). Wisdom through the ages. In R. J. Sternberg (Ed.), *Wisdom: Its nature, origins, and development* (pp. 13–24). New York: Cambridge University Press.

Rogers, C. R. (1951). *Client-centered therapy*. Boston: Houghton Mifflin.

Rogers, C. R. (1957). The necessary and sufficient conditions of therapeutic personality change. *Journal of Consulting Psychology, 21*, 95–103.

Rosenbaum, R. L., & Horowitz, M. J. (1983). Motivation for psychotherapy: A factorial and conceptual analysis. *Psychotherapy: Theory, Research, and Practice, 20*, 346–354.

Rowan, J. (1990). *Subpersonalities: The people inside us*. London: Routledge.

Russell, B. (1972). *A history of Western philosophy*. New York: Simon & Schuster.

Rychlak, J. F. (1982). Some psychotherapeutic implications of logical phenomenology. *Psychotherapy: Theory, Research and Practice, 19*, 259–265.

Saakvitne, K. W., & Pearlman, L. A. (1996). *Transforming the pain: A workbook on vicarious traumatization*. New York: W. W. Norton.

Sahakian, W. S. (1976). Philosophical psychotherapy. In W. S. Sahakian (Ed.), *Psychotherapy and counseling: Techniques in intervention* (pp. 286–302). Chicago: Rand McNally.

Samenow, S. E. (1998). *Straight talk about criminals*. Northvale, NJ: Jason Aronson.

Sarason, B. R., Sarason, I. G., & Pierce, G. R. (1990). *Social support: An interactional view*. New York: Wiley.

Scharfstein, B. (1989). *The dilemma of context*. New York: New York University Press.

Schofield, W. (1964). *Psychotherapy: The purchase of friendship*. Englewood Cliffs, NJ: Prentice-Hall.

Schotte, D. E., & Clum, G. A. (1987). Problem-solving skills in suicidal psychiatric patients. *Journal of Consulting and Clinical Psychology, 55*, 49–54.

Schwartz, R. C. (1995). *Internal family systems therapy*. New York: Guilford Press.

Segal, H. (1977). Countertransference. *International Journal of Psychoanalytic Psychotherapy, 6*, 31–37.

Seligman, M. E. P. (1990). *Learned optimism*. New York: Alfred A. Knopf.

Selmi, P. M., Klein, M. H., Greist, J. H., Sorrell, S. P., & Erdman, H. P. (1990). Computer-administered cognitive-behavioral therapy for depression. *American Journal of Psychiatry, 147*, 51–56.

Sennett, R., & Cobb, J. (1972). *The hidden injuries of class*. New York: Random House.

Sexton, T. L., & Whiston, S. C. (1994). The status of the counseling relationship: An empirical review, theoretical implications, and research directions. *Counseling Psychologist, 22*, 6–78.

Shedler, J., Mayman, M., & Manis, M. (1993). The illusion of mental health. *American Psychologist, 48*, 1117–1131.

Silverman, W. H. (1996). Cookbooks, manuals, and paint-by-numbers: Psychotherapy in the 90s. *Psychotherapy, 33*, 207–215.

Simon, R. (1985, September–October). Take it or leave it: An interview with Carl Whitaker. *Family Therapy Networker*, p. 27.

Singer, B. A., & Luborsky, L. (1977). Countertransference: The status of clinical versus quantitative research. In A. S. Gurman & A. M. Razin (Eds.), *Effective psychotherapy: A handbook of research* (pp. 433–451). New York: Pergamon.

Singer, M. T., & Lalich, J. (1996). *"Crazy" therapies: What are they? Do they work?* San Francisco: Jossey-Bass.

Skinner, B. F. (1971). *Beyond freedom and dignity*. New York: Knopf.

Slife, B. D. (1987). Can cognitive psychology account for metacognitive functions of mind? *Journal of Mind and Behavior, 8*, 195–208.

Slife, B. D., & Weaver, C. A. (1992). Depression, cognitive skill, and metacognitive skill in problem solving. *Cognition and Emotion, 6*, 1–22.

Smith, M. L., & Glass, G. V. (1977). Meta-analysis of psychotherapy outcome studies. *American Psychologist, 32*, 752–760.

Snyder, C. R. (1994). *The psychology of hope*. New York: Free Press.

Stein, D. M., & Lambert, M. J. (1995). Graduate training in psychotherapy: Are therapy outcomes enhanced? *Journal of Consulting and Clinical Psychology, 63*, 182–196.

Sternberg, R. J. (1986). Intelligence, wisdom, and creativity: Three is better than one. *Educational Psychologist, 21*(3), 175–190.

Sternberg, R. J. (Ed.). (1990). *Wisdom: Its nature, origins, and development*. New York: Cambridge University Press.

Sternberg, R. J., & Williams, W. M. (1997). Does the Graduate Record Examination predict meaningful success in the graduate training of psychologists? *American Psychologist, 52*, 630–641.

Stiles, W. B., Shapiro, D. A., & Elliott, R. (1986). "Are all psychotherapies equivalent?" *American Psychologist, 41*, 165–180.

Storr, A. (1989). Countertransference. In F. Flach (Ed.), *Psychotherapy* (pp. 104–113). New York: W. W. Norton.

Stotland, E. (1969). *The psychology of hope*. San Francisco: Jossey-Bass.

Strean, H. S. (1993). *Resolving counterresistances in psychotherapy*. New York: Brunner/Mazel.

Strupp, H. H. (1978). The therapist's theoretical orientation: An overrated variable. *Psychotherapy: Theory, Research, and Practice, 15*, 314–317.

Strupp, H. H. (1988). What is therapeutic change? *Journal of Cognitive Psychotherapy, 2*(2), 75–82.

Strupp, H. H. (1996). The tripartite model and the *Consumer Reports* study. *American Psychologist, 51*, 1017–1024.

Strupp, H. H. (1997). Research, practice, and managed care. *Psychotherapy, 34*(1), 91–94.

Strupp, H. H., & Hadley, S. W. (1979). Specific versus nonspecific factors in psychotherapy. *Archives of General Psychiatry, 36*, 1125–1136.

Tjeltveit, A. C. (1989). The ubiquity of models of human beings in psychotherapy: The need for rigorous reflection. *Psychotherapy, 26*, 1–10.

Townsend, J. T., & Busemeyer, J. R. (1989). Approach-avoidance: Return to dynamic decision behavior. In C. Izawa (Ed.), *Current issues in cognitive processes: The Tulane Floweree symposium on cognition* (pp. 107–133). Hillsdale, NJ: Lawrence Erlbaum.

Van Kaam, A. (1966). *Existential foundations of psychology*. Pittsburgh, PA: Duquesne University Press.

Van Wagoner, S. L., Gelso, C. L., Hayes, J. A., & Diemer, R. A. (1991). Countertransference and the reputedly excellent therapist. *Psychotherapy, 28*, 411–421.

Wachtel, P. L. (1977). *Psychoanalysis and behavior therapy: Toward an integration*. New York: Basic Books.

Walrond-Skinner, S. (1986). *Dictionary of psychotherapy*. New York: Routledge & Kegan Paul.

Wampold, B. E., Mondin, G. W., Moody, M., Stich, F., Benson, K., & Ahn, H. (1977). A meta-analysis of outcome studies comparing bona fide psychotherapies: Empirically, "all must have prizes." *Psychological Bulletin, 122*(3), 203–215.

Wann, T. W. (Ed.). (1964). *Behaviorism and phenomenology: Contrasting bases for modern psychology*. Chicago: University of Chicago Press.

Waters, L. (1997). [Letter to the editor]. *Psychotherapy, 34*, 99.

Watson, D. L., & Tharp, R. G. (1989). *Self-directed behavior: Self-modification for personal adjustment*. Pacific Grove, CA: Brooks/Cole.

Watzlawick, P., Weakland, J. H., & Fisch, R. (1974). *Change: Principles of problem formation and problem resolution*. New York: W. W. Norton.

Wegner, D. M., & Vallacher, R. R. (1977). *Implicit psychology: An introduction to social cognition*. New York: Oxford University Press.

Weiner, M. F. (1982). *The therapeutic impasse*. New York: Free Press.

Weisman, A. D. (1979). *Coping with cancer*. New York: McGraw-Hill.

Wessells, M. G. (1982). *Cognitive psychology*. New York: Harper & Row.

Whiston, S. C., & Sexton, T. L. (1993). An overview of psychotherapy outcome research: Implications for practice. *Professional Psychology: Research and Practice*, *24*(1), 43–51.

Whitaker, C. (1976). The hindrance of theory in clinical work. In P. D. Guerin (Ed.), *Family therapy: Theory and practice* (pp. 154–164). New York: Gardner Press.

Whitaker, C. (1989). *Midnight musings of a family therapist*. New York: Norton.

Whitaker, C. A., & Bumberry, W. M. (1988). *Dancing with the family: A symbolic-experiential approach*. New York: Brunner/Mazel.

Whitehead, A. N. (1925). *Science and the modern world*. New York: Free Press.

Whitehead, A. N. (1938). *Modes of thought*. New York: Capricorn Books.

Wolfe, B. E., & Goldfried, M. R. (1988). Research on psychotherapy integration: Recommendations and conclusions from an NIMH workshop. *Journal of Consulting and Clinical Psychology*, *56*, 448–451.

Wolpe, J. (1958). *Psychotherapy by reciprocal inhibition*. Stanford, CA: Stanford University Press.

Yalom, I. D. (1980). *Existential psychotherapy*. New York: Basic Books.

Yalom, I. D. (1989). *Love's executioner and other tales of psychotherapy*. New York: HarperCollins.

Yalom, I. D. (1995). *Theory and practice of group psychotherapy*. New York: Basic Books.

Zajonc, R. B. (1980). Feeling and thinking: Preferences need no inferences. *American Psychologist*, *35*, 151–175.

AUTHOR INDEX

SUBJECT INDEX

ABOUT THE AUTHOR

Fred J. Hanna, PhD, is a professor in the Department of Counseling and Human Services at Johns Hopkins University in Baltimore, Maryland. He has served on the editorial boards of six scholarly journals and has published nearly 50 scholarly and professional articles. In addition to many years of therapy practice, he has served as a consultant to a wide variety of community agencies and school systems on the subject of difficult clients. His research interests have focused on seeking the active ingredients of psychotherapeutic change. He has also developed clinical techniques aimed at positive change for victims of oppression; criminal personalities; persons with addictive behaviors; and defiant, aggressive adolescents. An experienced world traveler, he spent nearly two years studying and learning from the worldviews of many remote and varied cultures, mostly in Asia.